The Gospel of Matthew

The Gospel of Matthew

ROBERT T. FORTNA

*The Scholars Version Annotated
with Introduction and Greek Text*

SANTA ROSA CALIFORNIA

The Gospel of Matthew

Published in 2005 by Polebridge Press

Library of Congress Cataloging-in-Publication Data
Fortna, Robert Tomson.
  The Gospel of Matthew : the Scholars Version annotated with introduction and Greek text / Robert T. Fortna.
    p. cm.
  Includes bibliographical references and indexes.
  ISBN 0-944344-60-7
  1. Bible. N.T. Matthew--Criticism, Redaction. I. Bible. N.T. Matthew. English. Scholars. 2004. II. Bible. N.T. Matthew. Greek. 2005. III. Title.

  BS2575.52.F67 2005
  226.2'077--dc22

                                                          2004058637

For William, Nicholas, and Benjamin

Contents

The Gospel of Matthew

The Scholars Version

Editor in Chief
Robert W. Funk

General Editors

Daryl D. Schmidt
Texas Christian University

Julian V. Hills
Marquette University

Editors, Apocryphal Gospels

Ron Cameron
Wesleyan University

Karen L. King
Harvard University

Translation Panel

Harold Attridge, *Yale University*

Edward F. Beutner, *Catholic Diocese of Superior, Wisconsin*

J. Dominic Crossan, *Emeritus, DePaul University*

Jon B. Daniels, *Phoenix, Arizona*

Arthur J. Dewey, *Xavier University*

Robert T. Fortna, *Emeritus, Vassar College*

Ronald F. Hock, *University of Southern California*

Roy W. Hoover, *Emeritus, Whitman College*

Arland D. Jacobson, *Concordia College*

John S. Kloppenborg, *University of Toronto*

Helmut Koester, *Harvard University*

Lane C. McGaughy, *Willamette University*

Marvin W. Meyer, *Chapman College*

Robert J. Miller, *Juniata College*

Stephen J. Patterson, *Eden Theological Seminary*

Bernard Brandon Scott, *Phillips Theological Seminary*

Philip Sellew, *University of Minnesota*

Chris Shea, *Ball State University*

Mahlon H. Smith, *Rutgers University*

To the Reader

(Please read this first)

I have tried to address this book to the widest possible readership—from the neophyte or merely curious to serious students of scripture to the occasional Biblical scholar (but I don't intend to enter into scholarly debate). In any case I hope you will find its brisk style comfortable to read.

This is a not quite a standard commentary. Since I place *comments* on the English text of Matthew at the bottom of each page, sometimes verse by verse, it may appear to be. But the comments are *selective,* sometimes supplying only such background information as the meaning of unusual words or phrases, historical context, or parallels in Mark and Luke.

And only part of the time do I express an opinion about the *meaning* of the text. Instead I frequently ask questions and leave them for you the reader to consider. Read Matthew for yourself—don't let me read it for you. A commentator need not try to appear omniscient.

We make use of a fresh English translation of the original Greek text of Matthew, known as the *Scholars Version,* "SV" for short (more on it in Section 7 of the Introduction). Often, in the comments we'll consider the question how the Greek has been translated into modern American English—why SV reads as it does. And I explain a number of unusual translations of important words or phrases in six *Translation Notes,* interspersed where appropriate among the comments as cameo essays. By these means I hope to take you inside the translation process and help you see the so-called linguistic world of the Gospel of Matthew.

The *Greek text* appears on alternate pages, on the left, facing the English of the Scholars Version on the right. If you don't know Greek, as many readers won't, don't be intimidated. The left-hand pages can simply be ignored without loss. But if you know even a little Greek, it may be helpful to compare SV's English with the Greek that you recognize. Frequently I transliterate a

1

Greek word or phrase—for example, *êngiken* in the last comment on 3:2 to point up SV's way of putting it in English.

In a small number of cases, when the various ancient Greek manuscripts of Matthew differ significantly, we have to ask which "reading" is better. Just below the Greek I show the most significant alternative readings in *Text-critical Notes*, so that you can try to make up your own mind on the question. (See further, Introduction, section 6.)

A word about what I'll be calling this ancient author and his book: I don't refer to the *author* as "Matthew," although that is most commonly done. I prefer not to perpetuate the false impression that we know who the author was. The book was originally anonymous, and only later was it held to have been written by the apostle Matthew. That name is a pseudonym. Rather, I'll refer to the writer of this gospel simply as *the author* or *the evangelist*. (I explain this perhaps unfamiliar use of the word "evangelist" in the Introduction, section 1.) Even though he is anonymous, I believe we can speak of that author as male; I give my reasons for this in section 3 of the Introduction.

But for convenience I follow tradition in calling *the document* by the name Matthew. Some speak of it more neutrally as "the first gospel," since it comes at the head of the four-gospel canon, just as John is often called the fourth gospel. But to call Matthew first is confusing, since that could imply that it was the earliest of the gospels to be written, which I'm convinced it was not (see Introduction, section 2).

The text is of course divided into *chapters*, to make this very long gospel easier to deal with. The original document had no such divisions. They were introduced well after Matthew was written, perhaps as late as the sixteenth century. And later still, the chapters were divided into *verses* (abbreviated as "vss," or "vs" for a single verse). A colon separates chapter and verse numbers—for example, "3:1" means the first verse of chapter 3. Verses often comprise one sentence, with a single discrete idea. But occasionally they divide naturally into two units of thought. In that case, a letter after the verse number is conventionally used to indicate part of a verse. For example, the first part of verse thirty-four in chapter 5 would be called 5:34a and the latter part 5:34b.

Our *method for interpreting* Matthew will be to look first at the author's "sources" if possible (see Introduction, 2), then to notice how he has altered those earlier texts, and so to determine what his special concerns are. This method is called Redaction Criticism, and it allows us to look over the author's shoulder, so to speak, as he makes his own, often quite distinctive, use of traditional material. If used alone, it can be faulted for focusing too much on the evangelist's changes to his sources, and not enough on the end result. It's equally—maybe more—important, to view the gospel as an integral literary whole. So we'll try to balance these two approaches. In any case, when looking at redaction, we'll employ the broad definition used by Prof. Ingo Broer and include sociological and political factors.

Following the example of Ulrich Luz, I have attempted to deal with difficult theological questions in five *Interpretive Notes*, inserted where appropriate as cameos.

At almost the end of the book you'll find a *Bookshelf* that lists works I have cited and suggests materials for further study. Very occasionally I refer in the comments to one of these books, by author's name, a shortened title, and where necessary a location within that book: for instance, "Davies & Allison, *Matthew*, second paragraph of Introduction 1.2." But generally the reader will not be distracted by bibliographic references.

Finally, there is a *Glossary* of terms that may be unfamiliar, together with the *Abbreviations* that I use.

Note: I have made several corrections to the SV found in its hitherto most recent form (Miller, *The Complete Gospels* [1994], 55–114), and in several places I believe the translation can be improved. In these matters, Prof. Daryl Schmidt, author of an earlier volume in this series, has been a wise and helpful consultant, but I am responsible for the changes actually made. Tom Hall, who tirelessly and without recompence copy-read the entire book, has suggested many further improvements, for which I am most grateful. I am also indebted to Char Matejovsky of Polebridge Press for her practiced and deft mid-wifing of this manuscript to publication.

Whether you use this volume sporadically or systematically, I hope that you find it usable and that it engages your involvement with the Gospel of Matthew.

Robert T. Fortna
The Feast of St. Matthew 2004
Poughkeepsie NY

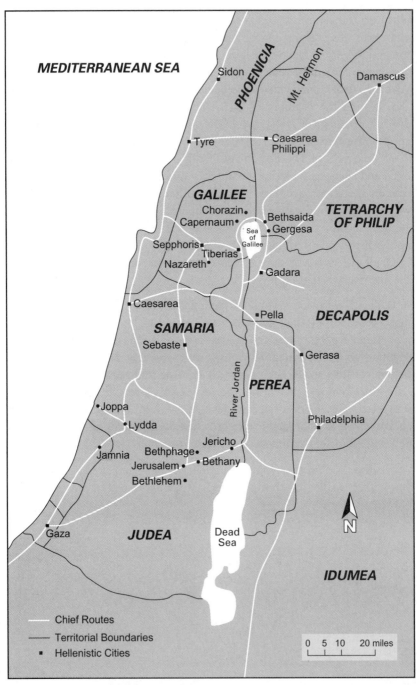

Palestine in the First Century CE

INTRODUCTION

1. Matthew: What kind of book?
   The pre-eminent gospel
   A synoptic gospel
   Title: "The Gospel of Matthew"? Or "... according to Matthew"?
   Genre

2. Sources of Matthew
   Mark
   "Q"
   "M"

3. Author—Place—Date
   Who
   When
   Where

4. Structure—Purpose—Audience
   How organized
   Why written
   For whom

5. Special Features
   Use of the Old Testament
   "Heaven"
   Peter and the other disciples
   Pharisees and Pilate

6. The Greek Text

7. The Scholars Version
   Name
   Tone
   Diction
   Principles of translation

1. Matthew: What kind of book?

The pre-eminent gospel

Four gospels head the New Testament canon—the officially recognized books—and from the beginning the Gospel of Matthew has had first place. It was held that the apostle Matthew wrote it (see further below, section 3), and that "Mark" and "Luke" were only associates of apostles—of Peter and Paul, respectively. (John's Gospel was also attributed to an apostle, but it was placed last as different and more "spiritual" than the other three.) Matthew is the longest gospel and gives the most comprehensive account of Jesus' career, and especially of his teaching. For these reasons, evidently, it has—almost without exception—been the leading gospel.

A synoptic gospel

Matthew, Mark, and Luke are alike in very many ways, and especially in contrast to John. Sometimes they share the same language, word for word, in Greek. And when not quite the same, they are usually very close in wording. So at first they were thought to be three independent eyewitness accounts, and because they have so much in common they are collectively called *the synoptic gospels*—from the Greek word meaning "seeing together," as with the same eyes. In fact they are not three independent accounts. And we now believe that none of the gospel writers was an eyewitness. (Luke 1:2, at least, makes it clear for that gospel.) Instead we understand the similarities to result from one author's copying from an earlier one. The earlier gospel is therefore called a "source" for the later one. On the sources underlying Matthew, see section 2.

Title: "The Gospel of Matthew"? Or ". . . according to Matthew"?

The distinction between these two titles may seem trivial. What does it matter whether we say The Gospel *of* or *according to Matthew*? It matters because the word *gospel* here is used in two rather different ways.

The English word "gospel" translates the Greek *euangelion* (in older English, sometimes simply "evangel"). The main part of this word (*-angelion*) means *a message* (an "angel" was simply one who brought a message). But the emphasis is on what kind of message it is. The Greek prefix (*eu-*) means "good." So the message is *good news*. And not just any good news but something to be proclaimed. It is the message that Jesus is the Anointed, was raised from the dead, and will come again.

The longer title—"The Gospel according to Matthew"—is the ancient one. In fact, in the Greek New Testament our gospel is called simply "According to Matthew," followed by "According to Mark," and so forth. They belong to the first block of the canon, called simply The Gospel. That is, the four gospel books are seen as four versions of the one Gospel—where that word expresses the *content* of these books, namely the Christian Good News.

In this earliest use there could be only one Gospel. Paul, the first Christian writer, warns: "If anyone proclaims to you a gospel contrary to what you received, let that one be cursed" (Gal 1:9). He is not speaking of books (there was none yet) but of the Christian message itself, which the books would eventually express. So the titles—"The Gospel according to Matthew," ". . . according to Mark," and so forth—mean that they are various expressions of the one Gospel. Each of them is understood to set forth one and the same message, even though in a rather different way.

The shorter title is a modern one, and far more common—the Gospel of Matthew, the Gospel of Mark, and so forth. In this phrasing "Gospel" identifies a *genre*, a *type of book* (as distinct from a letter, for example, or an apocalypse). A *gospel* is any book that sets forth *the Gospel*. In this sense the NT contains four gospels. Among scholars today the word is used almost exclusively in this way entirely, and usually with a lower-case g, except in the gospel titles.

There is, then, an important difference between these two titles. The first sentence of Mark—which reads *The beginning of the gospel of Jesus the Anointed*—doesn't refer to itself as a book (a gospel) but to *the* Gospel it proclaims. So, properly, it is the Gospel according to Mark. But it's cumbersome always to say *according to,* so the word came to have the modern meaning, and we call it simply the Gospel of Mark, and hence the present commentary's title—*The Gospel of Matthew.*

Thus, at the head of the New Testament canon stands the Gospel. It consists of one Gospel . . . and four gospels.

Genre

Some argue that there is no single genre that can be called a gospel, no one literary classification, which all the gospels typify. Of course all four proclaim the good news; all tell the story of Jesus' life and its significance. But beyond this similarity in content, is there one literary type called gospel? Are the four gospels, despite their differences, nevertheless the same kind of book? No, not quite. One of them (Mark, the earliest) sets the pattern the others will follow. But each is unique.

What *kind* of gospel, then, was Matthew intended to be? What is its primary focus? Davies & Allison (p. 3) suggest several possibilities, all of them apt to some degree: history, myth, apocalyptic teaching, and moral instruction. Let us consider them in order.

Matthew's narrative blends *history* with legend and myth. (We consider myth below.) History here does not necessarily mean factual history in the modern sense. The stories about Jesus' life, based on the collective memories of the early Christians and passed on orally for a number of decades, came to include a good deal of what must be considered legend. For example, John the Baptist's objection when Jesus comes to him to be baptized (Matt 3:14–15) and the account of the guards posted at Jesus' tomb (27:62–66). On the other hand, Matthew does contain what we would call factual history. That John baptized Jesus and that Jesus was crucified can hardly be disputed . . . despite details in those accounts that may be legendary (for example, John the Baptist's clothing, reminiscent of Elijah's in 2 Kgs 1:8, or the soldiers' gambling for Jesus' clothes [Psalm 22:18]). Thus, history in Matthew may interweave both fact and legend.

But there is also *myth* in Matthew. Here "myth" is not to be understood as an account that's simply untrue or incredible, but as an imaginative, symbolic story that isn't (merely) factual. Myth seeks to convey theological truth, like the story of Yahweh in the Garden of Eden (Gen 2). Similarly, in Matthew's account of what happened at Jesus' baptism (3:16) and his subsequent testing in the wilderness (4:1–11), the stage is peopled not by historical figures like John, the Judean crowds, and the human Jesus. Rather, God's son, God's spirit and voice, and the devil play out the scene. They are mythic figures. They seek to embody theological truth, not empirical fact.

Matthew contains a good deal of *apocalyptic teaching* (see the Glossary), in scattered sayings of Jesus and especially in chapter 24: the "final agonies" (vss 4–8) and the coming of the son of Adam (29–31); also the last judgment (the end of chap 25).

But it is Davies & Allison's fourth category, *moral instruction*, that seems to me to describe the basic character of this gospel best. The evangelist has organized and codified the teachings of Jesus. As we'll see, much of that teaching comprises five long speeches (like the "Sermon on the Mount") that seem to constitute new Torah, the new Christian Law: detailed instruction for discipleship and for the church. In some cases Jesus makes traditional Jewish teaching more stringent; in 5:27–28, for example, the prohibition against adultery is made to include simple lust. Sometimes the author or in his tradition has evidently softened Jesus' original teaching—as in the case of divorce, where infidelity on the woman's part is acceptable grounds (5:31-32, 19:9).

In the risen Jesus' last words he directs the disciples to teach "all peoples . . . to observe everything I have commanded" (28:20), just as God did through Moses. In other words, Matthew is a kind of Christian Manual of Discipline. And, of course, it does all this in the context of proclaiming the good news of Jesus Christ.

A further word about historicity in Matthew, in particular the possibility of getting back to the so-called *historical Jesus*—what he actually said and did. That cannot be done by taking Matthew (or the other gospels) at face value. Clearly, many additions, and in some cases inventions and distortions, entered the oral Jesus-tradition between his lifetime and the writing of the gospels up to 60 years later, and the authors themselves invented some of the material. Thus, Jesus now proclaims that he is Messiah and Son of God, and predicts his eventual fate. Thus we hear a Jesus who, I believe, never spoke in this way. Stories about him, too, were added in to the tradition—gratuitous miracles like his walking on the sea or causing a coin to be found in a fish's mouth, legends of the ripping of the temple veil and the earthquake at the moment of his death. Some of this invented material comes to our author already in written form, via his sources, and some was probably still oral or he himself created.

To separate what is historical fact from these alterations is a complicated task. One such attempt—made over a period of a decade and more, by a large group of scholars working collaboratively—is published as the two reports of the Jesus Seminar: *The Five Gospels* (1993), which deals with Jesus' teaching, and *The Acts of Jesus* (1998), on the deeds and events of his lifetime. Robert W. Funk, founder and organizer of the Jesus Seminar, is principal editor of both volumes.

2. Sources of Matthew

It is not possible to recover with any precision the sources of *Mark*, the earliest gospel, but we can diagram the sources of *Matthew*, along with those of Luke.

As the diagram displays, Mark and Q are each sources for both Matthew and Luke, and the principal ones. Mark provides much of their narrative, and Q most of their sayings. (On Q, see below.) Additional material called M appears only in Matthew, and L indicates material peculiar to Luke. We also find editorial work in both Matthew and Luke that stems from the evangelists themselves—habits of language, repeated themes or "motifs," and theological interests. In the case of Matthew, these become evident to the careful reader.

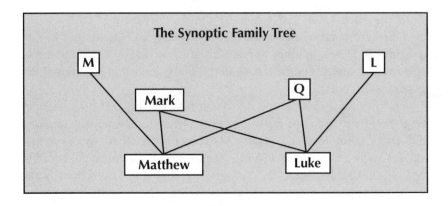

Scholars call this material "redaction"—that is, creative editing. It derives not from any of the sources, but from the evangelist himself.

Mark

The overwhelming majority of scholars hold that the Gospel of Mark must be a "source" lying behind Matthew and Luke, for several reasons: First, virtually all of Mark is found in either Matthew or Luke, and most of it in both. Second, although they are very differently organized they keep the material from Mark in much the same order. And third, they often follow Mark word-for-word or paraphrase it in improved Greek.

Not quite all modern Biblical scholars agree, but by far the most likely explanation seems to be that Mark is the earliest gospel, and a document that the authors of Matthew and Luke extensively revised. In other words, it is their source. But where they chose to do some retouching or "redacting," the material from Mark appears quite differently in Matthew and Luke. So it's difficult to see how "Luke" might have copied from our author, or vice versa. They must have used Mark independently of each other.

There is some evidence that calls this last assertion in question—the so-called Minor Agreements between Matthew and Luke, where they treat Markan material identically, or in some way agree against Mark. For example, both omit Mark 3:21 (Jesus' relatives think he is "out of his mind; see comment on Matt 12:22) and two complete story units, Mark 4:26–29 (the parable of seed growing in secret; see on Matt13:24–30) and 8:22–26 (the blind man of Bethsaida; see on Matt 16:13–20). These suggest to some scholars that perhaps after all the author of Matthew knew Luke (or the other way around). But even if their copies of Mark were identical to ours—and we can't be sure that was so—these agreements are not numerous or striking enough to suggest a form of interdependence between the two authors. They are rightly called "minor."

Where did Mark's gospel get its information? From oral traditions about Jesus. That is, separate, individual stories about him and recollections of what he had said. (See Schmidt, p. 7). This is how all the memories of Jesus were handed on for several decades after his death in about 30 CE. They were probably not written down as a continuous account until the author of Mark put them together, probably about 70 CE.

"Q"

Secondly, there is a source called simply Q. The authors of Matthew and Luke have used a great deal of common material that is not found in Mark and that often displays verbatim agreement. So it must have come from a written source that the two evangelists used, much the same as they used Mark. But it consists almost exclusively of *sayings* of Jesus, whereas Mark provided mainly narrative. This must be another source for Matthew and Luke. As they did with Mark, the two evangelists used it in such different ways that one of them could hardly have copied from the other. Thus, while they share this source, they must have used it independently.

This Q source is hypothetical. There is no longer a copy of it. But to account for all the sayings that Matthew and Luke share, it must have existed in written form. (Presumably it failed to survive because it was so completely contained in Matthew and Luke. Mark, also found in both, barely survived.) We know what Q must have contained, but not what it was called. The German scholars who first deduced its existence called it simply a Source—in German *Quelle*, so "Q" for short. It's sometimes called the Sayings Source—or the Logia Source, which means the same thing. Some call it the Saying Gospel.

It is lost, then, but we have two versions of the material it contained. And it can be reconstructed with some confidence.

"M"

Finally, both Matthew and Luke contain some material that is found only in one or the other. Some of it the authors themselves may have created. But probably much was tradition that has come down to only one or the other of them. In many cases this may have been still oral tradition. And probably this material had not yet been gathered together. It is simply a body of material that is *special* to Matthew or to Luke. For present purposes we lump it all together and call it simply *Special Matthew* and *Special Luke*—"M" and "L" for short. So Special Matthew was not a definable source for the evangelist in the way Mark and Q were. It is miscellaneous material, perhaps collected by the author himself, and so it found its way into his gospel. The components of M can be listed, but their wording, before he used them, can't easily be recovered.

There may be traces of the *Gospel of John* in Matthew. For example, Matt 11:27b ("No one knows the son except the Father, nor does anyone know the Father except the son—and anyone to whom the son wishes to reveal him") is decidedly Johannine in diction, and in content recalls John 3:34—36a. But such resonances are so few that our author can hardly have made use of the "Fourth Gospel," which quite likely was written somewhat later. Parallel oral tradition best accounts for them.

About the middle of the last century, a monastic library was unearthed in Upper Egypt. The oldest document in this library, and for NT purposes the most important, is a work that calls itself the *Gospel of Thomas*. It is made up entirely of sayings of Jesus. (In that way it resembles Q, but most of the material is entirely different.) A number of its sayings have close parallels in Matthew and the other synoptic gospels, and its earliest form it may even be older than Matthew. But it was not a source known to our evangelist. Or conversely, even though like Matthew it characteristically uses "Heaven's" domain instead of "God's" (see p. 19). Matthew was almost certainly not a source for Thomas—not even for its second-century expansion. So, in considering the teaching of Jesus, it's useful to compare passages in Thomas with their parallels in Matthew. See, for example, the comments on The Leased Vineyard (21:33–46). The Scholars Version text of Thomas, together with an introduction and commentary, can be found in Miller, *The Complete Gospels*, 301-22. When the parallels or contrasts are significant, I quote the Thomas material in a comment.

3. Author—Date—Place

Who was this author?

This "evangelist," as he can be called? (Note that this term has little of its modern sense, as for instance in "televangelist," or "evangelical" Christianity. Evangelist simply means the author of a gospel, one who puts the evangel, the good news, in writing.) Who was he? We simply don't know his name. Together with all the other gospels, Matthew was originally anonymous. Unlike modern authors, the evangelists chose not to claim authorship, perhaps because of the sacred nature of their writing. But at some point in the second century the anonymous authors were assigned names, and the gospels became pseudonymous—falsely named, after apostles (Matthew, John) or associates of apostles (Mark, Luke). This was done in an attempt to give the earliest four a special authority and authenticity among the many gospels that were beginning to circulate, most of which were considered unreliable or even heretical. (But then they too acquired apostolic names, such as Peter, Thomas, and James.)

Our gospel was assigned to the apostle Matthew. Just why, we don't know. In 9:9 the author has changed the name Levi (according to Mark 2:14) to Matthew, and that may have suggested to those looking for an apostolic name that he was subtly referring to himself. But he cannot be the apostle Matthew, for had he been an eyewitness of what appears in the gospel he would not have relied so heavily on Mark and Q. He would have told the story from his own memory. Therefore we have no idea of the author's name. Though "for convenience" he is customarily called Matthew, I choose—perhaps a bit perversely—to break with a usage implying that we know his identity. Instead I refer to him as "the evangelist" or "our author." But the gospel itself I call simply Matthew, since we have no other name for it. (As I've said, to speak of the First Gospel is cumbersome—and also ambiguous, for it comes first in the canon, not in order of writing.)

But apart from his name, what can we know about him from his book? Certainly he was a *Jew*—that is, of course, a Christian Jew. He is unusually familiar with many passages of the Hebrew Scriptures—the "Old Testament" (OT), as Christians would later call it. Further, he seems to have accurate knowledge of what came to be called rabbinic tradition. (Eventually it would be collected and written down as the Mishnah and the Talmud.) The Rabbis interpreted scripture, mostly Torah, the first five books of the OT. And they were mostly Pharisees or scholars or both (see Glossary). Sometimes—by no means always—they tightened the rules governing Jewish behavior. Our author has Jesus say, *they invent heavy burdens and lay them on people's shoulders* (23:4).

Only in this gospel is Jesus depicted as acquainted with this rabbinic tradition (see for example the comments on 5:22 and 5:28). And the extended *polemic against* the Pharisees and scholars that makes up most of chapter 23 is largely unparalleled in Mark and Q. This suggests that the author was far more intimately connected with the Pharisaic brand of Judaism than the other evangelists. Was he, then, like Paul earlier, a *former Pharisee and scholar*? That might explain the intensity of the condemnation of that group. A recent convert away from a sect often becomes virulently opposed to it.

Because of the evangelist's detailed knowledge of Jewish interpretation of the Law it seems to me highly likely that that author was a *male*, and all the more so if a former Pharisee. Hence, I speak of the evangelist as "he."

Some have suggested that the evangelist was not an individual but a number of people, who can be called "the school of Matthew." This is possible, but I know of no way to verify the proposal. And if it were true, it would offer little help in understanding Matthew. So I believe we may as well envision a singular "Matthew" as the author.

When was Matthew written?

Ancient books listed no publication date. In fact, when speaking of them, the idea of publication is an anachronism. A book was handwritten as a single copy, called its "autograph." And we can only approximate a book's date of authorship. We have to try to box it in—what is the earliest and what is the latest possible date? Mark was most probably written about 70 CE. So if indeed our evangelist used Mark as a source, that date defines one end of the time span for the book's authoring. On the other hand, the gospel is quoted as an authoritative writing early in the second century. Thus it is a reasonable guess—no more than that—that the evangelist wrote his gospel at some point *around 90* CE.

And where?

Probably in the so-called Diaspora (which began with the fall of Judea in 587 BCE and has continued ever since)—that is, not in Palestine but in one of the many Jewish communities scattered throughout the Greco-Roman world. For this reason the author writes in Greek, the common language of that world. And in quoting the Bible he most often depends on the Septuagint (abbreviated LXX), the standard Greek translation of the Hebrew scriptures used by Diaspora Jews. Some Greek was undoubtedly used in Palestine, but it was not the primarily language of the inhabitants. Since Persian times— fourth century BCE—their language had been Aramaic, a Semitic language akin to Hebrew.

If in the Diaspora, where? Probably in a city, and clearly one that had a considerable Jewish population. But since that was true in most of the cities of the Mediterranean world, it is as with the question of his name: we unfortunately can't know more. If Antioch, on the upper east end of the Mediterranean, was the gospel's provenance (that is often suggested, and perhaps the mention of Syria in 4:24 lends a bit of support) it would tell us a good deal about the gospel's social setting. (See Balch.)

4. Structure — Purpose — Audience

How organized?

Like other ancient authors, who didn't usually provide an outline displaying the plan of their book, even a table of contents, the evangelist gives no explicit indication of his gospel's structure. (Chapter divisions in books of the Bible represent a rough attempt to break the story into somewhat more manageable parts, often at quite logical points, but as I've said they were introduced much later.) The story may fall naturally into sections, but it lacks section headings. (Those that appear in most NT's are the modern creation of the translators or editors.) One episode follows another, with at most a minor transitional element (for example, *In due course*, 3:1; *And it happened*, 9:10). It is on the basis of content alone that we must search for structure in Matthew—at least the skeleton of an outline. And if we can determine some such underlying format it will of course help us better understand the evangelist's work as a whole.

Scholars will perhaps always argue about how our gospel is structured; nevertheless it exhibits clearer structural clues than we find in any of the other gospels. From those clues we can extract a kind of outline that I think makes most sense of Matthew. More than a century ago a few scholars observed that in Matthew—and only in Matthew—Jesus presents five long speeches or discourses. The author has gathered their contents from various sources. Each has a particular subject, and all five end with the same formula: *When Jesus had finished* [or *concluded*].... This appears at 7:28, 11:1, 13:53, 19:1, and 26:1. These five speeches are sometimes called sermons. But they are not really discourses that were delivered as such. Rather, each constitutes an extensive collection of sayings from the Jesus tradition on a common theme, strung together for a single purpose. They are the evangelist's creations. (One such speech was already assembled in Mark 13—the so-called apocalyptic discourse—and re-used in Matthew 24 (also Luke 21). Luke similarly has a brief sort-of-sermon (Luke 6:20—49), the "Sermon on the Plain," probably from Q, and it became the kernel of Matthew's "Sermon on the Mount." Based on the concluding formulas, we can identify these five collections:

Chapters 5–7	What Heaven's Empire Demands–the "Sermon on the Mount"
Chapter 10	Instructions for the Disciples' Mission
Chapter 13	Most of the Parables
Chapter 18	Instructions for the Church
Chapters 23–25	The Time of the End

For each of these "sermons" the author lays Mark aside, but the sections of narrative that alternate with them tend to resume Mark, and often its order. Yet even there we find the evangelist gathering from various points in Mark a certain kind of story—as in chapters 8—9 he collects accounts of most of Jesus' miracles. The author's mind is an orderly one, and his exposition of the Christian message and all it entails is carefully, indeed methodically, ordered.

Many have noted an obvious parallel between the five-part structure of Matthew and the so-called five Books of Moses, which also consist of both discourse and narrative. And even the concluding formula mentioned above resembles one that appears several times in those books when God or Moses has finished speaking (see Exod 31:18, 34:33, Num 16:31, Deut 31:1, 32:45). Thus the gospel may be, as it were, a kind of Christian Pentateuch, and Matthew may have been the one evangelist who imagined his work as forming the kernel of a Christian canon of scripture paralleling the Hebrew Bible. The three other gospel writers evidently had no such ambition. If the opening phrase of the gospel (1:1) is taken at face value, it means that this is the Book of Genesis about Jesus (see comment on that verse).

Some interpreters (David Bauer, for example) doubt that the author intended a parallel to the five Books of Moses. They point out that nowhere does he call attention to such a structure; at best it is implicit. Further, they ask, could his hearers/readers have been expected to recognize this format? Even though this gospel presupposes a Jewish Christian audience, perhaps not. But I believe it will be helpful to understand what was very possibly in his mind as he put his gospel together.

Why written?

What was the author's purpose? Even if, as just now suggested, he hoped his gospel to be preserved and become part of a Christian canon, it was pretty obviously written for more specific reasons—perhaps to settle certain theological and ecclesiastical issues or to meet particular needs of the author's young church.

One such question would have been the relation of Christianity to on-going, non-Christian Judaism. By the time Matthew was being written, Christianity was becoming less a movement within Judaism than a competing religion. On the one hand, then, the author clearly wants to show the *continuity* between Christianity and Judaism, and especially continuity with the Jewish scriptures. As I suggested earlier, the evangelist may have been like Paul a convert from Pharisaism (see the comment on 13:52) and thereafter hostile to it (chapter. 23). But far from attempting to deny the Jewishness of Christianity, he emphasizes it.

On the other hand, he seems to suggest that Christianity reinterprets Judaism and indeed *supplants* it. That would explain why he quotes so many Biblical passages—commonly with an introductory formula such as, *This happened so that the word spoken by the prophet ... would come true* (see for example, 1:22, 2:15). In Christ the scriptures have now been fulfilled; their predictive role is complete.

If in fact Matthew presents Christianity as *a new and truer Judaism*, that would explain the so-called antitheses in 5:21-48. Each takes the form, "As you know, our ancestors were told . . . But I tell you . . . ." In every case an older ethical expectation is replaced with a more demanding one. Not only the act of adultery is condemned, but the lust that would give rise to it (5:27-28).

The evangelist *expanded Mark* (his gospel is roughly half again as long). But he set out also *to revise* it—to correct and improve on it. In 3:3, for example, he corrects the error in Mark 1:2-3 (the first part of the quotation that follows ". . . Isaiah the prophet wrote" is not from Isaiah but Malachi).

Sometimes he seems to *ignore* important aspects of Mark. He largely expunges "the messianic secret," an important Markan motif evidently of that author's invention, that depicts Jesus silencing all christological recognition by those who witness his miracles. In Mark the secret is revealed in a theological epiphany only at the moment of Jesus' death (Mark 15:39). In Matthew merely vestiges of the theme remain (see for example 9:30, 17:9), and their presence is a bit puzzling, since our evangelist seems to have had little interest in the idea. He reports apocalyptic events immediately following Jesus' death (27:51b-52), but they have no christological significance. Rather, it is the *resurrection* of Jesus—which Mark does not depict—that in Matthew puts everything into focus.

For whom?

It will help us better understand the evangelist's purpose if we consider what audience his gospel addresses. Quite obviously it was an organized body of Christians, a congregation—in Greek an *ekklêsia*, usually translated into English as "church." Although common in Paul's letters, among the gospels that word appears only in Matthew (16:18; 18:15, 17, 21). It does not mean a building, and in some cases not even a particular congregation. It's a Hebrew idea, and at first Christians thought of themselves as simply members of a movement within Judaism, gathered into community with one another. Our evangelist's congregation was clearly made up largely of

Christians Jews. In some sense they were still Jews, but the author has written a polemic against Jews who were not Christians—some of whom, particularly Pharisees, persecuted Christians. In the eyes of Jewish authorities, of course, the Christians were separatists, even heretics—and as such unacceptable or even dangerous within Judaism, and therefore needing to be disciplined. The evangelist's counter-attack would have been welcome to his reader's ears.

In trying to picture this author's "implied" reader, the individual he imagines himself addressing, we should remind ourselves that his audience would be, as that word suggests, mostly hearers. Probably few could read, and in any case a book, laboriously hand-written one copy at a time, would have been owned only by the rich, or by a community. This reader/hearer is obviously a practicing Christian, and most likely a Christian Jew—one who has set him- or herself off from mainstream Judaism. To speak of a Christian Jew seems strange for us; the phrase sounds like a contradiction. Virtually all Christians today are Gentiles, people lacking a Jewish heritage, and the sectarian division between Christian and non-Christian Jews has long since become a total separation. Like Jesus, however all the earliest Christians were Jews. In the mind of the author, then, such a church member is a Christian Jew in need of a text that comprehensively lays out the ideas and demands of Christianity.

The gospel sets forth Christianity, but not for the first time. Matthew can hardly have been written primarily for those about to be baptized into the church. Rather, it is an extensive, almost exhaustive, exposition of Jesus' teaching. And an interpretation, of course, for a church that needs—the evangelist believes—a comprehensive presentation of the good news. And an accessible one, a logically organized one.

It is also likely, but less clear, that in the evangelist's time his church included *Christian Gentiles.* He not only shows that Jesus had some dealings with Gentiles, but in the case of the "Canaanite" woman (15:21–28) he has Jesus commend her persistence in seeking help for her sick daughter.

What was the sociological situation of the author's congregation? Probably mixed. If there were poor members, there were also some who were not poor. In 19:23-24 he retains the vivid saying about a camel and the difficulty the rich will have in reaching Heaven's domain (Mark 10:23–25). But he spiritualizes Q's congratulation (or blessing) of the poor (see the comment on 5:3). Richard A. Horsley (*Politics of Plot*) argues convincingly that Jesus' original message to those politically and economically oppressed can still be heard in the Gospel of Mark, and was evidently addressed to a very similar audience. This, I believe, is no longer so true in the case of Matthew. (For disagreement with this, see Carter, *Margins.*)

5. Special Features

Use of the Old Testament

All the evangelists quote the Hebrew Scriptures (what Christians would come to call the Old Testament). That was their Bible. But our author uses it far more often and purposefully than do the other evangelists. He is especially concerned with Christianity's relation to the Hebrew Scriptures. As noted earlier, he often claims not only that a prophecy is fulfilled in the life of Jesus, but also that the event takes place *in order to fulfill* it. In other words, what can be called a "divine necessity" is at work. Reflecting the common Christian belief that the Bible in countless ways predicted the Messiah, the Anointed, Matthew presents the Jewish scriptures as a preview of what would happen in the lifetime of Jesus, and shows those predictions having come true.

This extraordinary theological claim—that the gospel replaces Judaism (see above, p. 17)—is found nowhere in Mark or Luke, a few times in John, but a dozen times in Matthew. For example: *This happened so the Lord's prediction spoken by the prophet would come true: "Out of Egypt I have called my son."* (2:15).

Because of the expense and rarity of books in ancient times (and until the invention of the printing press), it's unlikely that our evangelist, or anyone in his community, had his own copy of the Bible to consult. Rather, he would have made use of one or more collections of what are called *testimonies* —passages that seemed to Christians to bear on the story of Jesus, indeed to prophesy it (though not all were from what we think of as the prophetic books—a number come from the Psalms, for example). But someone has had access to the entire Bible, or large portions of it, to have drawn up such collections. As already observed, these passages most often depend on the LXX.

"Heaven"

Probably the most obvious difference of Matthew from the other Synoptics, apart from its unique structure, is the use of the word *heaven.* (The Greek is plural, strictly "the heavens"; but the singular is more common English, and it makes little difference.) It appears more than eighty times here (compared to seven times in Mark, thirty in Luke, seventeen in John). "Heavenly Father" or "Father in heaven" is especially characteristic of Matthew, but found only once in the other gospels (Luke 11:13—Q).

The most common use of *heaven* in Matthew, almost half of its instances, is in the phrase *heaven's imperial rule* or *heaven's domain,* the Scholars Version's translation (see below, section 7) of the more common "kingdom of heaven."

It corresponds to the "kingdom of God" in the rest of the NT—mainly Mark and Luke. Since "Kingdom of heaven" appears nowhere in the rest of the NT it is clearly the author's alteration. (See further the Translation Note on "Heaven's Imperial Rule," p. 46.)

Why was this done? At first sight, very simply—it reflects the author's fundamental Jewishness. According to Jewish custom, he wants to *avoid* using the word "God." Much earlier in Judaism it had been forbidden to pronounce "YHWH," the ancient name of God (see Glossary). And gradually that avoidance of God's name grew to include the generic word "God." Instead, one "went around" the word (what is called *periphrasis*), substituting a less sacred or less loaded word—in this case, "heaven." Moderns of course sometimes do the same thing... "for heaven's sake," "heaven only knows," "gosh," and so forth. The modern Jewish convention of writing "G-d" has the same intent. Why "heaven"? Because while the word can mean simply "sky" God was thought to dwell in heaven, not (except very rarely) on earth, and certainly not in the underworld. These were the regions of the three-tiered first-century cosmology: a flat earth with a palace above and a dungeon below.

So it is apparently his understanding of God's kingdom that forces the change. Unlike the teaching of Jesus, the kingdom comes for Matthew to have as its locus, its ideal character, something non-terrestrial. Thus, in the so-called Lord's Prayer the evangelist sets up an almost Platonic parallel between God's rule in heaven and on earth (6:10), the one ideal, the other imperfect—or rather as yet unrealized. And he thereby implies not simply that the Kingdom/Empire is God's but also that heaven is its natural place. This is a major departure, for in Jesus' teaching the kingdom of God was breaking in *on the earth.* By seeming to locate the Kingdom ideally in heaven, our author de-radicalizes both Jesus' theological message and his challenge of Rome's imperial rule. To alter in this way Jesus' teaching, in what became the predominant gospel, has had a subtle and most unfortunate effect on much later Christian thought, I'm sorry to say. In the comments I will often revert to "God" when that is what "heaven" means.

Peter and the other disciples

The disciple Simon, nicknamed The Rock, is especially prominent in Matthew. He is more frequently named here than in Mark or Luke, and is the subject of some unique traditions. To give but a few examples, he tries to walk on water after seeing Jesus do so (14:28-31); Jesus indicates what his name implies (16:17-19); he alone receives the word about paying the temple tax (17:24–26). And he is sometimes singled out in an episode in which the other two synoptic gospels mention only the disciples as a group (see for instance, 15:15).

And compared to Mark, Matthew portrays all the disciples in a better light. In 20:21, for example, it's the mother of the disciples James and John (not, as in Mark 10:37, her sons) who makes the inappropriate request that they be assigned places of honor in Jesus' reign. Still more striking is Jesus' assurance that the twelve will sit on twelve thrones and judge the tribes of Israel (19:28).

Pharisees and Pilate

Our evangelist continually deprecates the members of this first-century Jewish group, to whom he frequently applies the Greek for *hypocrite*. That designation is variously rendered in SV—for example as *phony pietist, impostor, fraud*. This animosity, which almost certainly does not go back to Jesus, is evident especially in chapter 23. The same damning is directed also at *scholars* (the "scribes" of older translations), who in many cases were also Pharisees. (See Glossary for these terms, and the Interpretive Note that follows chapter 23.)

If the Pharisees represent Jesus' enemies in Matthew's portrayal, Pontius Pilate, the Roman Governor, has become Jesus' protector. In fact Pilate—who ruled over Palestine from 26 to 36 CE—resented his assignment to that backwater region of the empire. In the end he was removed from his assignment because of persistent complaints to Rome of his brutality. So it is hardly likely that he did his best to save Jesus from execution. But beginning with Mark, and as the first century progressed, he is shown in an increasingly positive light—arguing for Jesus' innocence and in Matthew absolving himself of all blame in his death, as if helpless when confronted by Jewish insistence. See esp. 27:24. This is due most likely to a Christian attempt to curry Rome's favor in the face of incipient persecution.

6. The Greek text

The original Greek document—written (or dictated) by the author and, being handwritten, the only one of its kind—has of course long since worn out and disappeared. The earliest surviving manuscript of the whole of Matthew is from the fourth century! (If this seems discouraging, consider that the oldest manuscript of non-Biblical ancient documents is from the ninth century.) Some fragments, or quotations in other documents, are earlier;

yet of the entire gospel we have only copies of copies of copies. Hundreds of manuscripts are available today and all of them differ from one another by various degrees, for in the process of copying, changes inevitably occurred. Until the development of the printing press in the fifteenth century, books were not published—produced in identical copies—but laboriously transcribed from another manuscript, that is, another *handwritten* document. Changes naturally proliferated. No doubt some were accidental (copyist's errors), but some were intentional—attempts to correct what seemed to be an error in the text being copied, or editorial "improvements," to make it say what the copyist thought it should. (The most common improvements made Matthew read like Luke, especially in places where Luke had more information than Matthew.) Those changes would of course be preserved in any copies made from that manuscript. That explains why no two manuscripts of the gospel are exactly alike. They all show "variant readings"—some minor, some major. In almost every verse of every chapter of Matthew there are several such variant readings. One naturally wonders which is the correct, the original reading . . . and whether that can be determined. All too often it's not clear which of the variant readings is the oldest, the more nearly original.

Most of the differences are negligible, but some are not. It is the task of "textual criticism" to recover as nearly as possible the original wording for each set of variations. Textual criticism—the term "criticism" here has no negative connotation—is the science that examines all the available manuscripts with a critical, that is, a discerning eye, to try to determine the most likely reading of the original text.

Here is an example. In Matt 4:17 many manuscripts read: "Change your ways because" before *Heaven's imperial rule. . . .* But a few lack that clause. It was probably inserted editorially to repeat John the Baptist's earlier announcement. See further the Text-Critical Note.

Another example: in 5:22, most manuscripts read . . . *those who say to a companion, 'You moron,' will be subject to the sentence of the court.* But some have "without cause" after *companion.* Which did the author write, the shorter or the longer version of the sentence? If the shorter is original, some copyist has evidently added "without cause," to soften the warning. If the longer reading was original, why was "without cause" omitted?

These aren't crucial issues, but they illustrate what text-critics must decide—in other words, what to print in their edition of Greek Matthew. Simply counting the number of manuscripts with a certain reading doesn't answer the question, because the change could have taken place rather early, and then been copied for generations, by the great majority of later copyists. On what basis, then, can such questions be decided?

In general, the reading that best explains how the other variants arose is the most likely to be original. For example, one rule of thumb is that the *shorter reading* is original. It's often easier to understand why a copyist would have added something—if it makes sense—than left it out. Thus in both the examples we looked at, the longer reading appears to be secondary. Of course this rule does not apply if the shorter reading is shorter by accident (see the Text-Critical Note on 12:47).

But the shorter reading is not always the better. A more important rule of thumb is that the *more difficult* reading is earlier—one with a problem that a copyist is not likely to have created. This may seem odd, since we're naturally inclined to prefer the reading that makes the most sense. But that is sometimes misguided. For example, in Matthew 13:35, where some manuscripts have . . . *so what was spoken through the prophet Isaiah would come true,* others lack "Isaiah." The problem is that the quotation that follows is not from Isaiah but from Ps 78:2. So the variant that lacks "Isaiah" makes more sense. But who has created the problem? The evangelist or a later copyist? Was "Isaiah" the evangelist's mistake, which a copyist corrected? Or did a copyist insert the mistake, and if so, Why? In this case, probably the former. Copyists can of course copy incorrectly—but they do so by accident, or to improve. It's more likely that "Isaiah" is original and the copyist has omitted it for accuracy. So the "harder" reading, the one that is less palatable and in this case slightly longer is the more likely.

A copyist may try to improve the text to make Matthew, in our case, conform to one or more of the other gospels. This kind of correction is sometimes called *attraction.* See, for example, the Text-Critical Note on 1:25.

The translation used in this book (see the following section) had to begin from an agreed-upon edition of the Greek text. And that could be determined only after detailed and often highly intricate study. The Greek printed here, page by page and facing its English translation, is a fresh edition, complied by comparing existing modern reconstructions of the text of Matthew verse by verse and making fresh evaluations of all the important variant readings. A subcommittee of the SV translators had to do this text-critical work before the translation could be made.

Where there seem to be significant variant readings I call them to your attention in a *Text-Critical Note.* The manuscript evidence for most of these variant readings can be found in any recent edition of Aland, *Novum*

Testamentum. In a few cases I have departed from the Greek used by the translators—for example at 4:17 (above) or 12:6 (taking "something" as the more difficult reading).

7. The Scholars Version

Name

This "version" (that is, translation) of Matthew has an ambiguous name. The Scholars Version (SV) was created not *for* scholars but *by* scholars—and for anyone, as opposed to a translation intended specifically for Christian use, public or private. (The same is true of the series this book belongs to, "The Scholars Bible"). And it's often rather different from other modern translations of Matthew. They are sometimes overly decorous. This version is freer, more vernacular—closer, the scholars believe, to the everyday, street language of a Greek-speaking first-century audience.

Tone

SV's down-to-earth tone, what might be called its *voice*, seeks to let the oral quality of the original storyteller shine through. For this reason SV is both more vivid and more colloquial than most other modern versions. This is particularly the case when translating the sayings of Jesus. He spoke Aramaic, a Semitic language with pungent expressions. Likely enough, he also spoke some Greek. In either case his language was direct, even blunt. A few examples:

- When silencing a "demon" (believed to inhabit a sick person) he says *Shut up!*—not the stiff "Be silent."
- *I swear to you* or *You can bet* instead of "Truly I tell you" or, more conventionally, "Amen, I say to you).
- After a parable—told in vivid, plain language—it is not "He who has ears to hear, let him hear," but *Anyone here with two ears had better listen.*

SV is a product of the Jesus Seminar. It is intended for every reader, whether an amateur Bible student or a professional, or something in between. It seeks to make the text of Matthew clear to modern American readers. It's not a word-for-word translation (known technically as "formal correspondence"), attempting to follow the Greek as closely as possible. Instead SV uses "dynamic equivalence"—that is, giving the sense of the Greek but not bound by what is simplistically called a literal reading. The translators believe that such a rendering presents both more clearly and more accurately what the Greek means. Sometimes, in the comments, I will show what a more conventional translation would be, following the Greek more closely but in an unimaginative way. Such a reading (which I often simply call literal) may in fact obscure what the Greek means, even camouflaging what SV seeks to make clear. Of course all translation involves some interpretation, and the Greek may "suffer in translation," as the saying goes. SV doesn't seek to be definitive; and often there are other ways the Greek can be understood.

It should be noted that the *section headings* that break up the chapters of SV Matthew into narrative units are not part of the Greek text. Rather, they are the translators' creations, representing their understanding of the text's structure and the essence of a particular section. And that of course involves interpretation. It would be useful for you as reader to imagine how you might subdivide the chapter differently and how you would characterize each section.

Throughout this book quotations from the other gospels are also from SV.

Diction

SV uses certain English words and phrases that may be surprising to those familiar with other versions. For example SV uses:

1. *toll collector* for what has most often been "tax collector." Roman income from occupied Palestine was derived largely from road tolls.

2. *pagan* or *foreigner* for "Gentile."

3. *trust* rather than "faith." Faith can mean simply "belief," without the loyalty that the Greek *pistis* most often includes.

4. *Congratulations* and *Damn you* for "Blessed" and "Woe." See the Translation Note.

5. *change your ways* for "repent."

6. Even *you are to be as liberal <in your love> as your heavenly Father is,* instead of "Be perfect. . . ."

In addition, see the Translation Notes, especially on *the Anointed* (for "Christ"), *Judeans* (for "Jews"), *imperial Rule* (for "Kingdom"), *son of Adam* (for "son of Man").

Principles of translation

Some rules and principles that guided the translation:

1. *Inclusive language* is used to override the sexism that modern ears perceive in the collective use of the masculine gender.

   a. The Greek word *anthrôpos* has in the past always been translated "man," even though the Greek word includes both men and women. In contemporary English it should be rendered "human being" or "person" (in the plural, "people," "the public," "humankind," and so forth).

   b. In 16:24, most versions use the third-person masculine pronoun: "If anyone wants to come after me *he* should deny *himself*, pick up *his* cross and follow me." SV here, as elsewhere, has used second person: *If any of you wants to come after me you should deny yourself, pick up your cross, and follow me!*
   This avoids gender-specific pronouns and the awkward "he or she."
   For another way around "his or her," consider 25:29b:
   from those who don't have, even what they do have will be taken away—instead of "from the one who doesn't have, even what he has . . ." Or, 16:27b: *all people according to their deeds*

   c. For "brother" in Greek, SV will frequently use *brother and sister,* as in NRSV. (In fact, Jesus probably made such a change himself. In what is reported at 12:50 he broadens "your mother and brothers" of the preceding vss 48–49 to *my brother and sister and mother.)*
   And "brother" sometimes becomes *friend* (5:24), *companion* (28:10). Or the plural can be *family* (23:8).

   d. God is usually not spoken of as a male. See the comment on 6:33.

2. The so-called *historical present,* found usually in narrative, is a bit like colloquial English: "Then I say to him . . . 'n' he says to me." This usage is commonly found in Mark, less often in Matthew. It evidently is intended to involve the reader/hearer in the narrative, to give a sense of immediacy. The SV translators have decided to keep the oral quality of the present tense, even when a past tense appears on either side of it. For example, 26:40–45:
   [40]And he *returns* to the disciples and *finds* them sleeping, and *says* to Peter . . . [42]Again for a second time he went away and

prayed . . . ⁴³And once again he came and found them sleeping, since their eyes had grown heavy. ⁴⁴And leaving them again, he went away and prayed, repeating the same words for a third time. ⁴⁵Then he *comes* to the disciples and *says* . . . .

3. The *imperfect tense* sometimes conveys what is habitual or typical or even "inceptive"(he began to . . .) See for instance 5:2: *(this is what he would teach them)*; also 9:34 and13:34. One of the postulates behind SV is that we seldom and perhaps never have Jesus' exact words, and more seldom still those spoken on an identifiable occasion. Rather, where the conventional translation is "he was teaching them," we often have only the kind of thing Jesus used to teach or would have been likely to teach. See further the comment on 9:11.

4. Some *particles* (words or brief phrases often used to introduce a paragraph) have been more creatively rendered than usually, since they have no single translation. Here are three examples:
   a. Greek *gar*, which commonly introduces an explanation of preceding material, has in the past always been translated "for" or "because." SV renders it in various ways, depending on the context: *Clearly* (3:3), *Just remember* (11:18), *for his part* (14:4), *For instance* (15:2), *After all* (19:14), *You know* (24:5). And sometimes I simply leave it untranslated.
   b. *idou* (traditionally "Behold") is translated, for example, *About that time* (2:1), *Out of nowhere* (4:11), *Just then* (8:24), *Suddenly* (8:32), *The next thing you know* (9:2), *As you'll see* (28:20).
   c. *euthus/eutheôs* ("Immediately") can appear as *right then and there* (4:20), *at that precise moment* (8:13), or more often *right away*. But sometimes a phrase determined by the context is used instead *(Jesus reached right out and took hold of [Peter]*, 14:31). In Mark, the word appears more than 40 times, and often means simply, "The next thing that happened was . . . ." Our evangelist has eliminated about half of these cases.
   d. *oun* ("Therefore") is often given no translation, or rendered, for example, "So," "Then," "This means," "Well, then," "To sum up."

The effect of all this, as the translators intended, is to make Matthew alive—less "biblical," more accessible to the modern American reader—so that one can almost read Matthew as if for the first time.

In the comments I often call attention to issues that translating the Greek raises. I want to engage the reader in grappling with the meaning of the text itself so as to understand some of the problems a translator faces.

SV is an evolving translation as corrections and improvements arise. I have made some of these, in most cases noted in the Comments.

Note: Within SV these textual marks are used:

( ) Parentheses enclose material the translators take to be the evangelist's explanation to the reader. For example, 27:33: . . . *the place known as Golgotha (which means "Place of the Skull")*. Or an aside, as in 9:6: *(he then says to the paralytic, "Get up, pick up your bed and go home")*. There is no such punctuation in the Greek.

< > Words the translators think to be implied by the author but not actually in the text are indicated with pointed brackets. See, for instance, 27:54: *The <Roman> officer . . .*

Some *verses are missing* (17:21, 18:11, 21:44, 23:14). This is because the editors of our Greek text believe they were inserted after the original manuscript was written. When verse numbers were eventually introduced, the text contained the verses and accordingly they were numbered.

Besides OT quotations, which are indented, often *Jesus' words* appear in the same way, when they can be isolated from the surrounding prose—principally the parables, in chap. 13 and elsewhere.

The Gospel of Matthew

P¹, one of the oldest fragments of the Gospel of Matthew, contains Matt 1:1, 9, 12, 14, and 20 and dates to the third century CE. Photograph courtesy of The University Museum, University of Pennsylvania (neg. #S4–140073).

1 Βίβλος γενέσεως Ἰησοῦ Χριστοῦ υἱοῦ Δαυὶδ υἱοῦ Ἀβραάμ.

²Ἀβραὰμ ἐγέννησεν τὸν Ἰσαάκ, Ἰσαὰκ δὲ ἐγέννησεν τὸν Ἰακώβ, Ἰακὼβ δὲ ἐγέννησεν τὸν Ἰούδαν καὶ τοὺς ἀδελφοὺς αὐτοῦ, ³Ἰούδας δὲ ἐγέννησεν τὸν Φάρες καὶ τὸν Ζάρα ἐκ τῆς Θαμάρ, Φάρες δὲ ἐγέννησεν τὸν Ἑσρώμ, Ἑσρὼμ δὲ ἐγέννησεν τὸν Ἀράμ, ⁴Ἀρὰμ δὲ ἐγέννησεν τὸν Ἀμιναδάβ, Ἀμιναδὰβ δὲ ἐγέννησεν τὸν Ναασσών, Ναασσὼν δὲ ἐγέννησεν τὸν Σαλμών, ⁵Σαλμὼν δὲ ἐγέννησεν τὸν Βόες ἐκ τῆς Ῥαχάβ, Βόες δὲ ἐγέννησεν τὸν Ἰωβὴδ ἐκ τῆς Ῥούθ, Ἰωβὴδ δὲ ἐγέννησεν τὸν Ἰεσσαί, ⁶Ἰεσσαὶ δὲ ἐγέννησεν τὸν Δαυὶδ τὸν βασιλέα.

Δαυὶδ δὲ ἐγέννησεν τὸν Σολομῶνα ἐκ τῆς τοῦ Οὐρίου, ⁷Σολομὼν δὲ ἐγέννησεν τὸν Ῥοβοάμ, Ῥοβοὰμ δὲ ἐγέννησεν τὸν Ἀβιά, Ἀβιὰ δὲ ἐγέννησεν τὸν Ἀσάφ, ⁸Ἀσὰφ δὲ ἐγέννησεν τὸν Ἰωσαφάτ, Ἰωσαφὰτ δὲ ἐγέννησεν τὸν Ἰωράμ, Ἰωρὰμ δὲ ἐγέννησεν τὸν Ὀζίαν, ⁹Ὀζίας δὲ ἐγέννησεν τὸν Ἰωαθάμ, Ἰωαθὰμ δὲ ἐγέννησεν τὸν Ἀχάζ, Ἀχὰζ δὲ ἐγέννησεν τὸν Ἑζεκίαν, ¹⁰Ἑζεκίας δὲ ἐγέννησεν τὸν Μανασσῆ, Μανασσῆς δὲ ἐγέννησεν τὸν Ἀμώς, Ἀμὼς δὲ ἐγέννησεν τὸν Ἰωσίαν, ¹¹Ἰωσίας δὲ ἐγέννησεν τὸν Ἰεχονίαν καὶ τοὺς ἀδελφοὺς αὐτοῦ ἐπὶ τῆς μετοικεσίας Βαβυλῶνος.

¹²Μετὰ δὲ τὴν μετοικεσίαν Βαβυλῶνος Ἰεχονίας ἐγέννησεν τὸν Σαλαθιήλ, Σαλαθιὴλ δὲ ἐγέννησεν τὸν Ζοροβαβέλ, ¹³Ζοροβαβὲλ δὲ

• **Chaps. 1–2** This birth and infancy narrative resembles the stories about Moses (Exod 1–2), for example, or Samuel (1 Sam 1–2). Luke 1–2 also gives a birth narrative for Jesus, but it is almost totally different from this one. Since Mark has no such narrative, these two accounts seem to be late creations in the developing Jesus tradition. Not even the author of John knows it. Is this therefore legend? And if so does it have the function of myth—myth not as untruth but on the contrary seeking to convey theological meaning? (On legend and myth, see Glossary.) If so, its purpose is not to present (mere) historical fact but to affirm for all to see that Jesus is the Messiah, or "Christ"—that is, "the Anointed."

• **1:1a** The terse Hebraic Greek says, word for word, "Book [or Scroll] of genesis of Jesus Anointed." There are three ways to understand the intent of these opening words:

a) As translated here, taking the first half of the verse as a title for the gospel as a whole, paralleling the Greek title of the first book of the Hebrew Scriptures. And, therefore, perhaps intending to begin a Christian canon?

b) Since the word *genesis* will be translated "birth" in vs 18, the words could be translated: *An account of the birth of Jesus,...* hence a title for the first two chapters of the gospel.

c) Taking *biblos genesis* to mean "genealogy": *The ancestors of Jesus,...* a title for 1:2–17.

Which of these three possibilities is best? Are perhaps two or all three to be understood simultaneously? In other words, is our author deliberately ambiguous?

the Anointed: See Translation Note, p.34.

• **1:1b** *descended from:* Greek, "son of."

David: The great king. Since the Anointed was often imagined as a second David who would appear, he naturally is descended from David.

Abraham: The chief ancestor of Israel. God had promised him that all peoples would be blessed through him (Gen 12:3; Gal 3:8). Therefore the genealogy begins with him, whereas in Luke it traces Jesus' ancestry back all the way to Adam.

• **1:2–17** This genealogy is largely incompatible with the one in Luke 3:23–38, using many different names. Both genealogies are "kerygmatic." That is, each presents a proclamation (Greek, *kerygma*) that Jesus is the Anointed—by telling his ancestry.

It is especially noteworthy in containing the names of four women, besides

1 The Book of Genesis of Jesus the Anointed, descended from David and from Abraham.

²Abraham was the father of Isaac, Isaac of Jacob, Jacob of Judah and his brothers, ³and Judah and Tamar were the parents of Perez and Zerah. Perez was the father of Hezron, Hezron of Ram, ⁴Ram of Amminadab, Amminadab of Nahshon, Nahshon of Salmon, ⁵and Salmon and Rahab were the parents of Boaz. Boaz and Ruth were the parents of Obed. Obed was the father of Jesse, ⁶and Jesse of David the king.

David and Uriah's wife were the parents of Solomon. ⁷Solomon was the father of Rehoboam, Rehoboam of Abijah, Abijah of Asaph, ⁸Asaph of Jehoshaphat, Jehoshaphat of Joram, Joram of Uzziah, ⁹Uzziah of Jotham, Jotham of Ahaz, Ahaz of Hezekiah, ¹⁰Hezekiah of Manasseh, Manasseh of Amos, Amos of Josiah, ¹¹and Josiah was the father of Jechoniah and his brothers at the time of the exile to Babylon.

¹²After the Babylonian exile, Jechoniah was the father of Salathiel, Salathiel of Zerubbabel, ¹³Zerubbabel of Abiud, Abiud of

Jesus' ancestors

Mary—most unusual in ancient Jewish genealogies. And in one way or another the four are anomalous, as we'll see (vss 3, 5, & 6b). Our evangelist has evidently inserted their names into an older list; there is no equivalent in the OT sources or in Luke.

• **1:2** *was the father of:* The Greek is an active verb, meaning "sired," "fathered" (in KJV "begat"). The genealogy is not simply a list of names, then, but a compressed historical account. But repeating the verb seems too laborious. So the genealogy continues simply, "Isaac [was the father] of Jacob, Jacob of Judah and his brothers. . . ."

Jacob [was the father] of Judah and his brothers: According to Genesis, Jacob of course had twelve sons. But it is only *Judah* who matters here. David at first was king of the tribe descended from him, which was the southern part of what he then made into a united Israel. And after Israel split again in two, *Judah* survived by 135 years the destruction of the northern kingdom in 722 BCE. So it was Judah that eventually gave its name to the Roman district of Judea. Jesus was from the northern district, Galilee. But according to this story of his birth—and Luke's as well—he was born in David's birthplace, Bethlehem of Judea (see 2:1).

• **1:3** *Judah and Tamar:* Tamar is the first of four women. Like the others (vss 5–6), Tamar represents embarrassment, here even scandal: She was Judah's daughter-in-law (Gen 38).

• **1:5** *Rahab:* A heroine to Israel but a non-Israelite and a prostitute (Josh 2).

Ruth: Not immoral but awkward in Jesus' ancestry, since this great-grandmother of King David was a Moabite (Ruth 1:4).

• **1:6** *David the king:* From this point, the genealogy is a royal one.

Uriah's wife: That is, Bathsheba. David raped her and had her husband killed. By her he subsequently sired *Solomon* (2 Sam 11). She like Ruth was a non-Israelite.

• **1:7–11** There are some discrepancies with the OT, particularly in the Hebrew. For example, some names are wrong: *Asaph* for *Asa*, *Amos* for *Amon*, *Jechoniah* for *Jehoahaz*. Four generations are skipped between *Joram* and *Uzziah*. And *Josiah* was not *the father of Jechoniah* but his grandfather.

• **1:11** *Jechoniah and his brothers:* This neatly summarizes a chaotic succession in the waning years of the kingdom of Judah.

the exile to Babylon: Beginning in 587 BCE, when Judah was finally conquered.

• **1:12–15** Most of these names are unknown in the OT.

ἐγέννησεν τὸν Ἀβιούδ, Ἀβιοὺδ δὲ ἐγέννησεν τὸν Ἐλιακίμ, Ἐλιακὶμ
δὲ ἐγέννησεν τὸν Ἀζώρ, ¹⁴Ἀζὼρ δὲ ἐγέννησεν τὸν Σαδώκ, Σαδὼκ
δὲ ἐγέννησεν τὸν Ἀχίμ, Ἀχὶμ δὲ ἐγέννησεν τὸν Ἐλιούδ, ¹⁵Ἐλιοὺδ
δὲ ἐγέννησεν τὸν Ἐλεάζαρ, Ἐλεάζαρ δὲ ἐγέννησεν τὸν Ματθάν,
Ματθὰν δὲ ἐγέννησεν τὸν Ἰακώβ, ¹⁶Ἰακὼβ δὲ ἐγέννησεν τὸν Ἰωσὴφ
τὸν ἄνδρα Μαρίας, ἐξ ἧς ἐγεννήθη Ἰησοῦς ὁ λεγόμενος Χριστός.

¹⁷Πᾶσαι οὖν αἱ γενεαὶ ἀπὸ Ἀβραὰμ ἕως Δαυὶδ γενεαὶ
δεκατέσσαρες, καὶ ἀπὸ Δαυὶδ ἕως τῆς μετοικεσίας Βαβυλῶνος γενεαὶ
δεκατέσσαρες, καὶ ἀπὸ τῆς μετοικεσίας Βαβυλῶνος ἕως τοῦ Χριστοῦ
γενεαὶ δεκατέσσαρες.

Birth of Jesus ¹⁸Τοῦ δὲ Ἰησοῦ Χριστοῦ ἡ γένεσις οὕτως ἦν. μνηστευθείσης τῆς
μητρὸς αὐτοῦ Μαρίας τῷ Ἰωσήφ, πρὶν ἢ συνελθεῖν αὐτοὺς εὑρέθη ἐν
γαστρὶ ἔχουσα ἐκ πνεύματος ἁγίου. ¹⁹Ἰωσὴφ δὲ ὁ ἀνὴρ αὐτῆς, δίκαιος
ὢν καὶ μὴ θέλων αὐτὴν δειγματίσαι, ἐβουλήθη λάθρα ἀπολῦσαι
αὐτήν.

²⁰Ταῦτα δὲ αὐτοῦ ἐνθυμηθέντος ἰδοὺ ἄγγελος κυρίου κατ' ὄναρ
ἐφάνη αὐτῷ λέγων, Ἰωσὴφ υἱὸς Δαυίδ, μὴ φοβηθῇς παραλαβεῖν
Μαριὰμ τὴν γυναῖκά σου· τὸ γὰρ ἐν αὐτῇ γεννηθὲν ἐκ πνεύματός
ἐστιν ἁγίου. ²¹τέξεται δὲ υἱόν, καὶ καλέσεις τὸ ὄνομα αὐτοῦ Ἰησοῦν·
αὐτὸς γὰρ σώσει τὸν λαὸν αὐτοῦ ἀπὸ τῶν ἁμαρτιῶν αὐτῶν.

²²Τοῦτο δὲ ὅλον γέγονεν ἵνα πληρωθῇ τὸ ῥηθὲν ὑπὸ κυρίου διὰ
τοῦ προφήτου λέγοντος,

1:18 Some MSS have a more literal term for *birth* here (*gennêsis* instead of
genesis). But the meaning is the same. A few MSS lack *Jesus* here. If original,
why would it have been dropped? Possibly, therefore, the shorter reading
is original.

• **1:16** *Jacob was the father of Joseph:* A Jacob
as the father of this Joseph is otherwise
unknown. Are he and his son—grandfather
and father of Jesus—meant to remind us of
the patriarchs Jacob and his son Joseph?

*Joseph, the husband of Mary, who was the
mother of Jesus:* The anomaly is that both
Matthew and Luke trace Jesus' ancestry
through Joseph, yet he is not named the
father of Jesus. In Luke's case Mary is Jesus'
only natural parent. In Matthew, the basis
for a virginal conception of Jesus is at best
ambiguous (see below on 1:18–25). Perhaps
the geneology was originally independent of
the account of Jesus' birth, and the evangelist here attempts to resolve the tension. Joseph will name Jesus (vs 25), which probably
means that he adopts him as his son.

• **1:17** *fourteen:* Possibly having symbolic
meaning, but we can only speculate what
that is. The last third of this genealogy in
fact names only thirteen generations.

• **1:18** *birth:* The most probable Greek word
here (*genesis*—see Text-Critical Note) was

coupled with "book"/"account" in vs 1. And
it is a cognate of the term "generation" in
vs 17. In Greek, then, this account of Jesus'
birth picks up the language of both the title
in vs 1 and the geneology of vss 2–17.

the Anointed: Here, oddly, no definite article
appears in the Greek, so perhaps the phrase
should be thought of here not as a title but a
name, as in the usual phrase "Jesus Christ."

was engaged: In fact, bound by the first
stage of the marriage contract, a bit like
what "betrothed" used to mean. So Joseph is
already *her husband* (vs 19) even though they
had not yet "slept together."

found to be pregnant: Under Jewish law this
would allow Joseph to divorce her, to "expose her publicly" (next verse.)

by the holy spirit: This is said for the reader's
benefit. Joseph learns it only in vs 20. There
is no article with "spirit" in the Greek. But
perhaps this is the terse Hebraizing style
of vs 1. The point here is that this birth is
special. It does not mean, as in Luke's parallel story, a miraculous, asexual conception,

Eliakim, Eliakim of Azor, [14]Azor of Zadok, Zadok of Achim, Achim of Eliud, [15]Eliud of Eleazar, Eleazar of Matthan, Matthan of Jacob. [16]And Jacob was the father of Joseph, the husband of Mary, who was the mother of Jesus. Jesus is known as the Anointed.

[17]In sum, the generations from Abraham to David come to fourteen, those from David to the Babylonian exile number fourteen, and those from the Babylonian exile to the Anointed amount to fourteen also.

[18]The birth of Jesus the Anointed took place as follows: While his **Birth of Jesus** mother Mary was engaged to Joseph, but before they slept together, she was found to be pregnant by the holy spirit. [19]Since Joseph her husband was a decent man and did not wish to expose her publicly, he planned to break off their engagement quietly.

[20]While he was thinking about these things, a messenger of the Lord surprised him in a dream with these words: "Joseph, descendant of David, don't hesitate to take Mary as your wife, since the holy spirit is responsible for her pregnancy. [21]She will give birth to a son and you will name him Jesus—the name means 'he will save his people from their sins.'"

[22]All of this has happened so the prediction of the Lord given by the prophet would come true:

---

which would make no sense in this author's Jewish context (see Miller, *Born Divine,* pp. 205–206). Rather, it implies that although the biological father (as we would say) of Jesus was unknown, Joseph is to treat the child as his own. See vss 20–21a. The evangelist does not regard Jesus to have been illegitimate (as a later Rabbinic tradition held, whether as fact or polemic). He justifies this unusual birth by using a "prediction" from Isaiah, rather differently from Luke (see further below on vss 22 and 23).

• **1:20** *a messenger of the Lord:* See Glossary.

surprised him: Usually translated, "Behold, [the angel] appeared to him."

in a dream: Often in the OT and in this gospel this is how God's will becomes known.

the holy spirit is responsible for her pregnancy: More literally, "what has been begotten in her is from a holy spirit."

• **1:21** *he will save his people from their sins:* This good news is the heart of the birth story. Along with our author's message as a whole, it accounts for the fact that this book is

called a "gospel" (see Introduction, p. 7).

he will save: "Yeshua," the Semitic form of "Jesus," means "Yah[weh] saves." Yahweh is of course the proper name of Israel's God. Does this mean that God will save his people through Jesus? or that Jesus himself will save? Perhaps for the evangelist there is no difference.

his people: Does this mean Yahweh's chosen, Israel, or Jesus' followers?

from their sins: This very Pauline idea has little expression in Matthew, apart from Jesus' word over the cup at the last supper in 26:28.

• **1:22** *this has happened so the prediction of the Lord given by the prophet would come true:* A formula like this occurs many times in Matthew. Biblical prophecy is not only fulfilled; these events take place *in order to* fulfill scripture. Or, put another way, this had to happen—and so it did. For the early Christians the Hebrew Scriptures (the OT), read with the eyes of faith, contained the biography of the Anointed. See Introduction,

²³Ἰδοὺ ἡ παρθένος ἐν γαστρὶ ἕξει

καὶ τέξεται υἱόν,

καὶ καλέσουσιν τὸ ὄνομα αὐτοῦ Ἐμμανουήλ,

ὅ ἐστιν μεθερμηνευόμενον Μεθ' ἡμῶν ὁ θεός.

²⁴Ἐγερθεὶς δὲ ὁ Ἰωσὴφ ἀπὸ τοῦ ὕπνου ἐποίησεν ὡς προσέταξεν αὐτῷ ὁ ἄγγελος κυρίου καὶ παρέλαβεν τὴν γυναῖκα αὐτοῦ, ²⁵καὶ οὐκ ἐγίνωσκεν αὐτὴν ἕως οὗ ἔτεκεν υἱόν· καὶ ἐκάλεσεν τὸ ὄνομα αὐτοῦ Ἰησοῦν.

1:25 Some MSS read "to her firstborn son" instead of *to a son,* probably by "attraction" to Luke 2:7 (see Introduction, p. 23).

---

p. 19, on the Matthean theme of prophecy fulfillment.

• **1:23** Isa 7:14b, more or less according to the Greek OT (LXX).

A virgin: The OT reads "the virgin" because it probably refers to the young wife of Ahaz (king of Judah, 735–715 BCE). In the Hebrew the word was simply "young woman" and she was already pregnant, so neither conception nor birth would be exceptional. The Greek translation raises the possibility of a miraculous birth, but Luke's understanding of this passage should not influence us. Very likely our author is chiefly concerned with the birth of Jesus, not his conception, and with the Hebrew name to

---

Translation Note: "The Anointed"

This phrase, a royal title, involves three languages. It began in Hebrew as *mashiach* and was used of the Israelite king after he had been crowned (as we would say) by being anointed with oil. Very occasionally the term was simply brought into Greek as *messias,* and it survives in John 1:41, 4:25—and in English as Messiah. But almost always, as in the Greek version of the OT (known as LXX), the word was translated into Greek as *christos,* one who has been anointed with chrism. This is the almost universal form in the Greek NT, whether as title *(Iêsous ho christos)* or eventually a name by itself. In English for some reason the Greek term—like Messiah—was not usually translated, but simply transliterated as "Christ." So SV at last completes the translation process: "the Anointed [one]." This restores the word's vividness and a dimension that the term "Christ" has long since lost.

After the Hebrew monarchy disappeared, and with it—in the 6th century BCE—the Jews' independence, the expectation arose that in good time God would restore the monarchy and independent nationhood, and the hoped-for figure of a new king would appear.

²³Behold, a virgin will conceive a child
and she will give birth to a son,
and they will name him Emmanuel

(which means "God with us").

²⁴Joseph got up and did what the messenger of the Lord told him:
he took <Mary as> his wife. ²⁵He did not have sex with her until she
had given birth to a son. Joseph named him Jesus.

---

be assigned to him.

Emmanuel (which means "God with us"): The
name "Jesus" has just been interpreted (vs
21). Now the symbolic name in Isa 7:14 is
applied to him. In Isaiah it meant God's
presence to judge. Here it means to bless,
to save.

• **1:24–25** Despite the fact that Mary is the
only known parent of Jesus, Joseph is the
central character in this story. He both receives the divine message and obeys it.

• **1:25** *have sex with her:* Greek, "know her."

Joseph named him Jesus: See comment on
vs 16, and the instruction Joseph received
in vs 21.

With time and the failure of such a restoration the expectation became
more and more urgent and the role the messiah would play when he
came more pivotal. He would bring in God's new age, when the Jews'
sufferings would be vindicated and their enemies punished.

Much of this is riding on our evangelist's use of the term, most of
all its apocalyptic connotation. But also the divinity that was somehow
associated with the title; Israelite kings were often called sons of God
in a special sense (Psalm 2:7–8), and this is taken literally in the case
of the Messiah. Soon after his death, and because of his purported
resurrection, Jesus was recognized as the Anointed one and (especially
for Gentiles) the Son of God, whose coming initiated a new age—but
not in the expected political sense—and whose return would complete
that restoration.

It can be doubted whether Jesus in his lifetime claimed this title,
indeed whether he wanted any exalted title for himself. His purpose
was to proclaim the breaking in of God's kingdom, God's domain,
rather than to preside over it. But after the resurrection, and in light
of it, the title easily enough was applied to him. He is the Christ, his
followers Christians, and the ongoing institution Christianity.

2 Τοῦ δὲ Ἰησοῦ γεννηθέντος ἐν Βηθλέεμ τῆς Ἰουδαίας ἐν ἡμέραις Ἡρῴδου τοῦ βασιλέως, ἰδοὺ μάγοι ἀπὸ ἀνατολῶν παρεγένοντο εἰς Ἱεροσόλυμα ²λέγοντες, Ποῦ ἐστιν ὁ τεχθεὶς βασιλεὺς τῶν Ἰουδαίων; εἴδομεν γὰρ αὐτοῦ τὸν ἀστέρα ἐν τῇ ἀνατολῇ καὶ ἤλθομεν προσκυνῆσαι αὐτῷ.

³Ἀκούσας δὲ ὁ βασιλεὺς Ἡρῴδης ἐταράχθη καὶ πᾶσα Ἱεροσόλυμα μετ᾽ αὐτοῦ, ⁴καὶ συναγαγὼν πάντας τοὺς ἀρχιερεῖς καὶ γραμματεῖς τοῦ λαοῦ ἐπυνθάνετο παρ᾽ αὐτῶν ποῦ ὁ Χριστὸς γεννᾶται.

⁵Οἱ δὲ εἶπαν αὐτῷ, Ἐν Βηθλέεμ τῆς Ἰουδαίας· οὕτως γὰρ γέγραπται διὰ τοῦ προφήτου·

⁶Καὶ σύ Βηθλέεμ, γῆ Ἰούδα,
οὐδαμῶς ἐλαχίστη εἶ ἐν τοῖς ἡγεμόσιν Ἰούδα·
ἐκ σοῦ γὰρ ἐξελεύσεται ἡγούμενος,
ὅστις ποιμανεῖ τὸν λαόν μου τὸν Ἰσραήλ.

⁷Τότε Ἡρῴδης λάθρᾳ καλέσας τοὺς μάγους ἠκρίβωσεν παρ᾽ αὐτῶν τὸν χρόνον τοῦ φαινομένου ἀστέρος, ⁸καὶ πέμψας αὐτοὺς εἰς Βηθλέεμ εἶπεν, Πορευθέντες ἐξετάσατε ἀκριβῶς περὶ τοῦ παιδίου· ἐπὰν δὲ εὕρητε, ἀπαγγείλατέ μοι, ὅπως κἀγὼ ἐλθὼν προσκυνήσω αὐτῷ.

⁹Οἱ δὲ ἀκούσαντες τοῦ βασιλέως ἐπορεύθησαν.

Καὶ ἰδοὺ ὁ ἀστήρ, ὃν εἶδον ἐν τῇ ἀνατολῇ, προῆγεν αὐτούς, ἕως ἐλθὼν ἐστάθη ἐπάνω οὗ ἦν τὸ παιδίον. ¹⁰ἰδόντες δὲ τὸν ἀστέρα ἐχάρησαν χαρὰν μεγάλην σφόδρα. ¹¹καὶ ἐλθόντες εἰς τὴν οἰκίαν εἶδον τὸ παιδίον μετὰ Μαρίας τῆς μητρὸς αὐτοῦ, καὶ πεσόντες προσεκύνησαν αὐτῷ καὶ ἀνοίξαντες τοὺς θησαυροὺς αὐτῶν

• **2:1** *Bethlehem:* Not mentioned till now. Perhaps the evangelist begins to follow a different tradition here. The town is of great significance in both this gospel and in Luke since it was David's hometown (1 Sam 16:1), and the Anointed would be not only descended from him (1:1) but like him—only greater. In this gospel Joseph and Mary are evidently living in Bethlehem, and so of course Jesus is born there. (In Luke they live in Nazareth, and it must explained, in Luke 2:1–5, how they came to be in Bethlehem for Jesus' birth.) Later on (Matt 2:21–23) the evangelist has to account for the fact that Jesus was known to come from Nazareth.

Judea: The southern part of Palestine. Nazareth, where Jesus must have grown up (and some would say was in fact born), is in Galilee, in the north.

Herod: "The Great." From about 37 to 4 BCE, he was king over Judea and Galilee under Roman control.

About that time: The Greek has *idou*; see Introduction, p. 27.

astrologers: In Greek, "magi," the ancient equivalent of sacred astronomers; they knew how to *observe* the stars. Like modern astrologers they found astral evidence of earthly events. Jesus' star, for instance, showed him to be a *newborn king*.

from the East: These wise men, as they might be called, were believed to have come from Persia, more or less the ancient equivalent of Iran. Despite later tradition, they are not called kings.

Jerusalem: Herod's capital. Bethlehem is about 5 miles to the southwest..

• **2:2** *the newborn king of the Judeans:* Jesus is to be like David, king of the people of Judah/Judea.

the Judeans: Usually translated "the Jews." See Translation Note, p. 41.

2 Jesus was born at Bethlehem, Judea, when Herod was king. About that time astrologers from the East showed up in Jerusalem. ²"Tell us," they said, "where the newborn king of the Judeans is. We have observed his star at its rising and have come to honor him."

Astrologers from the east

³When this news reached King Herod, he was visibly shaken, and all Jerusalem along with him. ⁴He called together all the ranking priests and scholars, and pressed them for information: "Where is the Anointed supposed to be born?"

⁵They replied, "At Bethlehem, Judea. This is how it is put by the prophet:

⁶And you, Bethlehem, in the province of Judah,
you are by no means least among the leaders of Judah.
Out of you will come a leader
who will shepherd my people Israel."

⁷Then Herod called the astrologers together secretly and ascertained from them the precise time the star became visible. ⁸Then he sent them to Bethlehem with these instructions: "Go make a careful search for the child. When you find him, report back to me, so I can also go and honor him."

⁹They listened to what the king had to say and continued on their way.

And there guiding them on was the star that they had observed in the East: it led them on until it came to a standstill above where the child lay. ¹⁰Once they saw the star <come to a stop> they were beside themselves with joy. ¹¹And they arrived at the house and saw the child with his mother Mary. They fell down and honored him.

---

his star at its rising: In Greek, "in the East," but how could it lead the "astrologers from the East" westwards? Evidently the phrase means a new star, something very important to observers of the sky.

• **2:3** *Herod . . . was visibly shaken:* That Jesus is to be *king of the Judeans* (vs 2) is of course a threat to his role and authority.

• **2:4** *ranking priests and scholars:* Usually translated "high priests and scribes" (see Glossary); but there was only one "high priest" at a time, in this case, Caiaphas—see 26:3.

Where is the Anointed supposed to be born? That is, according to scriptural prediction—particularly that of the prophets, which these authorities could interpret.

• **2:6** The prophecy is quoted, with some adaptation, from Mic 5:2.

• **2:7** *Herod . . . ascertained . . . the precise time the star became visible:* So he could be sure to have Jesus killed—see vss 16–18. The astrolo-gers would certainly have made note of *the precise time the star became visible.*

• **2:8** *so I can also go and honor him:* Not at all his real intent.

• **2:9** *there:* Greek, *idou* again; see above on vs 1.

that they had observed in the East: See on vs 2.

it led them on until it came to a standstill: In the ancient world it was believed that stars were lights that moved on the under-surface of the dome called "sky" and could become stationary. See Gen 1:14–17.

where the child lay: There is no mention of an inn or a manger as in Luke 2:7.

• **2:11** *gold, pure incense, and myrrh:* Because of the three costly gifts in *their treasure chests* the astrologers are often thought of as "three kings."

προσήνεγκαν αὐτῷ δῶρα, χρυσὸν καὶ λίβανον καὶ σμύρναν. ¹²καὶ χρηματισθέντες κατ' ὄναρ μὴ ἀνακάμψαι πρὸς Ἡρῴδην, δι' ἄλλης ὁδοῦ ἀνεχώρησαν εἰς τὴν χώραν αὐτῶν.

Flight to Egypt

¹³Ἀναχωρησάντων δὲ αὐτῶν ἰδοὺ ἄγγελος κυρίου φαίνεται κατ' ὄναρ τῷ Ἰωσὴφ λέγων, Ἐγερθεὶς παράλαβε τὸ παιδίον καὶ τὴν μητέρα αὐτοῦ καὶ φεῦγε εἰς Αἴγυπτον καὶ ἴσθι ἐκεῖ ἕως ἂν εἴπω σοι· μέλλει γὰρ Ἡρῴδης ζητεῖν τὸ παιδίον τοῦ ἀπολέσαι αὐτό.

¹⁴Ὁ δὲ ἐγερθεὶς παρέλαβεν τὸ παιδίον καὶ τὴν μητέρα αὐτοῦ νυκτὸς καὶ ἀνεχώρησεν εἰς Αἴγυπτον, ¹⁵καὶ ἦν ἐκεῖ ἕως τῆς τελευτῆς Ἡρῴδου· ἵνα πληρωθῇ τὸ ῥηθὲν ὑπὸ κυρίου διὰ τοῦ προφήτου λέγοντος,

Ἐξ Αἰγύπτου ἐκάλεσα τὸν υἱόν μου.

Murder of the babies

¹⁶Τότε Ἡρῴδης ἰδὼν ὅτι ἐνεπαίχθη ὑπὸ τῶν μάγων ἐθυμώθη λίαν, καὶ ἀποστείλας ἀνεῖλεν πάντας τοὺς παῖδας τοὺς ἐν Βηθλέεμ καὶ ἐν πᾶσι τοῖς ὁρίοις αὐτῆς ἀπὸ διετοῦς καὶ κατωτέρω, κατὰ τὸν χρόνον ὃν ἠκρίβωσεν παρὰ τῶν μάγων. ¹⁷τότε ἐπληρώθη τὸ ῥηθὲν διὰ Ἰερεμίου τοῦ προφήτου λέγοντος,

¹⁸Φωνὴ ἐν Ῥαμὰ ἠκούσθη,
κλαυθμὸς καὶ ὀδυρμὸς πολύς·
Ῥαχὴλ κλαίουσα τὰ τέκνα αὐτῆς,
καὶ οὐκ ἤθελεν παρακληθῆναι,
ὅτι οὐκ εἰσίν.

Return to Nazareth

¹⁹Τελευτήσαντος δὲ τοῦ Ἡρῴδου ἰδοὺ ἄγγελος κυρίου φαίνεται κατ' ὄναρ τῷ Ἰωσὴφ ἐν Αἰγύπτῳ ²⁰λέγων, Ἐγερθεὶς παράλαβε τὸ παιδίον καὶ τὴν μητέρα αὐτοῦ καὶ πορεύου εἰς γῆν Ἰσραήλ· τεθνήκασιν γὰρ οἱ ζητοῦντες τὴν ψυχὴν τοῦ παιδίου.

2:18 *mourning:* Some MSS have "dirges and mourning," which is closer to the Septuagint (LXX) of Jeremiah 31:15. Original, or a later correction?

• **2:12** *advised in a dream not to return to Herod:* To thwart his plan (vss 16–18).
  in a dream: That is, by God.
• **2:13** *a messenger . . . in a dream:* As in 1:20.
  to Egypt: Just as Jacob/Israel and his sons went down into Egypt, fleeing the famine in the land of Canaan/Israel (Gen 46).
• **2:15** *This happened so the Lord's prediction . . . would come true:* For this formula see above on 1:22.
  Out of Egypt I have called my son: A quotation from Hos 11:1. In that context it refers not

to the Anointed but to Israel and its exodus from Egypt. But that did not matter to those who found Jesus' story foretold in the scriptures. In fact, he is probably to be understood as reliving Israel's history, with his twelve disciples embodying the New Israel (see comment on 19:28).
  my son: As the "voice from the sky" at Jesus' baptism would declare (3:17).
• **2:16** *duped by the astrologers:* Actually, by God, who had "advised them in a dream" (vs 12).

Then they opened their treasure chests and presented him with gifts—gold, pure incense, and myrrh. ¹²And because they had been advised in a dream not to return to Herod, they journeyed back to their own country by a different route.

¹³After ‹the astrologers› had departed, a messenger of the Lord appeared in a dream to Joseph, saying, "Get up, take the child and his mother and flee to Egypt. Stay there until I give you instructions. For Herod is determined to hunt the child down and destroy him."

Flight to Egypt

¹⁴So Joseph got up and took the child and his mother under cover of night and set out for Egypt. ¹⁵There they would remain until Herod's death. This happened so the Lord's prediction spoken by the prophet would come true:

Out of Egypt I have called my son.

¹⁶When Herod realized he had been duped by the astrologers, he was outraged. He then issued instructions to kill all the children two years old and younger in Bethlehem and the surrounding region. This corresponded to the time ‹of the star› that he had learned from the astrologers. ¹⁷With this event the prediction made by Jeremiah the prophet came true:

Murder of the babies

¹⁸In Ramah the sound of mourning
and bitter grieving was heard:
Rachel weeping for her children.
She refused to be consoled:
They were no more.

¹⁹After Herod's death, a messenger of the Lord appeared in a dream to Joseph in Egypt: ²⁰"Get up, take the child and his mother, and return to the land of Israel; those who were seeking the child's life are dead."

Return to Nazareth

This corresponded . . .: That is, the *two years* did.

the time ‹of the star› that he had learned from the astrologers: In vs 7.

• **2:17** *the prediction . . . came true:* Here, unusually, the element of "divine necessity" is not expressed (as it is in vs 15). It's surprising that the evangelist does not depict this murder as foreshadowed in Pharaoh's killing of the Hebrew boys (Exod 1:22).

• **2:18** This verse is taken from Jer 31:15. There it is not prediction but reference to a past event, evidently Rachel's mourning for the exile of the Northern kingdom of Israel, represented by her sons, Joseph and Benjamin. It powerfully expresses the almost unbearable loss of one's child.

Ramah: A place NNW of Jerusalem, perhaps modern Ramallah.

• **2:19** *Herod's death:* In 4 BCE.

• **2:20** *those who were seeking the child's life:* Herod and his henchmen (see vs 16).

²¹Ὁ δὲ ἐγερθεὶς παρέλαβεν τὸ παιδίον καὶ τὴν μητέρα αὐτοῦ καὶ εἰσῆλθεν εἰς γῆν Ἰσραήλ. ²²ἀκούσας δὲ ὅτι Ἀρχέλαος βασιλεύει τῆς Ἰουδαίας ἀντὶ τοῦ πατρὸς αὐτοῦ Ἡρώδου ἐφοβήθη ἐκεῖ ἀπελθεῖν· χρηματισθεὶς δὲ κατ' ὄναρ ἀνεχώρησεν εἰς τὰ μέρη τῆς Γαλιλαίας, ²³καὶ ἐλθὼν κατῴκησεν εἰς πόλιν λεγομένην Ναζαρέτ· ὅπως πληρωθῇ τὸ ῥηθὲν διὰ τῶν προφητῶν ὅτι Ναζωραῖος κληθήσεται.

• **2:21** Often, when a divine command is followed, the words of the command (vs 20) are repeated precisely.

• **2:22** *Archelaus ... king of Judea:* Herod's eldest son, who inherited the most important part of his father's kingdom, Judea and Samaria. He ruled ten years, until 6 CE, when Rome removed him from power for his savage suppression of unrest.

  Galilee: Greek: "the territories of the Galilee." The region was under the rule of Herod Antipas, brother of Archelaus.

• **2:23** *Nazareth:* Where Jesus would grow up. In the hill country of Galilee.

  that he would be called a Nazorean: There is no very clear source for this quotation, but perhaps it refers to the promise at the birth of Samson in Judg 13:5, that he was to be "a Nazirite to God." In any case Jesus is often recognized as coming "from Nazareth" (21:11). And see 26:71, where Peter is identified in this way with Jesus.

²¹So he got up, took the child and his mother, and returned to the land of Israel. ²²He heard that Archelaus was the king of Judea in the place of his father Herod; as a consequence, he was afraid to go there. He was instructed in a dream to go to Galilee; ²³and he went and settled in a town called Nazareth, so that the prophecy spoken through the prophets might be fulfilled, that he would be called a Nazorean.

Translation Note: "The Judeans"

This is used in SV where "the Jews" has usually been the translation. The Greek word *Ioudaioi* in fact basically means the people of Judea, the Roman name for ancient Judah. And generalizing from it the word, singular or plural, can refer to Jews living anywhere—people originally from Judea. So the Greek makes no such distinction (Jew and Judean) as there is in English. Similarly, the place-name *Ioudaia* can mean either Judea or Jewry.

But "the Jews" is sometimes used in the NT in ways that have led to vicious anti-Semitism over the centuries. And next to the Gospel of John, Matthew is the NT book most responsible for this anti-Judaism. In the story of Jesus' arrest, trial, and execution "the people" are often mentioned, without distinguishing between them and their leaders. Most notably, at the time of Jesus' trial by Pilate "all the people" are depicted eagerly accepting the blame for Jesus' death—"blame his blood on us and on our children" (27:25). And "children" has usually been understood to apply to all future Jews, no matter how far removed from the 1st century. (Hence the frequent horrific view of Jews as simply "Christ-killers.") But that verse is certainly the creation of the evangelist. In fact, the responsibility for killing Jesus rested entirely on Pilate acting as Roman governor, however some Jewish leaders, wanting to be rid of Jesus, may have influenced him.

For this reason the translators of SV have chosen to avoid speaking collectively of "the Jews" who were Jesus' contemporaries and co-religionists. Instead to say simply *Judeans*. In Matthew the phrase is most often used in the title, "King of the Judeans."

In the comments I sometimes use the word Jew or Jewish, mostly to designate the Judeans' religion. And in SV Matthew, see the exception in 28:15.

3 Ἐν δὲ ταῖς ἡμέραις ἐκείναις παραγίνεται Ἰωάννης ὁ βαπτιστὴς κηρύσσων ἐν τῇ ἐρήμῳ τῆς Ἰουδαίας ²λέγων, Μετανοεῖτε· ἤγγικεν γὰρ ἡ βασιλεία τῶν οὐρανῶν.

³Οὗτος γάρ ἐστιν ὁ ῥηθεὶς διὰ Ἠσαΐου τοῦ προφήτου λέγοντος,

Φωνὴ βοῶντος ἐν τῇ ἐρήμῳ·
Ἑτοιμάσατε τὴν ὁδὸν κυρίου,
εὐθείας ποιεῖτε τὰς τρίβους αὐτοῦ.

⁴Αὐτὸς δὲ ὁ Ἰωάννης εἶχεν τὸ ἔνδυμα αὐτοῦ ἀπὸ τριχῶν καμήλου καὶ ζώνην δερματίνην περὶ τὴν ὀσφὺν αὐτοῦ, ἡ δὲ τροφὴ ἦν αὐτοῦ ἀκρίδες καὶ μέλι ἄγριον. ⁵τότε ἐξεπορεύετο πρὸς αὐτὸν Ἰεροσόλυμα καὶ πᾶσα ἡ Ἰουδαία καὶ πᾶσα ἡ περίχωρος τοῦ Ἰορδάνου, ⁶καὶ ἐβαπτίζοντο ἐν τῷ Ἰορδάνῃ ποταμῷ ὑπ' αὐτοῦ ἐξομολογούμενοι τὰς ἁμαρτίας αὐτῶν.

⁷Ἰδὼν δὲ πολλοὺς τῶν Φαρισαίων καὶ Σαδδουκαίων ἐρχομένους ἐπὶ τὸ βάπτισμα εἶπεν αὐτοῖς, Γεννήματα ἐχιδνῶν, τίς ὑπέδειξεν ὑμῖν φυγεῖν ἀπὸ τῆς μελλούσης ὀργῆς; ⁸ποιήσατε οὖν καρπὸν ἄξιον τῆς μετανοίας ⁹καὶ μὴ δόξητε λέγειν ἐν ἑαυτοῖς, Πατέρα ἔχομεν τὸν Ἀβραάμ. λέγω γὰρ ὑμῖν ὅτι δύναται ὁ θεὸς ἐκ τῶν λίθων

3:7 A few important mss add "his" before *baptism*, simply making explicit what is to be taken for granted.

• **3:1–12** Our author now begins to follow Mark (1:2–8). See Introduction, p. 12. Everything up to this point is unique to Matthew.

• **3:1** *In due course:* Greek, "in those days." But we jump here from Jesus' infancy to his adulthood.

the Baptist: That is, one who baptizes, immersing those who sought him out.

the wilderness: The land on either side of the river Jordan (vs 6), much of it desert, desolate and forbidding.

Judea: The region, whether ethnically or geographically. The Greek for "Judea" (*Ioudaia*) also means "Jewry." See Translation Note, p. 41.

• **3:2** *Change your ways:* More traditionally translated "Repent." Here there is no mention of forgiveness, as there is in Mark 1:4. Instead John is a prophet of doom.

Heaven's imperial rule is closing in: On John's lips this announcement is not good news, as it is in Mark 1:14, but a threat. It is Jesus who will proclaim the good news (using at first the same words—4:17; see 4:23–24).

Heaven's imperial rule: Our author's first use of this all-important phrase. See Translation Note, p. 46.

is closing in: The Greek uses a perfect tense, *ēngiken,* which has a double temporal meaning: something has happened with present and permanent effect. So we could translate "has come near" or even "has arrived." SV's phrase tries to include both these meanings.

• **3:3** *this is the person described by Isaiah the prophet:* The author makes the identification explicit; it's only implied in Mark 1:2–4.

A voice of someone . . . : The evangelist omits Mark's first quote ("Here is my messenger whom I send on ahead of you to prepare your way"), probably because it is not from Isaiah but Mal 3:1—correcting Mark's famous mistake. Consequently John is not portrayed here as Jesus' messenger, the forerunner who prepares his way (for that, see 11:10). Rather the crowds are to *make ready the way of the Lord* (that is, of Jesus). That is what John shouts, in the words of Isaiah.

A voice of someone shouting in the wilderness: This word-grouping subtly alters Isa 40:3. There the voice does not shout in the wilderness. Rather through the wilderness is where people are to "make ready the way of the Lord, make his paths straight." In Matthew, only John is *in the wilderness.* That is where he "shouted." What he calls for, mak-

3 In due course John the Baptist appears in the wilderness of Judea, ²calling out: "Change your ways because Heaven's imperial rule is closing in."

³Clearly this is the person described by Isaiah the prophet:

A voice of someone shouting in the wilderness:
"Make ready the way of the Lord;
make his paths straight."

⁴Now this same John wore clothes made of camel hair and had a leather belt around his waist; his diet consisted of locusts and raw honey. ⁵Then Jerusalem, and all Judea, and all the region around the Jordan streamed out to him, ⁶and got baptized in the Jordan river by him, admitting their sins.

⁷When he saw that many of the Pharisees and Sadducees were coming for baptism, <John> said to them, "You spawn of Satan! Who warned you to flee from the impending doom? ⁸Well then, start producing fruit suitable for a change of heart, ⁹and don't even think of saying to yourselves, 'We have Abraham for our father.' Let me tell you, God can raise up children for Abraham right out of these rocks.

---

ing ready for the Lord (Jesus), is evidently to be done everywhere.

- **3:4** His *clothes* were reminiscent of the prophet Elijah (2 Kgs 1:8), who was sometimes expected to return and prepare for the Anointed. John's *diet* was that of someone subsisting in the *wilderness.*

  wore clothes made of camel hair: Perhaps a better translation of the Hebrew than that he "was hairy" (NRSV).

- **3:5–6** Was this a means of preparing "the way of the Lord"? In part, certainly.

- **3:5** *the Jordan river:* Flowing south from the Sea of Galilee to the Dead Sea.

- **3:7–10** Here the author lays Mark aside momentarily and turns to material paralleled only in Luke (3:7-9), from the hypothetical document called Q (Introduction, p. 11).

- **3:7** *Pharisees and Sadducees:* In Luke 3:7, John speaks the menacing words "to the crowds" generally. Our author often singles out these two groups (see Glossary), and esp. the *Pharisees,* for criticism and denunciation.

  spawn of Satan: Otherwise translated "brood of snakes," "vipers' nest," or "generation of vipers." The image may have in mind snakes slithering away from a fire in the desert, with John's warning of "impending

doom" thought of as fire. In any case, it is an image of evil; hence *of Satan,* a name not in the Greek here, but used by Jesus—and only Jesus—elsewhere (4:10, 16:23). John names the members of the two Judean sects children of the devil.

Who warned you . . .? Have they come to John for the wrong reasons?

the impending doom: John warns of a coming "eschatological" event. In fact an "apocalyptic" one. See Glossary.

doom: Greek: "wrath," that is, of God.

- **3:8** *fruit:* That is, deeds.

  a change of heart: Identical with a "change [of one's] ways" in vs 2. More commonly translated "repentance."

- **3:9** *We have Abraham for our father:* That is, we are Jews, members of God's chosen people.

  God can raise up children for Abraham right out of these rocks: Does this mean that Gentiles can be as good as Jews in God's eyes?

τούτων ἐγεῖραι τέκνα τῷ Ἀβραάμ. ¹⁰ἤδη δὲ ἡ ἀξίνη πρὸς τὴν ῥίζαν τῶν δένδρων κεῖται· πᾶν οὖν δένδρον μὴ ποιοῦν καρπὸν καλὸν ἐκκόπτεται καὶ εἰς πῦρ βάλλεται.

¹¹Ἐγὼ μὲν ὑμᾶς βαπτίζω ἐν ὕδατι εἰς μετάνοιαν, ὁ δὲ ὀπίσω μου ἐρχόμενος ἰσχυρότερός μού ἐστιν, οὗ οὐκ εἰμὶ ἱκανὸς τὰ ὑποδήματα βαστάσαι· αὐτὸς ὑμᾶς βαπτίσει ἐν πνεύματι ἁγίῳ καὶ πυρί· ¹²οὗ τὸ πτύον ἐν τῇ χειρὶ αὐτοῦ καὶ διακαθαριεῖ τὴν ἅλωνα αὐτοῦ καὶ συνάξει τὸν σῖτον αὐτοῦ εἰς τὴν ἀποθήκην, τὸ δὲ ἄχυρον κατακαύσει πυρὶ ἀσβέστῳ.

John baptizes Jesus

¹³Τότε παραγίνεται ὁ Ἰησοῦς ἀπὸ τῆς Γαλιλαίας ἐπὶ τὸν Ἰορδάνην πρὸς τὸν Ἰωάννην τοῦ βαπτισθῆναι ὑπ' αὐτοῦ. ¹⁴ὁ δὲ Ἰωάννης διεκώλυεν αὐτὸν λέγων, Ἐγὼ χρείαν ἔχω ὑπὸ σοῦ βαπτισθῆναι, καὶ σὺ ἔρχῃ πρός με;

¹⁵Ἀποκριθεὶς δὲ ὁ Ἰησοῦς εἶπεν πρὸς αὐτόν, Ἄφες ἄρτι, οὕτως γὰρ πρέπον ἐστὶν ἡμῖν πληρῶσαι πᾶσαν δικαιοσύνην. τότε ἀφίησιν αὐτόν.

¹⁶Βαπτισθεὶς δὲ ὁ Ἰησοῦς εὐθὺς ἀνέβη ἀπὸ τοῦ ὕδατος· καὶ ἰδοὺ ἠνεῴχθησαν οἱ οὐρανοί, καὶ εἶδεν πνεῦμα θεοῦ καταβαῖνον ὡσεὶ περιστερὰν ἐρχόμενον ἐπ' αὐτόν· ¹⁷καὶ ἰδοὺ φωνὴ ἐκ τῶν οὐρανῶν λέγουσα, Οὗτός ἐστιν ὁ υἱός μου ὁ ἀγαπητός, ἐν ᾧ εὐδόκησα.

• **3:10b** The same words are found on Jesus' lips at 7:19. See comment there.

• **3:11** *carry his sandals:* In Mark and Luke "bend down and untie his sandal straps."

   baptize you with holy spirit and fire: As in Luke 3:16. Mark has simply ". . . holy spirit."

   holy spirit: No article in the Greek here. The Greek word also means "wind," and together with *fire* it sets up the image of threshing in the next verse.

• **3:12** *pitchfork . . . threshing floor:* The picture is familiar to any peasant farmer. For the evangelist, threshing—separating wheat from chaff by tossing it up to let the wind blow the chaff aside—stands for the last judgment and the separation of good people and bad. Like the trees without fruit of vs 10, the chaff is thrown into *a fire that can't be put out.* The fierce conflagration of burning chaff, once ignited, can't be stopped till everything is consumed. So the punishment here threatened is virtually endless.

• **3:13** *Jesus comes from Galilee:* His derivation, despite the "christological" legend of his birth in Bethlehem.

• **3:14–15** *I'm the one who needs to be baptized by you.* These two verses are unique to Matthew and probably reflect not historical fact but

¹⁰Even now the axe is aimed at the root of the trees. So every tree not producing choice fruit gets cut down and tossed into the fire.

¹¹"I baptize you with water to signal a change of heart, but someone more powerful than I am will succeed me. I am not fit to carry his sandals. He'll baptize you with holy spirit and fire. ¹²His pitchfork is in his hand, and he'll make a clean sweep of his threshing floor, and gather his wheat into the granary, but the chaff he'll burn in a fire that can't be put out."

¹³Then Jesus comes from Galilee to John at the Jordan to get baptized by him. ¹⁴And John tried to stop him with these words: "I'm the one who needs to get baptized by you, yet you come to me?"

John baptizes Jesus

¹⁵In response, Jesus said to him, "Let it go for now. After all, in this way we are doing what is fitting and right." Then John deferred to him.

¹⁶After Jesus had been baptized, he got right up out of the water, and believe it or not the skies opened up, he saw God's spirit coming down on him like a dove, and it perched on him, ¹⁷and there was a voice from the sky that said, "This is my favored son—I fully approve of him!"

---

the embarrassment of Christians in competition with followers of John in the late first century. By receiving John's baptism Jesus could be seen as subordinate to him. This saying, very likely legendary, serves to rule out any such claim.

• **3:15** *we are doing what is fitting and right:* Better than the more literal rendering, "we must fulfill all righteousness."

• **3:16–17** *the skies opened up:* Letting a revelation by God take place. Not experienced by Jesus alone, as it is in Mark 1:11, here it becomes a public event; the words about God's *favored son* are spoken to everyone.

Presumably a crowd was present. Only Jesus, it seems, *saw God's spirit coming down on him like a dove.*

This is my ... son: Mark gives Jesus the title Son of God at the very beginning (1:1). Here it is announced at last. Luke's genealogy made Jesus' divine sonship plain (Luke 3:38), but not Matthew's.

With vss 16 and 17 and the next passage (4:1–11), we move for a while into mythology. See Glossary, and Introduction, p. 8.

Translation Note:

"Heaven's imperial rule"/"Heaven's domain"

After "Son of Adam," these phrases represented the most difficult issue for the translators.

In the other gospels we find always *"God's* imperial rule," *"God's* domain." Our evangelist has substituted *Heaven's for God's,* as typical of his usage (see Introduction, p. 19). (The Greek for "heaven" is actually plural, *tôn ouranôn,* literally, "of the heavens"; however, the singular is more common English, and it makes little difference.)

But what about the strange terms *imperial rule and domain?* They replace the usual "kingdom"—"the kingdom of heaven" in Matthew, "the kingdom of God" elsewhere. Why avoid that word?

One reason is that kingdom is not an element of modern Americans' experience. We are a republic and so have no king. Further, to think of God as king is not gender-inclusive. But chiefly, the word "kingdom" is not strong enough. For the Greek word *basileia* means "empire" more basically than "kingdom." In Greek the Roman emperor was a *basileus,* his domain was a *basileia*. When Jesus spoke of God's empire, the pivotal term in his message, he was laying it over against Caesar's empire, which thereby he challenged in a subtly but provocatively political way. (Some scholars hold that Jesus used the term ironically, suggesting that God's *basileia* evokes the very opposite of empire.)

So why not simply "the empire of God," or in Matthew "the empire of heaven"? For a couple of reasons. The word empire suggests domination and exploitation, true of Rome's hegemony but not God's. And, like kingdom, it also implies a geographic territory, whereas God's empire cannot be mapped. The sense at the kernel of "God's empire" is authority, the recognition of God's power and legitimacy, over against any other. To convey this, SV part of the time uses "imperial rule." At other points, wanting to convey the extent of God's reign it uses "domain."

Hence, *heaven's imperial rule, heaven's domain.* The translators are not entirely satisfied with this rendering; the phrase suffers in translation. Perhaps "empire" would be as good after all. I'll sometimes use that in the comments.

Jesus is tested

4 Τότε ὁ Ἰησοῦς ἀνήχθη εἰς τὴν ἔρημον ὑπὸ τοῦ πνεύματος πειρασθῆναι ὑπὸ τοῦ διαβόλου. ²καὶ νηστεύσας τεσσεράκοντα ἡμέρας καὶ νύκτας τεσσεράκοντα, ὕστερον ἐπείνασεν.

³Καὶ προσελθὼν ὁ πειράζων εἶπεν αὐτῷ, Εἰ υἱὸς εἶ τοῦ θεοῦ, εἰπὲ ἵνα οἱ λίθοι οὗτοι ἄρτοι γένωνται.

⁴Ὁ δὲ ἀποκριθεὶς εἶπεν, Γέγραπται,

Οὐκ ἐπ' ἄρτῳ μόνῳ ζήσεται ὁ ἄνθρωπος,
ἀλλ' ἐπὶ παντὶ ῥήματι ἐκπορευομέν διὰ στόματος θεοῦ.

⁵Τότε παραλαμβάνει αὐτὸν ὁ διάβολος εἰς τὴν ἁγίαν πόλιν καὶ ἔστησεν αὐτὸν ἐπὶ τὸ πτερύγιον τοῦ ἱεροῦ, 6 καὶ λέγει αὐτῷ, Εἰ υἱὸς εἶ τοῦ θεοῦ, βάλε σεαυτὸν κάτω· γέγραπται γὰρ ὅτι

Τοῖς ἀγγέλοις αὐτοῦ ἐντελεῖται περὶ σοῦ
καὶ ἐπὶ χειρῶν ἀροῦσίν σε,
μήποτε προσκόψῃς πρὸς λίθον τὸν πόδα σου.

⁷Ἔφη αὐτῷ ὁ Ἰησοῦς, Πάλιν γέγραπται,

Οὐκ ἐκπειράσεις κύριον τὸν θεόν σου.

⁸Πάλιν παραλαμβάνει αὐτὸν ὁ διάβολος εἰς ὄρος ὑψηλὸν λίαν καὶ δείκνυσιν αὐτῷ πάσας τὰς βασιλείας τοῦ κόσμου καὶ τὴν δόξαν αὐτῶν ⁹καὶ εἶπεν αὐτῷ, Ταῦτά σοι πάντα δώσω, ἐὰν πεσὼν προσκυνήσῃς μοι.

• **4:1–11** These three episodes are often called Jesus' "temptations," as if Jesus were enticed to sin. Rather, *the devil* puts him to a kind of trial: Is he really *God's son,* as God has just declared (3:17)? If so, it is in one sense God who is tested. Of course it is also God who tests (vs 1).

The dramatis personae are not historical, earthly beings but the Son of God and the devil, with God just offstage. This, then, constitutes a mythical event, one that vividly asserts Jesus' anointed and divine status.

• **4:1** *guided into the wilderness by the spirit:* In Mark 1:12 the spirit "drives" him out, hurls him.

the wilderness: A place of terror for most people. See on 3:1. Where did this testing take place? Probably a pointless question for a mythological event. But when we next learn of Jesus' whereabouts he is going back to Galilee (vs 12).

by the spirit: Guided by God, that is,

guided . . . by the spirit to be put to the test. Just as "Satan" tested Job with God's consent (Job 1:6–12). In fact Jesus calls him Satan in vs 10. But the meaning of the title had changed from God's prosecuting attorney—"accuser"—to the prince of darkness. So the scenes that follow are depicted as a trial that the devil forces Jesus to endure. Jesus will also be "tested" by the authorities in 16:1, 19:3, and 22:35.

• **4:2** *forty days and forty nights:* Like the Israelites' forty-year wandering and testing "in the wilderness" (Exod). And Elijah's forty-day fast (1 Kgs 19:8).

he was famished: And so utterly vulnerable, or so the devil hopes.

• **4:3–10** The tests themselves don't appear in Mark. (We only hear that Jesus was "put to the test by Satan.") They are parallel to Luke 4:3–13 and so, one assumes, from Q.

4 Then Jesus was guided into the wilderness by the spirit to be put to the test by the devil. ²And after he had fasted 'forty days and forty nights,' he was famished.

³And the tester confronted him and said, "To prove you are God's son, order these stones to turn into bread."

⁴<Jesus> responded, "It is written,

Human beings are not to live on bread alone,
but on every word that comes out of God's mouth."

⁵Then the devil conducts him to the holy city, sets him on the pinnacle of the temple, ⁶and says to him, "To prove you are God's son, jump off; remember, it is written,

'To his heavenly messengers he will give orders about you,' and
'with their hands they will catch you,
so you won't even stub your toe on a stone.'"

⁷Jesus said to him, "Elsewhere it is written,

You are not to put the Lord your God to the test."

⁸Again the devil takes him to a very high mountain and shows him all the empires of the world and their splendor, ⁹and says to him, "I'll give you all these, if you will kneel down and worship me."

• **4:3–4** The first test.

• **4:3** *To prove you are God's son:* Greek, "If you are God's son." Does *the tester* doubt this and insist on being convinced? Or is he, so to speak, only playing devil's advocate—to see if Jesus doubts?

order these stones to turn into bread: Not just to feed his own hunger. Rather, a messianic sign. Can Jesus feed his people? That would prove that he is the savior Israel had long been waiting for.

• **4:4** *It is written . . . :* Jesus refuses to obey the devil's order. Instead he answers him with a Biblical quotation, from Deut 8:3.

Human beings: Usually mistranslated "man." See Introduction, p. 26.

but by every word that comes out of God's mouth: In this gospel Jesus is both faithful to Torah and reveals new law. Both come *out of God's mouth.* His rejoinder evidently silences the devil on this score.

• **4:5–7** The second test. In Luke, this and the third test are reversed. But little seems to hang on either order.

• **4:5** *the holy city:* Jerusalem.

the pinnacle of the temple: Evidently a high and prominent site in the temple's precincts.

• **4:6** *remember, it is written . . . :* Now the tester himself quotes scripture (Ps 91:11–12).

• **4:7** *Elsewhere it is written . . . :* Jesus matches his quotation, his a more fundamental one, because it comes from Torah (Deut 6:16).

You are not to put the Lord your God to the test: Does this mean that Jesus will not test God's promise? Or that the devil is not to test Jesus, Son of God? Or both?

• **4:8–10** The third test.

4:8 *all the empires of the world and their splendor:* On a flat earth they would be visible from *a very high mountain.*

¹⁰Τότε λέγει αὐτῷ ὁ Ἰησοῦς, Ὕπαγε, Σατανᾶ· γέγραπται γάρ,

Κύριον τὸν θεόν σου προσκυνήσεις
καὶ αὐτῷ μόνῳ λατρεύσεις.

¹¹Τότε ἀφίησιν αὐτὸν ὁ διάβολος, καὶ ἰδοὺ ἄγγελοι προσῆλθον καὶ διηκόνουν αὐτῷ.

A voice
in Galilee
¹²Ἀκούσας δὲ ὅτι Ἰωάννης παρεδόθη ἀνεχώρησεν εἰς τὴν Γαλιλαίαν. ¹³καὶ καταλιπὼν τὴν Ναζαρὰ ἐλθὼν κατῴκησεν εἰς Καφαρναοὺμ τὴν παραθαλασσίαν ἐν ὁρίοις Ζαβουλὼν καὶ Νεφθαλίμ· ¹⁴ἵνα πληρωθῇ τὸ ῥηθὲν διὰ Ἠσαΐου τοῦ προφήτου λέγοντος,

¹⁵Γῆ Ζαβουλὼν καὶ γῆ Νεφθαλίμ,
ὁδὸν θαλάσσης, πέραν τοῦ Ἰορδάνου,
Γαλιλαία τῶν ἐθνῶν,
¹⁶ὁ λαὸς ὁ καθήμενος ἐν σκοτίᾳ
φῶς εἶδεν μέγα,
καὶ τοῖς καθημένοις ἐν χώρᾳ καὶ σκιᾷ θανάτου
φῶς ἀνέτειλεν αὐτοῖς.

¹⁷Ἀπὸ τότε ἤρξατο ὁ Ἰησοῦς κηρύσσειν καὶ λέγειν, Ἤγγικεν ἡ βασιλεία τῶν οὐρανῶν.

4:10 Instead of *Get out of here, Satan!* some MSS have "Get out of my sight [literally, 'behind me'], Satan!" identical to Jesus' curse of Peter in 16:23.
4:17 Most MSS read "Change your ways because" before *Heaven's imperial rule*. Are these words a later addition, conforming to John's proclamation in 3:2? I believe so; why would they have been omitted, if original?

• **4:10** *Get out of here, Satan!* As Jesus will say to Peter in 16:23

  You are to worship the Lord your God, and revere him alone: Deut 6:13.
• **4:11** Concluding the tests.

  Then the devil leaves him: Showing his failure (for Jesus it is, not surprisingly, a success) in questioning Jesus' divine sonship. The message from heaven at Jesus' baptism (3:17) is now three times confirmed.

  heavenly messengers [angels] *... look after him:* Following Mark again (1:13).
• **4:12–25** Here the gospel's long introduction (Jesus' preparation, 1:1–4:16) is coming to a close. At last the Jesus' public activity, his so-called ministry, begins. His message echoes the Baptist's "voice in the wilderness" (3:1–2), but there is a difference; see below on vs 17.

• **4:12–16** Jesus returns from the wilderness to Galilee.
• **4:12** *When ... John had been locked up:* As in Mark 6:17–29, we'll hear a detailed report of John's arrest and death only much later (14:3–12).

  When Jesus heard: Learning that the work of John had been cut short, he embarks on his own work. In Mark 1:14 John's arrest simply dates the start of that work. Here it motivates Jesus' initiative.
• **4:13** *He left Nazareth:* Having just returned there, his hometown. Later, he will not be accepted in Nazareth (13:54–58).

  to go and settle down in Capernaum-by-the-sea: The three other canonical gospels tell of Jesus' going to Capernaum. But not at this point in the story. And the rest of this passage is unique to Matthew.

[10]Finally Jesus says to him, "Get out of here, Satan! Remember, it is written,

You are to worship the Lord your God,
and revere him alone."

[11]Then the devil leaves him, and heavenly messengers arrive out of nowhere and look after him.

[12]When Jesus heard that John had been locked up, he headed for Galilee. [13]He left Nazareth to go and settle down in Capernaum-by-the-sea, in the territory of Zebulun and Naphtali.[14]<This happened> so that the word spoken through Isaiah the prophet would come true:

A voice in Galilee

[15]Land of Zebulun and of Naphtali,
the way to the sea, across the Jordan,
Galilee of the pagans!
[16]The people who languished in darkness
have seen a great light,
those who have wasted away in the shadow of death,
for them a light has risen.

[17]From that time on Jesus began to proclaim: "Heaven's imperial rule is closing in."

Capernaum, a large town on the northwest shore of the so-called Sea of Galilee, will be a base of his operations, about to begin. He will work mostly in towns on the sea's shoreline.

the sea [of Galilee]: The large lake in northern Palestine. About 14 miles from north to south, and 8 miles across at its widest.

in the territory of Zebulun and Naphtali: Capernaum was probably within the old borders of the tribe of Zebulun. The reason for naming the two ancient tribal territories is the Biblical citation that follows. Their regions were partly within Galilee.

• **4:14** *<This happened> so that the word spoken through ... the prophet would come true:* Chaps. 1–4 contain the densest cluster of this formula within Matthew, with six or seven examples. See Introduction, p. 19. I doubt that the author means it was Jesus' intent to fulfill prophecy; hence *<This happened>.*

• **4:15–16** This quotation from Isa 9:1–2 has been shortened.

4:15 *Land of Zebulun and of Naphthali:* The territory of these tribes of ancient Israel, stretching to the west from the Galilean lake.

Galilee-of-the-pagans is no place for a Messiah in the view of some (see John 7:52). But Matthew makes a virtue of necessity: Jesus' going to the obscure Galilee is the cause of its salvation.

pagans: Usually, Gentiles.

• **4:16** *languished / wasted away:* In both cases the Greek has simply "sat." SV interprets.

• **4:17** *From that time on Jesus began ...:* His public teaching now begins.

Heaven's imperial rule is closing in: No longer an apocalyptic warning, as on the Baptist's lips in 3:2. Rather, good news (see 4:23). And especially so without John's insistence on what is usually called repentance ("Change your ways"), a theme relatively rare in Matthew, compared for example to Luke. It's true that only a very few manuscripts lack the phrase (one word in Greek, *Metanoiete*), but the likelihood that scribes added it later seems to me greater than that they omitted it (see Text-Critical Note). And, incidentally, according to the Jesus Seminar repentance was not something that the historical Jesus called for.

¹⁸Περιπατῶν δὲ παρὰ τὴν θάλασσαν τῆς Γαλιλαίας εἶδεν δύο ἀδελφούς, Σίμωνα τὸν λεγόμενον Πέτρον καὶ Ἀνδρέαν τὸν ἀδελφὸν αὐτοῦ, βάλλοντας ἀμφίβληστρον εἰς τὴν θάλασσαν· ἦσαν γὰρ ἁλιεῖς. ¹⁹καὶ λέγει αὐτοῖς, Δεῦτε ὀπίσω μου, καὶ ποιήσω ὑμᾶς ἁλιεῖς ἀνθρώπων. ²⁰οἱ δὲ εὐθέως ἀφέντες τὰ δίκτυα ἠκολούθησαν αὐτῷ.

²¹Καὶ προβὰς ἐκεῖθεν εἶδεν ἄλλους δύο ἀδελφούς, Ἰάκωβον τὸν τοῦ Ζεβεδαίου καὶ Ἰωάννην τὸν ἀδελφὸν αὐτοῦ, ἐν τῷ πλοίῳ μετὰ Ζεβεδαίου τοῦ πατρὸς αὐτῶν καταρτίζοντας τὰ δίκτυα αὐτῶν, καὶ ἐκάλεσεν αὐτούς. ²²οἱ δὲ εὐθέως ἀφέντες τὸ πλοῖον καὶ τὸν πατέρα αὐτῶν ἠκολούθησαν αὐτῷ.

²³Καὶ περιῆγεν ἐν ὅλῃ τῇ Γαλιλαίᾳ διδάσκων ἐν ταῖς συναγωγαῖς αὐτῶν καὶ κηρύσσων τὸ εὐαγγέλιον τῆς βασιλείας καὶ θεραπεύων πᾶσαν νόσον καὶ πᾶσαν μαλακίαν ἐν τῷ λαῷ. ²⁴καὶ ἀπῆλθεν ἡ ἀκοὴ αὐτοῦ εἰς ὅλην τὴν Συρίαν· καὶ προσήνεγκαν αὐτῷ πάντας τοὺς κακῶς ἔχοντας ποικίλαις νόσοις καὶ βασάνοις συνεχομένους, δαιμονιζομένους καὶ σεληνιαζομένους καὶ παραλυτικούς, καὶ ἐθεράπευσεν αὐτούς. ²⁵καὶ ἠκολούθησαν αὐτῷ ὄχλοι πολλοὶ ἀπὸ τῆς Γαλιλαίας καὶ Δεκαπόλεως καὶ Ἱεροσολύμων καὶ Ἰουδαίας καὶ πέραν τοῦ Ἰορδάνου.

• **4:18–25** Jesus gathers his first audience . . . and followers.

• **4:18** *also known as Peter:* Premature, since the nicknaming of Simon is not depicted till 16:17–18. "Simon" never appears in this gospel without reference to the nickname, and most often "Peter" alone is used.

• **4:19** *Become my followers:* Literally, "Come after me." See the next verse.

I'll have you fishing for people!: What does this mean?

• **4:20** *followed him:* A verb used frequently in Matthew, sometimes literally, but most often it means "become a follower," that is, a disciple—one who has been taught by Jesus.

• **4:23–25** At this point in Mark (1:21) we read that Jesus "started teaching" but in fact the stories of his healings begin. Our evangelist saves the miracles to be gathered together in chaps. 8–9. Here he simply gives a summary of Jesus' work and the following it attracted.

• **4:23** *the good news:* At last this assessment of Jesus' message appears. In Mark it is used already at 1:1.

healing every disease and every ailment: An immediate expression of the good news.

• **4:24** *the whole of Syria:* Does this mean the huge Roman province (Luke 2:2 tells us its governor's name at the time Jesus was born) that included Judea and Galilee and extended

¹⁸As he was walking by the Sea of Galilee, he spotted two brothers, Simon, also known as Peter, and Andrew his brother, throwing their net in the sea, since they were fishermen. ¹⁹And Jesus says to them, "Become my followers and I'll have you fishing for people!" ²⁰So right then and there they abandoned their nets and followed him.

²¹When he had gone on a little farther, he caught sight of two other brothers, James, Zebedee's son, and his brother John, in the boat with Zebedee their father, mending their nets, and he also called out to them. ²²They abandoned their boat and their father right then and there and followed him.

²³And he toured all over Galilee, teaching in their synagogues, proclaiming the good news of <Heaven's> domain, and healing every disease and every ailment the people had. ²⁴And his reputation spread through the whole of Syria. They brought him everyone who was ill, who suffered from any kind of disease or was in intense pain, who was possessed, who was epileptic, or a paralytic; and he cured them. ²⁵And huge crowds followed him from Galilee and the Decapolis and Jerusalem and Judea and from across the Jordan.

---

to the north and northeast of them? Or only the more limited land, known as Aram in the OT? In either case such a claim is found only here in the gospels. Perhaps it indicates the extent of the church in our author's time, or even that he lived and wrote in Syria.

everyone who was ill . . . who was possessed, who was epileptic, or a paralytic: This detailing of those Jesus healed is a rough summary of the variety of healings Jesus performs in chaps. 8 and 9.

• **4:25** *huge crowds followed him:* A statement that is repeated a number of times in the gospel—at 8:1, 12:15, 13:2, 15:30, 19:2, 20:29. In Mark 3:7–8 there is a similar but slightly

more wide-ranging list of where Jesus' followers came from. Our evangelist makes it more coherent with his story by adding *the Decapolis,* a region encompassing a group of towns—perhaps not strictly "ten," as the name suggests—chiefly Gentile and Hellenistic, surrounding the Jordan River where it flows south out of the lake of Galilee. And he eliminates Mark's "Idumea" (in the far south) and "from around Tyre and Sidon" (the coast north of Galilee—see on 11:21 and 15:21).

**The first
discourse**

5 Ἰδὼν δὲ τοὺς ὄχλους ἀνέβη εἰς τὸ ὄρος, καὶ καθίσαντος αὐτοῦ προσῆλθαν αὐτῷ οἱ μαθηταὶ αὐτοῦ· ²καὶ ἀνοίξας τὸ στόμα αὐτοῦ ἐδίδασκεν αὐτοὺς λέγων,

Congratulations

³Μακάριοι οἱ πτωχοὶ τῷ πνεύματι,
ὅτι αὐτῶν ἐστιν ἡ βασιλεία τῶν οὐρανῶν.

⁴Μακάριοι οἱ πενθοῦντες,
ὅτι αὐτοὶ παρακληθήσονται.

⁵Μακάριοι οἱ πραεῖς,
ὅτι αὐτοὶ κληρονομήσουσιν τὴν γῆν.

⁶Μακάριοι οἱ πεινῶντες καὶ διψῶντες τὴν δικαιοσύνην,
ὅτι αὐτοὶ χορτασθήσονται.

⁷Μακάριοι οἱ ἐλεήμονες,
ὅτι αὐτοὶ ἐλεηθήσονται.

⁸Μακάριοι οἱ καθαροὶ τῇ καρδίᾳ,
ὅτι αὐτοὶ τὸν θεὸν ὄψονται.

• **Chaps. 5–7** The first of Jesus' five extensive discourses. (See Introduction, p. 15) It is usually known as the Sermon on the Mount. More precisely it details what is expected of Jesus' followers, and therefore might best be titled The Demands of God's Empire.

As we just saw in the comment on 4:23–25, Mark reports that at about this point Jesus began to teach. And in Mark 3:13, shortly after the list of where Jesus' followers came from (see on 4:25, just above), Jesus goes "up on the mountain" and gathers his chosen disciples. These two data in Mark may very well have suggested to our evangelist to insert at this point in the story a discourse of Jesus' teachings, with a mountain setting.

• **5:1** *Taking note of the crowds:* It appears that Jesus is avoiding the crowd, and speaking only to *his disciples.* Certainly the targeted audience of the five discourses is his particular followers, and for our author, members of the church. It applies, with the reinterpretation necessary in view of the twenty centuries intervening, to all Christians today. But it's interesting that at the end we learn that Jesus had been speaking to "the crowds" (7:28), that is, potential followers. And, in fact, this sermon has spoken powerfully to many non-Christians: a notable example is Mohandas Gandhi (see below on 5:39b–41).

the mountain: Not "a" mountain. But what mountain? Does the evangelist intend us to see a parallel to Exodus, where it is held that

God gave Moses the five books of the Law on Mount Sinai (or Horeb) to be communicated to the whole of Israel? And is that why there are five "sermons"?

when he had sat down: Traditionally the posture for teaching, as in Luke 4:20.

his disciples: The first time this word is used. It clearly does not mean those who have enthusiastically followed him because of his healings but rather those whom, so far at least, he has called to be his followers: specifically, Peter and Andrew, James and John. And, of course, all for whom this gospel is written.

• **5:2** *and this is what he would teach them:* Instead of the usual "... what he taught them." See Introduction, p. 27.

• **5:3–12** This list is in some ways parallel to Luke 6:20–23. But there are only four Congratulations there. They are briefer and use the second person ("you," not "the" or "those"). And there they announce good news. Luke's list is probably closer to Q and to the original sayings of Jesus. The author of Q may have been the first to assemble the list, for in the Gospel of Thomas, at any rate (see Introduction, p. 12), they are not gathered together.

• **5:3** *Congratulations!* See Translation Note, p. 63. A better rendering, esp. for Luke's list, than the usual "Blessed," from which the traditional title for these nine sayings is derived: the Beatitudes (from *beatus,* "blessed"

5 Taking note of the crowds, he climbed up the mountain, and when he had sat down, his disciples came to him. ²He then began to speak, and this is what he would teach them:

The first discourse

³Congratulations to the poor in spirit!
Heaven's domain belongs to them.
⁴Congratulations to those who grieve!
They will be consoled.
⁵Congratulations to the gentle!
They will inherit the earth.
⁶Congratulations to those who hunger and thirst for justice!
They will have a feast.
⁷Congratulations to the merciful!
They will receive mercy.
⁸Congratulations to those with undefiled hearts!
They will see God.

Congratulations

---

in Latin). In the context of Matthew the term is closer to praise than well wishing—praise for being pleasing to God.

the poor in spirit: In Luke (6:20), "you poor." If that was original, our evangelist has shifted to a more general expression—to include not simply the literally poor (if in fact there were any such in his community). The switch from 2d person ("you") to 3d ("the") does the same. Perhaps he had in mind the Ten Commandments, but with a positive, not negative thrust. If so, this means "*Be* poor in spirit" and expresses a Christian virtue. The congratulation, then, commends the attaining of the virtue.

Heaven's domain belongs to them: As their reward. On *Heaven's domain,* see Translation Note. In Luke this is not reward but consolation, and Thom 54 has something mid-way between Matthew and Luke: "Congratulations to the poor, for to you belongs Heaven's domain."

• **5:4** *those who grieve:* In Luke, "you who weep now." But the meaning is quite different there ("for you will laugh"). Here grief is evidently religious: Those who regret their sins, perhaps.

They will be consoled: Here (and in vs 9) the passive voice is used. This is almost certainly the "divine passive" and means "God will console them."

• **5:5** *the gentle:* A far better translation than the usual "meek." This has no counterpart

in Luke and could not be turned back into one of Luke's reassurances to the oppressed. Evidently the entire verse, taken from Ps 37:11, has been added by our author.

• **5:6** *those who hunger and thirst for justice:* In the parallel (Luke 6:21a) simply "you who are hungry." By adding "for justice," the phrase no longer has to do with a socio-economic fact but promotes an ethical virtue.

They will have a feast: Their reward at the messianic banquet in "heaven"? Thom 69b: "Congratulations to those who go hungry, so the stomach of the one in want may be filled."

• **5:7–9** Like vs 5, these three also lack parallels in Luke's list, and presumably in Q. They depend mostly on Proverbs or the Psalms. They have been added to the earlier tradition of Q.

• **5:7** Taken almost verbatim from Prov 14:21b, where however it is "those who are *merciful* to the poor"). If there were no poor in the evangelist's church, mercy in general becomes the virtue.

• **5:8** *those with undefiled hearts:* Traditionally, "pure of heart." A phrase from Pss 24:4 and 73:1.

They will see God: This is surprising for a traditional Jew like our author. It was held that no one could see God, except Moses. Did Christianity count its adherents equal to Moses?

⁹Μακάριοι οἱ εἰρηνοποιοί,
ὅτι αὐτοὶ υἱοὶ θεοῦ κληθήσονται.

¹⁰Μακάριοι οἱ δεδιωγμένοι ἕνεκεν δικαιοσύνης,
ὅτι αὐτῶν ἐστιν ἡ βασιλεία τῶν οὐρανῶν.

¹¹Μακάριοί ἐστε ὅταν ὀνειδίσωσιν ὑμᾶς καὶ διώξωσιν καὶ
εἴπωσιν πᾶν πονηρὸν καθ' ὑμῶν ἕνεκεν ἐμοῦ. ¹²χαίρετε καὶ
ἀγαλλιᾶσθε, ὅτι ὁ μισθὸς ὑμῶν πολὺς ἐν τοῖς οὐρανοῖς· οὕτως γὰρ
ἐδίωξαν τοὺς προφήτας τοὺς πρὸ ὑμῶν.

Salt & light　　¹³Ὑμεῖς ἐστε τὸ ἅλας τῆς γῆς· ἐὰν δὲ τὸ ἅλας μωρανθῇ, ἐν τίνι
ἁλισθήσεται; εἰς οὐδὲν ἰσχύει ἔτι εἰ μὴ βληθὲν ἔξω καταπατεῖσθαι
ὑπὸ τῶν ἀνθρώπων.

¹⁴Ὑμεῖς ἐστε τὸ φῶς τοῦ κόσμου. οὐ δύναται πόλις κρυβῆναι
ἐπάνω ὄρους κειμένη· ¹⁵οὐδὲ καίουσιν λύχνον καὶ τιθέασιν αὐτὸν
ὑπὸ τὸν μόδιον ἀλλ' ἐπὶ τὴν λυχνίαν, καὶ λάμπει πᾶσιν τοῖς ἐν τῇ
οἰκίᾳ. ¹⁶οὕτως λαμψάτω τὸ φῶς ὑμῶν ἔμπροσθεν τῶν ἀνθρώπων,
ὅπως ἴδωσιν ὑμῶν τὰ καλὰ ἔργα καὶ δοξάσωσιν τὸν πατέρα ὑμῶν
τὸν ἐν τοῖς οὐρανοῖς.

**Law &
prophets**　　¹⁷Μὴ νομίσητε ὅτι ἦλθον καταλῦσαι τὸν νόμον ἢ τοὺς προφήτας·
οὐκ ἦλθον καταλῦσαι ἀλλὰ πληρῶσαι. ¹⁸ἀμὴν γὰρ λέγω ὑμῖν· ἕως
ἂν παρέλθῃ ὁ οὐρανὸς καὶ ἡ γῆ, ἰῶτα ἓν ἢ μία κεραία οὐ μὴ παρέλθῃ

5:11 A few mss add "and tell lies" after *gossip*.

• **5:9** *those who work for peace:* Possibly from the Greek version (LXX) of Prov 10:10.

• **5:10** *those who have suffered persecution:* So far the list has used the present tense ("those who grieve," "who hunger and thirst," etc.). The past tense here reflects the experience of the prophets in Israel's past, and, probably the recent repression of Christians in the author's time, as in vss 11–12. Thom 69a reads: "Congratulations to those who have been persecuted in their hearts: they are the ones who have truly come to know the Father."

• **5:11–12** These two verses comprise the concluding "beatitude"—very close to Luke 6:22–23—which does not recommend a virtue or model behavior but announces good news, like every one in Luke's list.

• **5:11** *Congratulations to you:* For the first time the second-person *you*, as always in Luke 6.
when they denounce you ... and spread malicious gossip about you: A summary of what Q must have read, behind Luke 6:22. Thom 68 has: "Congratulations to you when you are hated and persecuted."
because of me: Changed perhaps from "because of the Son of Adam" (Luke 6:22), to

leave no question that it is persecution of Christians.

• **5:12** A fitting conclusion to the so-called beatitudes (vss 3–12).
Rejoice and be glad! Slightly more decorous than Luke's "Rejoice ... and jump for joy."
Remember, this is how they persecuted the prophets who preceded you: "Persecute" is reiterated, and "the prophets" are perhaps not just in the distant past, like "the ancestors" in Luke, but persecuted Christian prophets in the Matthean community. Here alone in the author's list we have not reward but consolation, as in Luke.
Even so, the list is a Table of Christian Virtues, a kind of new Ten Commandments (but with only nine items). Unlike Moses' Decalogue, these are positive demands, not primarily a list of "Don'ts."

• **5:13** *the salt of the earth:* This means more than the phrase in its modern, popular use. It may include something of the same solidity and natural goodness, but it has greater pungency, implies a fundamental spark.
But if salt loses its zing: Refers of course not to the chemistry of salt but to the all-too-likely failure of disciples—and Christians

⁹Congratulations to those who work for peace!
  They will be known as God's children.
¹⁰Congratulations to those who have suffered persecution for
  the sake of justice!
  Heaven's domain belongs to them.

¹¹"Congratulations to you when they denounce you and persecute you and spread malicious gossip about you because of me! ¹²Rejoice and be glad! In heaven you will be more than compensated. Remember, this is how they persecuted the prophets who preceded you.

¹³"You are the salt of the earth. But if salt loses its zing, how will it be made salty? It then has no further use than to be thrown out and stomped on.

Salt & light

¹⁴"You are the light of the world. A city sitting on top of a hill can't be hidden. ¹⁵Nor do people light a lamp and put it under a bushel basket but rather on a lampstand, where it sheds light for everyone in the house. ¹⁶That's how your light is to shine in the presence of others, so they can see your good deeds and acclaim your Father in the heavens.

¹⁷"Don't imagine that I have come to annul the Law or the Prophets. I have come not to annul but to fulfill. ¹⁸I swear to you that until the world disappears, not one iota, not one serif, will disappear

Law & prophets

---

ever since—to provide what they esp. are called to give.

- **5:14** *You are the light of the world:* Unique to Matthew. This light must shine—like *a city sitting on top of a mountain,* which obviously *can't be concealed.* Compare Thom 32: "A city built on a high hill and fortified cannot fall, nor can it be hidden."
- **5:15** A more homely saying (almost identical to Luke 11:33), reinforces the uselessness of light that is hidden.
- **5:16** *your Father:* The phrase "your [heavenly] Father" or "your Father in [the] heaven[s]" (spoken to the disciples alone) appears more than ten times in this gospel, with no parallel in Mark or Luke. It is appears once in Mark (11:25=Matt 6:14) and twice, evidently, in Q (Luke 6:36=Matt 5:48; Luke 12:30=Matt 6:32). So it is a favorite expression in this gospel, and evidently a prerogative of the disciples alone. See 5:9, 45.
- **5:17–48** The rest of chap. 5 defines the Christian Judaism of the Matthean church—at once (according to the German title of a monograph by Ingo Broer) both Freedom from the Law and Radicalizing the Law.

- **5:17–20** Found only in this gospel.
- **5:17** *I have come:* In Matthew this assertion appears here and at 10:35, never in Mark or Luke, frequently in John. If original, it does not necessarily mean "I have come from God" or "from above," as in John. In this context it can simply express Jesus' mission in proclaiming God's empire.

  not to annul but to fulfill: Paul, esp. in his Letter to the Romans, could agree with what this affirms but not with what it denies.

  the Law [and] the Prophets: That is, the whole of Jewish scripture in the first century CE. The Writings, had not yet been fully accepted into what would become the three-fold Jewish canon.
- **5:18** *I swear to you:* See Translation Note, p. 61.

  until the world disappears: That is, until the last judgment.

  not one iota, not one serif, will disappear: In Greek, "one iota . . . will no not disappear"; the double negative is emphatic.

  iota . . . serif: The most negligible marks in a text. The evangelist takes the wording, even the spelling, of the law in a way that today we would call fundamentalist.

ἀπὸ τοῦ νόμου, ἕως ἂν πάντα γένηται. ¹⁹ὃς ἐὰν οὖν λύσῃ μίαν τῶν
ἐντολῶν τούτων τῶν ἐλαχίστων καὶ διδάξῃ οὕτως τοὺς ἀνθρώπους,
ἐλάχιστος κληθήσεται ἐν τῇ βασιλείᾳ τῶν οὐρανῶν· ὃς δ' ἂν ποιήσῃ
καὶ διδάξῃ, οὗτος μέγας κληθήσεται ἐν τῇ βασιλείᾳ τῶν οὐρανῶν.
²⁰λέγω γὰρ ὑμῖν ὅτι ἐὰν μὴ περισσεύσῃ ὑμῶν ἡ δικαιοσύνη πλεῖον
τῶν γραμματέων καὶ Φαρισαίων, οὐ μὴ εἰσέλθητε εἰς τὴν βασιλείαν
τῶν οὐρανῶν.

On anger   ²¹Ἠκούσατε ὅτι ἐρρέθη τοῖς ἀρχαίοις, Οὐ φονεύσεις· ὃς δ' ἂν
φονεύσῃ, ἔνοχος ἔσται τῇ κρίσει. ²²ἐγὼ δὲ λέγω ὑμῖν ὅτι πᾶς ὁ
ὀργιζόμενος τῷ ἀδελφῷ αὐτοῦ ἔνοχος ἔσται τῇ κρίσει· ὃς δ' ἂν
εἴπῃ τῷ ἀδελφῷ αὐτοῦ, Ῥακά, ἔνοχος ἔσται τῷ συνεδρίῳ· ὃς δ'
ἂν εἴπῃ, Μωρέ, ἔνοχος ἔσται εἰς τὴν γέενναν τοῦ πυρός. ²³ἐὰν οὖν
προσφέρῃς τὸ δῶρόν σου ἐπὶ τὸ θυσιαστήριον κἀκεῖ μνησθῇς ὅτι ὁ
ἀδελφός σου ἔχει τι κατὰ σοῦ, ²⁴ἄφες ἐκεῖ τὸ δῶρόν σου ἔμπροσθεν
τοῦ θυσιαστηρίου καὶ ὕπαγε πρῶτον διαλλάγηθι τῷ ἀδελφῷ σου, καὶ
τότε ἐλθὼν πρόσφερε τὸ δῶρόν σου.

²⁵Ἴσθι εὐνοῶν τῷ ἀντιδίκῳ σου ταχύ, ἕως ὅτου εἶ μετ' αὐτοῦ ἐν
τῇ ὁδῷ, μήποτέ σε παραδῷ ὁ ἀντίδικος τῷ κριτῇ καὶ ὁ κριτὴς τῷ
ὑπηρέτῃ καὶ εἰς φυλακὴν βληθήσῃ· ²⁶ἀμὴν λέγω σοι, οὐ μὴ ἐξέλθῃς
ἐκεῖθεν, ἕως ἂν ἀποδῷς τὸν ἔσχατον κοδράντην.

On lust   ²⁷Ἠκούσατε ὅτι ἐρρέθη, Οὐ μοιχεύσεις. ²⁸ἐγὼ δὲ λέγω ὑμῖν ὅτι πᾶς

5:22 Some MSS add "without cause" after *companion,* softening the threat.
5:25 Some MSS insert "will turn you over" after the second *judge,* making
explicit what is already clearly implied.

---

not until it all happens: This redundant
clause adds further emphasis.
• **5:19** *these regulations:* Including perhaps the
growing oral Law of "the rabbis."
• **5:20** *religion:* Often translated "righteousness." What this author takes to be basic to
Christianity.
scholars and Pharisees: A combination of two
Jewish groups found a number of times in
this gospel, mostly in chap. 23. See comment
there and Glossary.
• **5:21–48** The rest of the chapter is com-
posed of six brief sections, each with the
formula "As you know.... But I tell you...."
This structure gives shape to each of the
six sections of 5:21–48. In every case Jesus
gives a new and stricter directive than the
traditional one. The warnings seem to be
arranged in an order of increasing severity. Each section has to do with a separate
topic: anger, lust, and so forth. These are
sometimes called the Antitheses—On the
one hand, as you know.... On the other, I
tell you....

• **5:21** *As you know our ancestors were told:* The
first of six uses of this formula, variously
translated in vss 27, 31, 33, 38, and 43.
As you know: Strictly, "You have heard," evidently via public reading of the scriptures or
the rabbis' citing of unwritten law..
our ancestors were told: Traditionally translated "that it was said of old." God told
Moses, and he told the people, who passed
it down.
You must not kill: The sixth of the Ten Commandments, found in Exod 20:13 and Deut
5:17.
Whoever kills will be subject to judgment: This
quotation is not found in our Hebrew Scriptures. But there is a command that one who
kills is to be put to death (Exod 21:12).
• **5:22** *But I tell you:* The "I" is emphatic ("I, I
myself, tell you").
those who are [merely] *angry with a companion:* Greek: "with a brother," probably
any fellow Christian. This saying, when understood strictly, can lead to the unhealthy
belief that anger in itself is wrong. The two

from the Law—not until it all happens. ¹⁹Whoever ignores one of the most trivial of these regulations, and teaches others to do so, will be called trivial in Heaven's domain. But whoever acts on <these regulations> and teaches <others to do so>, will be called great in Heaven's domain. ²⁰Let me tell you: unless your religion goes beyond that of the scholars and Pharisees, you won't set foot in Heaven's domain.

²¹"As you know, our ancestors were told, 'You must not kill' and 'Whoever kills will be subject to judgment.' ²²But I tell you: those who are angry with a companion will be brought before a tribunal. And those who say to a companion, 'You moron,' will be subject to the sentence of the court. And whoever says, 'You idiot,' deserves the fires of Gehenna. ²³So, even if you happen to be offering your gift at the altar and recall that your friend has some claim against you, ²⁴leave your gift there at the altar. First go and be reconciled with your friend, and only then return and offer your gift.

On anger

²⁵"You should come to terms quickly with your opponent while you are both on the way <to court>, or else your opponent will hand you over to the judge, and the judge <will turn you over> to the bailiff, and you'll be thrown in jail. ²⁶I swear to you, you'll never get out of there until you've paid the last dime.

²⁷"You know that we once were told, 'You are not to commit adultery.' ²⁸But I tell you: Those who leer at a woman and desire her

On lust

---

examples that follow depict contempt and abusiveness as expressions of the kind of anger that Jesus forbids.

brought before a tribunal: As in vs 21, "subject to judgment."

You moron: In Greek, *raka*, evidently an Aramaic term of humiliation. In Rabbinic interpretation, this and other kinds of slander were not to be brought before a court.

subject to the sentence of the court: The court here is the Sanhedrin, the Jewish Council.

You idiot: Still more strongly dismissive.

deserves the fires of Gehenna: Damnation.

Gehenna: See Glossary.

• **5:23–24** Our author has evidently put this saying alongside vss 21–22. The two sayings don't exactly fit together.

• **5:23** *offering your gift at the altar:* In fulfillment of Jewish requirement.

has some claim against you: Not, as we would expect, "against whom you have some claim" and so at whom you are angry. Is the friends' claim against you that you have angrily dismissed him?

• **5:24** *First ... only then ...:* Ethical behavior takes precedence over ritual.

• **5:25–26** Another instruction, here about resolving someone's anger toward oneself.

• **5:25** *come to terms:* Or "settle."

on the way <to court>: The Greek says only, "in the street"; the words *opponent* and *judge* provide the context.

• **5:26** *dime:* In Greek, *kodrantēs,* a Roman copper coin of insignificant value.

• **5:27** *we once were told:* An equivalent to "our ancestors were told," above.

You are not to commit adultery: The seventh commandment (Exod 20:14, Lev 5:18).

• **5:28** Jesus does not give a new law, but interprets it to include much more than the literal act of adultery. This kind of reading of a commandment is sometimes found in Rabbinic tradition.

ὁ βλέπων γυναῖκα πρὸς τὸ ἐπιθυμῆσαι αὐτὴν ἤδη ἐμοίχευσεν αὐτὴν ἐν τῇ καρδίᾳ αὐτοῦ. ²⁹εἰ δὲ ὁ ὀφθαλμός σου ὁ δεξιὸς σκανδαλίζει σε, ἔξελε αὐτὸν καὶ βάλε ἀπὸ σοῦ· συμφέρει γάρ σοι ἵνα ἀπόληται ἓν τῶν μελῶν σου καὶ μὴ ὅλον τὸ σῶμά σου βληθῇ εἰς γέενναν. ³⁰καὶ εἰ ἡ δεξιά σου χεὶρ σκανδαλίζει σε, ἔκκοψον αὐτὴν καὶ βάλε ἀπὸ σοῦ· συμφέρει γάρ σοι ἵνα ἀπόληται ἓν τῶν μελῶν σου καὶ μὴ ὅλον τὸ σῶμά σου εἰς γέενναν ἀπέλθῃ.

On divorce   ³¹Ἐρρέθη δέ, Ὃς ἂν ἀπολύσῃ τὴν γυναῖκα αὐτοῦ, δότω αὐτῇ ἀποστάσιον. ³²ἐγὼ δὲ λέγω ὑμῖν ὅτι πᾶς ὁ ἀπολύων τὴν γυναῖκα αὐτοῦ παρεκτὸς λόγου πορνείας ποιεῖ αὐτὴν μοιχευθῆναι, καὶ ὃς ἐὰν ἀπολελυμένην γαμήσῃ μοιχᾶται.

On oaths   ³³Πάλιν ἠκούσατε ὅτι ἐρρέθη τοῖς ἀρχαίοις, Οὐκ ἐπιορκήσεις, ἀποδώσεις δὲ τῷ κυρίῳ τοὺς ὅρκους σου. ³⁴ἐγὼ δὲ λέγω ὑμῖν μὴ ὀμόσαι ὅλως· μήτε ἐν τῷ οὐρανῷ, ὅτι θρόνος ἐστὶν τοῦ θεοῦ, ³⁵μήτε ἐν τῇ γῇ, ὅτι ὑποπόδιόν ἐστιν τῶν ποδῶν αὐτοῦ, μήτε εἰς Ἱεροσόλυμα, ὅτι πόλις ἐστὶν τοῦ μεγάλου βασιλέως, ³⁶μήτε ἐν τῇ κεφαλῇ σου ὀμόσῃς, ὅτι οὐ δύνασαι μίαν τρίχα λευκὴν ποιῆσαι ἢ μέλαιναν. ³⁷ἔστω δὲ ὁ λόγος ὑμῶν ναὶ ναί, οὒ οὔ· τὸ δὲ περισσὸν τούτων ἐκ τοῦ πονηροῦ ἐστιν.

On retribution   ³⁸Ἠκούσατε ὅτι ἐρρέθη, Ὀφθαλμὸν ἀντὶ ὀφθαλμοῦ καὶ ὀδόντα ἀντὶ ὀδόντος. ³⁹ἐγὼ δὲ λέγω ὑμῖν μὴ ἀντιστῆναι τῷ πονηρῷ·

• **5:29–30** This double saying is found also at 18:8–9, in slightly different form and context. How should it be understood? Perhaps as a dire warning only.

• **5:29** Attaching this to vs 28 is probably suggested by "leer."

right eye: As in most cultures, the right eye is superior to the left. Maybe this means "*Even* if your *right* eye . . ."?

gets you into trouble: Greek, "causes you to stumble."

to have your whole body thrown into Gehenna: To be condemned, that is, at the last judgment.

• **5:31** *Whoever divorces . . . :* This is not strictly a quotation but a summation of Deut 24:1. Perhaps the evangelist depends here on a Rabbinic restatement of the Biblical text.

a bill of divorce: Not a document that frees her but a notice that she has been discarded.

• **5:32** Jesus evidently forbade divorce altogether. If so, *except in the case of infidelity,* here and in 19:9, has been added later—probably to ease his strict prohibition. That phrase is not found in the parallel saying in Luke 16:18, or in Mark 10:11. It probably refers only to a wife's misbehavior.

infidelity: Usually translated "adultery" but can include any extra-marital behavior.

makes her the victim of adultery: If she subsequently remarries. The new husband cannot marry a woman still married to another. This has usually been subtly and justly mistranslated as "makes her an adulteress."

and whoever marries a divorced woman commits adultery: The converse of the first half of the verse, typical of Jewish teaching, esp. poetry. Did Jesus sometimes speak in verse, like the OT prophets or the authors of the Psalms?

• **5:33** *You must not break an oath:* Or "swear falsely." The quotation is from Lev 19:12.

Oaths sworn in the name of God must be kept: A paraphrase of Num 30:2.

in the name of: See Glossary.

• **5:34a** *Don't swear at all:* Jesus requires strict honesty, so that all oath-taking is unnecessary,

• **5:34b–37** A series of amplifications of Jesus' ban.

• **5:34b–35** *Don't invoke . . . :* To swear by *heaven, earth,* or *Jerusalem* is to swear in some way by God, which Jesus forbids.

• **5:35b** *the great king:* Either the king of Judea or God himself, as in 35a.

have already committed adultery with her in their hearts. ²⁹And if your right eye gets you into trouble, rip it out and throw it away! You would be better off to lose a part of your body, than to have your whole body thrown into Gehenna. ³⁰And if your right hand gets you into trouble, cut it off and throw it away! You would be better off to lose a part of your body, than to have your whole body wind up in Gehenna.

On divorce

³¹"We once were told, 'Whoever divorces his wife should give her a bill of divorce.' ³²But I tell you: Everyone who divorces his wife (except in the case of infidelity) makes her the victim of adultery; and whoever marries a divorced woman commits adultery.

On oaths

³³ "You also know that our ancestors were told, 'You must not break an oath,' and 'Oaths sworn in the name of God must be kept.' ³⁴But I tell you: Don't swear at all. Don't invoke heaven, because it is the throne of God, ³⁵and don't invoke earth, because it is God's footstool, and don't invoke Jerusalem, because it is the city of the great king. ³⁶You shouldn't swear by your head either, since you aren't able to turn a single hair either white or black. ³⁷Rather, your responses should be simply 'Yes' and 'No.' Anything beyond that is inspired by the evil one.

On retribution

³⁸"As you know, we once were told, 'An eye for an eye' and 'A tooth for a tooth.' ³⁹But I tell you: Don't react violently against the one who is evil.

- **5:36–37** Don't swear even *by your head:* It's unnecessary. Your word should be enough.
- **5:38–42** A dense passage often misunderstood for its brevity.
- **5:38** *'An eye for an eye' and 'A tooth for a tooth':* From Exod 21:24 and Lev 24:20, the famous *lex talionus* (law of retaliation). For its time, it represented an advance on uncontrolled vengeance—*only* an eye for an eye . . . not a

life for an eye. Yet Jesus rules out even that.
- **5:39a** *Don't react violently against:* In the KJV, the Greek was translated simply "don't resist." So Jesus appears to call for passivity in the face of violence. But that ignored the verb's prefix (*anti*). In fact it means Don't respond in kind to violence.
  the one who is evil: That is, the one who treats you violently.

Translation Note: "I swear to you"

This is a translation of what word-for-word is "Amen. I tell you," a strange expression. The Hebrew word means "So be it." To put it at the beginning of a statement is characteristic of Jesus and connotes something like Now hear this! "Verily [*or* Truly] I say to you" doesn't quite do it. It is more than just telling something with authority. *Amen* adds a strong note of insistence, with overtones of a mild oath. SV's choice expresses the appropriate urgency. (In 18:13, more vernacularly, "You can bet.")

ἀλλ' ὅστις σε ῥαπίζει εἰς τὴν δεξιὰν σιαγόνα, στρέψον αὐτῷ καὶ τὴν ἄλλην·

⁴⁰καὶ τῷ θέλοντί σοι κριθῆναι καὶ τὸν χιτῶνά σου λαβεῖν, ἄφες αὐτῷ καὶ τὸ ἱμάτιον·

⁴¹Καὶ ὅστις σε ἀγγαρεύσει μίλιον ἕν, ὕπαγε μετ' αὐτοῦ δύο.

⁴²Τῷ αἰτοῦντί σε δός, καὶ τὸν θέλοντα ἀπὸ σοῦ δανίσασθαι μὴ ἀποστραφῇς.

On love of enemies

⁴³Ἠκούσατε ὅτι ἐρρέθη, Ἀγαπήσεις τὸν πλησίον σου καὶ μισήσεις τὸν ἐχθρόν σου. ⁴⁴ἐγὼ δὲ λέγω ὑμῖν, ἀγαπᾶτε τοὺς ἐχθροὺς ὑμῶν καὶ προσεύχεσθε ὑπὲρ τῶν διωκόντων ὑμᾶς, ⁴⁵ὅπως γένησθε υἱοὶ τοῦ πατρὸς ὑμῶν τοῦ ἐν οὐρανοῖς, ὅτι τὸν ἥλιον αὐτοῦ ἀνατέλλει

• **5:39b–41** Three extraordinary directives that illustrate the meaning of vs 39a. They are lapidary, each comprising a single sentence and telling how Christians should respond to violence or oppression. In each case Jesus addresses the victim, the recipient of the violence: "When someone slaps you," "is determined to sue you," "conscripts you."

slaps you on the right cheek: The blow would be given by the right hand (the left hand could not be used) and on the recipient's *right cheek.* So it necessarily means a backhanded *slap,* intended to remind you of your inferiority, to put you in your place—typically given to a woman or a child or a slave, or any subject of the Roman occupation of Palestine.

turn the other [cheek]: Usually taken to epitomize Christian passivity, even servility. But is that what is expressed when the one slapped responds by presenting the left cheek? Is this passive resistance? Or is it active resistance, yet non-violent? (It was so taken by Gandhi, the foundation of the radically effective principle of active non-violent resistance.) What would the response communicate to the one who had slapped?

• **5:40** The second directive evidently concerns a garment that has been pawned for some money, and the loan was never repaid. And it involves one who has only a *shirt* to pawn. This was a long garment, like a loose tunic.

determined to sue you: For only a shirt, or whatever pittance it could have been pawned for! Far easier to let the matter drop. But this *someone is determined* to take

you to court.

your coat along with it: In other words, all that you wear. Respond to the plaintiff with nudity. What would that communicate? (In Luke 6:29b it is a *coat* that is pawned and a *shirt* that is not to be withheld. A poor person might pawn his coat during the day—it was required that he could have it back during the night, for warmth—wearing only his ankle-length shirt in the day's heat. This order makes more sense. Perhaps our author has inadvertently reversed it. Was the practice—or the manner of dress—not relevant in his community?)

• **5:41** The third instruction.

conscripts you for one mile: The first and last words here explain the situation. This is a soldier who presses (*conscripts*) you into service. He can compel you to carry his gear. And for a *mile,* a Roman military unit of distance—but only a mile, according to the rules of Roman occupation of Palestine. Otherwise, those occupied might become rebellious.

go a second mile: Greek: "two [miles]." Usually, taken to mean doing more than is expected. But for a Jew that would be collaboration with the Roman oppressor. Here it is doing what the soldier could not safely allow. So what would this act say?

• **5:42** Thom 95 reads: "If you have money, don't lend it at interest. Rather, give [it] to someone from whom you won't get it back." Does Jesus merely propose charity? or an egalitarian community?

• **5:43** *You know that we once were told:* The formula, for the last time.

You are to love your neighbor: Lev 19:18,

When someone slaps you on the right cheek, turn the other as well.

⁴⁰If someone is determined to sue you for your shirt, let that person have your coat along with it.

⁴¹Further, when anyone conscripts you for one mile, go a second mile.

⁴²Give to anyone who begs from you; and don't turn away the one who tries to borrow from you.

⁴³"You know that we once were told, 'You are to love your neighbor' and 'You are to hate your enemy.' ⁴⁴But I tell you: Love your enemies and pray for your persecutors. ⁴⁵You'll then become children of your Father in the heavens. <God> causes the sun to rise on both the bad and the good, and sends rain on both the just and

On love of enemies

---

concluding with the words, "as yourself."

You are to hate your enemy: This cannot be found in the Hebrew scriptures. In fact, in Lev 19:34 there is the command to "love the alien who resides with you." But there is also the command to "utterly destroy" the enemy (for example, Deut 7:2).

• **5:44** *Love your enemies and pray for your per-*

secutors: The nearly impossible command of Jesus. Perhaps the best examples of those who taught and practiced it in our times are Martin Luther King, Jr., and Desmond Tutu.

• **5:45** *You'll then become children of your Father in the heavens:* As by right the disciples are meant to be; see above on 5:16.

Translation Note:

"Congratulations!" / "Damn you!"

The first of these phrases takes the place of what has generally been translated "Blessed," now an archaic and entirely religious word. As Jesus used it, the term (put into Greek as *makarios*) probably meant Lucky, Fortunate (Luke 6:20–23) and had a primarily socio-political sense. In the parallel list in Matthew 5:3–12 it has come to mean Pleasing to God. To convey all this the translators of SV have aptly chosen Congratulations, a word that like *makarios* confers what it pronounces. (Or in 13:16, "How privileged!")

The other phrase, often used in tandem with the first (Luke 6:24–26), has ordinarily appeared as "Woe!"—even more outdated. "Damn you," whether intended theologically or only emotionally, comes closest to the Greek (*ouai*) in modern diction. It will offend those who want Jesus' words only in decorous English.

ἐπὶ πονηροὺς καὶ ἀγαθοὺς καὶ βρέχει ἐπὶ δικαίους καὶ ἀδίκους. ⁴⁶ἐὰν
γὰρ ἀγαπήσητε τοὺς ἀγαπῶντας ὑμᾶς, τίνα μισθὸν ἔχετε; οὐχὶ καὶ οἱ
τελῶναι τὸ αὐτὸ ποιοῦσιν; ⁴⁷καὶ ἐὰν ἀσπάσησθε τοὺς ἀδελφοὺς ὑμῶν
μόνον, τί περισσὸν ποιεῖτε; οὐχὶ καὶ οἱ ἐθνικοὶ τὸ αὐτὸ ποιοῦσιν;
⁴⁸Ἔσεσθε οὖν ὑμεῖς τέλειοι ὡς ὁ πατὴρ ὑμῶν ὁ οὐράνιος τέλειός
ἐστιν.

5:47 Instead of *pagans* some MSS repeat "toll collectors" here from vs 46.

• **5:46** *toll collectors:* See comments on 9:9 and 9:10.

• **5:47** *pagans:* In the past usually translated "Gentiles."

5:48 *To sum up:* Greek, *oun;* see Introduction, p. 27.

　genuine: The word (*teleios*) also means "mature" or "perfect."

the unjust. [46]Tell me, if you love those who love you, why should you be commended for that? Even the toll collectors do as much, don't they? [47]And if you greet only your friends, what have you done that is exceptional? Even the pagans do as much, don't they? [48]To sum up, you are to be as genuine <in your love> as your heavenly Father.

**Piety
in public**

6 Προσέχετε δὲ τὴν δικαιοσύνην ὑμῶν μὴ ποιεῖν ἔμπροσθεν τῶν ἀνθρώπων πρὸς τὸ θεαθῆναι αὐτοῖς· εἰ δὲ μή γε, μισθὸν οὐκ ἔχετε παρὰ τῷ πατρὶ ὑμῶν τῷ ἐν τοῖς οὐρανοῖς.

²Ὅταν οὖν ποιῇς ἐλεημοσύνην, μὴ σαλπίσῃς ἔμπροσθέν σου, ὥσπερ οἱ ὑποκριταὶ ποιοῦσιν ἐν ταῖς συναγωγαῖς καὶ ἐν ταῖς ῥύμαις, ὅπως δοξασθῶσιν ὑπὸ τῶν ἀνθρώπων· ἀμὴν λέγω ὑμῖν, ἀπέχουσιν τὸν μισθὸν αὐτῶν.

³Σοῦ δὲ ποιοῦντος ἐλεημοσύνην μὴ γνώτω ἡ ἀριστερά σου τί ποιεῖ ἡ δεξιά σου, ⁴ὅπως ᾖ σου ἡ ἐλεημοσύνη ἐν τῷ κρυπτῷ· καὶ ὁ πατήρ σου ὁ βλέπων ἐν τῷ κρυπτῷ ἀποδώσει σοι.

**Prayer
in public**

⁵Καὶ ὅταν προσεύχησθε, οὐκ ἔσεσθε ὡς οἱ ὑποκριταί, ὅτι φιλοῦσιν ἐν ταῖς συναγωγαῖς καὶ ἐν ταῖς γωνίαις τῶν πλατειῶν ἑστῶτες προσεύχεσθαι, ὅπως φανῶσιν τοῖς ἀνθρώποις· ἀμὴν λέγω ὑμῖν, ἀπέχουσιν τὸν μισθὸν αὐτῶν.

⁶Σὺ δὲ ὅταν προσεύχῃ, εἴσελθε εἰς τὸ ταμεῖόν σου καὶ κλείσας τὴν θύραν σου πρόσευξαι τῷ πατρί σου τῷ ἐν τῷ κρυπτῷ· καὶ ὁ πατήρ σου ὁ βλέπων ἐν τῷ κρυπτῷ ἀποδώσει σοι.

⁷Προσευχόμενοι δὲ μὴ βατταλογήσητε ὥσπερ οἱ ἐθνικοί, δοκοῦσιν γὰρ ὅτι ἐν τῇ πολυλογίᾳ αὐτῶν εἰσακουσθήσονται. ⁸μὴ οὖν ὁμοιωθῆτε αὐτοῖς· οἶδεν γὰρ ὁ πατὴρ ὑμῶν ὧν χρείαν ἔχετε πρὸ τοῦ ὑμᾶς αἰτῆσαι αὐτόν.

⁹Οὕτως οὖν προσεύχεσθε ὑμεῖς·

Πάτερ ἡμῶν ὁ ἐν τοῖς οὐρανοῖς,
ἁγιασθήτω τὸ ὄνομά σου·

• **Chap. 6** The original reader/hearer would probably not have recognized a shift from what we call chap. 5 to this one. Those divisions were made long after the gospel was written, but often quite logically. We do pass here from the radical demands of the empire of God, to instruction about how Christians are to behave in contrast to their culture.

• **6:1** *flaunt your religion:* "Do your righteousness," defined entirely in religious terms.

• **6:2–4** In these three verses "you" and "your" are in the singular and so are addressed to individuals, unlike much of the rest of the chapter, which is obviously composite.

• **6:2** *toot your own horn:* "Sound a trumpet before yourself."

phony pietists: Greek: "hypocrites."

in houses of worship and on the street: That is, in public, whether indoors or out.

houses of worship: Greek, "synagogues."

• **6:3** *don't let your left hand in on what your right hand is up to:* Identical to Thom 62. An often

quoted, but cryptic saying of Jesus. The evangelist interprets it in vs 4a but does not explain what it means to hide one's charity even from oneself.

• **6:4** *your Father:* With vs 1, framing the passage.

will applaud you: Similar to "recognition" in vs 1. Does it mean reward you in "heaven" or in the future on earth?

• **6:5–8** Unique to this gospel.

• **6:5** *when you pray:* This phrase opens each of the first three verses of this section. But the evangelist is apparently assembling once disparate sayings.

phonies: See comment on vs 2.

stand up and pray: The conventional posture.

in houses of worship and on street corners: As in vs 2.

I swear to you. See Translation Note.

their prayers . . . answered: Ironic—receiving not what they supposedly were asking

6 "Take care that you don't flaunt your religion in public to be noticed by others. Otherwise, you will have no recognition from your Father in the heavens.

Piety in public

²"For example, when you give to charity, don't bother to toot your own horn as some phony pietists do in houses of worship and on the street. They are seeking human recognition. I swear to you, their grandstanding is its own reward.

³"Instead, when you give to charity, don't let your left hand in on what your right hand is up to, ⁴so your acts of charity may remain hidden. And your Father, who has an eye for the hidden, will applaud you.

⁵"And when you pray, don't act like phonies. They love to stand up and pray in houses of worship and on street corners, so they can show off in public. I swear to you, their prayers have been answered!

Prayer in public

⁶"When you pray, go into a room by yourself and shut the door behind you. Then pray to your Father, the hidden one. And your Father, with his eye for the hidden, will applaud you.

⁷"And when you pray, you should not babble on as the pagans do. They imagine that the length of their prayers will command attention. ⁸So don't imitate them. After all, your Father knows what you need before you ask.

⁹"Instead, you should pray like this:

> Our Father in the heavens,
> your name be revered;

---

of God. Rather, they got their wish to be noticed.

• **6:7** *babble on as the pagans do:* It's not clear just what this refers to.

command attention: Human or divine?

• **6:8** Is Jesus saying that prayer for oneself is unnecessary, even inappropriate? And is he suggesting a difference between what you might want and *what you need?*

• **6:9b–13** The so-called Lord's Prayer or Pater Noster ("Our Father"). This is the familiar version. A shorter form is found in Luke 11:2b–4. It must have come from Q, the "Sayings Gospel." And in the case of most differences between the two versions Luke's is probably closer to Q's wording. Did Jesus compose this prayer or was it constructed out of his sayings after his death? Even if the latter, it obviously is older than either Matthew or Luke, and probably older than Q. So at the least it represents a very early form of Christian prayer.

• **6:9b** *Our:* Making the prayer liturgical, for use in corporate worship. Luke 11:2b has simply "Father." Furthermore, our author suggests that regarding God as "your Father" is a special prerogative of the disciple. See above on 5:16.

Father: A way of regarding God relatively rare in the OT but common in the authentic teaching of Jesus. The word very likely translates the Aramaic *Abba*, whose intimacy in this context is remarkable. Not unlike "Papa."

in the heavens: That is, the sky, from which the Biblical notion of heaven derives—at the top of the three-story universe of heaven, earth, and underworld. The evangelist, evidently, adds the phrase to qualify the intimacy of "Father"; it is lacking in Luke.

your name be revered: A prayer that this might happen among humans. God's "name" is God's very self.

¹⁰ἐλθέτω ἡ βασιλεία σου·
γενηθήτω τὸ θέλημά σου,
ὡς ἐν οὐρανῷ καὶ ἐπὶ γῆς·
¹¹Τὸν ἄρτον ἡμῶν τὸν ἐπιούσιον δὸς ἡμῖν σήμερον·
¹²Καὶ ἄφες ἡμῖν τὰ ὀφειλήματα ἡμῶν,
ὡς καὶ ἡμεῖς ἀφήκαμεν τοῖς ὀφειλέταις ἡμῶν·
¹³Καὶ μὴ εἰσενέγκῃς ἡμᾶς εἰς πειρασμόν,
ἀλλὰ ῥῦσαι ἡμᾶς ἀπὸ τοῦ πονηροῦ.

¹⁴Ἐὰν γὰρ ἀφῆτε τοῖς ἀνθρώποις τὰ παραπτώματα αὐτῶν, ἀφήσει καὶ ὑμῖν ὁ πατὴρ ὑμῶν ὁ οὐράνιος· ¹⁵ἐὰν δὲ μὴ ἀφῆτε τοῖς ἀνθρώποις, οὐδὲ ὁ πατὴρ ὑμῶν ἀφήσει τὰ παραπτώματα ὑμῶν.

On fasting   ¹⁶Ὅταν δὲ νηστεύητε, μὴ γίνεσθε ὡς οἱ ὑποκριταὶ σκυθρωποί, ἀφανίζουσιν γὰρ τὰ πρόσωπα αὐτῶν ὅπως φανῶσιν τοῖς ἀνθρώποις νηστεύοντες· ἀμὴν λέγω ὑμῖν, ἀπέχουσιν τὸν μισθὸν αὐτῶν.

¹⁷Σὺ δὲ νηστεύων ἄλειψαί σου τὴν κεφαλὴν καὶ τὸ πρόσωπόν σου νίψαι, ¹⁸ὅπως μὴ φανῇς τοῖς ἀνθρώποις νηστεύων ἀλλὰ τῷ πατρί σου τῷ ἐν τῷ κρυφαίῳ· καὶ ὁ πατήρ σου ὁ βλέπων ἐν τῷ κρυφαίῳ ἀποδώσει σοι.

6:12 For *have forgiven* many MSS read "we forgive," so that our forgiveness need not necessarily be prior to God's forgiving us, slightly softening what Jesus says.
6:13 At the end of the prayer many MSS add "For yours is the kingdom, the power, and the glory. Amen." This probably reflects later use of the prayer in public worship.

• **6:10** *Impose . . . enact:* "May [your empire] come," "may [your will] be done." In the Greek these are divine passives, calling on God to accomplish these things: the SV rendering is correct.

your imperial rule: See Translation Note, above, pp. 46–47; conventionally translated "your kingdom."

enact your will . . .: The author's addition, perhaps for rhetorical effect, making the petition three-fold. This third request mainly summarizes the second.

on earth as <you do> in heaven: Suggesting a parallel reality, the ideal *in heaven.* This focus on *heaven* in a way makes the earthly manifestation of God's kingdom and God's will less urgent, even less important, than it was in Jesus' original teaching. See Introduction, p. 20.

• **6:11** *the bread we need for the day:* That is, one assumes, "for today," combining the two Greek words *epiousion* and *sêmeron.* But this can also be read, "give us today the bread [we need] for tomorrow." Luke has "each day."

• **6:12** *debts:* Metaphorical, at least for the evangelist. Vss 14–15 show that he understands "debt" to mean what has usually been called "sin," whether our sin against God or a neighbor's sin against us. Luke has "sins" here but "[those] indebted to us" in the next clause.

to the extent that we ourselves have forgiven: The operative Greek word, *hôs,* has usually been rendered simply "as." And the verb has been treated as present in tense. Thus: "just as we too forgive," indicating a parallel between divine and human forgiveness. But the Greek makes God's forgiveness conditional. It depends on our prior forgiveness ("insofar as we ourselves have [already] forgiven") and is in proportion to it (*to the extent that*). This is made clear in vss 14–15. If this seems to be a denial of grace, perhaps it means that unless one has known what it is to forgive, one cannot really accept forgiveness.

• **6:13** *we beg:* The verb for *don't subject us* is not an imperative like the others, but a subjunctive, which is less direct, more

¹⁰impose your imperial rule,

enact your will—

on earth as <you do> in heaven.

¹¹Provide us with the bread we need for the day.

¹²Forgive our debts

to the extent that we ourselves have forgiven those in debt

to us.

¹³And, we beg, don't subject us to testing,

but rescue us from the evil one.

¹⁴"For if you forgive others their failures and offenses, your heavenly Father will also forgive yours. ¹⁵And if you don't forgive the failures and mistakes of others, your Father won't forgive yours.

¹⁶"When you fast, don't look gloomy, as showoffs do. As you know, they distort their appearance so as to appear in public to be fasting. I swear to you, they have been paid in full.

On fasting

¹⁷"When you fast, dress your hair and wash your face, ¹⁸so you don't display your fasting. But it will be recognized by your Father, the hidden one, and your Father, who has an eye for the hidden, will applaud you.

---

courteous. Whether intentional or not (if the prayer is an assemblage of once separate elements, the subjunctive may have been preserved more or less accidentally), it suggests a distinctive translation. I prefer "we beg" to the translators' original "please," which seems too me too bland.

testing: The extreme test for the early Christians was persecution and the possibility of martyrdom. That of course would have severely raised the temptation to renounce Christianity. But the word does not primarily mean temptation. The prayer asks that we be spared the test of persecution. See 4:1–11, the story of Jesus' testing by the devil in the wilderness.

but rescue us from the evil one: Not in Luke.

from the evil one: Or simply "from evil."

• **6:14–15** Explaining vs 12. This seems to make God's forgiveness dependent on prior human action, not entirely consistent with Jesus' teaching about God's goodness (or Paul's, about grace). Does it mean that unless one learns the very difficult lesson of how to forgive, once cannot accept, even receive, God's forgiveness?

• **6:15** Something like this is used at the end of the parable of the unforgiving slave (18:35).

• **6:16–18** Unique to Matthew.

• **6:16** *When you fast:* As was common in the Judaism of Jesus' time.

showoffs: "Hypocrites." Sometimes SV translates it "phonies."

they distort their appearance: We aren't told what this meant; evidently the evangelist's audience would have understood. (In Esther 14:1–3 the queen, "in distress and mourning," covers her head with ashes and dung.) There is a kind of word-play in Greek with the next phrase (*so as to appear*) that our translation tries to replicate in English: more literally, "they make their faces unseemly (*aphanizousin*) so that they may seem (*phanôsin*) to be fasting." Does it mean applying something disfiguring to the hair and face? The directive to "[anoint your head] and wash your face" in the next verse suggests this.

have been paid in full: "Have their reward." Ironic, as in vs 5. They got the public recognition they wanted, but not God's (vs 18).

• **6:17–18** As in vss 2–4 and unlike most of chap. 6 till now, "you" and "your" here are addressed to an individual, not a group.

• **6:17** *dress your hair:* Greek: "anoint your head," expressing joy. Difficult to put into modern English, but it seems to mean more than simply "comb your hair."

6:18 *the hidden one:* As opposed to public recognition. Literally, "(who is) in secret."

applaud you: See on vs 4.

On possessions

¹⁹Μὴ θησαυρίζετε ὑμῖν θησαυροὺς ἐπὶ τῆς γῆς, ὅπου σὴς καὶ βρῶσις ἀφανίζει καὶ ὅπου κλέπται διορύσσουσιν καὶ κλέπτουσιν· ²⁰θησαυρίζετε δὲ ὑμῖν θησαυροὺς ἐν οὐρανῷ, ὅπου οὔτε σὴς οὔτε βρῶσις ἀφανίζει καὶ ὅπου κλέπται οὐ διορύσσουσιν οὐδὲ κλέπτουσιν· ²¹ὅπου γάρ ἐστιν ὁ θησαυρός σου, ἐκεῖ ἔσται καὶ ἡ καρδία σου.

Eye & light

²²Ὁ λύχνος τοῦ σώματός ἐστιν ὁ ὀφθαλμός. ἐὰν οὖν ᾖ ὁ ὀφθαλμός σου ἁπλοῦς, ὅλον τὸ σῶμά σου φωτεινὸν ἔσται· ²³ἐὰν δὲ ὁ ὀφθαλμός σου πονηρὸς ᾖ, ὅλον τὸ σῶμά σου σκοτεινὸν ἔσται. εἰ οὖν τὸ φῶς τὸ ἐν σοὶ σκότος ἐστίν, τὸ σκότος πόσον.

Two masters

²⁴Οὐδεὶς δύναται δυσὶ κυρίοις δουλεύειν· ἢ γὰρ τὸν ἕνα μισήσει καὶ τὸν ἕτερον ἀγαπήσει, ἢ ἑνὸς ἀνθέξεται καὶ τοῦ ἑτέρου καταφρονήσει. οὐ δύνασθε θεῷ δουλεύειν καὶ μαμωνᾷ.

On anxieties

²⁵Διὰ τοῦτο λέγω ὑμῖν, μὴ μεριμνᾶτε τῇ ψυχῇ ὑμῶν τί φάγητε ἢ τί πίητε, μηδὲ τῷ σώματι ὑμῶν τί ἐνδύσησθε. οὐχὶ ἡ ψυχὴ πλεῖόν ἐστιν τῆς τροφῆς καὶ τὸ σῶμα τοῦ ἐνδύματος; ²⁶ἐμβλέψατε εἰς τὰ πετεινὰ τοῦ οὐρανοῦ ὅτι οὐ σπείρουσιν οὐδὲ θερίζουσιν οὐδὲ συνάγουσιν εἰς ἀποθήκας, καὶ ὁ πατὴρ ὑμῶν ὁ οὐράνιος τρέφει αὐτά· οὐχ ὑμεῖς μᾶλλον διαφέρετε αὐτῶν; ²⁷τίς δὲ ἐξ ὑμῶν μεριμνῶν δύναται προσθεῖναι ἐπὶ τὴν ἡλικίαν αὐτοῦ πῆχυν ἕνα; ²⁸καὶ περὶ ἐνδύματος τί μεριμνᾶτε; καταμάθετε τὰ κρίνα τοῦ ἀγροῦ πῶς αὐξάνουσιν· οὐ κοπιῶσιν οὐδὲ νήθουσιν· ²⁹λέγω δὲ ὑμῖν ὅτι οὐδὲ Σολομὼν ἐν πάσῃ τῇ δόξῃ αὐτοῦ περιεβάλετο ὡς ἓν τούτων. ³⁰εἰ δὲ τὸν χόρτον τοῦ ἀγροῦ σήμερον ὄντα καὶ αὔριον εἰς κλίβανον βαλλόμενον ὁ θεὸς οὕτως ἀμφιέννυσιν, οὐ πολλῷ μᾶλλον ὑμᾶς, ὀλιγόπιστοι; ³¹μὴ οὖν μεριμνήσητε λέγοντες, Τί φάγωμεν; ἤ, Τί πίωμεν; ἤ, Τί περιβαλώμεθα; ³²πάντα γὰρ ταῦτα τὰ ἔθνη ἐπιζητοῦσιν· οἶδεν γὰρ ὁ πατὴρ ὑμῶν ὁ οὐράνιος ὅτι χρῄζετε τούτων ἁπάντων. ³³ζητεῖτε δὲ πρῶτον τὴν βασιλείαν [τοῦ θεοῦ] καὶ τὴν δικαιοσύνην αὐτοῦ, καὶ ταῦτα πάντα προστεθήσεται ὑμῖν. ³⁴μὴ οὖν μεριμνήσητε εἰς τὴν αὔριον, ἡ γὰρ αὔριον μεριμνήσει ἑαυτῆς· ἀρκετὸν τῇ ἡμέρᾳ ἡ κακία αὐτῆς.

6:25 Some MSS lack and drink—omitted because food in what follows does not strictly include drink?

• **6:20** *gather . . . in heaven:* How is this to be accomplished?
• **6:22–23a** A bit of first-century CE physiology?
• **6:23a** *clouded:* In Greek, "bad."
• **6:23b** *If the light within you is darkness:* What is meant is surely moral, not physiological.
• **6:24ab** Perhaps a common proverb.
• **6:24c** *both God and a bank account:* The proverb is applied to the moral life.

   a bank account: In Greek *mammon,* borrowed from Aramaic. It means simply money. The

translation here of course applies to modern middle-class life.
• **6:25** *That's why I tell you:* Referring to vs 24c. But originally the two sayings would have had nothing to do with each other. See the next comment.

   To *keep worrying about . . . food and clothing:* In Jesus' context hardly a question of being enslaved to one's money (vs 24), but in the Matthean church . . .?

   life: In Greek, *psychê,* meaning not a part of a person, such as mind or soul. In the Jewish

¹⁹"Don't acquire possessions here on earth, where moths and corrosion eat away and where robbers break in and steal. ²⁰Instead, gather your nest egg in heaven, where neither moth nor corrosion eats away and where no robbers break in or steal. ²¹As you know, where your treasure is that is where your heart will be as well.

On possessions

²²"The eye is the body's lamp. It follows that if your eye is clear, your whole body will be flooded with light. ²³If your eye is clouded, your whole body will be shrouded in darkness. If, then, the light within you is darkness, how dark that can be!

Eye & light

²⁴"No one can be a slave to two masters. No doubt that slave will either hate one and love the other, or be devoted to one and disdain the other. You can't be enslaved to both God and a bank account!

Two masters

²⁵"That's why I tell you: Don't keep worrying about your life—what you're going to eat and drink, or about your body—what you're going to wear. There is more to living than food and clothing, isn't there? ²⁶Take a look at the birds of the sky: they don't plant or harvest, or gather into barns. Yet your heavenly Father feeds them. You're worth more than they, aren't you? ²⁷Can any of you add one hour to life by worrying about it? ²⁸Why worry about clothes? Notice how the wild lilies grow: they don't slave and they never spin. ²⁹Yet let me tell you, even Solomon at the height of his glory was never decked out like one of them. ³⁰If God dresses up the grass in the field, which is here today and tomorrow is thrown into an oven, won't <God take care of> you even more, you who have so little trust? ³¹So don't worry. Don't say, 'What am I going to eat?' or 'What am I going to drink?' or 'What am I going to wear?' ³²These are all things pagans go after. After all, your heavenly Father is aware that you need them. ³³You are to seek <God's> domain, and <God's> justice first, and all these things will come to you as a bonus. ³⁴So don't fret about tomorrow. Let tomorrow fret about itself. The troubles that the day brings are enough.

On anxieties

---

understanding of the human being, all parts were inseparable, and so, interchangeable.

body: In Greek, *soma.* Spoken of here as if only the outward self ("what you're going to wear"). But of course eating and drinking have just as much to do with the body.

living: The Greek repeats the two terms just used (*psychê* and *sôma*). SV rightly treats them as one.

• **6:26–30** The argument is the classical one, from less to greater. Also at 7:11, 10:29–30, 12:11–12.

• **6:26** *sky:* The same word as for "heaven."

• **6:27** *one hour:* The Greek uses a unit of linear measurement—literally a "cubit," about 18

inches.

• **6:30** *who have so little trust:* Greek: "of little faith." Evidently all these things should be taken for granted.

• **6:32** *pagans:* "[Other] nations/peoples." In other words, Gentiles.

his justice: In this context, better than the common translation, "righteousness."

• **6:33** *<God's> domain and <God's> justice:* Instead of the usual "his domain and his justice," even though SV retains "Father" in vs 32. See Introduction, p. 26.

On judging **7** Μὴ κρίνετε, ἵνα μὴ κριθῆτε· ²ἐν ᾧ γὰρ κρίματι κρίνετε κριθήσεσθε, καὶ ἐν ᾧ μέτρῳ μετρεῖτε μετρηθήσεται ὑμῖν. ³τί δὲ βλέπεις τὸ κάρφος τὸ ἐν τῷ ὀφθαλμῷ τοῦ ἀδελφοῦ σου, τὴν δὲ ἐν τῷ σῷ ὀφθαλμῷ δοκὸν οὐ κατανοεῖς; ⁴ἢ πῶς ἐρεῖς τῷ ἀδελφῷ σου, Ἄφες ἐκβάλω τὸ κάρφος ἐκ τοῦ ὀφθαλμοῦ σου, καὶ ἰδοὺ ἡ δοκὸς ἐν τῷ ὀφθαλμῷ σοῦ; ⁵ὑποκριτά, ἔκβαλε πρῶτον ἐκ τοῦ ὀφθαλμοῦ σοῦ τὴν δοκόν, καὶ τότε διαβλέψεις ἐκβαλεῖν τὸ κάρφος ἐκ τοῦ ὀφθαλμοῦ τοῦ ἀδελφοῦ σου.

Pearls to pigs ⁶Μὴ δῶτε τὸ ἅγιον τοῖς κυσὶν μηδὲ βάλητε τοὺς μαργαρίτας ὑμῶν ἔμπροσθεν τῶν χοίρων, μήποτε καταπατήσουσιν αὐτοὺς ἐν τοῖς ποσὶν αὐτῶν καὶ στραφέντες ῥήξωσιν ὑμᾶς.

Ask,
seek, knock ⁷Αἰτεῖτε καὶ δοθήσεται ὑμῖν, ζητεῖτε καὶ εὑρήσετε, κρούετε καὶ ἀνοιγήσεται ὑμῖν· ⁸πᾶς γὰρ ὁ αἰτῶν λαμβάνει καὶ ὁ ζητῶν εὑρίσκει καὶ τῷ κρούοντι ἀνοιγήσεται. ⁹ἢ τίς ἐστιν ἐξ ὑμῶν ἄνθρωπος, ὃν αἰτήσει ὁ υἱὸς αὐτοῦ ἄρτον, μὴ λίθον ἐπιδώσει αὐτῷ; ¹⁰ἢ καὶ ἰχθὺν αἰτήσει, μὴ ὄφιν ἐπιδώσει αὐτῷ; ¹¹εἰ οὖν ὑμεῖς πονηροὶ ὄντες οἴδατε δόματα ἀγαθὰ διδόναι τοῖς τέκνοις ὑμῶν, πόσῳ μᾶλλον ὁ πατὴρ ὑμῶν ὁ ἐν τοῖς οὐρανοῖς δώσει ἀγαθὰ τοῖς αἰτοῦσιν αὐτόν.

Golden rule ¹²Πάντα οὖν ὅσα ἐὰν θέλητε ἵνα ποιῶσιν ὑμῖν οἱ ἄνθρωποι, οὕτως καὶ ὑμεῖς ποιεῖτε αὐτοῖς· οὗτος γάρ ἐστιν ὁ νόμος καὶ οἱ προφῆται.

Two gates ¹³Εἰσέλθατε διὰ τῆς στενῆς πύλης· ὅτι πλατεῖα ἡ πύλη καὶ εὐρύχωρος ἡ ὁδὸς ἡ ἀπάγουσα εἰς τὴν ἀπώλειαν καὶ πολλοί εἰσιν οἱ εἰσερχόμενοι δι᾽ αὐτῆς· ¹⁴τί στενὴ καὶ τεθλιμμένη ἡ ὁδὸς ἡ ἀπάγουσα εἰς τὴν ζωήν καὶ ὀλίγοι εἰσὶν οἱ εὑρίσκοντες αὐτήν.

By their fruits ¹⁵Προσέχετε ἀπὸ τῶν ψευδοπροφητῶν, οἵτινες ἔρχονται πρὸς

7:13 Some mss insert "is the gate" after *Wide*.
7:14 Many mss insert "is the gate" after *Narrow*.

• **Chap. 7** Unlike the beginning of chap. 6, no break in the content occurs here. The chapter division, when it was made much later, broke the text into blocks of approximately similar length.
• **7:1–2** Roughly parallel to Luke 6:37–38. The second half of vs 2 is also parallel to Mark at 4:24.
• **7:1** *pass judgment . . . be judged* The first verb is in the present tense and means "Don't keep on passing judgment" or, better, "Stop passing judgment." The second is in the aorist tense and means more or less "be once and for all judged" . . . at the last judgment, perhaps.
• **7:3–5** A separate saying, aptly combined by the evangelist with vss 1–2. In Luke 6 the two sayings are separated. "You" is singular in this saying but plural in vss 1–2 and from

vs 6 onward.
• **7:3** The image is of course absurd. It's not only hypocritical but in fact impossible to see anything, with a *timber in your . . . eye*.
  friend: In Greek, "brother."
  timber: A log.
• **7:4** *when you have:* The usual translation reproduces the idiomatic Greek "and behold!"
• **7:5** *phony:* As in 6:2, "hypocrite."
• **7:6** Very similar to Thom 93.
  The words *sacred* and *pearls* may have constituted a pun in Aramaic. The first part of the saying is similar to Jesus' reply to the Canaanite woman in 15:26.
  tear you to shreds: Evidently a wild boar is in mind.
• **7:9–11** Providing the assurance for vss 7–8.
• **7:10** *Of course no one would!* There is no such phrase in the Greek. But the questions in vss

7 "Don't pass judgment, so you won't be judged. ²Don't forget, the **On judging**
judgment you hand out will be the judgment you get back. And the
standard you apply will be the standard applied to you. ³Why do you
notice the sliver in your friend's eye, but overlook the timber in your
own? ⁴How can you say to your friend, 'Let me get the sliver out of
your eye,' when you have that timber in your own? ⁵You phony, first
take the timber out of your own eye and then you'll see well enough
to remove the sliver from your friend's eye.

⁶"Don't offer to dogs what is sacred, and don't throw your pearls **Pearls to pigs**
to pigs, or they'll trample them underfoot and turn and tear you to
shreds.

⁷"Ask—it'll be given to you; seek—you'll find; knock—it'll be **Ask,**
opened for you. ⁸Everyone who asks receives; everyone who seeks **seek, knock**
finds; and for the one who knocks it is opened. ⁹Who among you
would hand a son a stone when it's bread he's asking for? ¹⁰Again,
who would hand him a snake when it's fish he's asking for? Of
course no one would! ¹¹So if you, worthless as you are, know how
to give your children good gifts, isn't it much more likely that your
Father in the heavens will give good things to those who ask him?

¹²"Consider this: Treat people in ways you want them to treat **Golden rule**
you. This sums up <the whole of> the Law and the Prophets.

¹³"Try to get in through the narrow gate. Wide and smooth is **Two gates**
the road that leads to destruction. The majority are taking that
route. ¹⁴How narrow and rough is the road that leads to life! Only a
minority discover it.

¹⁵"Be on the lookout for phony prophets, who make their pitch **By their fruits**

9–10 are clearly formulated to expect the
answer No: "You wouldn't hand your son a
stone, would you? . . ."
- **7:11** *worthless:* Evidently this description of
humans is to be understood in comparison
to God's goodness and in contrast to *good
gifts.* It seems a better translation than the
usual "evil."
    isn't it much more likely? Again, as in 6:28–30,
the reasoning is classic, from less to greater.
    your Father in the heavens: Luke 11:13 has
"the heavenly Father."
- **7:12** The traditional name for this saying,
the Golden Rule, indicates that it epitomizes
Jesus' ethical teaching. Self-interest can best
identify what constitutes ethical treatment
of others. See also 22:37–39.
    Consider this: Greek *oun.* Usually translated
"Therefore," which makes little sense here.

*This sums up <the whole of> the Law and the
Prophets:* Not found in the parallel version
in Luke 6:31. It is probably our author's addition, expressing his Jewish way of understanding Christianity. Compare 22:40 ("On
these . . . depends everything in the Law and
the Prophets").
    This sums up: In Greek, simply "This is."
- **7:13** *get in:* Presumably, into God's Empire,
the so-called kingdom of God.
    destruction: At the last judgment?
- **7:14** *life:* In the new age.
- **7:15–16** Unique to this gospel.
- **7:15** *phony prophets:* Perhaps traveling
teachers who claim to be Christian.
    make their pitch: From the context this ap-
propriately interprets the Greek, which says
only "come to you."

ὑμᾶς ἐν ἐνδύμασιν προβάτων, ἔσωθεν δέ εἰσιν λύκοι ἅρπαγες. ¹⁶ἀπὸ τῶν καρπῶν αὐτῶν ἐπιγνώσεσθε αὐτούς. μήτι συλλέγουσιν ἀπὸ ἀκανθῶν σταφυλὰς ἢ ἀπὸ τριβόλων σῦκα; ¹⁷οὕτως πᾶν δένδρον ἀγαθὸν καρποὺς καλοὺς ποιεῖ, τὸ δὲ σαπρὸν δένδρον καρποὺς πονηροὺς ποιεῖ. ¹⁸οὐ δύναται δένδρον ἀγαθὸν καρποὺς πονηροὺς ποιεῖν οὐδὲ δένδρον σαπρὸν καρποὺς καλοὺς ποιεῖν. ¹⁹πᾶν δένδρον μὴ ποιοῦν καρπὸν καλὸν ἐκκόπτεται καὶ εἰς πῦρ βάλλεται. ²⁰ἄρα γε ἀπὸ τῶν καρπῶν αὐτῶν ἐπιγνώσεσθε αὐτούς.

Invocation without obedience

²¹Οὐ πᾶς ὁ λέγων μοι, Κύριε κύριε, εἰσελεύσεται εἰς τὴν βασιλείαν τῶν οὐρανῶν, ἀλλ᾽ ὁ ποιῶν τὸ θέλημα τοῦ πατρός μου τοῦ ἐν τοῖς οὐρανοῖς. ²²πολλοὶ ἐροῦσίν μοι ἐν ἐκείνῃ τῇ ἡμέρᾳ, Κύριε κύριε, οὐ τῷ σῷ ὀνόματι ἐπροφητεύσαμεν, καὶ τῷ σῷ ὀνόματι δαιμόνια ἐξεβάλομεν, καὶ τῷ σῷ ὀνόματι δυνάμεις πολλὰς ἐποιήσαμεν; ²³καὶ τότε ὁμολογήσω αὐτοῖς ὅτι Οὐδέποτε ἔγνων ὑμᾶς· ἀποχωρεῖτε ἀπ᾽ ἐμοῦ οἱ ἐργαζόμενοι τὴν ἀνομίαν.

Foundations

²⁴Πᾶς οὖν ὅστις ἀκούει μου τοὺς λόγους τούτους καὶ ποιεῖ αὐτούς, ὁμοιωθήσεται ἀνδρὶ φρονίμῳ, ὅστις ᾠκοδόμησεν αὐτοῦ τὴν οἰκίαν ἐπὶ τὴν πέτραν· ²⁵καὶ κατέβη ἡ βροχὴ καὶ ἦλθον οἱ ποταμοὶ καὶ ἔπνευσαν οἱ ἄνεμοι καὶ προσέπεσαν τῇ οἰκίᾳ ἐκείνῃ, καὶ οὐκ ἔπεσεν, τεθεμελίωτο γὰρ ἐπὶ τὴν πέτραν. ²⁶καὶ πᾶς ὁ ἀκούων μου τοὺς λόγους τούτους καὶ μὴ ποιῶν αὐτοὺς ὁμοιωθήσεται ἀνδρὶ μωρῷ, ὅστις ᾠκοδόμησεν αὐτοῦ τὴν οἰκίαν ἐπὶ τὴν ἄμμον· ²⁷καὶ κατέβη ἡ βροχὴ καὶ ἦλθον οἱ ποταμοὶ καὶ ἔπνευσαν οἱ ἄνεμοι καὶ προσέκοψαν τῇ οἰκίᾳ ἐκείνῃ, καὶ ἔπεσεν καὶ ἦν ἡ πτῶσις αὐτῆς μεγάλη.

²⁸Καὶ ἐγένετο ὅτε ἐτέλεσεν ὁ Ἰησοῦς τοὺς λόγους τούτους, ἐξεπλήσσοντο οἱ ὄχλοι ἐπὶ τῇ διδαχῇ αὐτοῦ· ²⁹ἦν γὰρ διδάσκων αὐτοὺς ὡς ἐξουσίαν ἔχων καὶ οὐχ ὡς οἱ γραμματεῖς αὐτῶν.

• **7:16** *by what they produce:* "By their fruits."

• **7:17–20** Somewhat similar teaching is found at Luke 6:43–45.

• **7:17** Another version of this saying, together with vs 16a, appears in 12:33.

• **7:19** Among the gospels this warning is found only here and at 3:10b (spoken by the Baptist).

the fire: Probably a symbol for the last judgment.

• **7:20** Restating vs 16a.

• **7:21** *Master:* Or "Lord." Perhaps both senses are intended here.

my Father in heaven: In Matthew Jesus refers to God in this way a number of times. The phrase isn't used in Mark. Luke has simply "my Father."

• **7:22** *On that day:* Evidently the day of judg-ment.

prophesied . . . exorcised demons . . . performed miracles: A valid summary of Jesus' public activity.

use your name: See "In the name of" in the Glossary.

exorcised demons: "Demons," or bad spirits, were believed to inhabit people and cause them to be sick, either physically or men-tally. To "exorcise" was literally to throw the demons out.

• **7:23** *tell . . . honestly:* A happy translation of the Greek verb.

you subverters of the Law: More literally, "you who practice lawlessness," whether speaking of intent or effect.

• **7:24–29** A double metaphor about house building, also found in Luke 6:47–49. It

disguised as sheep; inside they are really voracious wolves. ¹⁶You'll know who they are by what they produce. Since when do people pick grapes from thorns, or figs from thistles? ¹⁷Every healthy tree produces choice fruit, but the rotten tree produces spoiled fruit. ¹⁸A healthy tree cannot produce spoiled fruit, any more than a rotten tree can produce choice fruit. ¹⁹Every tree that does not produce choice fruit gets cut down and tossed on the fire. ²⁰Remember, you'll know who they are by what they produce.

²¹"Not everyone who addresses me as 'Master, master,' will get into Heaven's domain—only those who carry out the will of my Father in heaven. ²²On that day many will address me: 'Master, master, didn't we use your name when we prophesied? Didn't we use your name when we exorcised demons? Didn't we use your name when we performed all those miracles?' ²³Then I will tell them honestly: 'I never knew you; get away from me, you subverters of the Law!'

Invocation without obedience

²⁴"Everyone who pays attention to these words of mine and acts on them will be like a shrewd builder who erected a house on bedrock. ²⁵Later the rain fell, and the torrents came, and the winds blew and pounded that house, yet it did not collapse, since its foundation rested on bedrock. ²⁶Everyone who listens to these words of mine and doesn't act on them will be like a careless builder, who erected a house on the sand. ²⁷When the rain fell, and the torrents came, and the winds blew and pounded that house, it collapsed. Its fall was colossal."

Foundations

²⁸And so, when Jesus had finished this discourse, the crowds were astonished at his teaching, ²⁹since he had been teaching them on his own authority, unlike their <own> scholars.

---

graphically illustrates Jesus' declaration in vs 21b: "only those who carry out the will of my Father in heaven" will enter "God's domain." For our evangelist, the way to do God's will is to *pay attention to [Jesus'] words* (vs 24).

• **7:28–29** Thus ends the so-called Sermon on the Mount, the first of five extended discourses. It can be epitomized as *What God's Empire Demands.*

• **7:28** *when Jesus had finished . . .:* A formula that concludes each of the five discourses—here and at 11:1, 13:53, 19:1, and 26:1. It is found several times in the Pentateuch—see Introduction, p. 16.

this discourse: "These words." Chaps. 5–7 can hardly be a speech that Jesus gave at one time, but, as we've seen, a massive compos-

ite probably created by the evangelist. It fits his plan of writing a kind of "manual of discipline" for the church.

the crowds: At the beginning of the discourse (5:1) Jesus left the crowds and talked only to the disciples. Why is his audience here so much wider? Or why was his audience at first so restricted? Perhaps the distinction is not an entirely real one; the crowds were potential disciples.

• **7:29** *on his own authority:* That is, not merely explaining scripture or traditional interpretation, as the *scholars* did.

**Jesus
cures a leper**

8 Καταβάντος δὲ αὐτοῦ ἀπὸ τοῦ ὄρους ἠκολούθησαν αὐτῷ ὄχλοι πολλοί. ²καὶ ἰδοὺ λεπρὸς προσελθὼν προσεκύνει αὐτῷ λέγων, Κύριε, ἐὰν θέλῃς δύνασαί με καθαρίσαι.

³Καὶ ἐκτείνας τὴν χεῖρα ἥψατο αὐτοῦ λέγων, Θέλω, καθαρίσθητι· καὶ εὐθέως ἐκαθαρίσθη αὐτοῦ ἡ λέπρα. ⁴καὶ λέγει αὐτῷ ὁ Ἰησοῦς, Ὅρα μηδενὶ εἴπῃς, ἀλλὰ ὕπαγε σεαυτὸν δεῖξον τῷ ἱερεῖ καὶ προσένεγκον τὸ δῶρον ὃ προσέταξεν Μωϋσῆς, εἰς μαρτύριον αὐτοῖς.

**Officer's
servant**

⁵Εἰσελθόντος δὲ αὐτοῦ εἰς Καφαρναοὺμ προσῆλθεν αὐτῷ ἑκατόνταρχος παρακαλῶν αὐτὸν ⁶καὶ λέγων, Κύριε, ὁ παῖς μου βέβληται ἐν τῇ οἰκίᾳ παραλυτικός, δεινῶς βασανιζόμενος.

⁷Καὶ λέγει αὐτῷ, Ἐγὼ ἐλθὼν θεραπεύσω αὐτόν.

⁸Ἀποκριθεὶς δὲ ὁ ἑκατόνταρχος ἔφη, Κύριε, οὐκ εἰμὶ ἱκανὸς ἵνα μου ὑπὸ τὴν στέγην εἰσέλθῃς, ἀλλὰ μόνον εἰπὲ λόγῳ, καὶ ἰαθήσεται ὁ παῖς μου. ⁹καὶ γὰρ ἐγὼ ἄνθρωπός εἰμι ὑπὸ ἐξουσίαν, ἔχων ὑπ' ἐμαυτὸν στρατιώτας, καὶ λέγω τούτῳ, Πορεύθητι, καὶ πορεύεται, καὶ ἄλλῳ, Ἔρχου, καὶ ἔρχεται, καὶ τῷ δούλῳ μου, Ποίησον τοῦτο, καὶ ποιεῖ.

¹⁰Ἀκούσας δὲ ὁ Ἰησοῦς ἐθαύμασεν καὶ εἶπεν τοῖς ἀκολουθοῦσιν, Ἀμὴν λέγω ὑμῖν, παρ' οὐδενὶ τοσαύτην πίστιν ἐν τῷ Ἰσραὴλ εὗρον. ¹¹λέγω δὲ ὑμῖν ὅτι πολλοὶ ἀπὸ ἀνατολῶν καὶ δυσμῶν ἥξουσιν καὶ ἀνακλιθήσονται μετὰ Ἀβραὰμ καὶ Ἰσαὰκ καὶ Ἰακὼβ ἐν τῇ βασιλείᾳ τῶν οὐρανῶν, ¹²οἱ δὲ υἱοὶ τῆς βασιλείας ἐκβληθήσονται εἰς τὸ σκότος

• **Chaps. 8–9** A block of miracle stories, for the most part. It can be surmised that the evangelist has collected them here to be exemplary of what the church is to do after Jesus' lifetime. (See, for example, comments on 8:18–22, 9:8, and 9:14.) This then leads up to the second discourse, about the disciples' responsibility to spread the good news of God's empire (chap. 10). The miracle stories have been gathered from various sources: Mark, Q, and the author's own tradition (M). Often they have been abbreviated—streamlined, we might say, for efficiency; our author is producing a big book, or scroll, rather, and his work would have filled a scroll about as big as could comfortably be held. There are nine miracles here and seven others in chaps. 12, 14, 15, 17, and 20. How did the author choose the stories to use here? All but one are healings, and in most cases the people healed are in some way outsiders or without status: a leper, a Roman officer's servant, Peter's mother-in-law, and so forth. Another criterion may have been the reply Jesus will make to John in 11:4–5: "The blind see again and the lame walk; lepers are cleansed and the deaf hear; the dead are raised, and the poor have the good news

preached to them." Perhaps the chief consideration was simply structure: three groups of three healings each, separated by words of Jesus having to do with discipleship. These then prepare for Jesus' instructions to the twelve disciples (chap. 10).

• **8:1–4** The Markan version of this story (1:40–45) is longer. Luke 5:12–16 is also a parallel.

• **8:1** In this introduction to the first miracle the narrative momentarily parallels Mark again, which it has not done since 4:23. In other words, chaps. 5–7 are an insertion into the Markan chronology, which nevertheless the evangelist is more or less following.
the mountain and *crowds*: As in 5:1.

• **8:2** *sir*: A Greek term of address to a superior, *kyrie*. Translated "Master" when on the lips of disciples, as in vss 21 and 25 below.
clean: It was held that leprosy (whatever the term meant in Jesus' time) made one ritually unclean.

• **8:3** *Okay*: Greek: "I want to," "I will."
you're clean: Jesus orders the cleansing (literally, "Be cleansed") . . . and so it takes place.

• **8:4** *See that you don't tell anyone*: A theme very important in Mark. It has become known as

8 When he came down from the mountain, huge crowds followed him. ²Just then a leper appeared, bowed down to him, and said, "Sir, if you want to, you can make me clean."

³And he stretched out his hand, touched him, and says, "Okay—you're clean!" At once his leprosy was cleansed away. ⁴Then Jesus warns him: "See that you don't tell anyone, but go, have a priest examine <your skin>. Then offer the gift that Moses commanded, as evidence <of your cure>."

⁵When he had entered Capernaum, a <Roman> officer approached him and pleaded with him: ⁶"Sir, my servant boy was struck down with paralysis and is in terrible pain."

⁷And he said to him, "I'll come and cure him."

⁸And the officer replied, "Sir, I don't deserve to have you in my house, but only say the word and my boy will be cured. ⁹After all, I myself am under orders, and I have soldiers under me. I order one to go, and he goes; I order another to come, and he comes; and <I order> my slave to do something, and he does it."

¹⁰As Jesus listened he was amazed and said to those who followed, "I swear to you, I have not found such trust in a single Israelite! ¹¹I predict that many will come from east and west and dine with Abraham and Isaac and Jacob in Heaven's domain, ¹²but those who

---

the "messianic secret," since Jesus' healings are understood, after his own time, as signs of his having been the Anointed. And in Mark the secrecy is imposed until, following Peter's recognition of his messianic standing, Jesus can make clear how his life will end, and that his messiahship is one of suffering and dying (Mark 8:31–32). Our author retains only some of the many expressions of this theme in Mark.

offer the gift that Moses commanded: As in Lev 14.

as evidence: Presumably to the priests.

• **8:5–13** There is a similar story in Luke 7:1–10, none in Mark. It is the only healing, and one of the very few narratives, in what we know of Q

• **8:5** *Capernaum:* See 4:13.

<Roman> *officer:* The Greek term, "ruler of a hundred," translates the Latin term for the Roman military rank, *centurion.*

• **8:6** *Sir:* See comment on vs 2.

my servant boy was struck down: The Greek continues, "in the house" or "at home," so the servant is evidently no common slave.

• **8:7** *cure:* Or "heal."

• **8:8** *to have you in my house:* Greek—"for you to come under my roof."

Say the word: As is clear in the next verse, the military mind perceives Jesus as having sufficient authority within God's chain of command to accomplish the boy's cure simply by giving the order from a distance.

• **8:10** *I swear to you:* See Translation Note.

trust: Usually a more apt translation than "faith." But this gospel, like Luke, at times emphasizes not so much trust in Jesus as belief in him. Which is meant here?

• **8:11–12** The evangelist has inserted this pronouncement, taking it from a different part of Q (see Luke 13:28–30).

• **8:11** *I predict:* Or perhaps simply, "I tell you."

Many . . . from east and west: Evidently Gentiles, like this officer.

dine with Abraham and Isaac and Jacob: A great meal, at which all the righteous of Israel will be gathered, is a frequent image for the coming of the empire of God.

in a single Israelite: The officer is of course a Gentile.

• **8:12** *those who think heaven's domain belongs to them:* Greek: "the sons of the empire." The expression "sons of," deriving from Hebrew, can connote almost anyone, and almost any relation between the "sons" and what follows it. As here, the context must indicate

τὸ ἐξώτερον· ἐκεῖ ἔσται ὁ κλαυθμὸς καὶ ὁ βρυγμὸς τῶν ὀδόντων.

¹³Καὶ εἶπεν ὁ Ἰησοῦς τῷ ἑκατοντάρχῃ, Ὕπαγε, ὡς ἐπίστευσας γενηθήτω σοι. καὶ ἰάθη ὁ παῖς ἐν τῇ ὥρᾳ ἐκείνῃ.

Peter's mother-in-law

¹⁴Καὶ ἐλθὼν ὁ Ἰησοῦς εἰς τὴν οἰκίαν Πέτρου εἶδεν τὴν πενθερὰν αὐτοῦ βεβλημένην καὶ πυρέσσουσαν· ¹⁵καὶ ἥψατο τῆς χειρὸς αὐτῆς, καὶ ἀφῆκεν αὐτὴν ὁ πυρετός, καὶ ἠγέρθη καὶ διηκόνει αὐτῷ.

At day's end

¹⁶Ὀψίας δὲ γενομένης προσήνεγκαν αὐτῷ δαιμονιζομένους πολλούς· καὶ ἐξέβαλεν τὰ πνεύματα λόγῳ καὶ πάντας τοὺς κακῶς ἔχοντας ἐθεράπευσεν, ¹⁷ὅπως πληρωθῇ τὸ ῥηθὲν διὰ Ἠσαΐου τοῦ προφήτου λέγοντος,

Αὐτὸς τὰς ἀσθενείας ἡμῶν ἔλαβεν
καὶ τὰς νόσους ἐβάστασεν.

Foxes have dens

¹⁸Ἰδὼν δὲ ὁ Ἰησοῦς ὄχλους περὶ αὐτὸν ἐκέλευσεν ἀπελθεῖν εἰς τὸ πέραν. ¹⁹καὶ προσελθὼν εἷς γραμματεὺς εἶπεν αὐτῷ, Διδάσκαλε, ἀκολουθήσω σοι ὅπου ἐὰν ἀπέρχῃ.

²⁰Καὶ λέγει αὐτῷ ὁ Ἰησοῦς, Αἱ ἀλώπεκες φωλεοὺς ἔχουσιν καὶ τὰ πετεινὰ τοῦ οὐρανοῦ κατασκηνώσεις, ὁ δὲ υἱὸς τοῦ ἀνθρώπου οὐκ ἔχει ποῦ τὴν κεφαλὴν κλίνῃ.

²¹Ἕτερος δὲ τῶν μαθητῶν εἶπεν αὐτῷ, Κύριε, ἐπίτρεψόν μοι πρῶτον ἀπελθεῖν καὶ θάψαι τὸν πατέρα μου.

²²Ὁ δὲ Ἰησοῦς λέγει αὐτῷ, Ἀκολούθει μοι καὶ ἄφες τοὺς νεκροὺς θάψαι τοὺς ἑαυτῶν νεκρούς.

Rebuking wind & wave

²³Καὶ ἐμβάντι αὐτῷ εἰς πλοῖον ἠκολούθησαν αὐτῷ οἱ μαθηταὶ αὐτοῦ. ²⁴καὶ ἰδοὺ σεισμὸς μέγας ἐγένετο ἐν τῇ θαλάσσῃ, ὥστε τὸ

8:13 At the end of the verse some mss read "The Roman official returned to his house and found that at that very moment the boy [had been restored to] good health"—clumsily conflating this story with the ending of John 4:46b–53a.

8:18 Most mss read "huge" *crowds*. Was it perhaps added later to enhance the impression of Jesus' popularity? Why would it be omitted, if original?

---

the meaning.

where it is utterly dark: "Outer darkness," that is, not just relatively dark.

There'll be weeping and grinding of teeth: This warning appears five more times in Matthew: 13:42, 50; 22:13; 24:51; 25:30. To the evangelist it signifies Hell.

• **8:13** *Your trust will be the measure of the results:* Greek, "may it happen for you <just> as you have trusted."

at that precise moment: An instantaneous healing and at a distance.

• **8:14–15** Equally brief in Mark 1:30–31.

• **8:14** *Peter's house:* In Capernaum? See vs 5. In Mark and Luke, Peter is called by his given name, Simon.

• **8:15b** *Then she got up and started looking after*

him: Was this his motive for healing her? Or simply evidence of the healing?

• **8:16–17** This abbreviates, summarizes Mark 1:32–34. It rounds out the first group of three healings, having primarily a transitional purpose

• **8:16** *demon-possessed:* See on 7:22.

• **8:17** The evangelist inserts this prophecy fulfillment, quoting Isa 53:4, and, unusually, with no apparent reference to Jesus suffering and death.

In this way . . . prophecy came true: More often the formula, "so that . . . [the prophecy] would come true" is used, as for example in 4:14.

• **8:18–22** The first interlude in the chain of miracles that comprises chaps. 8 and 9. Just

think Heaven's domain belongs to them will be thrown where it is utterly dark. There'll be weeping and grinding of teeth out there."

¹³And Jesus said to the officer, "Be on your way. Your trust will be the measure of the results." And the boy was cured at that precise moment.

¹⁴And when Jesus came to Peter's house, he noticed <Peter's> mother-in-law lying sick with a fever. ¹⁵He touched her hand and the fever disappeared. Then she got up and started looking after him.

Peter's mother-in-law

¹⁶In the evening, they brought many who were demon-possessed to him. He drove out the spirits with a command, and all those who were ill he cured. ¹⁷In this way Isaiah's prophecy came true:

At day's end

He took away our illnesses
and carried off our diseases.

¹⁸When Jesus saw the crowds around him, he gave orders to cross over to the other side. ¹⁹And one scholar came forward and said to him, "Teacher, I'll follow you wherever you go."

Foxes have dens

²⁰And Jesus says to him, "Foxes have dens, and birds of the sky have nests, but the son of Adam has nowhere to rest his head."

²¹Another disciple said to him, "Master, first let me go and bury my father."

²²But Jesus says to him, "Follow me, and leave it to the dead to bury their own dead."

²³When he got into a boat, his disciples followed him. ²⁴And just then a great storm broke on the sea, so that the boat was being

Rebuking wind & wave

---

as the miracles Jesus performs are perhaps examples for the church to follow, so too this teaching pertains to all who would *follow* Jesus.

- **8:18** *the other side:* Of the Sea of Galilee, presumably from Capernaum (vs 5).
- **8:19–22** Parallel to Luke 9:57–60.
- **8:19** *scholar:* See Glossary.

  Teacher: The scholar wants to *follow* Jesus as a disciple, that is, accept his teaching. He makes the further step of intending to follow Jesus literally. He will accompany Jesus, an itinerant teacher traveling along with his disciples, *wherever* [he would] *go*.
- **8:20** *son of Adam:* This phrase is used here for the first time—and about 30 times after this. See Translation Note, pp. 80–81. It is a title

for Jesus.

nowhere to rest his head: Jesus identifies an aspect of what Dietrich Bonhoeffer has called "the cost of discipleship."

- **8:21** *go and bury my father:* A solemn requirement for a pious Jew.
- **8:22** *the dead . . . their own dead:* The former phrase is obviously not to be taken literally. So what does Jesus' saying mean?
- **8:23–27** The miracles now resume. This is the only miracle story in chaps. 8–9 that is not strictly a healing, though the ancient mind might have seen it as healing an illness in nature. It is a slightly abbreviated version of Mark 4:35–41 and Luke 8:22–25.
- **8:24** *just then:* In Greek, *idou*, usually translated too stiffly and mechanically as "behold!"

Translation Note: "The Son of Adam"

Together with "Heaven's imperial rule," this phrase posed the greatest difficulty to the translators and finds the least consensus among them.

The strange Greek *(ho huios tou anthrôpou)* has always been translated more or less word-for-word as "the son of Man," or with two capitals, the Son of Man. ("The son of the man" would be still more literal.) It's a curious, puzzling phrase. In Matthew it is used as a title, both by the evangelist and by Jesus himself, and it clearly refers to Jesus and only to him. Sometimes the author replaces the phrase when it occurs in Q or Mark with a simple pronoun indicating Jesus—for example, at 5:11 or in the first prediction of the passion, 16:21. And sometimes the reverse, as at 16:13—Jesus' question to the disciples at Caesarea Philippi.

The title can suggest the trials of Jesus' *earthly ministry* ("Foxes have dens, and birds of the sky have nests, but the son of Adam has nowhere to rest his head"—8:20) and, especially, his coming *suffering and death* ("The son of Adam is about to be turned over to his enemies, and they will end up killing him"—17:23). But it can also express Jesus' *appearance* at the end of the age ("the son of Adam [will come] on clouds of heaven with great power and splendor"—24:30).

Our author has suppressed an earlier usage in the tradition, a phrase meaning any human being. Mark 2:27 (SV) reads: "The sabbath day was created for Adam and Eve . . . not Adam and Eve for the sabbath day; so the son of Adam has control over the sabbath day." This is Semitic poetry and "son of Adam" means simply a human being. But Matthew 12:8 has only the second part of this saying and intends the phrase to refer to Jesus alone.

How did the phrase arise and become this mysterious title? It has a considerable biblical background. The prophet Ezekiel hears God habitually addressing him as "son of man," meaning simply human being and perhaps *mere* human being. For example, in Ezekiel 2:1 NRSV has "mortal." In chapter 7 of the book of Daniel, the seer has a vision of "one like a son of man" (NRSV: "like a human being") who goes up to heaven and beholds "the ancient of days." In the book's coded language this means that Israel—the people and the nation, in distinction to their oppressor empires, represented by animals—will be vindicated before God.

So both the ordinary sense of the phrase and an apocalyptic one have OT precedent. But it's the latter that takes off in Jewish speculation, and the corporate meaning of Daniel's phrase (Israel depicted as an individual) is forgotten. Before long Son of Man became an arcane figure of the future, who like the Anointed would one day appear to consummate Israel's unhappy earthly history and usher in a new age, whether on earth or in heaven. (Eventually this figure will play a major role in non-canonical books like Enoch.)

Evidently Jesus used the phrase in its simple, ordinary sense, for that is how we find it entering the tradition of his teaching. That he used it in an apocalyptic sense is highly unlikely, and if he spoke of a suffering Son of Man, it may have included both himself and his followers and would not have predicted in detail his eventual arrest and death (see the comment on 16:21–23). Our evangelist, however, applies it solely to Jesus.

But why SV's unusual rendering, "the son of Adam"? There was considerable debate among the translators how the phrase could best be expressed in modern, understandable English. Women's issues are a principal concern, and both nouns are problematic. By the standards of inclusive language, the Greek word for "man" (*anthrôpos*) has simply been mistranslated. It does not mean a male person but any human. So "man" is wrong.

The word "son" is a different kind of problem. It is not strictly a mistranslation; *huios* is not ordinarily a generic term meaning any offspring, male or female. The word means simply a male child, and as a title for Jesus, it poses no difficulty---apart from the profound theological one of his very maleness. But what is to be done with *tou anthrôpou*? "Son of the human [or Human]" seemed too bland. It was decided to use the Biblical name, Adam. While it seems to connote a male human being, in fact the Hebrew word *'adham* means just the same as *anthrôpos:* a human being. Thus "son of Adam" was arrived at as a title for the man Jesus. It has the advantage of being concise, vivid, and also Biblical.

But this decision was not unanimous. Some translators felt that while retaining a sonorous quality it had lost the mystery befitting a title. And though not a problem in Matthew, when the phrase refers to any human being it sounds even less inclusive than "son of Man." Nor does it interpret what the phrase means. So "the human one" was the choice of the minority, and when applied to Jesus, the Human One, or even the Truly Human One (see Walter Wink's recent book).

In the end, the translators agreed that this phrase is the most problematic in the gospels. The reader will have to recognize that "son of Adam" carries a heavy load of meaning not immediately obvious in the phrase itself.

πλοῖον καλύπτεσθαι ὑπὸ τῶν κυμάτων, αὐτὸς δὲ ἐκάθευδεν. ²⁵καὶ προσελθόντες ἤγειραν αὐτὸν λέγοντες, Κύριε, σῶσον, ἀπολλύμεθα.

²⁶Καὶ λέγει αὐτοῖς, Τί δειλοί ἐστε, ὀλιγόπιστοι; τότε ἐγερθεὶς ἐπετίμησεν τοῖς ἀνέμοις καὶ τῇ θαλάσσῃ, καὶ ἐγένετο γαλήνη μεγάλη.

²⁷Οἱ δὲ ἄνθρωποι ἐθαύμασαν λέγοντες, Ποταπός ἐστιν οὗτος ὅτι καὶ οἱ ἄνεμοι καὶ ἡ θάλασσα αὐτῷ ὑπακούουσιν;

Demons of Gadara

²⁸Καὶ ἐλθόντος αὐτοῦ εἰς τὸ πέραν εἰς τὴν χώραν τῶν Γαδαρηνῶν ὑπήντησαν αὐτῷ δύο δαιμονιζόμενοι ἐκ τῶν μνημείων ἐξερχόμενοι, χαλεποὶ λίαν, ὥστε μὴ ἰσχύειν τινὰ παρελθεῖν διὰ τῆς ὁδοῦ ἐκείνης. ²⁹καὶ ἰδοὺ ἔκραξαν λέγοντες, Τί ἡμῖν καὶ σοί, υἱὲ τοῦ θεοῦ; ἦλθες ὧδε πρὸ καιροῦ βασανίσαι ἡμᾶς; ³⁰ἦν δὲ μακρὰν ἀπ᾽ αὐτῶν ἀγέλη χοίρων πολλῶν βοσκομένη. ³¹οἱ δὲ δαίμονες παρεκάλουν αὐτὸν λέγοντες, Εἰ ἐκβάλλεις ἡμᾶς, ἀπόστειλον ἡμᾶς εἰς τὴν ἀγέλην τῶν χοίρων.

³²Καὶ εἶπεν αὐτοῖς, Ὑπάγετε.

Οἱ δὲ ἐξελθόντες ἀπῆλθον εἰς τοὺς χοίρους· καὶ ἰδοὺ ὥρμησεν πᾶσα ἡ ἀγέλη κατὰ τοῦ κρημνοῦ εἰς τὴν θάλασσαν καὶ ἀπέθανον ἐν τοῖς ὕδασιν. ³³οἱ δὲ βόσκοντες ἔφυγον, καὶ ἀπελθόντες εἰς τὴν πόλιν ἀπήγγειλαν πάντα καὶ τὰ τῶν δαιμονιζομένων. ³⁴καὶ ἰδοὺ πᾶσα ἡ πόλις ἐξῆλθεν εἰς ὑπάντησιν τῷ Ἰησοῦ, καὶ ἰδόντες αὐτὸν παρεκάλεσαν ὅπως μεταβῇ ἀπὸ τῶν ὁρίων αὐτῶν.

8:28 Mss differ widely in naming the people into whose territory Jesus comes. Some have "Gerasenes" and others "Gergesenes." Some of the same confusion is to be found at Mark 5:1 and Luke 8:26. There were at least three places on the east side of the Jordan with similar names. See Comment.

---

storm: Literally, a shaking or tossing, which on land would be an earthquake.

• **8:28–34** The story is much condensed compared to Mark 5:1–20 and Luke 8:26–39.

• **8:28** *the region of the Gadarenes:* Gadara was one of the Hellenistic cities of the Decapolis (see above on 4:25), south of the Sea of Galilee, but not on the eastern shore of the lake, as the story implies. Mark 5:1 has "the region of the Gerasenes," of a Decapolis site farther south and also not on the shore. Per-

haps that was a mistake for Gergesenes (see Gergesa on Map of Palestine; also the Text-Critical Note).

demoniacs: That is, people thought to be possessed by demons. See above on 7:22.

the tombs: In Jewish eyes, a place of uncleanness and dereliction. These demoniacs are in a state of hopeless dementia.

hard to deal with: Or "violent."

• **8:29** *What do you want with us?* In Greek, "What to us and to you?"—a Hebraism.

swamped by the waves; but he was asleep. ²⁵And they came and woke him up, and said to him, "Master, save us! We are going to drown!"

²⁶He says to them, "Why are you so cowardly? You have so little trust!" Then he got up and rebuked the winds and the sea, and there was a great calm.

²⁷And everyone marveled, saying, "What kind of person is this, that even the winds and the sea obey him?"

²⁸And when he came to the other side, to the region of the Gadarenes, he was met by two demoniacs who came out from the tombs. They were so hard to deal with that no one could pass along that road. ²⁹And just then they shouted, "What do you want with us, you son of God? Did you come here ahead of time to torment us?" ³⁰And a large herd of pigs was feeding off in the distance. ³¹And the demons kept bargaining with him: "If you drive us out, <at least> send us into the herd of pigs."

³²And he said to them, "Get out <of him>!"

And they came out and went into the pigs, and suddenly the whole herd rushed down the bluff into the sea and drowned in the water. ³³The herdsmen ran off, and went into town and reported everything, especially about the demoniacs. ³⁴And what do you know, the whole town came out to meet Jesus. And when they saw him, they begged him to move on from their district.

**Demons
of Gadara**

---

son of God: An idea first expressed in the story of Jesus' baptism (3:17). And finally in the high priest's question at his trial by the Council (26:63).

Did you come . . . ahead of time? Nothing in Mark or Luke corresponds to this. What does it mean? "Before the judgment," perhaps? "Before the coming of God's kingdom"?

• **8:31** *bargaining with him:* An unusual rendering for the usual "pleading."

send us into the herd of pigs: It was thought that when demons were exorcised they had to find another place to dwell. Regarded by Jews as ritually unclean, *pigs* are an appropriate destiny for demons.

• **8:32** *suddenly:* Usually, "Behold!" (Greek *idou*)

drowned: Did the demons die with them?

• **8:34** *And what do you know:* Again *idou*.

A paralytic

9 Καὶ ἐμβὰς εἰς πλοῖον διεπέρασεν καὶ ἦλθεν εἰς τὴν ἰδίαν πόλιν. ²καὶ ἰδοὺ προσέφερον αὐτῷ παραλυτικὸν ἐπὶ κλίνης βεβλημένον. καὶ ἰδὼν ὁ Ἰησοῦς τὴν πίστιν αὐτῶν εἶπεν τῷ παραλυτικῷ, Θάρσει, τέκνον, ἀφίενταί σου αἱ ἁμαρτίαι.

³Καὶ ἰδού τινες τῶν γραμματέων εἶπαν ἐν ἑαυτοῖς, Οὗτος βλασφημεῖ.

⁴Καὶ ἰδὼν ὁ Ἰησοῦς τὰς ἐνθυμήσεις αὐτῶν εἶπεν, Ἱνατί ἐνθυμεῖσθε πονηρὰ ἐν ταῖς καρδίαις ὑμῶν; ⁵τί γάρ ἐστιν εὐκοπώτερον, εἰπεῖν, Ἀφίενταί σου αἱ ἁμαρτίαι, ἢ εἰπεῖν, Ἔγειρε καὶ περιπάτει; ⁶ἵνα δὲ εἰδῆτε ὅτι ἐξουσίαν ἔχει ὁ υἱὸς τοῦ ἀνθρώπου ἐπὶ τῆς γῆς ἀφιέναι ἁμαρτίας – τότε λέγει τῷ παραλυτικῷ, Ἐγερθεὶς ἆρόν σου τὴν κλίνην καὶ ὕπαγε εἰς τὸν οἶκόν σου.

⁷Καὶ ἐγερθεὶς ἀπῆλθεν εἰς τὸν οἶκον αὐτοῦ. ⁸ἰδόντες δὲ οἱ ὄχλοι ἐφοβήθησαν καὶ ἐδόξασαν τὸν θεὸν τὸν δόντα ἐξουσίαν τοιαύτην τοῖς ἀνθρώποις.

Jesus dines with sinners

⁹Καὶ παράγων ὁ Ἰησοῦς ἐκεῖθεν εἶδεν ἄνθρωπον καθήμενον ἐπὶ τὸ τελώνιον, Μαθθαῖον λεγόμενον, καὶ λέγει αὐτῷ, Ἀκολούθει μοι. καὶ ἀναστὰς ἠκολούθησεν αὐτῷ.

¹⁰Καὶ ἐγένετο αὐτοῦ ἀνακειμένου ἐν τῇ οἰκίᾳ, καὶ ἰδοὺ πολλοὶ τελῶναι καὶ ἁμαρτωλοὶ ἐλθόντες συνανέκειντο τῷ Ἰησοῦ καὶ τοῖς μαθηταῖς αὐτοῦ.

¹¹Καὶ ἰδόντες οἱ Φαρισαῖοι ἔλεγον τοῖς μαθηταῖς αὐτοῦ, Διὰ τί μετὰ τῶν τελωνῶν καὶ ἁμαρτωλῶν ἐσθίει ὁ διδάσκαλος ὑμῶν;

• **9:1–8** The series of Jesus' miracle stories continues. The chapter change here was evidently made to break in two the long series of stories between Jesus' first and second discourses, chaps. 5–7 and 10. The first story parallels Mark 2:1–12 and Luke 5:17–26, but in a shortened version.

• **9:1** *the boat:* The one in which he had come to the east side of the lake (8:23).

to his own town: Returning to Capernaum. See 4:13.

• **9:2** *The next thing you know:* Another translation of *idou* ("Behold"). Also *At that* in the next verse.

• **9:3** *blasphemes:* To presume to forgive sins is to act like God. See Mark 2:7 ("Who can forgive sins except the one God?").

• **9:4** *he knew what they were thinking:* By intuition or divine inspiration?

harbor evil thoughts: The Greek has "consider evil in your hearts." In Jesus' culture the heart was the seat of both the mind and the will. So were the scholars thinking how they could trap him?

• **9:5** *Which is easier . . . ?* How would Jesus have answered this question?

• **9:6** *so that you may realize:* The "you" is plural. Is Jesus still speaking to the scholars, or our author to readers?

the son of Adam: See Translation Note, p. 80. Our author surely understands Jesus as speaking of himself. But see vs 8.

9:8 *humans:* We'd expect "a human," meaning Jesus. Very likely the author wants to suggest that what Jesus once did ought to be repeated by latter-day disciples, that is, by the church.

• **9:9–17** The second group of three miracles complete, our author creates another panel of Jesus' teaching in the two-chapter compilation of miracle stories. The other was in 8:18–22. As before, there are lessons for the church here. With these episodes the author resumes for the moment the narrative of Mark 2, also found in Luke 5.

• **9:9** *tollbooth:* Usually translated "tax office." Since passage on Roman roads was not free, the toll was itself a widespread form of

9 After he got on board the boat, he crossed over and came to his own town. ²The next thing you know, some people were bringing him a paralytic lying on a bed. When Jesus noticed their trust, he said to the paralytic, "Take courage, child, your sins are forgiven."

A paralytic

³At that some of the scholars said to themselves, "This fellow blasphemes!"

⁴Because he knew what they were thinking, Jesus said, "Why do you harbor evil thoughts? ⁵Which is easier: To say, 'Your sins are forgiven'? or to say, 'Get up and walk'? ⁶But so that you may realize that on earth the son of Adam has authority to forgive sins . . ." (he says to the paralytic) "Get up, pick up your bed and go home."

⁷And he got up and went home. ⁸When the crowds saw this, they became fearful, and extolled God for giving such authority to humans.

⁹As Jesus was walking along there, he caught sight of a man sitting at the tollbooth, one named Matthew, and he says to him, "Follow me." And he got up and followed him.

Jesus dines with sinners

¹⁰And it happened while he was dining in <Matthew's> house that many toll collectors and sinners showed up just then, and they dined with Jesus and his disciples.

¹¹And when the Pharisees saw this, they began to question his disciples: "Why does your teacher eat with toll collectors and sinners?"

---

taxation. And its collectors were evidently regarded by other Jews as betraying their own people.

Matthew: In the parallel stories in Mark and Luke, this man is named Levi. But all the lists of "the twelve" have Matthew but no Levi. Until modern times *Matthew* was taken to be our author's reference to himself, which led to the assignment of our gospel to that disciple as author. We now understand that a disciple of Jesus cannot have written the gospel; rather, it was anonymous (see Introduction, p. 13).

• **9:10** *in <Matthew's> house:* The Greek has simply "in the house." And it has been much debated whether it might instead mean Peter's house (8:14). Or even Jesus'—he has just come "to his own town" (9:1). Maybe the evangelist didn't know and so left it ambiguous.

toll collectors and sinners: Toll collectors worked for Rome's gain at the expense of their fellow Jews. (See comment on *tollbooth,* vs 9, just above.) They were therefore con-

sidered *sinners.* The phrase must mean "toll collectors and [other] sinners."

• **9:11** An objection to Jesus' behavior. See also vs 14.

when the Pharisees saw this, they began . . .: The author, whose grammar is more precise than we find in Mark, here uses the imperfect tense, which can express either what is typical ("they used to" or "they would," as sometimes in SV), or continuous ("they kept on . . ."). Here it seems to be what's called inceptive ("began to"), since the author uses the aorist tense, a past of actual event, to report that Jesus responded ("he said," in vs 12). That they only "began" to question may suggest that this objection was made again and again in the experience of the church. See the next comment.

Why does your teacher . . .? The question is put to the disciples, not directly to Jesus. (See the opposite just below, vs 14; also in 12:2, 15:2, where people complain to Jesus about the disciples.) Elsewhere the Pharisees have no reluctance to go directly to

**Feasting
& fasting**

¹²Ὁ δὲ ἀκούσας εἶπεν, Οὐ χρείαν ἔχουσιν οἱ ἰσχύοντες ἰατροῦ ἀλλ᾽ οἱ κακῶς ἔχοντες. ¹³πορευθέντες δὲ μάθετε τί ἐστιν, Ἔλεος θέλω καὶ οὐ θυσίαν· οὐ γὰρ ἦλθον καλέσαι δικαίους ἀλλὰ ἁμαρτωλούς.

¹⁴Τότε προσέρχονται αὐτῷ οἱ μαθηταὶ Ἰωάννου λέγοντες, Διὰ τί ἡμεῖς καὶ οἱ Φαρισαῖοι νηστεύομεν, οἱ δὲ μαθηταί σου οὐ νηστεύουσιν;

¹⁵Καὶ εἶπεν αὐτοῖς ὁ Ἰησοῦς, Μὴ δύνανται οἱ υἱοὶ τοῦ νυμφῶνος πενθεῖν ἐφ᾽ ὅσον μετ᾽ αὐτῶν ἐστιν ὁ νυμφίος; ἐλεύσονται δὲ ἡμέραι ὅταν ἀπαρθῇ ἀπ᾽ αὐτῶν ὁ νυμφίος, καὶ τότε νηστεύσουσιν.

¹⁶Οὐδεὶς δὲ ἐπιβάλλει ἐπίβλημα ῥάκους ἀγνάφου ἐπὶ ἱματίῳ παλαιῷ· αἴρει γὰρ τὸ πλήρωμα αὐτοῦ ἀπὸ τοῦ ἱματίου καὶ χεῖρον σχίσμα γίνεται. ¹⁷οὐδὲ βάλλουσιν οἶνον νέον εἰς ἀσκοὺς παλαιούς· εἰ δὲ μή γε, ῥήγνυνται οἱ ἀσκοὶ καὶ ὁ οἶνος ἐκχεῖται καὶ οἱ ἀσκοὶ ἀπόλλυνται· ἀλλὰ βάλλουσιν οἶνον νέον εἰς ἀσκοὺς καινούς, καὶ ἀμφότεροι συντηροῦνται.

**An official's
daughter/a
woman**

¹⁸Ταῦτα αὐτοῦ λαλοῦντος αὐτοῖς, ἰδοὺ ἄρχων εἷς ἐλθὼν προσεκύνει αὐτῷ λέγων ὅτι Ἡ θυγάτηρ μου ἄρτι ἐτελεύτησεν· ἀλλὰ ἐλθὼν ἐπίθες τὴν χεῖρά σου ἐπ᾽ αὐτήν, καὶ ζήσεται. ¹⁹καὶ ἐγερθεὶς ὁ Ἰησοῦς ἠκολούθησεν αὐτῷ καὶ οἱ μαθηταὶ αὐτοῦ.

²⁰Καὶ ἰδοὺ γυνὴ αἱμορροοῦσα δώδεκα ἔτη προσελθοῦσα ὄπισθεν ἥψατο τοῦ κρασπέδου τοῦ ἱματίου αὐτοῦ· ²¹ἔλεγεν γὰρ ἐν ἑαυτῇ, Ἐὰν μόνον ἅψωμαι τοῦ ἱματίου αὐτοῦ σωθήσομαι. ²²ὁ δὲ Ἰησοῦς στραφεὶς καὶ ἰδὼν αὐτὴν εἶπεν, Θάρσει, θύγατερ· ἡ πίστις σου σέσωκέν σε. καὶ ἐσώθη ἡ γυνὴ ἀπὸ τῆς ὥρας ἐκείνης.

Jesus with a criticism of him (for example, 19:3). Perhaps both reflect a complaint to or about latter-day Christian prophets. But it undoubtedly began with Jesus' practice of inclusive social activity as a sign of God's empire already present in his movement's activity.

eat with: In whose company the Law allowed a Jew to eat was an esp. important question.

• **9:12** *Since when do the able-bodied need a doctor? It's the sick who do:* For what has just been implied to be sin (*eat with . . . sinners*), Jesus uses the metaphor of illness. Not blame but cure is the appropriate response. An importance lesson for the church, so often judgmental.

• **9:13** *Go and learn what this means:* Jesus acts as authoritative teacher of the scriptures.

It's mercy I desire instead of sacrifice: Aptly quoting Hos 6:6 here, and also at 12:7.

I did not come to enlist religious people but sinners: Jesus' mission is to gather, to "call" into God's empire, not those thought of as "the

righteous" (*religions people*)—is this deliberate irony?—but those usually held to be unrighteous, *sinners.* They were sometimes so regarded only because they were too poor to fulfill the expected religious practices, such as going to offer sacrifice in Jerusalem three times a year. In that case, Jesus' saying is not only ethical, but socially revolutionary. How would it apply to our situation today?

• **9:14** *the disciples of John:* This is a second objection to Jesus' practice. Pharisees made the first (9:11). Evidently the evangelist does not regard followers of the Baptist as friends of Jesus, either. After John had been killed, their movement was a rival to the church.

but your disciples don't [fast]: A question about the practice of Jesus' followers that probably pertains more, or perhaps entirely, to the post-resurrection period—that is, the time of the church.

• **9:15** *The groom's friends:* In Greek, "the sons of the groom," a Hebraism.

groom: Representing the Anointed. This metaphor serves the evangelist's christo-

¹²When Jesus overheard, he said, "Since when do the able-bodied need a doctor? It's the sick who do. ¹³Go and learn what this means, 'It's mercy I desire instead of sacrifice.' After all, I did not come to enlist religious people but sinners."

¹⁴Then the disciples of John come up to him and ask: "Why do we fast, and the Pharisees fast, but your disciples don't?"

Feasting & fasting

¹⁵And Jesus said to them, "The groom's friends can't mourn as long as the groom is around, can they? But the days will come when the groom is taken away from them, and then they will fast.

¹⁶"Nobody puts a piece of unshrunk cloth on an old garment, since the patch pulls away from the garment and creates a worse tear. ¹⁷Nor do they pour young wine into old wineskins; otherwise the wineskins burst, the wine gushes out, and the wineskins are destroyed. Instead, they put young wine in new wineskins and both are preserved."

¹⁸Just as he was saying these things to them, one of the officials came, began to bow down to him and say, "My daughter has just died. But come and put your hand on her and she will live." ¹⁹And Jesus got up and followed him, along with his disciples.

An official's daughter/a woman

²⁰And just then a woman who had suffered from vaginal bleeding for twelve years came up from behind and touched the hem of his cloak. ²¹She had been saying to herself, "If I only touch his cloak, I'll be cured." ²²Then Jesus turned around, saw her, and said, "Take courage, daughter, your trust has cured you." And the woman was cured right then and there.

---

logical interest. In a first-century Palestinian wedding the final arrival of the groom is the moment expectantly waited for, when the festivities can begin. More to the point, and perhaps closer to an original meaning of Jesus, is the broader focus not on the groom but on the wedding itself as symbol of the new age. Then fasting is unthinkable.

But the days will come when the groom is taken away from them, and then they will fast: This applies not to a wedding, but to the church's experience of the loss of Jesus. Then they would *mourn*, when to *fast* might be sometimes appropriate. But, as contrasted to the Baptist's survivors the Christians did not generally fast because of the joy of Jesus' resurrection. And perhaps Jesus had not regularly fasted. Thom 104b is a bit different: "When the groom leaves the bridal suite, then let people fast and pray."

• **9:16–17** In both sayings, something new is here. To behave in the *old* way would do violence to the arrival of the kingdom.

• **9:17** *young:* Greek, "new."

• **9:17b** *Instead, they put young wine in new wineskins and both are preserved:* This conclusion, found in shorter and slightly different form in Mark, disturbs the balanced structure of the two sayings (vss 16 and 17a). It seems obvious and unnecessary, and perhaps was not original to Jesus.

• **9:18–26** Now the succession of miracles, begun in chap. 8, resumes with the final three, the first a double healing.

• **9:18** *one of the officials:* In Mark and Luke he is named Jairus. Why not here?

began to bow down to him: See on the imperfect tense in 9:11.

• **9:20–22** As an interruption (Why?) another healing—of a woman with a hemorrhage—now takes place. This is a greatly condensed form of the story in Mark 5:24b–34 and Luke 8:40–56, where also it comes in the midst of the healing of the official's daughter. In Mark, Jesus knows that someone has touched him and turns to find who it is. Why does our author omit it? Perhaps only to save space.

²³Καὶ ἐλθὼν ὁ Ἰησοῦς εἰς τὴν οἰκίαν τοῦ ἄρχοντος καὶ ἰδὼν τοὺς αὐλητὰς καὶ τὸν ὄχλον θορυβούμενον ²⁴ἔλεγεν, Ἀναχωρεῖτε, οὐ γὰρ ἀπέθανεν τὸ κοράσιον ἀλλὰ καθεύδει. καὶ κατεγέλων αὐτοῦ. ²⁵ὅτε δὲ ἐξεβλήθη ὁ ὄχλος εἰσελθὼν ἐκράτησεν τῆς χειρὸς αὐτῆς, καὶ ἠγέρθη τὸ κοράσιον. ²⁶καὶ ἐξῆλθεν ἡ φήμη αὕτη εἰς ὅλην τὴν γῆν ἐκείνην.

Two blind men

²⁷Καὶ παράγοντι ἐκεῖθεν τῷ Ἰησοῦ ἠκολούθησαν αὐτῷ δύο τυφλοὶ κράζοντες καὶ λέγοντες, Ἐλέησον ἡμᾶς, υἱὸς Δαυίδ.

²⁸Ἐλθόντι δὲ εἰς τὴν οἰκίαν προσῆλθον αὐτῷ οἱ τυφλοί, καὶ λέγει αὐτοῖς ὁ Ἰησοῦς, Πιστεύετε ὅτι δύναμαι τοῦτο ποιῆσαι;

Λέγουσιν αὐτῷ, Ναί κύριε.

²⁹Τότε ἥψατο τῶν ὀφθαλμῶν αὐτῶν λέγων, Κατὰ τὴν πίστιν ὑμῶν γενηθήτω ὑμῖν. ³⁰καὶ ἠνεῴχθησαν αὐτῶν οἱ ὀφθαλμοί. καὶ ἐνεβριμήθη αὐτοῖς ὁ Ἰησοῦς λέγων, Ὁρᾶτε μηδεὶς γινωσκέτω. ³¹οἱ δὲ ἐξελθόντες διεφήμισαν αὐτὸν ἐν ὅλῃ τῇ γῇ ἐκείνῃ.

Jesus cures a mute

³²Αὐτῶν δὲ ἐξερχομένων ἰδοὺ προσήνεγκαν αὐτῷ ἄνθρωπον κωφὸν δαιμονιζόμενον. ³³καὶ ἐκβληθέντος τοῦ δαιμονίου ἐλάλησεν ὁ κωφός. καὶ ἐθαύμασαν οἱ ὄχλοι λέγοντες, Οὐδέποτε ἐφάνη οὕτως ἐν τῷ Ἰσραήλ.

³⁴Οἱ δὲ Φαρισαῖοι ἔλεγον, Ἐν τῷ ἄρχοντι τῶν δαιμονίων ἐκβάλλει τὰ δαιμόνια.

Good crop, few workers

³⁵Καὶ περιῆγεν ὁ Ἰησοῦς τὰς πόλεις πάσας καὶ τὰς κώμας διδάσκων ἐν ταῖς συναγωγαῖς αὐτῶν καὶ κηρύσσων τὸ εὐαγγέλιον

9:34 A few mss lack this verse.

- **9:23–26** The healing of the official's daughter resumes. Our author has abbreviated a much longer story (twelve verses in Mark), omitting many particulars and somewhat blunting its effect.
- **9:23** *mourners with their flutes:* In Greek simply "flute players," customary after a death, together with *the crowd making a disturbance.*
- **9:24** *the girl hasn't died; she's sleeping:* If this is taken literally, there is far less of a miracle when Jesus raises the girl up. But sleep is often a metaphor for death. So what does Jesus mean?
- **9:26** *his reputation:* As a healer who can even raise the dead.
- **9:27–31** A more detailed version of this story, with some variations, appears at 20:29–34, with close parallels in Mark 10:46–

52 and Luke 18:35–43. In both cases Matthew has two nameless blind men, not simply the one Bartimaeus as in Mark. This intricate interweaving of traditions about healing blindness is hard to untangle.
- **9:27** *son of David:* This title, meaning of course "the Anointed," is used here for the first time since the opening of the gospel (1:1, where it was translated "descended from David"). It is the ill, demon-possessed, who most clearly recognize who Jesus is.
- **9:29** *Your trust will be the measure of your cure:* "May it happen for you according to your trust," similar to 8:13.
- **9:30** *their eyes were opened:* A "divine passive"—God, or Jesus, opened their eyes. Similarly with the mute in the next episode (vs 33).

²³And when Jesus came into the home of the official and saw the mourners with their flutes, and the crowd making a disturbance, ²⁴he said, "Go away; don't you see? the girl hasn't died; she's sleeping." And they started laughing at him. ²⁵When the crowd had been thrown out, he came in and took her by the hand and raised the little girl up. ²⁶And his reputation spread all around that region.

Two blind men

²⁷And when Jesus left there, two blind men followed him, crying out, "Have mercy on us, son of David."

²⁸When <Jesus> arrived home, the blind men came to him. Jesus says to them, "Do you trust that I can do this?"

They reply to him, "Yes, sir."

²⁹Then he touched their eyes, saying, "Your trust will be the measure of your cure." ³⁰And their eyes were opened. Then Jesus scolded them, saying, "See that no one finds out about it." ³¹But they went out and spread the news of him throughout that whole territory.

Jesus cures a mute

³²Just as they were leaving, they brought to him a mute who was demon-possessed. ³³And after the demon had been driven out, the mute started to speak. And the crowd was amazed and said, "Nothing like this has ever been seen in Israel."

³⁴But the Pharisees would say, "He drives out demons in the name of the head demon."

Good crop, few workers

³⁵And Jesus went about all the towns and villages, teaching in their synagogues and proclaiming the good news of <Heaven's>

---

scolded them, saying, "See that no one finds out about it": Scolded is often undertranslated "sternly charged them." But the Greek (*enebrimêthê*) is stronger than that and may anticipate the blind men's disobedience of what Jesus demands of them. The enjoining of silence (often called the "messianic secret") appears first at 8:4. But here (vs 31), as also occasionally later, Jesus' attempt to maintain secrecy is ignored.
• **9:32–34** This is almost the same story as in 12:22–24. There's an even briefer form of it in Luke 11:14–15.
• **9:32** *a mute who was demon-possessed:* That is, according to ancient belief, mute because of demon possession.
• **9:33** *Nothing like this has ever been seen in Israel:* Unlikely to be true, given that faith

healers were common in both Jewish and Greek society of the time. But the response expresses appropriate awe of Jesus' healing power.
• **9:34** *would say:* That is, whenever Jesus exorcised a demon. Or, "began to say." See Introduction, p. 27.

in the name of: See Glossary.

the head demon: Evidently Beelzebul, as in 12:27.
• **9:35–38** Concluding the collection of miracles comprising chaps. 8–9 is this summary of Jesus' work, with a saying that introduces chap. 10. What Jesus has done the Twelve are to do also . . . and the church that stems from them.

τῆς βασιλείας καὶ θεραπεύων πᾶσαν νόσον καὶ πᾶσαν μαλακίαν. ³⁶Ἰδὼν δὲ τοὺς ὄχλους ἐσπλαγχνίσθη περὶ αὐτῶν, ὅτι ἦσαν ἐσκυλμένοι καὶ ἐρριμμένοι ὡσεὶ πρόβατα μὴ ἔχοντα ποιμένα. ³⁷τότε λέγει τοῖς μαθηταῖς αὐτοῦ, Ὁ μὲν θερισμὸς πολύς, οἱ δὲ ἐργάται ὀλίγοι· ³⁸δεήθητε οὖν τοῦ κυρίου τοῦ θερισμοῦ ὅπως ἐκβάλῃ ἐργάτας εἰς τὸν θερισμὸν αὐτοῦ.

9:36 *vulnerable and helpless:* More literally, "weary and 'thrown'."

• **9:38** *the harvest boss:* Since it evidently refers to God, this crude phrase may seem inappropriate. But it properly maintains the metaphor of the empire of God as a dirty herd of *sheep* (the preceding verse) or a grain field needing sweaty *workers.*

Interpretive Note: Jesus' Healings

Apart from the nature miracles (see the Interpretative Note, p. 140), Jesus' healings, which are his most characteristic miracles, require some reflection, at the end of the evangelist's two-chapter collection of such stories. (The one exception—Rebuking wind and wave, 8:23–27—we'll deal with along with the other nature miracles.) That Jesus was in fact able to heal sickness and did so as a characteristic part of his public activity can hardly be denied. His 1st-century world, both Jewish and pagan, had many such healers, and we can imagine that much of these people's success was due to what we now know as psychosomatic illness—genuine illness, with a psychic, not a physical cause. A strong, charismatic figure, using either magical techniques or supportive, pastoral attention to the sufferer (and Jesus used both, perhaps—see Morton Smith) was often able to rid a sufferer of even long-standing disease.

For the 21st-century reader of these stories who wants a rational explanation of Jesus' evident power, this would explain stories we have just read, like those of Peter's mother-in-law, the paralytic, perhaps the woman with vaginal bleeding, blind and deaf people, and (in ch 17) the epileptic. In several of these stories we hear of people being under

imperial rule and healing every disease and ailment. ³⁶When he saw the crowd, he was moved by them because they were vulnerable and helpless, like sheep without a shepherd. ³⁷Then he said to his disciples, "Although the crop is good, still there are few to harvest it. ³⁸So beg the harvest boss to dispatch workers to the fields."

the power of demons. The authoritative command of an experienced exorcist can, demonstrably, bring about the immediate healing that Jesus is shown accomplishing, even when it involves insanity (at Gadara). Similarly, the power of guilt to cause illness may be released with a decisive pronouncement of absolution, as with the paralytic.

Understandably, legend will have supplied some of the miracle stories, or their details. I have in mind the healing of a leper (if his disease in Jesus' time is like what we call leprosy today) and of a withered hand, and the healings-at-a-distance (officer's servant, Canaanite woman's daughter).

To give this kind of scientific explanation of Jesus' power to heal, and to "explain away" some of the stories, will be unsatisfactory to some, even offensive ("A miracle is a miracle"). But in any case, the chief meaning of these stories is not chiefly Jesus' impressive capability, showing who he is—although the christological element is often present and can be affirmed by the believer—but to show Heaven's domain breaking in. His activity as healer is of a piece with his proclaimed message. For the theist, all causation is derived from God, however rationally it is explained; all healing, including the most technologically sophisticated, however secular it appears, derives from God's creativity and compassion.

The twelve

10 Καὶ προσκαλεσάμενος τοὺς δώδεκα μαθητὰς αὐτοῦ ἔδωκεν αὐτοῖς ἐξουσίαν πνευμάτων ἀκαθάρτων ὥστε ἐκβάλλειν αὐτὰ καὶ θεραπεύειν πᾶσαν νόσον καὶ πᾶσαν μαλακίαν. ²Τῶν δὲ δώδεκα ἀποστόλων τὰ ὀνόματά ἐστιν ταῦτα· πρῶτος Σίμων ὁ λεγόμενος Πέτρος καὶ Ἀνδρέας ὁ ἀδελφὸς αὐτοῦ, καὶ Ἰάκωβος ὁ τοῦ Ζεβεδαίου καὶ Ἰωάννης ὁ ἀδελφὸς αὐτοῦ, ³Φίλιππος καὶ Βαρθολομαῖος, Θωμᾶς καὶ Μαθθαῖος ὁ τελώνης, Ἰάκωβος ὁ τοῦ Ἀλφαίου καὶ Θαδδαῖος, ⁴Σίμων ὁ Καναναῖος καὶ Ἰούδας ὁ Ἰσκαριώτης ὁ καὶ παραδοὺς αὐτόν.

The second discourse: Instructions for the twelve

⁵Τούτους τοὺς δώδεκα ἀπέστειλεν ὁ Ἰησοῦς παραγγείλας αὐτοῖς λέγων, Εἰς ὁδὸν ἐθνῶν μὴ ἀπέλθητε καὶ εἰς πόλιν Σαμαριτῶν μὴ εἰσέλθητε· ⁶πορεύεσθε δὲ μᾶλλον πρὸς τὰ πρόβατα τὰ ἀπολωλότα οἴκου Ἰσραήλ.

⁷Πορευόμενοι δὲ κηρύσσετε λέγοντες ὅτι Ἤγγικεν ἡ βασιλεία τῶν οὐρανῶν.

⁸Ἀσθενοῦντας θεραπεύετε, νεκροὺς ἐγείρετε, λεπροὺς καθαρίζετε, δαιμόνια ἐκβάλλετε· δωρεὰν ἐλάβετε, δωρεὰν δότε. ⁹Μὴ κτήσησθε χρυσὸν μηδὲ ἄργυρον μηδὲ χαλκὸν εἰς τὰς ζώνας ὑμῶν, ¹⁰μὴ πήραν εἰς ὁδὸν μηδὲ δύο χιτῶνας μηδὲ ὑποδήματα μηδὲ ῥάβδον· ἄξιος γὰρ ὁ ἐργάτης τῆς τροφῆς αὐτοῦ.

10:3 A few MSS read "Lebbaeus" in place of *Thaddaeus.* Why? And many combine these two names as "Lebbaeus who is called Thaddaeus."

• **10:1** *twelve disciples:* It's not been indicated till now that Jesus' chosen disciples number twelve and as a body can be identified in that way. For example, in 20:17, 26:14. The number has obvious symbolism, reflecting the twelve tribes of Israel, which is explicit in 19:28. The first four of the twelve have already been heard of (4:18–22). Also Matthew, in 9:9. The others are spoken of only here, with the exception of Judas.

authority to drive out unclean spirits and to heal: In other words, to do what Jesus has just been doing in chaps. 8 and 9. See further, vs 8 below.

• **10:2** *apostles:* In this gospel the word is used only here. It means a disciple who is "sent out" with a mission (vs 5 below).

first: Only here among all the gospels is Peter so designated. Does it mean simply that he was first to be called by Jesus (4:18)? Or something more?

Rock: The Greek is the common noun, *petros*—a (any) rock. Our name "Peter" derives from this nickname. It is a translation of the Aramaic word for rock: *Kepha,* in the Greek spelled as "Kephas" (John 1:42 and several times in 1 Corinthians and Galatians). The actual nicknaming takes place at 16:18–19.

• **10:3** *Matthew the toll collector:* As in 9:9. In other lists of "the twelve" the name alone appears.

the son of Alphaeus: To distinguish him from the son of Zebedee (vs 2) and from Jesus' brother (13:55).

Thaddaeus: In the manuscripts there is considerable variation from this name. In part, at least, that was caused by the fact that Luke lacks it (9:15) and also Acts (1:13), both of which lists give instead another Judas, "son of James."

• **10:4** *Zealot:* The Greek word is *kananaios,* from the Aramaic word for "zealot." In first-century CE Palestine it meant a guerrilla warrior, one who supported armed revolution against Rome. This party was largely responsible for the Jewish revolt that began in 66 CE and ended disastrously in Rome's destruction of Jerusalem in 70. "Simon the Zealot" distinguishes this man from Rock/Peter, and from a number of others with the same rather common name; besides Jesus' brother (13:55), see 26:6, 27:62.

Judas: The Greek for Judah. Also the name of one of Jesus' brothers (13:55)

of Iscariot: It's unclear whether this was the name of a place, as perhaps suggested here,

10 And summoning his twelve disciples he gave them authority **The twelve** to drive out unclean spirits and to heal every disease and every ailment. ²The names of the twelve apostles were these: first, Simon, also known as Rock, and Andrew his brother, and James the son of Zebedee and John his brother, ³Philip and Bartholomew, Thomas, and Matthew the toll collector, James the son of Alphaeus, and Thaddaeus, ⁴Simon the Zealot, and Judas of Iscariot, the one who, in the end, turned him in.

⁵Jesus sent out these twelve after he had given them these **The second** instructions: "Don't travel foreign roads and don't enter a Samaritan **discourse:** town, ⁶but go rather to the lost sheep of the house of Israel. **Instructions for the twelve**

⁷"Go and announce: 'Heaven's imperial rule is closing in.'

⁸"Heal the sick, raise the dead, cleanse the lepers, drive out demons. You have received freely, so freely give. ⁹Don't carry gold or silver or copper coins for spending money, ¹⁰or a knapsack for the road, or two shirts, or sandals, or a staff. For 'the worker deserves to be fed.'

---

or had some more obscure meaning.

who, in the end, turned him in: Or "who would turn him in."

• **10:5** *these instructions:* This sermon, or discourse, is addressed to the apostles about to be sent out to proclaim the good news of God's empire, and esp. to continue Jesus' healing ministry. It comprises Instructions for the Apostolic Mission. It ends at 11:1.

foreign roads: "A Gentile road."

Samaritan: The only reference to Samaria in Matthew. (The parable of the good Samaritan is to be found only in Luke.) It was a section of Palestine that had very few Jews in it, compared to Judea and Galilee. But it was situated between those two regions. Its natives had a religion close to Judaism, but were nevertheless hated by Jews as not actually Jewish.

• **10:6** *to the lost sheep of the house of Israel:* What does the metaphor mean? To those Jews the religion or the system has left out? That would be consonant with Jesus' mission to the lost, the marginalized, the forgotten. In 15:24 he says he is sent only to them.

• **10:7** This, simply put, has been Jesus' message in everything he has been saying.

is closing in: See comment on 3:2.

• **10:8** This is what Jesus has been doing since the beginning of chap. 8.

• **10:9–15** These rules are based on Mark 6:8–11 and on Q (see Luke 9:3 and 10:4–8, 10–11)

but identical to none of those passages.

• **10:9** *don't carry gold or silver or copper coins:* Mark prohibits *copper*, Luke *silver.* For the author, evidently, not only is all extravagance ruled out, but the missionary will need no money at all. He is to trust entirely in God's care and to show "that God is working not through the rich and powerful but through the poor and powerless" (Davies & Allison, II, 171).

for spending money: Greek: "for your belts"—in our parlance, in your wallets.

• **10:10a** In other words, Travel light. Our author has excluded everything ruled out in either Mark or Q except bread—and that is to be provided by the people stayed with (vs 10b). His version of this Jesus tradition is therefore the most stringent.

don't take . . . sandals, or a staff: The itinerant missioner is make himself as poor as those he preaches to. These rules undoubtedly go back to Jesus himself and those he sent out to spread his proclamation to the marginalized peasants of Galilee.

two shirts: Nothing extra, for convenience. The *shirt* (Greek: *chitôn*) was a long tunic, the only clothing needed.

• **10:10b** *the worker deserves to be fed:* Evidently a common saying. The apostles were to be taken care of by those in the house or town they preached to—that is, when such people were "deserving" (see vs 11).

¹¹Εἰς ἢν δ' ἂν πόλιν ἢ κώμην εἰσέλθητε, ἐξετάσατε τίς ἐν αὐτῇ ἄξιός ἐστιν· κἀκεῖ μείνατε ἕως ἂν ἐξέλθητε. ¹²εἰσερχόμενοι δὲ εἰς τὴν οἰκίαν ἀσπάσασθε αὐτήν· ¹³καὶ ἐὰν μὲν ᾖ ἡ οἰκία ἀξία, ἐλθάτω ἡ εἰρήνη ὑμῶν ἐπ' αὐτήν, ἐὰν δὲ μὴ ᾖ ἀξία, ἡ εἰρήνη ὑμῶν πρὸς ὑμᾶς ἐπιστραφήτω. ¹⁴καὶ ὃς ἂν μὴ δέξηται ὑμᾶς μηδὲ ἀκούσῃ τοὺς λόγους ὑμῶν, ἐξερχόμενοι ἔξω τῆς οἰκίας ἢ τῆς πόλεως ἐκείνης ἐκτινάξατε τὸν κονιορτὸν τῶν ποδῶν ὑμῶν. ¹⁵ἀμὴν λέγω ὑμῖν, ἀνεκτότερον ἔσται γῇ Σοδόμων καὶ Γομόρρων ἐν ἡμέρα κρίσεως ἢ τῇ πόλει ἐκείνῃ.

Risks of discipleship

¹⁶Ἰδοὺ ἐγὼ ἀποστέλλω ὑμᾶς ὡς πρόβατα ἐν μέσῳ λύκων· γίνεσθε οὖν φρόνιμοι ὡς οἱ ὄφεις καὶ ἀκέραιοι ὡς αἱ περιστεραί. ¹⁷προσέχετε δὲ ἀπὸ τῶν ἀνθρώπων· παραδώσουσιν γὰρ ὑμᾶς εἰς συνέδρια καὶ ἐν ταῖς συναγωγαῖς αὐτῶν μαστιγώσουσιν ὑμᾶς· ¹⁸καὶ ἐπὶ ἡγεμόνας δὲ καὶ βασιλεῖς ἀχθήσεσθε ἕνεκεν ἐμοῦ εἰς μαρτύριον αὐτοῖς καὶ τοῖς ἔθνεσιν. ¹⁹ὅταν δὲ παραδῶσιν ὑμᾶς, μὴ μεριμνήσητε πῶς ἢ τί λαλήσητε· δοθήσεται γὰρ ὑμῖν ἐν ἐκείνῃ τῇ ὥρᾳ τί λαλήσητε· ²⁰οὐ γὰρ ὑμεῖς ἐστε οἱ λαλοῦντες ἀλλὰ τὸ πνεῦμα τοῦ πατρὸς ὑμῶν τὸ λαλοῦν ἐν ὑμῖν. ²¹παραδώσει δὲ ἀδελφὸς ἀδελφὸν εἰς θάνατον καὶ πατὴρ τέκνον, καὶ ἐπαναστήσονται τέκνα ἐπὶ γονεῖς καὶ θανατώσουσιν αὐτούς. ²²καὶ ἔσεσθε μισούμενοι ὑπὸ πάντων διὰ τὸ ὄνομά μου· ὁ δὲ ὑπομείνας εἰς τέλος οὗτος σωθήσεται. ²³ὅταν δὲ διώκωσιν ὑμᾶς ἐν τῇ πόλει ταύτῃ, φεύγετε εἰς τὴν ἑτέραν· ἀμὴν γὰρ λέγω ὑμῖν, οὐ μὴ τελέσητε τὰς πόλεις τοῦ Ἰσραὴλ ἕως ἔλθῃ ὁ υἱὸς τοῦ ἀνθρώπου.

Student & teacher

²⁴Οὐκ ἔστιν μαθητὴς ὑπὲρ τὸν διδάσκαλον οὐδὲ δοῦλος ὑπὲρ τὸν κύριον αὐτοῦ. ²⁵ἀρκετὸν τῷ μαθητῇ ἵνα γένηται ὡς ὁ διδάσκαλος αὐτοῦ καὶ ὁ δοῦλος ὡς ὁ κύριος αὐτοῦ. εἰ τὸν οἰκοδεσπότην

10:23 After *another* a few mss add "And when they persecute you [there], flee to yet another one."

- **10:11** *who is deserving:* That is, who will "welcome you, or listen to your words" (vs 14a).
- **10:13** *give it your peace blessing:* Greek, "send your peace upon it," perhaps simply by pronouncing "Shalom."
  withdraw your peace blessing: Why? From spite? or as a statement?
- **10:14** *shake the dust off your feet:* An act of rejection, wanting to take along nothing of that place, and perhaps a kind of curse too.
- **10:15** *Sodom and Gomorrah:* Traditionally places representing God's damnation. (See for example Gen 13:10: ". . . before the LORD destroyed Sodom and Gomorrah.") See further below on 11:23.
  on judgment day: At the end of the age, the so-called last judgment.
- **10:16–23** In Mark 13:9–12, part of that gospel's apocalyptic discourse, these trials are in store for disciples "at the end of the

age." Here they can evidently be expected at any time in the life of Christians. Matt 24:9–12, speaking of the end of the age, offers a similar but much abbreviated account.
- **10:16** *like sheep to a pack of wolves:* Evidently it was dangerous, at least by the evangelist's time, to preach Christianity in Jewish Palestine. The zealous Pharisee Paul's persecution of Christians before his acceptance of Jesus as the Anointed one (1 Cor 15:9) illustrates this danger.
  Therefore you must be as sly as a snake and as simple as a dove: Found only here and in Thom 39:3. What would such a combination consist of?
  simple: Or "guileless."
- **10:17** *beware of people:* Of any and everyone, that is.
  the Council: The Jewish "Sanhedrin," or ruling body.

¹¹"Whichever town or village you enter, find out who is deserving; stay there until you leave. ¹²When you enter a house, greet it. ¹³And if the house is deserving, give it your peace blessing, but if it is unworthy, withdraw your peace blessing. ¹⁴And if anyone does not welcome you or listen to your words, shake the dust off your feet as you leave that house or town. ¹⁵I swear to you, the land of Sodom and Gomorrah will be better off on judgment day than that town.

¹⁶"Look, I'm sending you out like sheep to a pack of wolves. Therefore you must be as sly as a snake and as simple as a dove. ¹⁷And beware of people, for they will turn you over to the Council and in the synagogues they will flog you. ¹⁸And you will be hauled up before governors and even kings on my account so you can make your case to them and to the nations. ¹⁹And when they lock you up, don't worry about how you should speak or what you should say. It will occur to you at that moment what to say. ²⁰For it is not you who are speaking but your Father's spirit speaking through you. ²¹One brother will turn in another to be put to death, and a father his child, and children will turn against their parents and kill them. ²²And you will be universally hated because of me. But those who hold out to the end will be saved. ²³When they persecute you in one town, flee to another. I swear to you, you certainly won't have exhausted the towns of Israel before the son of Adam comes.

²⁴"Students are not above their teachers, nor slaves above their masters. ²⁵It is appropriate for students to be like their teachers and slaves to be like their masters. If they have dubbed the master of

Risks of discipleship

Student & teacher

• **10:18** *hauled up before governors and even kings:* Perhaps the experience of some among the author's audience, as also in Mark and Luke.

hauled up before governors: As Jesus was, before Pilate, the Roman governor of Syria.

make your case to them and to the nations: An enormous responsibility; but the missionary should not fear—see vss 19–20.

the nations: Or "Gentiles."

• **10:19** *lock you up:* That is, "turn you in" as lawbreakers.

• **10:21** Reminiscent of Mic 7:6, but more drastic. See also below, vss 35–36.

• **10:22** *because of me:* "On account of my name," a Hebraism.

• **10:23** Found only in this gospel.

you certainly won't have exhausted the towns of Israel before the son of Adam comes: A promise that must have been made when the

Christian mission was still limited to Jews, whether by Jesus or—more likely—later, but before the evangelist's time. The survival of such predictions beyond their pertinence suggests how enduring Jesus traditions were, once they arose.

the son of Adam comes: Comes again, that is, returns at the end of the age. This was probably not a promise made by Jesus himself, but an apocalyptic idea introduced early in the handing down of the Jesus tradition

• **10:24–25** These sayings continue the theme of the possible fate of Jesus' disciples. The metaphors of teacher, master, and head of household are used to describe Jesus' relation to disciples.

• **10:24–25a** Probably from Q. Luke's version (6:40) is briefer and perhaps less original: "Students are not above their teacher. But those who are fully taught will be like their

Have no fear

Βεελζεβοὺλ ἐπεκάλεσαν, πόσῳ μᾶλλον τοὺς οἰκιακοὺς αὐτοῦ. ²⁶Μὴ οὖν φοβηθῆτε αὐτούς· οὐδὲν γάρ ἐστιν κεκαλυμμένον ὃ οὐκ ἀποκαλυφθήσεται καὶ κρυπτὸν ὃ οὐ γνωσθήσεται. ²⁷ὃ λέγω ὑμῖν ἐν τῇ σκοτίᾳ εἴπατε ἐν τῷ φωτί, καὶ ὃ εἰς τὸ οὖς ἀκούετε κηρύξατε ἐπὶ τῶν δωμάτων.

²⁸Καὶ μὴ φοβεῖσθε ἀπὸ τῶν ἀποκτεννόντων τὸ σῶμα, τὴν δὲ ψυχὴν μὴ δυναμένων ἀποκτεῖναι· φοβεῖσθε δὲ μᾶλλον τὸν δυνάμενον καὶ ψυχὴν καὶ σῶμα ἀπολέσαι ἐν γεέννῃ. ²⁹οὐχὶ δύο στρουθία ἀσσαρίου πωλεῖται; καὶ ἓν ἐξ αὐτῶν οὐ πεσεῖται ἐπὶ τὴν γῆν ἄνευ τοῦ πατρὸς ὑμῶν. ³⁰ὑμῶν δὲ καὶ αἱ τρίχες τῆς κεφαλῆς πᾶσαι ἠριθμημέναι εἰσίν. ³¹μὴ οὖν φοβεῖσθε· πολλῶν στρουθίων διαφέρετε ὑμεῖς.

³²Πᾶς οὖν ὅστις ὁμολογήσει ἐν ἐμοὶ ἔμπροσθεν τῶν ἀνθρώπων, ὁμολογήσω κἀγὼ ἐν αὐτῷ ἔμπροσθεν τοῦ πατρός μου τοῦ ἐν τοῖς οὐρανοῖς· ³³ὅστις δ' ἂν ἀρνήσηταί με ἔμπροσθεν τῶν ἀνθρώπων, ἀρνήσομαι κἀγὼ αὐτὸν ἔμπροσθεν τοῦ πατρός μου τοῦ ἐν τοῖς οὐρανοῖς.

Way of the cross

³⁴Μὴ νομίσητε ὅτι ἦλθον βαλεῖν εἰρήνην ἐπὶ τὴν γῆν· οὐκ ἦλθον βαλεῖν εἰρήνην ἀλλὰ μάχαιραν. ³⁵ἦλθον γὰρ διχάσαι

ἄνθρωπον κατὰ τοῦ πατρὸς αὐτοῦ
καὶ θυγατέρα κατὰ τῆς μητρὸς αὐτῆς
καὶ νύμφην κατὰ τῆς πενθερᾶς αὐτῆς,
³⁶καὶ ἐχθροὶ τοῦ ἀνθρώπου οἱ οἰκιακοὶ αὐτοῦ.

³⁷Ὁ φιλῶν πατέρα ἢ μητέρα ὑπὲρ ἐμὲ οὐκ ἔστιν μου ἄξιος, καὶ ὁ φιλῶν υἱὸν ἢ θυγατέρα ὑπὲρ ἐμὲ οὐκ ἔστιν μου ἄξιος· ³⁸καὶ ὃς οὐ λαμβάνει τὸν σταυρὸν αὐτοῦ καὶ ἀκολουθεῖ ὀπίσω μου, οὐκ

---

teacher." The saying originally spoke of an equality between teacher and student, master and slave.

• **10:25b** Unique to Matthew.

If they have dubbed the master of the house Beelzebul As is true of Jesus (for example in 9:34, 12:24).

Beelzebul: One of the names for the chief devil. Another is "Satan" (see on 3:7).

• **10:26–33** Closely parallel to Luke 12:2–9.

• **10:26** Very similar to Thom 5:2 and 6:5–6. Evidently referring to the apocalypse, that is, the "unveiling" at the end of the age, at the last judgment. See the extended metaphor of distinguishing the sheep from the goats in 25:31–46.

• **10:27** *What I say to you in darkness . . . and what you hear whispered . . .:* What might this refer to? Teachings of Jesus to the disciples in private that they are later to proclaim openly? One way to account for additions to the Jesus tradition after his lifetime was to maintain they had been told originally in se-

cret. (For example, additions to Mark known as Secret Mark; see Miller, *Complete Gospels,* 408–11.)

• **10:28** *those who kill the body but cannot kill the soul:* The enemies of the good news, evidently.

the one who can destroy both the soul and the body: That is, God.

Gehenna: Hell.

• **10:29–31** The reasoning here is from less to greater, as in 6:28–30.

• **10:29** *What do sparrows cost? A penny apiece?* Evidently to buy for sacrificing in the temple. NRSV has "two . . . for a penny," which is closer to the Greek, except that the value of the coin in question (*assarion*) cannot be very precisely given a modern equivalent. Curiously in Greek, Luke 12:6 has "five . . . for two *assarions*" (in SV, "a dime a dozen"). The point, of course, is that if sparrows, which are so cheap to buy, are taken care of by God, how much more will the disciple be.

• **10:31** *don't be so timid:* Or "stop being

the house 'Beelzebul,' how much more <likely will they malign> the members of his household.

Have no fear

²⁶"So don't be afraid of them. After all, there is nothing veiled that won't be unveiled, or hidden that won't be made known. ²⁷What I say to you in darkness, say in the light, and what you hear whispered in your ear, announce from the rooftops.

²⁸"Don't fear those who kill the body but cannot kill the soul; instead, you ought to fear the one who can destroy both the soul and the body in Gehenna. ²⁹What do sparrows cost? A penny apiece? Yet not one of them will fall to the earth without the consent of your Father. ³⁰As for you, even the hairs on your head have all been counted. ³¹So, don't be so timid: you're worth more than a flock of sparrows.

³²"Everyone who acknowledges me in public, I too will acknowledge before my Father in heaven. ³³But the one who disowns me in public, I too will disown before my Father in heaven.

Way of the cross

³⁴"Don't get the idea that I came to bring peace on earth. I did not come to bring peace but a sword. ³⁵After all, I have come

to pit a man against his father,
a daughter against her mother,
and a daughter-in-law against her mother-in-law.
    ³⁶Your enemies live under your own roof.

³⁷"If you love your father and mother more than me, you're not worthy of me; and if you love your son or daughter more than me, you're not worthy of me. ³⁸Unless you take your cross and come

---

afraid."
- **10:32–33** Esp. relevant to the late first-century CE situation of the church under persecution.
- **10:34–42** Mostly from Q, therefore unlike anything in Mark but parallel to Luke (12:51–53 and 14:26–27).
- **10:34** This saying has had a notorious use; but it is almost certainly not from Jesus. Did he ever say "I have come in order to . . .?" (see below). And if he did, in this case he surely said only that division was certain to be the result of his gathering followers. But more likely the saying originated after Jesus' time, reflecting the experience of Christians in conflict with their families.

  I came: While Jesus does not say where he has come from, his mission is clearly divinely mandated. Notice "the one who sent me" below in vs 40. See comment on "I have come" in 5:17.

  bring peace: The Hebrew phrase, used here in Greek, is "throw peace."

but a sword: The parallel in Luke 12:51 has "division," which is more nearly an alternative to "peace," and therefore probably more nearly original. Perhaps our author's audience experienced violent division.
- **10:35–36** The language here (*[man] against father,*" etc.) comes directly from Mic 7:6, which was paraphrased in vs 21 above.
- **10:37–39** Parallel to Luke 14:26–27, 17:33, no doubt via Q.
- **10:37** To follow Jesus is to *love* him more than one's closest kin. In Luke 14:26 and Thom 55 (=101) the wording is stronger: "Whoever does not hate father and mother. . . ."
- **10:38–39** Another version of these two sayings is found at 16:24–25.
- **10:38** To love Jesus, to be *worthy* of him, is to be ready to suffer a fate like his. This is the first reference in Matthew to the fact that Jesus would die on a *cross.*

ἔστιν μου ἄξιος. ³⁹ὁ εὑρὼν τὴν ψυχὴν αὐτοῦ ἀπολέσει αὐτήν, καὶ ὁ ἀπολέσας τὴν ψυχὴν αὐτοῦ ἕνεκεν ἐμοῦ εὑρήσει αὐτήν.

⁴⁰Ὁ δεχόμενος ὑμᾶς ἐμὲ δέχεται, καὶ ὁ ἐμὲ δεχόμενος δέχεται τὸν ἀποστείλαντά με. ⁴¹ὁ δεχόμενος προφήτην εἰς ὄνομα προφήτου μισθὸν προφήτου λήμψεται, καὶ ὁ δεχόμενος δίκαιον εἰς ὄνομα δικαίου μισθὸν δικαίου λήμψεται. ⁴²καὶ ὃς ἂν ποτίσῃ ἕνα τῶν μικρῶν τούτων ποτήριον ψυχροῦ μόνον εἰς ὄνομα μαθητοῦ, ἀμὴν λέγω ὑμῖν, οὐ μὴ ἀπολέσῃ τὸν μισθὸν αὐτοῦ.

• **10:39** Originally, perhaps, this saying circulated independently and used the finding and losing of *life* metaphorically. Coming after vs 38, losing one's life seems to be understood literally. The saying is paralleled in Luke 17:33.

• **10:40–41** To "accept" Jesus, these verses makes it clear, is to see him as *a prophet* and as *virtuous* (or "righteous").

 be treated like a prophet: "Have a prophet's reward."

• **10:42** *a cup of cool water:* The related saying

along with me, you're not worthy of me. [39]By finding your life, you'll lose it, and by losing your life for my sake, you'll find it.

[40]"The one who accepts you accepts me, and the one who accepts me accepts the one who sent me. [41]The one who accepts a prophet as a prophet will be treated like a prophet; and the one who accepts a virtuous person as a virtuous person will be treated like a virtuous person. [42]And whoever gives so much as a cup of cool water to one of these little ones, because the little one is a follower of mine, I swear to you, such a person certainly won't go unrewarded."

---

in Mark 9:41 views the disciples ("you") as receiving the water. Here the disciples are to give the water. Loving Jesus (vs 37), accepting him (40), is best displayed in caring, as he did, for *the little one*—that is, the helpless, the defenseless, the "sinner."

11 Καὶ ἐγένετο ὅτε ἐτέλεσεν ὁ Ἰησοῦς διατάσσων τοῖς δώδεκα μαθηταῖς αὐτοῦ, μετέβη ἐκεῖθεν τοῦ διδάσκειν καὶ κηρύσσειν ἐν ταῖς πόλεσιν αὐτῶν.

John queries Jesus   ²ˈΟ δὲ Ἰωάννης ἀκούσας ἐν τῷ δεσμωτηρίῳ τὰ ἔργα τοῦ Χριστοῦ πέμψας διὰ τῶν μαθητῶν αὐτοῦ ³εἶπεν αὐτῷ, Σὺ εἶ ὁ ἐρχόμενος ἢ ἕτερον προσδοκῶμεν;

⁴Καὶ ἀποκριθεὶς ὁ Ἰησοῦς εἶπεν αὐτοῖς, Πορευθέντες ἀπαγγείλατε Ἰωάννῃ ἃ ἀκούετε καὶ βλέπετε·

⁵Τυφλοὶ ἀναβλέπουσιν καὶ χωλοὶ περιπατοῦσιν,
λεπροὶ καθαρίζονται καὶ κωφοὶ ἀκούουσιν,
καὶ νεκροὶ ἐγείρονται
καὶ πτωχοὶ εὐαγγελίζονται.

⁶Καὶ μακάριός ἐστιν ὃς ἐὰν μὴ σκανδαλισθῇ ἐν ἐμοί.

Jesus praises John   ⁷Τούτων δὲ πορευομένων ἤρξατο ὁ Ἰησοῦς λέγειν τοῖς ὄχλοις περὶ Ἰωάννου, Τί ἐξήλθατε εἰς τὴν ἔρημον θεάσασθαι; κάλαμον ὑπὸ ἀνέμου σαλευόμενον; ⁸ἀλλὰ τί ἐξήλθατε ἰδεῖν; ἄνθρωπον ἐν μαλακοῖς ἠμφιεσμένον; ἰδοὺ οἱ τὰ μαλακὰ φοροῦντες ἐν τοῖς οἴκοις τῶν βασιλέων εἰσίν. ⁹ἀλλὰ τί ἐξήλθατε ἰδεῖν; προφήτην; ναί λέγω ὑμῖν, καὶ περισσότερον προφήτου.

¹⁰Οὗτός ἐστιν περὶ οὗ γέγραπται,

• **11:1** This verse belongs with chap. 10, completing the second discourse that began at 10:5b and consists of *Instructions for the Disciples' Mission.*

when Jesus had finished . . .: The formula that ends each of the five discourses. As in 7:28.

from there . . . their towns: Where and whose towns is not clear.

• **11:2–19** This block of three sections about John the Baptist is paralleled in Luke and, as with 10:34–42, just above, very likely stems from Q. The second discourse is finished, but having laid aside Mark in chap. 4, our author introduces other non-Markan material in this chapter.

• **11:2** *John was in prison:* The Baptist's arrest is recounted later (14:3) as a flashback, just as in Mark 6:17–18.

the Anointed: Jesus' title has not appeared since the stories of his birth, chaps. 1–2. But it will be used many times in the rest of Matthew. See Translation Note, p. 34.

sent his disciples: John is shown with a following, like Jesus. Note that it is John's *disciples* who are putting the questions to Jesus. They may represent members of a John-the-

Baptist movement in the time this gospel was written. If so, however, there is no claim that John was "the one who is to come" (next verse); on the contrary.

• **11:3** *the one who is to come:* The expected agent of God, the Anointed, who would usher in the new age.

or are we to wait for another? John wonders whether Jesus is the expected one. In the story of John's preaching in the wilderness and Jesus' baptism (3:11–17) it's implied that John already knew the answer to this question. This tradition, however, implies that in fact John had not known it.

• **11:5** A summary of Jesus' healings in chaps. 8–9. It is practically a quotation of Isa 35:35–36, together with 29:18.

the poor have the good news preached to them: Evidently the literally poor, unlike the first beatitude (5:3: "Heaven's domain belongs to [the poor in spirit]").

• **11:6** This must be aimed at John's latter-day followers, and of course to others.

Congratulations: See Translation Note, p. 63.

those who don't take offense at me: In part, at least, Christians in the time of this gospel's

11 And so when Jesus had finished instructing his twelve disciples, he moved on from there to teach and proclaim in their towns.

²While John was in prison he heard about what the Anointed had been doing and he sent his disciples ³to ask, "Are you the one who is to come, or are we to wait for another?"

⁴And so Jesus answered them, "Go report to John what you have heard and seen:

⁵The blind see again and the lame walk;
lepers are cleansed and the deaf hear;
the dead are raised,
and the poor have the good news preached to them.

⁶"Congratulations to those who don't take offense at me."

⁷After <John's disciples> had departed, Jesus began to talk about John to the crowds: "What did you go out to the wilderness to gawk at? A reed shaking in the wind? ⁸What did you really go out to see? A man dressed in fancy <clothes>? Look, those who wear fancy <clothes> are found where kings live. ⁹Come on, what did you go out to see? A prophet? Yes, that's what you went out to see, yet someone more than a prophet.

¹⁰"This is the one about whom it was written:

---

writing, as opposed to many—perhaps also Jews—who did "take offense."

• **11:7–30** The rest of the chapter is comprised of sayings of Jesus, mostly from Q, assembled by the evangelist, but not designated a discourse ("sermon") like chaps. 5–7 or 10. The author had at his disposal more sayings of Jesus than could be included in the five discourses, each of which had its own subject matter.

• **11:7–15** The issue now shifts from the question who Jesus is to the question of John's identity. John (or his followers) asked the former question (vs 3), which Jesus has indirectly answered (vs 5). Here Jesus both raises and answers the second.

• **11:7–9** The double question in each verse might also be translated: "Why did you go out? To gawk at . . .?"

• **11:7** *A reed shaking in the wind:* A trivial thing. Obviously no reason to venture into the God-forsaken wilderness. The imagery here and in vs 8 is identical to that in Thom 78.

• **11:8** *What did you really go out to see?:* Usually translated "But [*alla*] what did you go out to see?"

a man dressed in fancy <clothes>: Ridiculously out of place there.

• **11:9** *Come on:* In Greek, *alla*—repeated from vs 8—with the sense of "In fact." Jesus presses the question.

A prophet? Yes: Jesus answers his question . . . and then qualifies it: *someone more than a prophet*

• **11:10** *This is the one about whom it was written:* Here, for once, it is Jesus rather than the evangelist who cites scriptural prophecy. The prediction, adapted from Mal 3:1, is seen as if addressed to Jesus, a promise about himself. It was—Jesus says—fulfilled by John. In Matt 3:3 our author omitted the prophecy from Mark's introduction. So also at Luke 3:4. Here it is evidently from Q (as at Luke 7:27).

Here is my messenger, whom I send on ahead of you to prepare your way before you: John's followers evidently expected that he would prepare the way for God's appearance. John has done that—but for Jesus' appearance.

Ἰδοὺ ἐγὼ ἀποστέλλω τὸν ἄγγελόν μου
πρὸ προσώπου σου,
ὃς κατασκευάσει τὴν ὁδόν σου ἔμπροσθέν σου.

¹¹Ἀμὴν λέγω ὑμῖν· οὐκ ἐγήγερται ἐν γεννητοῖς γυναικῶν μείζων
Ἰωάννου τοῦ βαπτιστοῦ· ὁ δὲ μικρότερος ἐν τῇ βασιλείᾳ τῶν
οὐρανῶν μείζων αὐτοῦ ἐστιν. ¹²ἀπὸ δὲ τῶν ἡμερῶν Ἰωάννου τοῦ
βαπτιστοῦ ἕως ἄρτι ἡ βασιλεία τῶν οὐρανῶν βιάζεται, καὶ βιασταὶ
ἁρπάζουσιν αὐτήν. ¹³πάντες γὰρ οἱ προφῆται καὶ ὁ νόμος ἕως
Ἰωάννου ἐπροφήτευσαν· ¹⁴καὶ εἰ θέλετε δέξασθαι, αὐτός ἐστιν Ἠλίας
ὁ μέλλων ἔρχεσθαι. ¹⁵ὁ ἔχων ὦτα ἀκουέτω.

Children in the marketplaces

¹⁶Τίνι δὲ ὁμοιώσω τὴν γενεὰν ταύτην; ὁμοία ἐστὶν παιδίοις
καθημένοις ἐν ταῖς ἀγοραῖς ἃ προσφωνοῦντα τοῖς ἑτέροις
¹⁷λέγουσιν,

Ηὐλήσαμεν ὑμῖν
καὶ οὐκ ὠρχήσασθε,
ἐθρηνήσαμεν
καὶ οὐκ ἐκόψασθε.

¹⁸ἦλθεν γὰρ Ἰωάννης μήτε ἐσθίων μήτε πίνων, καὶ λέγουσιν,
Δαιμόνιον ἔχει. ¹⁹ἦλθεν ὁ υἱὸς τοῦ ἀνθρώπου ἐσθίων καὶ πίνων, καὶ
λέγουσιν, Ἰδοὺ ἄνθρωπος φάγος καὶ οἰνοπότης, τελωνῶν φίλος καὶ
ἁμαρτωλῶν. καὶ ἐδικαιώθη ἡ σοφία ἀπὸ τῶν ἔργων αὐτῆς.

Damn you, Chorazin

²⁰Τότε ἤρξατο ὀνειδίζειν τὰς πόλεις ἐν αἷς ἐγένοντο αἱ πλεῖσται
δυνάμεις αὐτοῦ, ὅτι οὐ μετενόησαν·

- **11:11–13** Three originally separate sayings are put alongside each other, with puzzling result.
- **11:11** John is the greatest human in history. But he stands outside *God's domain*. In that sense he is less than *the least* in it. Thom 46: "From Adam to John the Baptist, among those born of women, no one is ... greater than John the Baptist.... But I have said that whoever among you becomes a child ... will become greater than John."
- **11:12** The author includes this saying here, because it supports the thrust of this section, about John's role in God's plan. But it clearly had an independent origin, one of Jesus' many brief, memorable sayings, called "aphorisms" (see Glossary).

  From the time of John the Baptist until now: John's appearance marks the inauguration of the new age.

  the empire of Heaven has been suffering violence: A notoriously difficult saying, whose very translation is debatable. This rendering fits best, I believe, with the second half of the verse (*violent men are attempting*

to gain it by force). And it means that since John initiated the movement of the empire of Heaven, and Jesus took it up, it has been receiving the violence of those who would stamp it out. But it could instead mean "... has been breaking in violently." That is, the verb may be understood as either active or passive. If the latter version is correct, then is the violence of the verse's second half to be taken as good?

- **11:13** *the Prophets and even the Law predicted:* This has usually been rendered simply "the Prophets and the Law, ..." but surprisingly *the Law* comes second, after *the Prophets*. So SV is right to insert *even*.

  the Law predicted everything that was to happen: There is a prediction in Torah, the first five books of the OT, namely that God would send a prophet like Moses (Deut 18:15), and the evangelist surely understands that to have been fulfilled by the Baptist.

  everything that was to happen up to John's time: Our author, esp., cannot mean to say that *since* John's time the Hebrew Scriptures ceased to be relevant or authoritative. (5:17:

Here is my messenger
whom I send on ahead of you
to prepare your way before you.

¹¹"I swear to you, among those born of women no one has arisen who is greater than John the Baptist; yet the least in Heaven's domain is greater than he. ¹²From the time of John the Baptist until now Heaven's imperial rule has been suffering violence, and violent men are attempting to gain it by force. ¹³For the Prophets and even the Law predicted everything that was to happen up to John's time. ¹⁴And if you are willing to admit it, <John> is the Elijah who was to come. ¹⁵Anyone here with two ears had better listen!

¹⁶"What does this generation remind me of? It is like children sitting in marketplaces, who call out to others:

Children in the marketplaces

¹⁷We played the flute for you
but you wouldn't dance;
we sang a dirge
but you wouldn't mourn.

¹⁸"Just remember, John appeared on the scene neither eating nor drinking, and they say, 'He is demented.' ¹⁹The son of Adam appeared on the scene both eating and drinking, and they say, 'There's a glutton and a drunk, a crony of toll collectors and sinners.' Indeed, wisdom is vindicated by her deeds."

²⁰Then he began to denounce the towns where he had performed most of his miracles, because they had not changed their ways:

Damn you, Chorazin

"Don't imagine that I have come to annul the Law or the Prophets. I have come not to annul but to fulfill [the Law].")

• **11:14** *admit:* Greek: "accept."

<John> *is the Elijah who was to come:* According to 2 Kgs 2:11–12 Elijah didn't die but was taken up to heaven. So Jews at the time of Jesus and ever since have believed that Elijah would return, probably to usher in the new age. (For this reason a place is set for Elijah at the Passover Seder meal.) Jesus declares that the expectation has come to pass in the person of John.

• **11:15** *Anyone here with two ears had better listen!* Usually, "He who has ears to hear, let him hear." This is the way Jesus several times ends a body of teaching. It is comparable to our "Now hear this!" Found also at 13:9 and 43, and at Mark 4:9 etc.

• **11:16–19** This unit of tradition must be from Q. It's found also in Luke 7:31–35. It fits here as further mention of John.

• **11:16** *What does this generation remind me of?* Greek: What should I compare it to?

• **11:16b–17** A simile, a bit like a very brief parable. Its application to vss 18–19 is not entirely logical. Were the two sets of verses originally separate, combined later in the oral tradition?

children sitting in marketplaces: Evidently playing games that imitate adult practice, at a wedding or a funeral.

• **11:18** *John appeared on the scene neither eating nor drinking:* As at a funeral. John's way of life was ascetic.

they say, He is demented: Acting illogically, like the children of vs 17 who *wouldn't dance . . . wouldn't mourn.*

• **11:19** *son of Adam:* Jesus clearly refers to himself. And to his lifestyle.

eating and drinking: As at a wedding
toll collectors and sinners: See on 9:10.

Indeed, wisdom is vindicated by her deeds: Perhaps a common proverb. What does it mean here? Does Jesus imply that he personifies Wisdom and so is justified in the way he lives? Or that those who follow the teachings of wisdom can expect criticism from fools?

²¹Οὐαί σοι, Χοραζίν, οὐαί σοι, Βηθσαϊδά·

ὅτι εἰ ἐν Τύρῳ καὶ Σιδῶνι ἐγένοντο αἱ δυνάμεις αἱ γενόμεναι

ἐν ὑμῖν, πάλαι ἂν ἐν σάκκῳ καὶ σποδῷ μετενόησαν.

²²Πλὴν λέγω ὑμῖν, Τύρῳ καὶ Σιδῶνι ἀνεκτότερον ἔσται ἐν

ἡμέρᾳ κρίσεως ἢ ὑμῖν.

²³Καὶ σύ, Καφαρναούμ,

μὴ ἕως οὐρανοῦ ὑψωθήσῃ;

ἕως ᾅδου καταβήσῃ·

Ὅτι εἰ ἐν Σοδόμοις ἐγενήθησαν αἱ δυνάμεις αἱ γενόμεναι ἐν

σοί, ἔμεινεν ἂν μέχρι τῆς σήμερον.

²⁴Πλὴν λέγω ὑμῖν ὅτι γῇ Σοδόμων ἀνεκτότερον ἔσται ἐν

ἡμέρᾳ κρίσεως ἢ σοί.

Father & son   ²⁵ Ἐν ἐκείνῳ τῷ καιρῷ ἀποκριθεὶς ὁ Ἰησοῦς εἶπεν,

Ἐξομολογοῦμαί σοι, πάτερ, κύριε τοῦ οὐρανοῦ καὶ τῆς γῆς,

ὅτι ἔκρυψας ταῦτα ἀπὸ σοφῶν καὶ συνετῶν

καὶ ἀπεκάλυψας αὐτὰ νηπίοις·

²⁶Ναί ὁ πατήρ, ὅτι οὕτως εὐδοκία ἐγένετο ἔμπροσθέν σου.

²⁷Πάντα μοι παρεδόθη ὑπὸ τοῦ πατρός μου,

καὶ οὐδεὶς ἐπιγινώσκει τὸν υἱὸν εἰ μὴ ὁ πατήρ,

οὐδὲ τὸν πατέρα τις ἐπιγινώσκει εἰ μὴ ὁ υἱὸς

καὶ ᾧ ἐὰν βούληται ὁ υἱὸς ἀποκαλύψαι.

²⁸Δεῦτε πρός με πάντες οἱ κοπιῶντες καὶ πεφορτισμένοι,

κἀγὼ ἀναπαύσω ὑμᾶς.

²⁹Ἄρατε τὸν ζυγόν μου ἐφ᾽ ὑμᾶς καὶ μάθετε ἀπ᾽ ἐμοῦ,

ὅτι πραΰς εἰμι καὶ ταπεινὸς τῇ καρδίᾳ,

καὶ εὑρήσετε ἀνάπαυσιν ταῖς ψυχαῖς ὑμῶν·

³⁰Ὁ γὰρ ζυγός μου χρηστὸς καὶ τὸ φορτίον μου ἐλαφρόν

ἐστιν.

• **11:21** Evidently from Q; found at Luke 10:13.

Damn you: Traditionally, "Woe to you." The negative of "Congratulations." See that Translation Note, p. 63.

Chorazin . . . Bethsaida: Towns on the Sea of Galilee. They are not otherwise mentioned in Matthew. Evidently we are to assume that Jesus *performed . . . miracles* there too. *Chorazin* was north of Capernaum (see comment on 4:13) and *Bethsaida* probably still farther north and east, at the mouth of the Jordan river as it flows into the lake. (For *Bethsaida*, see below on 16:13–20, and 14:22 also.)

Tyre and Sidon: Cities on the Mediterranean coast north of Palestine, inhabited by Phoenicians, that is, pagan Gentiles. Since they are sometimes linked as a pair in the Hebrew Scriptures, usually for denunciation, Jesus'

saying is all the more poignant.

changed their ways: Sometimes translated "repented."

sackcloth and ashes: Traditionally used in the ritual of mourning. The pagans would have repented and converted to God's ways.

• **11:23** *Hell:* In Greek, "Hades."

Sodom: In Gen 19 this ancient town is usually paired with Gomorrah (as in 10:15). It was perhaps on the southeastern shore of the Dead Sea, or is now covered with water. Supposedly destroyed for its sins, it became a symbol of wickedness.

• **11:25–27** This passage is unique in the synoptic gospels, closely akin to what we find in the Gospel of John. It's been called a "thunderbolt" out of a clear Johannine sky.

• **11:25** *exclaimed:* Strictly "answered and said," but in the context it can't mean

²¹Damn you, Chorazin! Damn you, Bethsaida!

If the miracles done in you had been done in Tyre and Sidon,
    they would have <sat> in sackcloth and ashes
    and changed their ways long ago.
²²So I tell you, Tyre and Sidon will be better off
    on judgment day than you.
²³And you, Capernaum,
    you don't think you'll be exalted to heaven, do you?
    No, you'll go to Hell.
Because if the miracles done among you had been done in
    Sodom, Sodom would still be around.
²⁴So I tell you, the land of Sodom will be better off
    on judgment day than you.

²⁵At that point, Jesus exclaimed:

                                      Father & son

I praise you, Father, Lord of heaven and earth,
    because you have hidden these things from the wise and
        the learned
    but revealed them to the untutored;
²⁶yes indeed, Father, because this is the way you want it.
²⁷ My Father has turned everything over to me.
    No one knows the son except the Father,
        nor does anyone know the Father except the son
        —and anyone to whom the son wishes to reveal him.
²⁸All you who labor and are overburdened come to me,
    and I will refresh you.
²⁹Take my yoke upon you and learn from me,
    because I am meek and modest
    and your lives will find rest.
³⁰For my yoke is comfortable and my load is light.

"replied," since Jesus was already speaking. The Greek is sometimes simply the formula used by the evangelists for opening a new set of sayings.

Father: Only in this passage in Matthew does Jesus as an individual directly address God in this way (in vs 27, "My Father"). "Our Father" (6:9) is a different matter, of course.

these things: What does this refer to? The miracles that Jesus has done (vs 20)?

the untutored: "Babes."

• **11:27** Here Jesus no longer addresses God (as in vss 25–26) but evidently any who follow him.

My Father: See above on vs 25.

the Father: By itself as title for God this is rare in Matthew. (Elsewhere in 24:36 and 28:19.) Should "son" here be capitalized also?

• **11:28–30** Unique to Matthew in the New Testament. But Thom 90 reads: "Come to me, for my yoke is comfortable and my lordship is gentle, and you will find rest for yourselves."

• **11:28** *who labor and are overburdened:* Peasants, perhaps; they were often overworked and oppressed.

• **11:29** *Take my yoke upon you and learn from me:* Perhaps a metaphor for accepting the responsibilities of discipleship.

I am meek and modest: As opposed to the typical overlord.

Except for a few scattered passages, not since chap. 4 has the evangelist followed Mark. Now he does so, from Mark 2:23 more or less till the end, but with many insertions.

Son of Adam over the sabbath

12 Ἐν ἐκείνῳ τῷ καιρῷ ἐπορεύθη ὁ Ἰησοῦς τοῖς σάββασιν διὰ τῶν σπορίμων· οἱ δὲ μαθηταὶ αὐτοῦ ἐπείνασαν καὶ ἤρξαντο τίλλειν στάχυας καὶ ἐσθίειν. ²οἱ δὲ Φαρισαῖοι ἰδόντες εἶπαν αὐτῷ, Ἰδοὺ οἱ μαθηταί σου ποιοῦσιν ὃ οὐκ ἔξεστιν ποιεῖν ἐν σαββάτῳ.

³Ὁ δὲ εἶπεν αὐτοῖς, Οὐκ ἀνέγνωτε τί ἐποίησεν Δαυὶδ ὅτε ἐπείνασεν καὶ οἱ μετ᾽ αὐτοῦ, ⁴πῶς εἰσῆλθεν εἰς τὸν οἶκον τοῦ θεοῦ καὶ τοὺς ἄρτους τῆς προθέσεως ἔφαγον, ὃ οὐκ ἐξὸν ἦν αὐτῷ φαγεῖν οὐδὲ τοῖς μετ᾽ αὐτοῦ εἰ μὴ τοῖς ἱερεῦσιν μόνοις; ⁵ἢ οὐκ ἀνέγνωτε ἐν τῷ νόμῳ ὅτι τοῖς σάββασιν οἱ ἱερεῖς ἐν τῷ ἱερῷ τὸ σάββατον βεβηλοῦσιν καὶ ἀναίτιοί εἰσιν; ⁶λέγω δὲ ὑμῖν ὅτι τοῦ ἱεροῦ μεῖζόν ἐστιν ὧδε. ⁷εἰ δὲ ἐγνώκειτε τί ἐστιν, Ἔλεος θέλω καὶ οὐ θυσίαν, οὐκ ἂν κατεδικάσατε τοὺς ἀναιτίους. ⁸κύριος γάρ ἐστιν τοῦ σαββάτου ὁ υἱὸς τοῦ ἀνθρώπου.

Man with a crippled hand

⁹Καὶ μεταβὰς ἐκεῖθεν ἦλθεν εἰς τὴν συναγωγὴν αὐτῶν· ¹⁰καὶ ἰδοὺ ἄνθρωπος χεῖρα ἔχων ξηράν. καὶ ἐπηρώτησαν αὐτὸν λέγοντες, Εἰ ἔξεστιν τοῖς σάββασιν θεραπεῦσαι; ἵνα κατηγορήσωσιν αὐτοῦ.

¹¹Ὁ δὲ εἶπεν αὐτοῖς, Τίς ἔσται ἐξ ὑμῶν ἄνθρωπος ὃς ἕξει πρόβατον ἕν καὶ ἐὰν ἐμπέσῃ τοῦτο τοῖς σάββασιν εἰς βόθυνον, οὐχὶ κρατήσει αὐτὸ καὶ ἐγερεῖ; ¹²πόσῳ οὖν διαφέρει ἄνθρωπος προβάτου. ὥστε ἔξεστιν τοῖς σάββασιν καλῶς ποιεῖν.

¹³Τότε λέγει τῷ ἀνθρώπῳ, Ἔκτεινόν σου τὴν χεῖρα. καὶ ἐξέτεινεν καὶ ἀπεκατεστάθη ὑγιὴς ὡς ἡ ἄλλη.

12:6 Some MSS read "someone" instead of *something,* which as the more difficult reading is probably original (see Introduction, p. 23), since Jesus will refer to himself in vs 8. I depart from the last published SV here.

• **12:1** *About that time:* This is probably not a specific historical detail but an editorial transition that the evangelist uses to join originally separate stories. Also at 14:1.

was walking: Not the usual tense (imperfect) for continuous or habitual action, but the temporal phrase at the head of the sentence suggests it.

his disciples: In this depiction Jesus himself doesn't violate the sabbath, only his followers, and the authorities complain to Jesus about them (vs 2). Perhaps this has more to do with Christians of our author's time than those in the time of Jesus. See also 15:2 and, for the other way around, 9:11.

• **12:2** *what's not permitted on the sabbath day:* Evidently to *strip heads of grain* (vs 1) was understood as doing work and so not allowed under the Jewish law of the sabbath.

• **12:3–7** Referring to scriptural example is a typical practice of the Pharisees. For that reason, evidently, the evangelist portrays Jesus answering their objection in the same way.

• **12:3–4** In 1 Sam 21:1–6.

• **12:4** *the house of God:* This refers evidently, to a shrine containing the ark, before Solomon built the temple.

• **12:5–7** The author seems to have added these verses. Mark 2 and Luke 6 have no parallel. Mention of *the temple* suggests a situation long after the time of Moses. See the preceding comment.

• **12:5** There is nothing to this effect in the written *Law.* Perhaps the oral law—Rabbinic interpretation—is meant. But was it already in writing, so that it could be *read?*

• **12:6** *there's something greater than the temple here:* Perhaps it is God's empire. But if "someone" is original (see the Text-Critical Note) Jesus must be referring to himself.

• **12:7** *It's mercy I desire instead of sacrifice:* A quotation from Hos 6:6, as above in 9:13.

• **12:8** The evangelist has omitted the first half of this saying as it appears in Mark 2:27: "the sabbath day was created for Adam

12 About that time Jesus was walking through the grain fields on the sabbath. His disciples were hungry and began to strip heads of grain and chew them. ²When the Pharisees saw this, they said to him, "See here, your disciples are doing what's not permitted on the sabbath day."

³He said to them, "Haven't you read what David did when he and his companions were hungry? ⁴He went into the house of God, and ate the consecrated bread, which no one is permitted to eat—not even David or his companions—except the priests alone! ⁵Or haven't you read in the Law that during the sabbath day the priests violate the sabbath in the temple and are held blameless? ⁶Yet I say to you, there's something greater than the temple here. ⁷And if you had known what this means, 'It's mercy I desire instead of sacrifice,' you would not have condemned those who are blameless. ⁸Remember, the son of Adam is master of the sabbath day."

⁹And when he had moved on, he went into their synagogue. ¹⁰Just then a fellow with a crippled hand appeared, and they asked, "Is it permitted to heal on the sabbath day?"—so they could denounce him.

¹¹He replied, "If you had only a single sheep, and it fell into a ditch on the sabbath day, wouldn't you grab it and pull it out? ¹²A person is worth considerably more than a sheep. So, it is permitted to do good on the sabbath day."

¹³Then he says to the fellow, "Hold out your hand!" He held it out and it was restored to health like the other.

Son of Adam over the sabbath

Man with a crippled hand

---

and Eve, not Adam and Eve for the sabbath day." Perhaps he did so because it refers to humanity in general, but for him "the son of Adam" is a title that applies only to Jesus,.

the son of Adam is master of the sabbath day: The saying is identical to Luke 6:5b and almost identical to Mark 2:28.

the son of Adam: The author clearly means Jesus. Jesus himself probably meant that all human beings had control over the Sabbath, since it was ordained for their benefit.

• **12:9–14** One of the miracle stories not collected in chaps. 8–9. From Mark 3:1–6 and paralleled in Luke 6:6–11.

• **12:9** *their synagogue:* Whose? all Jews'? the Pharisees'? or simply the local people's?

• **12:10** As in Mark the healing story has been "invaded" by controversy about the sabbath, connecting it with the preceding episode.

crippled: In Greek, "dry" and often translated "withered." SV properly leaves open the question just what disability the man had.

they: Evidently still the Pharisees.

Is it permitted to heal on the sabbath day? Healing could be considered a form of work, and so not allowed on the sabbath. In Mark and Luke, Jesus asks the question of his critics. Here they pretend to consult him about the law, on which they were experts.

denounce him: In order to "get rid of him" (vs 14).

• **12:11–12** Jesus responds with his question to them. These two verses are not to be found in either Mark's or Luke's version of this story. But there is a similar question in Luke 14:5: "Suppose your son or your ox falls down a well . . . on the sabbath day." Evidently the evangelist has taken an independent saying in Q and conveniently put it into this context. Again the argument is from less to greater. (See on 6:26–30.)

• **12:12b** Jesus' answer to his opponents' question in vs 10 addresses the legal question not by citing Torah but applying the principle of humaneness.

Jesus withdraws

¹⁴Ἐξελθόντες δὲ οἱ Φαρισαῖοι συμβούλιον ἔλαβον κατ' αὐτοῦ ὅπως αὐτὸν ἀπολέσωσιν.

¹⁵Ὁ δὲ Ἰησοῦς γνοὺς ἀνεχώρησεν ἐκεῖθεν. καὶ ἠκολούθησαν αὐτῷ ὄχλοι πολλοί, καὶ ἐθεράπευσεν αὐτοὺς πάντας.

¹⁶Καὶ ἐπετίμησεν αὐτοῖς ἵνα μὴ φανερὸν αὐτὸν ποιήσωσιν, ¹⁷ἵνα πληρωθῇ τὸ ῥηθὲν διὰ Ἠσαΐου τοῦ προφήτου λέγοντος,

¹⁸Ἰδοὺ ὁ παῖς μου ὃν ᾑρέτισα,
ὁ ἀγαπητός μου εἰς ὃν εὐδόκησεν ἡ ψυχή μου·
θήσω τὸ πνεῦμά μου ἐπ' αὐτόν,
καὶ κρίσιν τοῖς ἔθνεσιν ἀπαγγελεῖ.
¹⁹Οὐκ ἐρίσει οὐδὲ κραυγάσει,
οὐδὲ ἀκούσει τις ἐν ταῖς πλατείαις τὴν φωνὴν αὐτοῦ.
²⁰Κάλαμον συντετριμμένον οὐ κατεάξει
καὶ λίνον τυφόμενον οὐ σβέσει,
ἕως ἂν ἐκβάλῃ εἰς νῖκος τὴν κρίσιν.
²¹καὶ τῷ ὀνόματι αὐτοῦ ἔθνη ἐλπιοῦσιν.

Beelzebul controversy

²²Τότε προσηνέχθη αὐτῷ δαιμονιζόμενος τυφλὸς καὶ κωφός, καὶ ἐθεράπευσεν αὐτόν, ὥστε τὸν κωφὸν λαλεῖν καὶ βλέπειν. ²³καὶ ἐξίσταντο πάντες οἱ ὄχλοι καὶ ἔλεγον, Μήτι οὗτός ἐστιν ὁ υἱὸς Δαυίδ;

²⁴Οἱ δὲ Φαρισαῖοι ἀκούσαντες εἶπον, Οὗτος οὐκ ἐκβάλλει τὰ δαιμόνια εἰ μὴ ἐν τῷ Βεελζεβοὺλ ἄρχοντι τῶν δαιμονίων.

²⁵Εἰδὼς δὲ τὰς ἐνθυμήσεις αὐτῶν εἶπεν αὐτοῖς, Πᾶσα βασιλεία μερισθεῖσα καθ' ἑαυτῆς ἐρημοῦται καὶ πᾶσα πόλις ἢ οἰκία μερισθεῖσα

12:15 Some MSS have simply "many," that is "many people," instead of "huge crowds."

• **12:15** *Aware of this:* The author has added this to the Markan text (3:7–12).
• **12:16** See Glossary on "the Messianic Secret."
  his identity: That he is the Anointed, God's chosen *servant* (vs 18).
• **12:17–21** Our author adds this quotation of Isa 42:1–4. For once the quote is not from the Greek text, the Septuagint—where the oracle has to do with Jacob/Israel—but with God's future Servant, as in the Hebrew text. It's hard to see how this prediction fits the secrecy imposed in vs 16. Is it implied that God's *servant* will work quietly, behind the scenes? Vs 19b may suggest this ("nor will anyone hear his voice . . ."), but not vs 18d ("He will announce justice . . .").
• **12:17** *<In this way> what was spoken . . . <came true>:* The usual citation formula—see Introduction, p. 19. Literally, "so as to fulfill, . . ." but it can hardly mean that this was Jesus'

intention. See the comment just above.
• **12:18** *justice for foreigners:* So they "will center their hope on him" (vs 21).
• **12:19** *He will not be contentious, or loud-mouthed:* A curious statement. Does it mean he will not be a troublemaker? Or, will not call attention to himself?
• **12:20** *break a crushed reed . . . snuff out a smoldering wick:* What is meant? Possibly that he will not harm those who are already oppressed and marginalized.
  a decisive victory: Over evil.
• **12:22–37** Here the author combines Mark 3:19b–30 with a similar but slightly different account from Q (see Luke 11:14–23), sometimes following the one more closely, sometimes the other.
• **12:22** A slightly longer version of this brief healing story is found in 9:32–34. But there the person was only mute. In Mark 3:22–30 there is no healing; Q reports a cure, but

¹⁴The Pharisees went out and hatched a plot against him, to get rid of him.

¹⁵Aware of this, Jesus withdrew from there, and huge crowds followed him, and he healed all of them.

Jesus withdraws

¹⁶And he warned them not to disclose his identity. ¹⁷<In this way> what was spoken through Isaiah the prophet <came> true:

¹⁸Here is my servant, whom I have selected,
my favored of whom I fully approve.
I will put my spirit upon him,
and he will announce justice for foreigners.
¹⁹He will not be contentious or loud-mouthed,
nor will anyone hear his voice on Main Street.
²⁰He is not about to break a crushed reed,
and he's not one to snuff out a smoldering wick,
until he brings forth a decisive victory,
²¹and foreigners will center their hope on him.

²²Then they brought to him a blind and mute person who was demon-possessed, and he cured him so the mute was able both to speak and to see. ²³And the entire crowd was beside itself and kept saying, "This can't be the son of David, can it?"

Beelzebul controversy

²⁴But when the Pharisees heard of it, they said, "This fellow drives out demons only in the name of Beelzebul, the head demon."

²⁵He knew what they were thinking, and said to them: "Every government divided against itself is devastated, and no town or

---

does not mention blindness. Perhaps the evangelist adds that detail to distinguish this story from the one in chap. 9. There too the charge was made that Jesus uses demons to drive out demons, but only in passing (9:34). Here the charge becomes central. In Mark (3:21) it is preceded by Jesus' family's trying to restrain him since "they thought he was out of his mind." Both our evangelist and the Lukan text omit this, one of the so-called Minor Agreements of Matthew and Luke against Mark (see Introduction, pp. 10–11). The explanation would seem to be not textual interdependence but a common pious concern to protect Jesus' image or his family's.

• **12:23** *kept saying:* Or "began to say."
can't . . . can it? The form of the crowd's question indicates that the answer clearly expected is No. The author uses irony: The reader/hearer understands that he is in fact "the son of David," the characters in the

story do not.
son of David: The Anointed. Here, for the first time on the lips of humans. More commonly it is uttered by demons or the demon-possessed (as at 9:27, 20:30–31).

• **12:24** In other words, anyone who deals with demons must be demonic himself.
the Pharisees: Mark 3:22 has "the scholars." Luke (11:15) reads only "some of them."
in the name of: See Glossary.
Beelzebul: A name sometimes given to the devil. Another spelling is "Beelzebub." It may derive in part from the old name for a non-Israelite god, Baal. A false god, of course, in Jewish eyes.

• **12:25–29** Jesus refutes the Pharisees' charge in three ways: showing that it's self-contradictory (25–26), hypocritical (27), and naive (29).

• **12:25–26** The first refutation: the charge makes no sense.

καθ᾽ ἑαυτῆς οὐ σταθήσεται. ²⁶καὶ εἰ ὁ Σατανᾶς τὸν Σατανᾶν ἐκβάλλει,
ἐφ᾽ ἑαυτὸν ἐμερίσθη· πῶς οὖν σταθήσεται ἡ βασιλεία αὐτοῦ;

²⁷Καὶ εἰ ἐγὼ ἐν Βεελζεβοὺλ ἐκβάλλω τὰ δαιμόνια, οἱ υἱοὶ ὑμῶν
ἐν τίνι ἐκβάλλουσιν; διὰ τοῦτο αὐτοὶ κριταὶ ἔσονται ὑμῶν. ²⁸εἰ δὲ ἐν
πνεύματι θεοῦ ἐγὼ ἐκβάλλω τὰ δαιμόνια, ἄρα ἔφθασεν ἐφ᾽ ὑμᾶς ἡ
βασιλεία τοῦ θεοῦ.

²⁹ἭἭ πῶς δύναταί τις εἰσελθεῖν εἰς τὴν οἰκίαν τοῦ ἰσχυροῦ καὶ τὰ
σκεύη αὐτοῦ ἁρπάσαι, ἐὰν μὴ πρῶτον δήσῃ τὸν ἰσχυρόν; καὶ τότε τὴν
οἰκίαν αὐτοῦ διαρπάσει.

³⁰Ὁ μὴ ὢν μετ᾽ ἐμοῦ κατ᾽ ἐμοῦ ἐστιν, καὶ ὁ μὴ συνάγων μετ᾽ ἐμοῦ
σκορπίζει. ³¹διὰ τοῦτο λέγω ὑμῖν, πᾶσα ἁμαρτία καὶ βλασφημία
ἀφεθήσεται τοῖς ἀνθρώποις, ἡ δὲ τοῦ πνεύματος βλασφημία οὐκ
ἀφεθήσεται. ³²καὶ ὃς ἐὰν εἴπῃ λόγον κατὰ τοῦ υἱοῦ τοῦ ἀνθρώπου,
ἀφεθήσεται αὐτῷ· ὃς δ᾽ ἂν εἴπῃ κατὰ τοῦ πνεύματος τοῦ ἁγίου, οὐκ
ἀφεθήσεται αὐτῷ οὔτε ἐν τούτῳ τῷ αἰῶνι οὔτε ἐν τῷ μέλλοντι.

³³Ἢ ποιήσατε τὸ δένδρον καλὸν καὶ τὸν καρπὸν αὐτοῦ καλόν,
ἢ ποιήσατε τὸ δένδρον σαπρὸν καὶ τὸν καρπὸν αὐτοῦ σαπρόν· ἐκ
γὰρ τοῦ καρποῦ τὸ δένδρον γινώσκεται. ³⁴γεννήματα ἐχιδνῶν, πῶς
δύνασθε ἀγαθὰ λαλεῖν πονηροὶ ὄντες; ἐκ γὰρ τοῦ περισσεύματος
τῆς καρδίας τὸ στόμα λαλεῖ. ³⁵ὁ ἀγαθὸς ἄνθρωπος ἐκ τοῦ ἀγαθοῦ
θησαυροῦ ἐκβάλλει ἀγαθά, καὶ ὁ πονηρὸς ἄνθρωπος ἐκ τοῦ πονηροῦ
θησαυροῦ ἐκβάλλει πονηρά. ³⁶λέγω δὲ ὑμῖν ὅτι πᾶν ῥῆμα ἀργὸν ὃ
λαλήσουσιν οἱ ἄνθρωποι ἀποδώσουσιν περὶ αὐτοῦ λόγον ἐν ἡμέρᾳ

• **12:25** *he knew what they were thinking:* This is
lacking in Mark 3:23. It's to be found in the Q
version of this teaching; see Luke 11:17–22.

• **12:26** *Satan:* The usual name for the devil
on Jesus' lips in Matthew. But see the next
verse, and 10:25.

• **12:27–28** The second answer to the Pharisees' charge in vs 24. Not found in Mark, but
in Luke 11:19–20.

• **12:27** *Even if:* Granting for the moment the
charge against him.

*in whose name do your own people drive
<them> out?* Whether *in Beelzebul's name* or
not, they too practice exorcism.

your own people: Greek: "your sons."

In that case, they will be your judges: Either
way they fall under the same criticism as
Jesus.

they will be your judges: Who will be? "Your
own people" or the demons? Evidently the
former.

• **12:28** *But if:* Completing the hypothetical
question of vs 27. Jesus makes a powerful
claim, albeit a conditional one and entrusts
it to the hearer to judge whether or not it is

true. Is it in fact by God's spirit that he can
drive out demons? If so hasn't *God's domain
… arrived?*

God's spirit: Luke (11:20), probably as in Q,
reads "God's finger." Our author has eliminated the suggestion that God has a human
body.

God's domain: The one instance of this
phrase in the gospel. Evidently the evangelist here forgot to change *God's* to
"Heaven's."

• **12:29** The third reply, a mini-parable. *To loot
… a powerful man's house* is a metaphor for
casting out demons.

• **12:30** An example of Semitic poetic parallelism. The two halves of the saying mean
much the same. It's interesting that Jesus'
role is described as *gather[ing]*. What does
that mean? And whom does it refer to? A
puzzling saying, esp. since it contradicts the
saying in Mark 9:40, which our author omits:
"Whoever is not against us is on our side."
Possibly the inclusive thrust of Jesus' movement gave way in the Matthean church,
under pressure of persecution and competi-

household divided against itself will survive. ²⁶So if Satan drives out Satan, he is divided against himself. In that case, how will his domain endure?

²⁷"Even if I drive out demons in Beelzebul's name, in whose name do your own people drive <them> out? In that case, they will be your judges. ²⁸But if by God's spirit I drive out demons, then for you God's imperial rule has arrived.

²⁹"Or how can someone enter a powerful man's house and steal his belongings, unless he first ties him up? Only then does he loot his house.

³⁰"The one who isn't with me is against me, and the one who doesn't gather with me scatters. ³¹That's why I tell you:

> Every offense and blasphemy will be forgiven humankind, but blasphemy of the spirit won't be forgiven. ³²And the one who speaks a word against the son of Adam will be forgiven; but the one who speaks a word against the holy spirit won't be forgiven, either in this age or in the one to come.

³³"If you make the tree choice, its fruit will be choice; if you make the tree rotten, its fruit will be rotten. After all, the tree is known by its fruit. ³⁴You spawn of Satan, how can your speech be good when you are corrupt? As you know, the mouth gives voice to what the heart is full of. ³⁵The good person produces good things out of a fund of good; and the evil person produces evil things out of a fund of evil. ³⁶Let me tell you: On judgment day people will have

---

tion, to this more exclusionist mentality, one that has often characterized the Christian church ever since.

• **12:31–37** The section the translators have entitled the "Beelzebul controversy" continues, the author at first (vss 31–32) following Mark. It's hard to see how the title can still apply. On the other hand, no appropriate heading for these verses suggests itself. It seems to be a collection of originally independent sayings, and some of them are obscure.

• **12:31** *the blasphemy of the spirit:* What this means is notoriously uncertain. Often understood as blasphemy "against the Spirit," as in the next verse. But there is no article ("the") in the Greek. And capitalization ("Spirit") represents a modern interpretation. There could be no such indicator in the Greek. The translators were right to leave this ambiguous.

• **12:32** *the holy spirit:* As in 1:18 and 28:19, the translators do not read this as a personified Holy Spirit. The formulation of that idea would take place later than this gospel. Nev-

ertheless, the meaning is that blasphemy against God's spirit is a denial of the very power of God and therefore cannot be forgiven. Do you agree with this?

• **12:33–35** These verses have some parallels to John the Baptist's words in 3:7b–8, 10.

• **12:33** A proverb, apparently. Another version appears at Luke 6:43–44. See also Matt 7:17, "Every healthy tree produces choice fruit, but the rotten tree produces spoiled fruit." It briefly interrupts the theme of good and evil speech (31–32), and being held accountable for it. That resumes in vss 34–37.

• **12:34** *spawn of Satan:* Jesus uses the Baptist's phrase. See comment on 3:7. To whom is this addressed? Perhaps the evangelist still has the Pharisees in mind. He has inserted it into the Q saying.

• **12:35** An application, evidently, of vs 33. It can be found also at Luke 6:45.

• **12:36** *thoughtless:* In the context, a deft translation for the usual "idle."

κρίσεως· ³⁷ἐκ γὰρ τῶν λόγων σου δικαιωθήσῃ, καὶ ἐκ τῶν λόγων σου καταδικασθήσῃ.

Request for a sign

³⁸Τότε ἀπεκρίθησαν αὐτῷ τινες τῶν γραμματέων καὶ Φαρισαίων λέγοντες, Διδάσκαλε, θέλομεν ἀπὸ σοῦ σημεῖον ἰδεῖν.

³⁹Ὁ δὲ ἀποκριθεὶς εἶπεν αὐτοῖς, Γενεὰ πονηρὰ καὶ μοιχαλὶς σημεῖον ἐπιζητεῖ, καὶ σημεῖον οὐ δοθήσεται αὐτῇ εἰ μὴ τὸ σημεῖον Ἰωνᾶ τοῦ προφήτου. ⁴⁰ὥσπερ γὰρ ἦν Ἰωνᾶς ἐν τῇ κοιλίᾳ τοῦ κήτους τρεῖς ἡμέρας καὶ τρεῖς νύκτας, οὕτως ἔσται ὁ υἱὸς τοῦ ἀνθρώπου ἐν τῇ καρδίᾳ τῆς γῆς τρεῖς ἡμέρας καὶ τρεῖς νύκτας. ⁴¹ἄνδρες Νινευῖται ἀναστήσονται ἐν τῇ κρίσει μετὰ τῆς γενεᾶς ταύτης καὶ κατακρινοῦσιν αὐτήν, ὅτι μετενόησαν εἰς τὸ κήρυγμα Ἰωνᾶ, καὶ ἰδοὺ πλεῖον Ἰωνᾶ ὧδε.

⁴²Βασίλισσα νότου ἐγερθήσεται ἐν τῇ κρίσει μετὰ τῆς γενεᾶς ταύτης καὶ κατακρινεῖ αὐτήν, ὅτι ἦλθεν ἐκ τῶν περάτων τῆς γῆς ἀκοῦσαι τὴν σοφίαν Σολομῶνος, καὶ ἰδοὺ πλεῖον Σολομῶνος ὧδε.

Return of an unclean spirit

⁴³Ὅταν δὲ τὸ ἀκάθαρτον πνεῦμα ἐξέλθῃ ἀπὸ τοῦ ἀνθρώπου, διέρχεται δι' ἀνύδρων τόπων ζητοῦν ἀνάπαυσιν καὶ οὐχ εὑρίσκει. ⁴⁴τότε λέγει, Εἰς τὸν οἶκόν μου ἐπιστρέψω ὅθεν ἐξῆλθον· καὶ ἐλθὸν εὑρίσκει σχολάζοντα σεσαρωμένον καὶ κεκοσμημένον. ⁴⁵τότε πορεύεται καὶ παραλαμβάνει μεθ' ἑαυτοῦ ἑπτὰ ἕτερα πνεύματα πονηρότερα ἑαυτοῦ καὶ εἰσελθόντα κατοικεῖ ἐκεῖ· καὶ γίνεται τὰ ἔσχατα τοῦ ἀνθρώπου ἐκείνου χείρονα τῶν πρώτων. οὕτως ἔσται καὶ τῇ γενεᾷ ταύτῃ τῇ πονηρᾷ.

• **12:38–45** These two sections are not found in Mark. They come from Q (see Luke 11:24–32).

• **12:38** *some of the scholars and Pharisees:* See on 5:20. Our author adds this. In Luke 11:29 (and so in Q?) Jesus speaks simply of "this generation" that "insists on a sign."

a sign from you: Evidently some proof, very likely a miracle, that would demonstrate Jesus' authority to speak and act as he does (that is, as the Anointed) by showing that God was behind it. Parallel versions of this saying (16:1, and Mark 8:11) indicate that "a sign from heaven" is expected. A sign *from you* is evidently the same.

• **12:39** *An evil and immoral generation:* The verse seems to castigate all of Jesus' contemporaries. As it probably does in Q (see on vs 38). Or is it a kind of exaggeration, since in Matthew it applies most clearly to the "scholars and Pharisees"?

and no sign will be given . . . except the sign of Jonah: In perhaps the earliest form of this saying (Mark 8:12), no exception is offered: "No sign will be given this generation"—period. Perhaps the Jonah clause was added after Jesus' time to soften his refusal. But *the sign of Jonah* is of course not of the sort called for. Two possible meanings are spelled out, one each in vss 40–41.

• **12:40** *just as Jonah was in the belly . . .:* This tale from the Hebrew Scriptures (Jonah 1) is not exactly a sign that God accomplished. Technically, in the Christian interpretation here, it's a "type." It is taken to foreshadow what God will do to Jesus, bringing about his death and burial. That, of course, will be a sign, when it occurs.

bowels: Greek: "heart," that is, the interior. This translation makes clear a correspon-

to account for every thoughtless word they utter. ³⁷Your own words will vindicate you, and your own words will condemn you."

³⁸Then some of the scholars and Pharisees responded to him, "Teacher, we would like to see a sign from you."

³⁹In response he said to them,

> An evil and immoral generation insists on a sign, and no sign will be given it, except the sign of Jonah the prophet. ⁴⁰For just as 'Jonah was in the belly of a sea monster for three days and three nights,' so the son of Adam will be in the bowels of the earth for three days and three nights. ⁴¹At judgment time, the citizens of Nineveh will come back to life along with this generation and condemn it, because they had a change of heart in response to Jonah's message. Yet take note: what is right here is greater than Jonah.

> ⁴²"At judgment time, the queen of the south will be brought back to life along with this generation, and she will condemn it, because she came from the ends of the earth to listen to Solomon's wisdom. Yet take note: what is right here is greater than Solomon.

> ⁴³When an unclean spirit leaves a person, it wanders through waterless places in search of a resting place. When it doesn't find one, ⁴⁴it then says, 'I will return to the home I left.' It then returns and finds it empty, swept, and refurbished. ⁴⁵Next, it goes out and brings back with it seven other spirits more vile than itself, who enter and settle in there. So that person ends up worse off than when he or she started. That's how it will be for this perverse generation."

---

dence with the sea monster's *belly.*

three days: See below on 27:63.

• **12:41** Another reference to Jonah—this time to Jonah 4.

At judgment time . . .: The end of the age, when all humans will be raised from the dead, both the good (in this case *the citizens of Nineveh*—capital of ancient Assyria, conqueror of Israel—whom Jonah refused to preach to but who nevertheless *had a change of heart*) and the bad (*this generation*).

condemn it: By comparison with the Ninevites, Jesus' contemporaries will be found guilty. Here again Jonah's story is not a sign. Rather, a warning.

change of heart: See on 3:8.

what is right here is greater: Evidently the inbreaking of God's empire. Also in the next verse. That is the sign that was asked for, but people can't see it.

• **12:42** A reference to the story in 1 Kgs 10:1–13 and 2 Chr 9:1–12.

• **12:43–45** In Luke 11:24–26, and probably in Q, this passage precedes the Request for a Sign. If so, why does the evangelist invert the order? In any case he makes a connection by adding "this generation" at the end of vs 45 as a catchword. It was evidently lacking in Q.

• **12:43** *When an unclean spirit leaves a person:* Having been exorcised, as for example Jesus did in healing the blind and mute person (12:22).

it wanders through waterless places in search of a resting place: Part of the ancient mythology of demons.

• **12:44** *home:* An "unclean spirit" needs to dwell within a person to do its work.

• **12:45d** *That's how it will be for this perverse generation:* Not found in the Lukan parallel

**True
relatives**

⁴⁶Ἔτι αὐτοῦ λαλοῦντος τοῖς ὄχλοις ἰδοὺ ἡ μήτηρ καὶ οἱ ἀδελφοὶ
αὐτοῦ εἱστήκεισαν ἔξω ζητοῦντες αὐτῷ λαλῆσαι. ⁴⁷εἶπεν δέ τις αὐτῷ,
Ἰδοὺ ἡ μήτηρ σου καὶ οἱ ἀδελφοί σου ἔξω ἑστήκασιν ζητοῦντές σοι
λαλῆσαι.

⁴⁸Ὁ δὲ ἀποκριθεὶς εἶπεν τῷ λέγοντι αὐτῷ, Τίς ἐστιν ἡ μήτηρ μου
καὶ τίνες εἰσὶν οἱ ἀδελφοί μου; ⁴⁹καὶ ἐκτείνας τὴν χεῖρα αὐτοῦ ἐπὶ
τοὺς μαθητὰς αὐτοῦ εἶπεν, Ἰδοὺ ἡ μήτηρ μου καὶ οἱ ἀδελφοί μου.
⁵⁰ὅστις γὰρ ἂν ποιήσῃ τὸ θέλημα τοῦ πατρός μου τοῦ ἐν οὐρανοῖς
αὐτός μου ἀδελφὸς καὶ ἀδελφὴ καὶ μήτηρ ἐστίν.

12:47 Many MSS omit this verse. In the Greek it ends with the same word as
vs 46 (*to speak*). Perhaps a scribe, looking away and then back again at the MS
he was copying, slipped accidentally from vs 46 to vs 48. Any later scribes
copying from a MS with that omission would of course reproduce it. The
resulting error is called haplography, literally, writing half of what's there—
in this case one verse instead of two. But just possibly a scribe, believing that
Jesus would know supernaturally that his relatives were seeking him and
thus not need to be told, deliberately omitted the verse as superfluous.

(11:26). How does the vivid image of the unclean spirit in the preceding verses parallel
the situation of "this generation"?
- **12:46–50** Found in Mark 3:31–35 and Luke
8:19–21, without major change here.
- **12:46** *his mother and brothers . . . had come to
speak to him:* Mark, at 3:21, says that his relatives came to get him because they thought
he was out of his mind. Why has our author
omitted this? (See comment on 12:22.)

   showed up outside: Outside what? Perhaps
the place where he had healed the blind
mute (in 12:22), that is, if the evangelist

intends to present an on-going itinerary for
Jesus. But we weren't told where that healing took place.
- **12:48** *who ever are they?* They are not truly
his "mother and brothers," as the chapter's
concluding verses explain.
- **12:49–50** The Jesus movement functioned
as a new kind of family.
- **12:50** *the will of my Father:* As Jesus has conveyed it, for example, in his first discourse
(chaps. 5–7, the "Sermon on the Mount").

⁴⁶While he was still speaking to the crowds, his mother and brothers showed up outside; they had come to speak to him. ⁴⁷Someone said to him, "Look, your mother and your brothers are outside wanting to speak to you."

⁴⁸In response he said to the one speaking to him, "My mother and my brothers—who ever are they?" ⁴⁹And he pointed to his disciples and said, "Here are my mother and my brothers. ⁵⁰For whoever does the will of my Father in heaven, that's my brother and sister and mother."

True relatives

The third discourse

13 Ἐν τῇ ἡμέρᾳ ἐκείνῃ ἐξελθὼν ὁ Ἰησοῦς τῆς οἰκίας ἐκάθητο παρὰ τὴν θάλασσαν· ²καὶ συνήχθησαν πρὸς αὐτὸν ὄχλοι πολλοί, ὥστε αὐτὸν εἰς πλοῖον ἐμβάντα καθῆσθαι, καὶ πᾶς ὁ ὄχλος ἐπὶ τὸν αἰγιαλὸν εἱστήκει. ³καὶ ἐλάλησεν αὐτοῖς πολλὰ ἐν παραβολαῖς λέγων,

Sower, seeds, soils

Ἰδοὺ ἐξῆλθεν ὁ σπείρων τοῦ σπείρειν. ⁴καὶ ἐν τῷ σπείρειν αὐτὸν ἃ μὲν ἔπεσεν παρὰ τὴν ὁδόν, καὶ ἐλθόντα τὰ πετεινὰ κατέφαγεν αὐτά. ⁵ἄλλα δὲ ἔπεσεν ἐπὶ τὰ πετρώδη ὅπου οὐκ εἶχεν γῆν πολλήν, καὶ εὐθέως ἐξανέτειλεν διὰ τὸ μὴ ἔχειν βάθος γῆς· ⁶ἡλίου δὲ ἀνατείλαντος ἐκαυματίσθη καὶ διὰ τὸ μὴ ἔχειν ῥίζαν ἐξηράνθη. ⁷ἄλλα δὲ ἔπεσεν ἐπὶ τὰς ἀκάνθας, καὶ ἀνέβησαν αἱ ἄκανθαι καὶ ἔπνιξαν αὐτά. ⁸ἄλλα δὲ ἔπεσεν ἐπὶ τὴν γῆν τὴν καλὴν καὶ ἐδίδου καρπόν, ὃ μὲν ἑκατόν, ὃ δὲ ἑξήκοντα, ὃ δὲ τριάκοντα.

⁹ὉΟ ἔχων ὦτα ἀκουέτω.

Why parables

¹⁰Καὶ προσελθόντες οἱ μαθηταὶ εἶπαν αὐτῷ, Διὰ τί ἐν παραβολαῖς λαλεῖς αὐτοῖς;

¹¹Ὁ δὲ ἀποκριθεὶς εἶπεν, Ὅτι ὑμῖν δέδοται γνῶναι τὰ μυστήρια τῆς βασιλείας τῶν οὐρανῶν, ἐκείνοις δὲ οὐ δέδοται. ¹²ὅστις γὰρ ἔχει, δοθήσεται αὐτῷ καὶ περισσευθήσεται· ὅστις δὲ οὐκ ἔχει, καὶ ὃ ἔχει ἀρθήσεται ἀπ' αὐτοῦ. ¹³διὰ τοῦτο ἐν παραβολαῖς αὐτοῖς λαλῶ, ὅτι βλέποντες οὐ βλέπουσιν καὶ ἀκούοντες οὐκ ἀκούουσιν οὐδὲ συνίουσιν, ¹⁴καὶ ἀναπληροῦται αὐτοῖς ἡ προφητεία Ἠσαΐου ἡ λέγουσα,

---

• **13:1** *the house:* In Mark 3:20 Jesus "goes home," but our author lacks that. See on 12:46.

• **13:2** *sat down:* To teach, as in 5:1. This sets the stage for the third of the five discourses into which the evangelist has gathered much of Jesus' teaching. It runs to vs 53 and consists of many of Jesus' parables.

• **13:3a** *many things:* In Mark 4 a number of parables follow. Our author uses them here and introduces others, the sabotage of weeds (vss 24–30) and four very brief ones (vss 33, 44–50). Six other parables, all of them of greater length, are saved for Jesus' teaching in Judea (chaps. 20–25).

in parables: That is, by telling a story—not for its own sake but to suggest something else that is at most hinted at in the story, usually about God's empire.

• **13:3b** *This sower:* Literally, "A sower," but since the absence of the article stresses his function, "this sower" is a felicitous rendering.

• **13:4** *along the path:* Probably the field's boundary.

• **13:8** *some<times> a hundredfold...sixty... thirty:* This could refer either to different parts of the field, or to different years (an extraordinary one, a normal one, and a poor one). In every case, however, even the third, the result is astounding. Is it significant that our evangelist has reversed the order of yield in Mark 4:8, which reads "thirty... sixty... a hundred"?

• **13:9** See comment on 11:15.

• **13:10–17** Supposedly Jesus is giving a public discourse. But since it is a construct of the evangelist, using traditional material, this interruption should not surprise us.

Once removed in time and place from Jesus' original situation (spoken to agrarian Galilean peasants, suffering under Rome's heavy occupation and Jerusalem's taxation), some of the parables would have become baffling and would need to be explained, as below in vss 18–23 (sower) and 37–43

13 That same day, Jesus left the house and sat beside the sea. [2]Huge crowds gathered around him, so he climbed into a boat and sat down, while the entire crowd stood on the seashore. [3]He told them many things in parables:

The third discourse

    This sower went out to sow. [4]While he was sowing, some <seed> fell along the path, and the birds came and ate it up. [5]Other seed fell on rocky ground where there wasn't much soil, and it came up right away because the soil had no depth. [6]When the sun came up it was scorched, and because it had no roots it withered. [7]Still others fell among thorns, and the thorns came up and choked it. [8]Other seed fell on good earth and started producing fruit, some<times> a hundredfold, some<times> sixty, and some<times> thirty.

Sower, seeds, soils

[9]"Anyone here with two ears had better listen!"

[10]And his disciples came up and said to him, "Why do you instruct them in parables?"

Why parables

[11]In response he said, "You have been given <the privilege of> knowing the secrets of Heaven's imperial rule, but it has not been granted to anyone else. [12]In fact, to those who have, more will be given, and then some; and from those who don't have, even what they do have will be taken away! [13]This is why I tell them parables: Because 'when they look they don't really see and when they listen they don't really hear or understand.' [14]In them the prophecy of Isaiah comes true, the one that says,

---

(weeds). Later the idea arose that they had been told only for the benefit of an in-group, and this was seen as a fulfillment of a *prophecy of Isaiah* (vss 13–15).

- **13:10** *them:* The crowds of vss 2–3.
- **13:11** *you have been given <the privilege of> knowing:* Greek, "to you it has been given to know."

    secrets: Greek, *mystêria*. A late, not original, understanding of the nature of parables.

    to anyone else: "To those people." This has sometimes been understood to mean the Jews, as opposed to Christians who can understand. But however critical of Jewish leadership, our author is not anti-Jewish. The phrase includes all, Jew or Gentile, who don't hear the church's proclamation of good news, as the allegorical interpretation of the sower parable, just below, will show.

- **13:12** An independent saying, found at Mark 4:25, used also at Matt 25:29. It's inserted here into the text of Mark 4:10–12. What does it mean in this context? That

only to those "with two good ears" (vs 9) will *more . . . be given?*

- **13:13** *When they look they don't really see . . .:* A Hebrew idiom here, from Isa 6:9, Jer 5:21; literally, "When they see they don't see and when they hear they don't hear."

    This is a significant change from Mark 4:12, where Jesus says he tells parables "so that [people] may look . . . but never . . . see, . . . otherwise they might turn around and find forgiveness!" That fairly accurately reproduces the sarcasm and bitterness of Isa 6:9, 10e. Our author, however, eases the wording of Mark's quotation, and does not treat it as a quotation. For him parables are not told in order to keep people from understanding, but in fact they won't understand. They are secrets conveyed to the disciples.

- **13:14–15** The evangelist now quotes the whole of Isa 6:9–10, using LXX (unlike Mark). Davies & Allison (II, 393–4) omit these verses as an early gloss, copied from Acts 28:26–27;

Ἀκοῇ ἀκούσετε καὶ οὐ μὴ συνῆτε,
καὶ βλέποντες βλέψετε καὶ οὐ μὴ ἴδητε.
¹⁵ἐπαχύνθη γὰρ ἡ καρδία τοῦ λαοῦ τούτου,
καὶ τοῖς ὠσὶν βαρέως ἤκουσαν
καὶ τοὺς ὀφθαλμοὺς αὐτῶν ἐκάμμυσαν,
μήποτε ἴδωσιν τοῖς ὀφθαλμοῖς
καὶ τοῖς ὠσὶν ἀκούσωσιν
καὶ τῇ καρδίᾳ συνῶσιν καὶ ἐπιστρέψωσιν
καὶ ἰάσομαι αὐτούς.

¹⁶Ὑμῶν δὲ μακάριοι οἱ ὀφθαλμοὶ ὅτι βλέπουσιν καὶ τὰ ὦτα ὑμῶν ὅτι ἀκούουσιν. ¹⁷ἀμὴν γὰρ λέγω ὑμῖν ὅτι πολλοὶ προφῆται καὶ δίκαιοι ἐπεθύμησαν ἰδεῖν ἃ βλέπετε καὶ οὐκ εἶδαν, καὶ ἀκοῦσαι ἃ ἀκούετε καὶ οὐκ ἤκουσαν.

Understanding the sower

¹⁸Ὑμεῖς οὖν ἀκούσατε τὴν παραβολὴν τοῦ σπείραντος.

¹⁹Παντὸς ἀκούοντος τὸν λόγον τῆς βασιλείας καὶ μὴ συνιέντος ἔρχεται ὁ πονηρὸς καὶ ἁρπάζει τὸ ἐσπαρμένον ἐν τῇ καρδίᾳ αὐτοῦ, οὗτός ἐστιν ὁ παρὰ τὴν ὁδὸν σπαρείς. ²⁰ὁ δὲ ἐπὶ τὰ πετρώδη σπαρείς, οὗτός ἐστιν ὁ τὸν λόγον ἀκούων καὶ εὐθὺς μετὰ χαρᾶς λαμβάνων αὐτόν, ²¹οὐκ ἔχει δὲ ῥίζαν ἐν ἑαυτῷ ἀλλὰ πρόσκαιρός ἐστιν, γενομένης δὲ θλίψεως ἢ διωγμοῦ διὰ τὸν λόγον εὐθὺς σκανδαλίζεται. ²²ὁ δὲ εἰς τὰς ἀκάνθας σπαρείς, οὗτός ἐστιν ὁ τὸν λόγον ἀκούων, καὶ ἡ μέριμνα τοῦ αἰῶνος καὶ ἡ ἀπάτη τοῦ πλούτου συμπνίγει τὸν λόγον καὶ ἄκαρπος γίνεται. ²³ὁ δὲ ἐπὶ τὴν καλὴν γῆν σπαρείς, οὗτός ἐστιν

---

but, as they acknowledge, there is no text-critical basis for this. Yet this is the only place in Matthew where Jesus himself seems to cite fulfilled prophecy. Therefore it makes the most sense to regard these verses not as original, but the evangelist's parenthesis, interrupting Jesus' speech. The quotation parallels some of the language of vs 13 more closely than the reader may readily recognize.
- **13:14** *the prophecy of Isaiah comes true:* An unusual way of citing prophecy in Matthew—see Introduction, p. 19, on prophecy fulfillment.
- **13:15** *mind:* Greek: "heart."
  this people: See above on *anyone else* in vs 11.
  otherwise . . . they might turn around and I would heal them: The hope is that this will happen, in contrast to Mark's form of the end of Isa 6:10, where parables are used to

prevent this. The author is not very confident of this (see the comment on vs 13) but can still hope for it.
  the mind . . . has grown dull: Greek, "the heart has gotten fat."
- **13:16–17** The author adds this from Q (Luke 10:23–24). It reasserts the good fortune of the disciples (vs 11).
- **13:16** Resuming Jesus' words after the author's parenthesis, this—in his rewriting of Q—contrasts the disciples' eyes that in fact *see* and their ears that *hear* with the eyes and ears of those to whom Jesus speaks only in parables (vs 13).
- **13:17** *righteous ones:* Luke has "kings." Probably our evangelist has made the change; the same phrase appears also at 23:29 (but not in the otherwise parallel Luke 11:47).
- **13:18–23** One of two explanations of a parable; the other is of the sabotage of weeds

You listen closely, yet you won't ever understand,
and you look intently but won't ever see.
[15]For the mind of this people has grown dull,
and their ears are hard of hearing,
and they have shut their eyes;
otherwise they might actually see with their eyes,
and hear with their ears,
and understand with their minds and turn around
and I would heal them.

[16]"How privileged are your eyes because they see, and your ears because they hear.[17]I swear to you, many prophets and righteous ones have longed to see what you see and didn't see it, and to hear what you hear and didn't hear it.

[18]"So you especially should pay attention to <the interpretation of> the sower.

Understanding the sower

[19]"When anyone listens to the message of <Heaven's> imperial rule and does not understand it, the evil one comes and steals away what was sown in the heart: this is the one who is sown 'along the path.' [20]The one who is sown 'on rocky ground' is the one who listens to the message and right away receives it happily. [21]However, this one lacks its own 'root' and so is short-lived. When distress or persecution comes because of the message, such a person becomes easily shaken. [22]And the one sown 'among thorns' is the one who listens to the message, but the worries of the age and the seductiveness of wealth 'choke' the message and it becomes fruitless. [23]The one who is sown 'on good earth' is the one who

---

(vss 37–43 below). These explanations treat the parables as allegories, applying them to the church's situation in the late first century as if they were hidden messages needing to be decoded. Here the parable is taken to illustrate the varied and mostly negative responses to the church's proclamation of *the message*. Some others, too, have been allegorized by our author or someone earlier in the transmission of the Jesus tradition. See for example, the leased vineyard (21:33–46) and the entrusted money (25:14–30). In fact, however, Jesus' parables were not allegories.
• **13:18** *So you especially should:* In Greek simply "You, therefore, . . ." *—you* is emphasized.
pay attention to <the interpretation of> the parable: The Greek is more blunt, "Hear the parable" . . . as if for the first time, since it would have made little sense without this *interpretation*.

• **13:19** *the evil one comes . . . :* Logically this should be "it is because the evil one has come. . . ."
heart: Here, perhaps the seat of the will.
this is the one who is sown: The seed is personified since in this interpretation it stands for those who hear "the message."
• **13:21** *persecution comes because of the message:* So far as we know, not a widespread experience of Christians earlier than the late first century.
becomes easily shaken: Or "quickly falls away." The Greek *skandalizō* derives from "stumbling block."
• **13:23** *here a hundred, there sixty, and there thirty:* Proclaiming the good news brings the church much adversity, but in the end it yields a prodigious harvest.

ὁ τὸν λόγον ἀκούων καὶ συνιείς, ὃς δὴ καρποφορεῖ καὶ ποιεῖ ὃ μὲν
ἑκατόν, ὃ δὲ ἑξήκοντα, ὃ δὲ τριάκοντα.

Sabotage
of weeds

²⁴Ἄλλην παραβολὴν παρέθηκεν αὐτοῖς λέγων,

Ὡμοιώθη ἡ βασιλεία τῶν οὐρανῶν ἀνθρώπῳ σπείραντι
καλὸν σπέρμα ἐν τῷ ἀγρῷ αὐτοῦ. ²⁵ἐν δὲ τῷ καθεύδειν τοὺς
ἀνθρώπους ἦλθεν αὐτοῦ ὁ ἐχθρὸς καὶ ἐπέσπειρεν ζιζάνια ἀνὰ
μέσον τοῦ σίτου καὶ ἀπῆλθεν. ²⁶ὅτε δὲ ἐβλάστησεν ὁ χόρτος καὶ
καρπὸν ἐποίησεν, τότε ἐφάνη καὶ τὰ ζιζάνια. ²⁷προσελθόντες
δὲ οἱ δοῦλοι τοῦ οἰκοδεσπότου εἶπον αὐτῷ, Κύριε, οὐχὶ καλὸν
σπέρμα ἔσπειρας ἐν τῷ σῷ ἀγρῷ; πόθεν οὖν ἔχει ζιζάνια; ²⁸ὁ δὲ
ἔφη αὐτοῖς, Ἐχθρὸς ἄνθρωπος τοῦτο ἐποίησεν. οἱ δὲ δοῦλοι
λέγουσιν αὐτῷ, Θέλεις οὖν ἀπελθόντες συλλέξωμεν αὐτά;
²⁹ὁ δέ φησιν, Οὔ, μήποτε συλλέγοντες τὰ ζιζάνια ἐκριζώσητε
ἅμα αὐτοῖς τὸν σῖτον. ³⁰ἄφετε συναυξάνεσθαι ἀμφότερα ἕως
τοῦ θερισμοῦ, καὶ ἐν καιρῷ τοῦ θερισμοῦ ἐρῶ τοῖς θερισταῖς,
Συλλέξατε πρῶτον τὰ ζιζάνια καὶ δήσατε αὐτὰ εἰς δέσμας πρὸς
τὸ κατακαῦσαι αὐτά, τὸν δὲ σῖτον συναγάγετε εἰς τὴν ἀποθήκην
μου.

Mustard
seed & leaven

³¹Ἄλλην παραβολὴν παρέθηκεν αὐτοῖς λέγων,

Ὁμοία ἐστὶν ἡ βασιλεία τῶν οὐρανῶν κόκκῳ σινάπεως, ὃν
λαβὼν ἄνθρωπος ἔσπειρεν ἐν τῷ ἀγρῷ αὐτοῦ· ³²ὃ μικρότερον
μέν ἐστιν πάντων τῶν σπερμάτων, ὅταν δὲ αὐξηθῇ μεῖζον τῶν
λαχάνων ἐστὶν καὶ γίνεται δένδρον, ὥστε ἐλθεῖν τὰ πετεινὰ τοῦ
οὐρανοῦ καὶ κατασκηνοῦν ἐν τοῖς κλάδοις αὐτοῦ.

³³Ἄλλην παραβολὴν ἐλάλησεν αὐτοῖς·

Ὁμοία ἐστὶν ἡ βασιλεία τῶν οὐρανῶν ζύμη, ἣν λαβοῦσα γυνὴ
ἐνέκρυψεν εἰς ἀλεύρου σάτα τρία ἕως οὗ ἐζυμώθη ὅλον.

• **13:24–30** Another agricultural parable. (It
takes the place of Mark 4:26–29, a parable
about seed growing in secret, which Luke
also lacks.) Its allegorical interpretation is in
vss 37–43.

Another version of the story also in Thom
57:

The Father's imperial rule is like a person
who had [good] seed. ²His enemy came
during the night and sowed weeds among
the good seed. ³The person did not let the
workers pull up the weeds, but said to
them, "No, otherwise you might go to pull
up the weeds and pull up the wheat along

with them." ⁴For on the day of the harvest
the weeds will be conspicuous, and will be
pulled up and burned.
• **13:24** spun out . . . for them: A nice way of
rendering "put before them" (as in vs 31).
them: The crowds again; see vs 34.
the empire of God is like: Some of the parables
have to do explicitly with God's kingdom.
• **13:30** Gather the weeds first: How? Jesus'
original hearers would have understood.
• **13:31–32** The parable of the mustard seed
is found at Mark 4:30–32 and, in a different
context, in Luke 13:18–19. In the Gospel of
Thom 20, there is a briefer version:

listens to the message and understands it, and who then 'produces fruit and yields here a hundred, there sixty, and there thirty.' "

²⁴He spun out another parable for them:

Heaven's imperial rule is like someone who sowed good seed in his field. ²⁵And while everyone was asleep, his enemy came and scattered weed seed around in his wheat and stole away. ²⁶And when the crop sprouted and produced heads, then the weeds also appeared. ²⁷The owner's slaves came and asked him, "Master, didn't you sow good seed in your field? Then why are there weeds <everywhere>?" ²⁸He replied to them, "Some enemy has done this." The slaves said to him, "Do you want us then to go and pull <the weeds>?" ²⁹He replied, "No, otherwise you'll root out the wheat at the same time as you pull the weeds. ³⁰Let them grow up together until the harvest, and at harvest time I'll say to the harvesters, 'Gather the weeds first and bind them in bundles to burn, but gather the wheat into my granary.'

³¹He put another parable before them with these words:

Heaven's imperial rule is like a mustard seed that a man took and sowed in his field. ³²Though it is the smallest of all seeds, yet when it has grown up it is the largest of garden plants and becomes a tree, so that the birds of the sky come and roost in its branches.

³³He told them another parable:

Heaven's imperial rule is like leaven that a woman took and concealed in fifty pounds of flour until it was all leavened.

[God's imperial rule] is like a mustard seed. <It's> the smallest of all seeds, but when it falls on prepared soil, it produces a <plant with> large branch<es> and becomes a shelter for the birds of the sky.

• **13:31** *the empire of Heaven is like:* See on vs 24.

• **13:32** *becomes a tree:* This is a considerable exaggeration.

• **13:33** For the parable of leaven the evangelist turns to Q (Luke 13:20–21). It is barely complete. A fuller version is in Thom 96:

The Father's imperial rule is like a woman who took a little leaven, [hid] it

in dough, and made it into large loaves of bread. Anyone here with two good ears had better listen!

leaven: In Jewish eyes, yeast was a symbol of uncleanness.

fifty pounds: Greek, three measures. Enough to make bread for perhaps a hundred people! If the version in Thomas is more original, our author or someone before him has introduced this detail. On the other hand, it may be original, typical of Jesus' use of exaggeration, and dropped out of the Thomas tradition as puzzling or superfluous.

³⁴Ταῦτα πάντα ἐλάλησεν ὁ Ἰησοῦς ἐν παραβολαῖς τοῖς ὄχλοις καὶ χωρὶς παραβολῆς οὐδὲν ἐλάλει αὐτοῖς, ³⁵ὅπως πληρωθῇ τὸ ῥηθὲν διὰ τοῦ προφήτου λέγοντος,

Ἀνοίξω ἐν παραβολαῖς τὸ στόμα μου,
ἐρεύξομαι κεκρυμμένα ἀπὸ καταβολῆς κόσμου.

³⁶Τότε ἀφεὶς τοὺς ὄχλους ἦλθεν εἰς τὴν οἰκίαν. καὶ προσῆλθον αὐτῷ οἱ μαθηταὶ αὐτοῦ λέγοντες, Διασάφησον ἡμῖν τὴν παραβολὴν τῶν ζιζανίων τοῦ ἀγροῦ.

Understanding the sabotage of weeds

³⁷Ὁ δὲ ἀποκριθεὶς εἶπεν, Ὁ σπείρων τὸ καλὸν σπέρμα ἐστὶν ὁ υἱὸς τοῦ ἀνθρώπου, ³⁸ὁ δὲ ἀγρός ἐστιν ὁ κόσμος, τὸ δὲ καλὸν σπέρμα οὗτοί εἰσιν οἱ υἱοὶ τῆς βασιλείας· τὰ δὲ ζιζάνιά εἰσιν οἱ υἱοὶ τοῦ πονηροῦ, ³⁹ὁ δὲ ἐχθρὸς ὁ σπείρας αὐτά ἐστιν ὁ διάβολος, ὁ δὲ θερισμὸς συντέλεια αἰῶνός ἐστιν, οἱ δὲ θερισταὶ ἄγγελοί εἰσιν. ⁴⁰ὥσπερ οὖν συλλέγεται τὰ ζιζάνια καὶ πυρὶ καίεται, οὕτως ἔσται ἐν τῇ συντελείᾳ τοῦ αἰῶνος· ⁴¹ἀποστελεῖ ὁ υἱὸς τοῦ ἀνθρώπου τοὺς ἀγγέλους αὐτοῦ, καὶ συλλέξουσιν ἐκ τῆς βασιλείας αὐτοῦ πάντα τὰ σκάνδαλα καὶ τοὺς ποιοῦντας τὴν ἀνομίαν ⁴²καὶ βαλοῦσιν αὐτοὺς εἰς τὴν κάμινον τοῦ πυρός· ἐκεῖ ἔσται ὁ κλαυθμὸς καὶ ὁ βρυγμὸς τῶν ὀδόντων. ⁴³Τότε οἱ δίκαιοι ἐκλάμψουσιν ὡς ὁ ἥλιος ἐν τῇ βασιλείᾳ τοῦ πατρὸς αὐτῶν. ὁ ἔχων ὦτα ἀκουέτω.

More parables

⁴⁴Ὁμοία ἐστὶν ἡ βασιλεία τῶν οὐρανῶν θησαυρῷ κεκρυμμένῳ ἐν τῷ ἀγρῷ, ὃν εὑρὼν ἄνθρωπος ἔκρυψεν, καὶ ἀπὸ τῆς χαρᾶς αὐτοῦ ὑπάγει καὶ πωλεῖ πάντα ὅσα ἔχει καὶ ἀγοράζει τὸν ἀγρὸν ἐκεῖνον.

13:35 *through the prophet*: A few mss read "through the prophet Isaiah." That is curious, since the quotation is Psalm 78:2–3. Could it therefore be original, as the "more difficult reading"? If so it is like the famous slip in Mark 1: 2–3, corrected in Matt 3:3 by the evangelist's omission but here by that of by a later scribe. In a number of mss *of the world* is lacking. Was that reading original and the phrase later added from 25:34? The meaning is the same.

• **13:34** *he would not say anything to them except by way of parable*: Not strictly true, of course.

• **13:35** Once the parables were understood as allegorical secrets hidden from hearers it was necessary to try to explain why Jesus would have taught in this way. So once again, as in vss 14–15 above, an OT prophecy is cited by way of explanation,

what was spoken . . . <came> true: The formula of 1:22, frequent in Matthew, but not meaning that this was Jesus' purpose.

the prophet: In this case quoting not a prophet—esp. not *Isaiah*, as the text may have read here (see the Text-Critical Note), but instead Ps 78:2.

• **13:36** Uniquely, this third discourse falls into two halves, the first spoken mainly (though not entirely) to the crowds, the second to the disciples alone. Some scholars see this as a turning point in the gospel, coming not so far from its center. But while the teaching from this point on is often directed only to the disciples, that is not always the case (see for example 15:10, 22:33). And the second discourse (chap. 10) was not a public one.

went into the house: The house of 13:1?

• **13:37–43** Compared with the interpretation of the sower parable (vss 18–23 above), there is even greater difference here between the

³⁴Jesus spoke all these things to the crowds in parables. And he would not say anything to them except by way of parable; ³⁵<in this way> what was spoken through the prophet <came> true:

I will open my mouth in parables,
I will utter matters kept secret
    since the foundation of the world.

³⁶Then he left the crowds and went into the house. His disciples came to him with this request: "Explain the parable of the weeds in the field to us."

³⁷This was his response: "The one who 'sows the good seed' is the son of Adam; ³⁸'the field' is the world; and 'the good seed' are those to whom <Heaven's> domain belongs, but 'the weeds' represent progeny of the evil one. ³⁹'The enemy' who sows <the weeds> is the devil, and 'the harvest' is the end of the present age; 'the harvesters' are the heavenly messengers. ⁴⁰Just as the weeds are gathered and destroyed by fire—that's how it will be at the end of the age. ⁴¹The son of Adam will send his messengers and they will gather all <those who set> snares and those who subvert the Law out of his domain ⁴²and throw them into the fiery furnace. People in that place will weep and grind their teeth. ⁴³Then those who are vindicated will be radiant like the sun in my Father's domain. Anyone here with two ears had better listen!

Understanding the sabotage of weeds

⁴⁴Heaven's imperial rule is like treasure hidden in a field: When someone finds it, that person covers it up again, and out of sheer joy goes and sells every last possession and buys that field.

More parables

---

allegorical explanation of the sabotage of weeds and the plain meaning of this story. The field is *the world*, but more specifically the church (*those to whom Heaven's domain belongs*). For the time being it is mixed, plagued with the presence among the faithful of *snares and the perverters of the Law*. But the assumed time frame is not so much the present life of the church as *the end of the present age*; and the chief actors are *the son of Adam*, with his *heavenly messengers*, and *the evil one, the devil*, with his *progeny*.

• **13:38** *those to whom <Heaven's> domain belongs:* Usually translated "the sons of the Kingdom." SV properly understands this Hebrew idiom and avoids using the non-inclusive "sons."

• **13:41** *snares:* Stumbling blocks, obstacles.
  those who subvert the Law: Literally, "those who practice lawlessness." See above on

7:23.

• **13:42** *the fiery furnace:* That is, Hell, where they will *weep and grind their teeth*. So it is not like the furnace of fire that Daniel and his three friends survived, for that was not punishment but test (Dan 3:19–30).

• **13:43** *those who are vindicated:* The "righteous" in most versions, but a more than ethical meaning is correct—those who are justified (*hoi dikaioi*) and are rewarded with the *Father's domain*.
  [they will be] radiant like the sun: Like those in Dan 12:3 who will be raised to everlasting life.
  Any one here . . .: See on 11:15.

• **13:44–52** These three brief sayings are unique to Matthew in the NT. They are similar in form to the stories that precede, but are not so much parables as similes.

⁴⁵Πάλιν ὁμοία ἐστὶν ἡ βασιλεία τῶν οὐρανῶν ἀνθρώπῳ ἐμπόρῳ ζητοῦντι καλοὺς μαργαρίτας· ⁴⁶εὑρὼν δὲ ἕνα πολύτιμον μαργαρίτην ἀπελθὼν πέπρακεν πάντα ὅσα εἶχεν καὶ ἠγόρασεν αὐτόν.

⁴⁷Πάλιν ὁμοία ἐστὶν ἡ βασιλεία τῶν οὐρανῶν σαγήνῃ βληθείσῃ εἰς τὴν θάλασσαν καὶ ἐκ παντὸς γένους συναγαγούσῃ· ⁴⁸ἣν ὅτε ἐπληρώθη ἀναβιβάσαντες ἐπὶ τὸν αἰγιαλὸν καὶ καθίσαντες συνέλεξαν τὰ καλὰ εἰς ἄγγη, τὰ δὲ σαπρὰ ἔξω ἔβαλον. ⁴⁹οὕτως ἔσται ἐν τῇ συντελείᾳ τοῦ αἰῶνος· ἐξελεύσονται οἱ ἄγγελοι καὶ ἀφοριοῦσιν τοὺς πονηροὺς ἐκ μέσου τῶν δικαίων ⁵⁰καὶ βαλοῦσιν αὐτοὺς εἰς τὴν κάμινον τοῦ πυρός· ἐκεῖ ἔσται ὁ κλαυθμὸς καὶ ὁ βρυγμὸς τῶν ὀδόντων.

⁵¹Συνήκατε ταῦτα πάντα;
λέγουσιν αὐτῷ, Ναί.
⁵²Ὁ δὲ εἶπεν αὐτοῖς,

Διὰ τοῦτο πᾶς γραμματεὺς μαθητευθεὶς τῇ βασιλείᾳ τῶν οὐρανῶν ὅμοιός ἐστιν ἀνθρώπῳ οἰκοδεσπότῃ, ὅστις ἐκβάλλει ἐκ τοῦ θησαυροῦ αὐτοῦ καινὰ καὶ παλαιά.

⁵³Καὶ ἐγένετο ὅτε ἐτέλεσεν ὁ Ἰησοῦς τὰς παραβολὰς ταύτας, μετῆρεν ἐκεῖθεν.

No respect at home ⁵⁴Καὶ ἐλθὼν εἰς τὴν πατρίδα αὐτοῦ ἐδίδασκεν αὐτοὺς ἐν τῇ συναγωγῇ αὐτῶν, ὥστε ἐκπλήσσεσθαι αὐτοὺς καὶ λέγειν, Πόθεν τούτῳ ἡ σοφία αὕτη καὶ αἱ δυνάμεις; ⁵⁵οὐχ οὗτός ἐστιν ὁ τοῦ τέκτονος υἱός; οὐχ ἡ μήτηρ αὐτοῦ λέγεται Μαριὰμ καὶ οἱ ἀδελφοὶ αὐτοῦ Ἰάκωβος καὶ Ἰωσὴφ καὶ Σίμων καὶ Ἰούδας; ⁵⁶καὶ αἱ ἀδελφαὶ

• **13:45–46** Compare Thom 76:1–2:
   The Father's imperial rule is like a merchant who had a supply of merchandise and then found a pearl. ²That merchant was prudent; he sold the merchandise and bought the single pearl for himself.
• **13:47–50** Only this third parable of the fishnet has an allegorical explanation, which in this case is attached to the parable itself (vss 49–50).
   Thom 8:1–3 has a similar parable, without allegorization:
   The human one is like a wise fisherman who cast his net into the sea and drew it up from the sea full of little fish. ²Among them the wise fisherman discovered a fine large fish. ³He threw all the little fish

back into the sea, and easily chose the large fish.
• **13:48** *collect the good fish . . .*: Much like the sabotage of weeds (vs 30, just above).
• **13:51b** *Of course:* Is this meant as irony? Someone has called it the funniest line in the NT. Or is the evangelist correcting the impression in Mark that the disciples generally misunderstood Jesus (for example, Mark 8:21)?
• **13:52** This verse has no parallel in other gospels. It is sometimes seen as the author's verbal self-portrait.
   That's why: What is Jesus explaining? What the comprehending disciples (vs 51) are like? Or is this perhaps only the author's way of introducing a saying?

⁴⁵Again, Heaven's imperial rule is like a trader looking for beautiful pearls. ⁴⁶When he finds one priceless pearl, he sells everything he owns and buys it.

⁴⁷Once more: Heaven's imperial rule is like a net that is cast into the sea and catches all kinds of fish. ⁴⁸When the net is full, they haul it ashore. Then they sit down and collect the good fish into baskets, but the worthless fish they throw away. ⁴⁹This is how the present age will end. God's messengers will go out and separate the evil from the righteous ⁵⁰and throw the evil into the fiery furnace. People in that place will weep and grind their teeth.

⁵¹"Do you understand all these things?"

"Of course," they replied.

⁵²He said to them,

That's why every scholar who is schooled in Heaven's imperial rule is like a proprietor who produces from his storeroom treasures old and new.

⁵³And so when Jesus had finished these parables, he moved on from there.

⁵⁴And when he came to his hometown and was teaching them in their synagogue, they were astounded and said so: "What's the source of this wisdom and these miracles? ⁵⁵This is the carpenter's son, isn't it? Isn't his mother called Mary? And aren't his brothers James and Joseph and Simon and Judas? ⁵⁶And aren't all his sisters

No respect at home

---

schooled in the empire of Heaven: Apparently an authority in the Christian traditions and their interpretation, such as this gospel contains.

proprietor: Of a house or an estate.

treasures old and new: What would this mean? Both Jewish and Christian truths?

• **13:53** This ends the third discourse (almost the whole of chap. 13), which includes many of the parables in the gospel. It was began with the gathering of several parables from Mark 4, but was considerably expanded.

when Jesus had finished these parables: The usual formula, as in 7:28 and 11:1.

At this point the evangelist jumps to Mark 6:1. The miracles in Mark 4 and 5 (from 4:35) have already been used in Matthew 8.

• **13:54** *his hometown:* Nazareth. The Greek word (*patris*) can mean "homeland," that is, Galilee. But the reference here to a single synagogue rules that out.

this wisdom and these miracles: A summary of Jesus' public activity of teaching and healing.

• **13:55** *the carpenter's son:* In Mark 6:1–4, the closely parallel story has simply "carpenter." Is the evangelist here seeking to dignify Jesus' standing and avoid the suggestion that he was a mere artisan? A carpenter in Jesus' world had a very low social standing, below that of a peasant because usually not a landowner.

αὐτοῦ οὐχὶ πᾶσαι πρὸς ἡμᾶς εἰσιν; πόθεν οὖν τούτῳ ταῦτα πάντα;
[57]καὶ ἐσκανδαλίζοντο ἐν αὐτῷ. ὁ δὲ Ἰησοῦς εἶπεν αὐτοῖς, Οὐκ ἔστιν
προφήτης ἄτιμος εἰ μὴ ἐν τῇ πατρίδι καὶ ἐν τῇ οἰκίᾳ αὐτοῦ. [58]καὶ οὐκ
ἐποίησεν ἐκεῖ δυνάμεις πολλὰς διὰ τὴν ἀπιστίαν αὐτῶν.

• **13:57** *were resentful of him:* That is, "took offense at him," "were scandalized by him."

No prophet goes without respect . . .: Perhaps a proverb current in Jesus' time. It appears in John 4:44 ("A prophet gets no respect on his own turf") and in Thom 31 ("No prophet is welcome on his home turf").

• **13:58** *he did not perform many miracles:* In Mark 6:5, Jesus was not "able" to perform any miracle.

neighbors of ours? So where did he get all this?" ⁵⁷And they were resentful of him. Jesus said to them, "No prophet goes without respect, except on his home turf and in his household!" ⁵⁸ And he did not perform many miracles there because of their lack of trust.

---

because of their lack of trust: In this gospel, unlike the Gospel of John, Jesus does not work miracles in order to evoke faith. At most they produce wonder. In fact it is almost the reverse; they depend on faith—that is, *trust,* not mere belief—on the part of those affected.

14 Ἐν ἐκείνῳ τῷ καιρῷ ἤκουσεν Ἡρῴδης ὁ τετραάρχης τὴν ἀκοὴν Ἰησοῦ, ²καὶ εἶπεν τοῖς παισὶν αὐτοῦ, Οὗτός ἐστιν Ἰωάννης ὁ βαπτιστής· αὐτὸς ἠγέρθη ἀπὸ τῶν νεκρῶν καὶ διὰ τοῦτο αἱ δυνάμεις ἐνεργοῦσιν ἐν αὐτῷ.

³ Ὁ γὰρ Ἡρῴδης κρατήσας τὸν Ἰωάννην ἔδησεν αὐτὸν καὶ ἐν φυλακῇ ἀπέθετο διὰ Ἡρῳδιάδα τὴν γυναῖκα Φιλίππου τοῦ ἀδελφοῦ αὐτοῦ· ⁴ἔλεγεν γὰρ ὁ Ἰωάννης αὐτῷ, Οὐκ ἔξεστίν σοι ἔχειν αὐτήν.

⁵Καὶ θέλων αὐτὸν ἀποκτεῖναι ἐφοβήθη τὸν ὄχλον, ὅτι ὡς προφήτην αὐτὸν εἶχον. ⁶γενεσίοις δὲ γενομένοις τοῦ Ἡρῴδου ὠρχήσατο ἡ θυγάτηρ τῆς Ἡρῳδιάδος ἐν τῷ μέσῳ καὶ ἤρεσεν τῷ Ἡρῴδῃ, ⁷ὅθεν μεθ' ὅρκου ὡμολόγησεν αὐτῇ δοῦναι ὃ ἐὰν αἰτήσηται.

⁸Ἡ δὲ προβιβασθεῖσα ὑπὸ τῆς μητρὸς αὐτῆς, Δός μοι, φησίν, ὧδε ἐπὶ πίνακι τὴν κεφαλὴν Ἰωάννου τοῦ βαπτιστοῦ.

⁹Καὶ λυπηθεὶς ὁ βασιλεὺς διὰ τοὺς ὅρκους καὶ τοὺς συνανακειμένους ἐκέλευσεν δοθῆναι, ¹⁰καὶ πέμψας ἀπεκεφάλισεν τὸν Ἰωάννην ἐν τῇ φυλακῇ. ¹¹καὶ ἠνέχθη ἡ κεφαλὴ αὐτοῦ ἐπὶ πίνακι καὶ ἐδόθη τῷ κορασίῳ, καὶ ἤνεγκεν τῇ μητρὶ αὐτῆς. ¹²καὶ προσελθόντες οἱ μαθηταὶ αὐτοῦ ἦραν τὸ πτῶμα καὶ ἔθαψαν αὐτόν καὶ ἐλθόντες ἀπήγγειλαν τῷ Ἰησοῦ.

¹³Ἀκούσας δὲ ὁ Ἰησοῦς ἀνεχώρησεν ἐκεῖθεν ἐν πλοίῳ εἰς ἔρημον τόπον κατ' ἰδίαν· καὶ ἀκούσαντες οἱ ὄχλοι ἠκολούθησαν αὐτῷ πεζῇ ἀπὸ τῶν πόλεων. ¹⁴καὶ ἐξελθὼν εἶδεν πολὺν ὄχλον καὶ ἐσπλαγχνίσθη ἐπ' αὐτοῖς καὶ ἐθεράπευσεν τοὺς ἀρρώστους αὐτῶν.

14:12 Some MSS read "buried it [that is, his body]" instead of *buried him* But it obviously makes no difference.

• **14:1–11** After he had killed the Baptist, Herod reacts to reports about Jesus. But the account of John's death has not yet been reported, only alluded to in 4:12. So—as in Mark—the beheading of John must now be told, in a flashback (vss 3–12). It is a slight abbreviation of Mark 6:17–29.

• **14:1** *Herod the tetrarch:* Herod Antipas, son of Herod the Great of chap. 2. Like two other of Herod's sons Antipas inherited part of his father's kingdom, in his case including Galilee. Each was called *Tetrarch* (strictly, "ruler of a fourth [of his father's former kingdom]") under Rome's control. This Herod is the local ruler over the region in which Jesus spent most of his career.

• **14:2** *This is John the Baptizer:* This view of Jesus is reported again in 16:14.

He's been raised from the dead: Ironic, since it will be Jesus who is raised. Or did the followers of John believe that their leader had been raised?

miraculous powers: In Greek *dynameis,* the usual NT word for what we commonly call miracles.

• **14:3** *Herodias:* Antipas had married her. (Why does the author omit that explanatory remark from Mark 6:17?) She was apparently his niece, not *his brother Philip's* [former] *wife.* So under Jewish law he could not have married her, as John had pointed out (vs 4).

• **14:4** *for his part:* The Greek particle *gar,* usually translated "for."

had said to him: Or "used to say"/"kept saying to him." The tense is imperfect.

It is not right: Whether morally or legally ("It's not allowed" is another translation). But in Jewish eyes there is no difference.

14 On that occasion Herod the tetrarch heard the rumor about Jesus ²and said to his servants, "This is John the Baptizer. He's been raised from the dead; that's why miraculous powers are at work in him."

³For Herod had arrested John, put him in chains, and thrown him in prison on account of Herodias, his brother Philip's wife. ⁴John, for his part, had said to him, "It is not right for you to have her."

⁵And while <Herod> wanted to kill him, he was afraid of the crowd because they regarded <John> as a prophet. ⁶On Herod's birthday, the daughter of Herodias danced for them and captivated Herod, ⁷so he swore an oath and promised to give her whatever she asked.

⁸Prompted by her mother, she said, "Give me the head of John the Baptist right here on a platter."

⁹The king was sad, but on account of his oath and his dinner guests, he ordered that it be done. ¹⁰And he sent and had John beheaded in prison. ¹¹<John's> head was brought on a platter and presented to the girl, and she gave it to her mother. ¹²Then his disciples came and got his body and buried him. Then they went and told Jesus.

¹³When Jesus got word of <John's death>, he went off quietly by boat to an isolated place. But the crowds heard of <his departure> and followed him on foot from the towns. ¹⁴When he stepped ashore, he saw this huge crowd, took pity on them, and healed their sick.

**Herod
beheads John**

• **14:5** *<Herod> wanted to kill him:* Like most autocrats, Herod did not like criticism.

they regarded <John> as a prophet: Not in Mark here. Our evangelist has taken it from a later scene in Mark (11:27–33), which he uses at 21:26.

• **14:6** *the daughter of Herodias:* Usually thought to have been named Salome.

• **14:8** *Give me the head of John the Baptist:* Even in his impassioned, and perhaps drunken, promise (vs 8) Herod had expected some little thing that a girl might ask, not this politically dangerous demand by his wife.

• **14:9** *sad:* Or "disturbed." Because of John's popular standing, vs 5.

on account of his oath and his dinner guests: To break it would cause him to be shamed before his *guests*.

• **14:10** *he sent and had John beheaded:* Literally,

"he beheaded John," similar to the wording in vs 3.

• **14:12** *his disciples:* Evidently there were two movements, one led by the Baptizer and one by Jesus. See John 1:35.

they went and told Jesus: As we heard earlier, in 4:12. The flashback that began with vs 3 now ends.

• **14:13** Jesus is evidently stunned by John's death. Does it represent for him more than loss (Jesus may have been a follower of the Baptist's)—perhaps the specter of martyrdom? His attempt to find solitude is thwarted by his growing reputation.

• **14:14** *and healed their sick:* This is lacking in Mark 6:30–44. The evangelist occasionally adds such a report, as for example in 9:35.

**Loaves &
fish for 5000**

¹⁵Ὀψίας δὲ γενομένης προσῆλθον αὐτῷ οἱ μαθηταὶ λέγοντες, Ἔρημός ἐστιν ὁ τόπος καὶ ἡ ὥρα ἤδη παρῆλθεν· ἀπόλυσον τοὺς ὄχλους, ἵνα ἀπελθόντες εἰς τὰς κώμας ἀγοράσωσιν ἑαυτοῖς βρώματα.

¹⁶Ὁ δὲ Ἰησοῦς εἶπεν αὐτοῖς, Οὐ χρείαν ἔχουσιν ἀπελθεῖν, δότε αὐτοῖς ὑμεῖς φαγεῖν.

¹⁷Οἱ δὲ λέγουσιν αὐτῷ, Οὐκ ἔχομεν ὧδε εἰ μὴ πέντε ἄρτους καὶ δύο ἰχθύας.

¹⁸Ὁ δὲ εἶπεν, Φέρετέ μοι ὧδε αὐτούς. ¹⁹καὶ κελεύσας τοὺς ὄχλους ἀνακλιθῆναι ἐπὶ τοῦ χόρτου, λαβὼν τοὺς πέντε ἄρτους καὶ τοὺς δύο ἰχθύας, ἀναβλέψας εἰς τὸν οὐρανὸν εὐλόγησεν καὶ κλάσας ἔδωκεν τοῖς μαθηταῖς τοὺς ἄρτους, οἱ δὲ μαθηταὶ τοῖς ὄχλοις.

²⁰Καὶ ἔφαγον πάντες καὶ ἐχορτάσθησαν, καὶ ἦραν τὸ περισσεῦον τῶν κλασμάτων δώδεκα κοφίνους πλήρεις. ²¹οἱ δὲ ἐσθίοντες ἦσαν ἄνδρες ὡσεὶ πεντακισχίλιοι χωρὶς γυναικῶν καὶ παιδίων.

**Jesus
departs**

²²Καὶ εὐθέως ἠνάγκασεν τοὺς μαθητὰς ἐμβῆναι εἰς τὸ πλοῖον καὶ προάγειν αὐτὸν εἰς τὸ πέραν, ἕως οὗ ἀπολύσῃ τοὺς ὄχλους. ²³καὶ ἀπολύσας τοὺς ὄχλους ἀνέβη εἰς τὸ ὄρος κατ' ἰδίαν προσεύξασθαι. ὀψίας δὲ γενομένης μόνος ἦν ἐκεῖ.

**Jesus walks
on the sea**

²⁴Τὸ δὲ πλοῖον ἤδη σταδίους πολλοὺς ἀπὸ τῆς γῆς ἀπεῖχεν βασανιζόμενον ὑπὸ τῶν κυμάτων, ἦν γὰρ ἐναντίος ὁ ἄνεμος. ²⁵τετάρτῃ δὲ φυλακῇ τῆς νυκτὸς ἦλθεν πρὸς αὐτοὺς περιπατῶν ἐπὶ τὴν θάλασσαν. ²⁶οἱ δὲ μαθηταὶ ἰδόντες αὐτὸν ἐπὶ τῆς θαλάσσης περιπατοῦντα ἐταράχθησαν λέγοντες ὅτι Φάντασμά ἐστιν, καὶ ἀπὸ τοῦ φόβου ἔκραξαν.

²⁷Εὐθὺς δὲ ἐλάλησεν ὁ Ἰησοῦς αὐτοῖς λέγων, Θαρσεῖτε, ἐγώ εἰμι· μὴ φοβεῖσθε.

²⁸Ἀποκριθεὶς δὲ αὐτῷ ὁ Πέτρος εἶπεν, Κύριε, εἰ σὺ εἶ, κέλευσόν με ἐλθεῖν πρὸς σὲ ἐπὶ τὰ ὕδατα.

²⁹Ὁ δὲ εἶπεν, Ἐλθέ.

• **14:15–21** This account is taken from the episode in Mark (6:35–44) that comes next after the report of John's death.

• **14:15** The disciples are acting like the deacons in Acts 6:1–6.

• **14:17** *five loaves of bread and two fish:* It's the bread that matters. The fish will be forgotten after vs 19.

• **14:19** The acts of Jesus with the *loaves of bread* here—*took, gave a blessing, breaking,* and *gave,* the acts of any host at the beginning of a meal—are in the Greek just those to be found when Jesus eats his last meal with his disciples (26:26). So is this episode to be understood not primarily as miracle but as sacrament, Jesus feeding his church with the

eucharist?

• **14:20** *everybody had more than enough to eat:* This, and also that they *picked up . . . leftovers,* is just like what happened to the Israelites in the wilderness when God gave them manna (Exod 16).

twelve baskets: See comment on 16:9b–10.

• **14:21** *not counting women and children:* Mark 6:44 gives the number of males as 5000. Our author realizes that *women and children* may have been present! And enhances the miracle.

• **14:22** *to the other side:* Evidently the other side of the lake from the unspecified place on the shore where he fed the 5000. In Mark 6, which the evangelist continues to follow,

¹⁵When it was evening the disciples approached him, and said, "This place is desolate and it's already late. Send the crowd away so that they can go to the villages and buy food for themselves."

¹⁶Jesus said to them, "They don't need to leave; give them something to eat yourselves."

¹⁷But they say to him, "We have nothing here except five loaves of bread and two fish!"

¹⁸He said, "Bring them here to me." ¹⁹And he told the crowd to sit down on the grass, and he took the five loaves and two fish, and looking up to the sky he gave a blessing, and breaking the bread apart he gave it to the disciples, and the disciples <gave it> to the crowd.

²⁰And everybody had more than enough to eat. Then they picked up twelve baskets full of leftovers. ²¹The number of people who had eaten came to about five thousand, not counting women and children.

²²And he made the disciples get right into a boat and go ahead of him to the other side, while he dispersed the crowds. ²³When he had dispersed the crowds, he went up the mountain privately to pray. He remained there alone well into the evening.

²⁴By this time the boat was already some distance from land and was being pounded by waves because the wind was against them. ²⁵About three o'clock in the morning he came toward them walking on the sea. ²⁶But when the disciples saw him walking on the sea, they were terrified. "It's a ghost," they said, and cried out in fear.

²⁷Jesus spoke right to them, saying, "Take heart, it's me! Don't be afraid."

²⁸In response Peter said, "Master, if it's really you, order me to come across the water to you."

²⁹He said, "Come on."

---

the boat's destination is Bethsaida (Mark 6:45). Why does he omit this? Is it because Jesus has denounced Bethsaida for failing to repent in the face of healings done there (11:21)?
- **14:23** Now at last Jesus succeeds in finding solitude. See vs 13.
  up the mountain: The Greek says clearly "the" mountain. A particular mountain? See on 5:1 for a possible resonance with Mount Sinai/Horeb of Exodus. Or does it mean simply "up into the hill country"?
- **14:24–33** Based on Mark 6:47–52.
- **14:24** some distance: Greek: "many stadia." A stadion was about 200 yards.
- **14:25** About three o'clock in the morning: In the

Greek, "at the fourth watch of the night." Commonly the night, from 6 in the evening to 6 in the morning, was divided into four watches, of about three hours each.
- **14:26** a ghost: Greek, phantasma. Perhaps not quite what we think of as a ghost, but a terrifying vision.
- **14:27** spoke right to them: The Greek euthus—usually "Right away he spoke to them"—conveys not so much speed as directness.
- **14:28–31** The probably legendary account of Peter's attempt to walk on the sea is unique to Matthew. Also several other stories involving him. See Introduction, p. 20.
- **14:28** if it's really you: Peter is not quite sure yet what he has seen.

Καὶ καταβὰς ἀπὸ τοῦ πλοίου ὁ Πέτρος περιεπάτησεν ἐπὶ τὰ ὕδατα καὶ ἦλθεν πρὸς τὸν Ἰησοῦν. ³⁰βλέπων δὲ τὸν ἄνεμον ἰσχυρὸν ἐφοβήθη, καὶ ἀρξάμενος καταποντίζεσθαι ἔκραξεν λέγων, Κύριε, σῶσόν με.

Cure of the sick

³¹Εὐθέως δὲ ὁ Ἰησοῦς ἐκτείνας τὴν χεῖρα ἐπελάβετο αὐτοῦ καὶ λέγει αὐτῷ, Ὀλιγόπιστε, εἰς τί ἐδίστασας; ³²καὶ ἀναβάντων αὐτῶν εἰς τὸ πλοῖον ἐκόπασεν ὁ ἄνεμος.

³³Οἱ δὲ ἐν τῷ πλοίῳ προσεκύνησαν αὐτῷ λέγοντες, Ἀληθῶς θεοῦ υἱὸς εἶ.

³⁴Καὶ διαπεράσαντες ἦλθον ἐπὶ τὴν γῆν εἰς Γεννησαρέτ. ³⁵καὶ ἐπιγνόντες αὐτὸν οἱ ἄνδρες τοῦ τόπου ἐκείνου ἀπέστειλαν εἰς ὅλην τὴν περίχωρον ἐκείνην καὶ προσήνεγκαν αὐτῷ πάντας τοὺς κακῶς ἔχοντας ³⁶καὶ παρεκάλουν αὐτὸν ἵνα μόνον ἅψωνται τοῦ κρασπέδου τοῦ ἱματίου αὐτοῦ· καὶ ὅσοι ἥψαντο διεσώθησαν.

• **14:30** *with the strong wind in his face:* Strictly, "seeing the . . . wind."

• **14:31** *reached right out:* See comment on vs 27.

says to him: One of the relatively few instances of the so-called historic present in this gospel. (It appears in vs 17 above and again below in 15:1.) It is very common in Mark.

trust: Usually mistranslated as "faith," which suggests mere religious belief.

hesitate: Or "doubt."

• **14:33** *God's son:* The first time that this messianic title appears on human lips. Till now

And Peter got out of the boat and walked on the water and came toward Jesus. ³⁰But with the strong wind in his face, he panicked. And when he began to sink, he cried out, "Master, save me."

³¹Jesus reached right out and took hold of him and says to him, "You have so little trust! Why did you hesitate?" ³²And by the time they had climbed into the boat, the wind had died down.

³³Then those in the boat bowed down to him, saying, "You really are God's son!"

³⁴Once they had crossed over they landed at Gennesaret. ³⁵And the local people recognized him and sent word into the whole surrounding area and brought him all who were ill. ³⁶And they begged him just to let them touch the fringe of his cloak. And all those who managed to touch <it> were cured.

Cure of the sick

---

only Satan, "the tester," in the temptation story (4:3, 6), and demons (8:29) have spoken it. It reappears in the story of Jesus' trial and execution (chaps. 26–27).

• **14:34** *Gennesaret:* Evidently a town or area on the lakeshore, perhaps SW of Capernaum.

• **14:36** *just to let them touch the fringe of his cloak:* Like the woman with a hemorrhage (9:21), they believe even his clothing has magic powers. And the evangelist believes that legend too.

Rules for handwashing

15 Τότε προσέρχονται τῷ Ἰησοῦ ἀπὸ Ἰεροσολύμων Φαρισαῖοι καὶ γραμματεῖς λέγοντες, ²Διὰ τί οἱ μαθηταί σου παραβαίνουσιν τὴν παράδοσιν τῶν πρεσβυτέρων; οὐ γὰρ νίπτονται τὰς χεῖρας αὐτῶν ὅταν ἄρτον ἐσθίωσιν.

³Ὁ δὲ ἀποκριθεὶς εἶπεν αὐτοῖς, Διὰ τί καὶ ὑμεῖς παραβαίνετε τὴν ἐντολὴν τοῦ θεοῦ διὰ τὴν παράδοσιν ὑμῶν; ⁴ὁ γὰρ θεὸς εἶπεν, Τίμα τὸν πατέρα καὶ τὴν μητέρα, καί, Ὁ κακολογῶν πατέρα ἢ μητέρα θανάτῳ τελευτάτω. ⁵ὑμεῖς δὲ λέγετε, Ὃς ἂν εἴπῃ τῷ πατρὶ ἢ τῇ μητρί, Δῶρον ὃ ἐὰν ἐξ ἐμοῦ ὠφεληθῇς, ⁶οὐ μὴ τιμήσει τὸν πατέρα αὐτοῦ· καὶ ἠκυρώσατε τὸν λόγον τοῦ θεοῦ διὰ τὴν παράδοσιν ὑμῶν. ⁷ὑποκριταί, καλῶς ἐπροφήτευσεν περὶ ὑμῶν Ἠσαΐας λέγων,

⁸Ὁ λαὸς οὗτος τοῖς χείλεσίν με τιμᾷ,
ἡ δὲ καρδία αὐτῶν πόρρω ἀπέχει ἀπ' ἐμοῦ·
⁹Μάτην δὲ σέβονταί με
διδάσκοντες διδασκαλίας ἐντάλματα ἀνθρώπων.

What comes out defiles

¹⁰Καὶ προσκαλεσάμενος τὸν ὄχλον εἶπεν αὐτοῖς, Ἀκούετε καὶ συνίετε· ¹¹οὐ τὸ εἰσερχόμενον εἰς τὸ στόμα κοινοῖ τὸν ἄνθρωπον, ἀλλὰ τὸ ἐκπορευόμενον ἐκ τοῦ στόματος τοῦτο κοινοῖ τὸν ἄνθρωπον.

¹²Τότε προσελθόντες οἱ μαθηταὶ λέγουσιν αὐτῷ, Οἶδας ὅτι οἱ Φαρισαῖοι ἀκούσαντες τὸν λόγον ἐσκανδαλίσθησαν;

¹³Ὁ δὲ ἀποκριθεὶς εἶπεν, Πᾶσα φυτεία ἣν οὐκ ἐφύτευσεν ὁ πατήρ μου ὁ οὐράνιος ἐκριζωθήσεται. ¹⁴ἄφετε αὐτούς· τυφλοί εἰσιν ὁδηγοὶ τυφλῶν· τυφλὸς δὲ τυφλὸν ἐὰν ὁδηγῇ, ἀμφότεροι εἰς βόθυνον πεσοῦνται.

15:14 Some MSS omit *of blind people,* and it may have been a later copyist's addition, for intensity.

• **15:1** *from Jerusalem:* As in Mark. Only here in Matthew are they so identified; its largely Jewish audience would take this for granted.

• **15:2** Our author greatly abbreviates Mark 7:2–5 here—again he may be assuming his reader is familiar with the Rabbinic practice it explains.

Why do your disciples . . .? See on 12:1.

the traditions of the elders: Rules of the scholars that had accumulated over the centuries. In the Matthean Jesus' eyes, contrary to the Rabbinic position, they do not have the weight of the Law.

wash their hands before they eat: Not a hygienic but a religious practice.

• **15:3** *God's commandment:* As opposed, per-haps, to what are merely "the traditions of the elders" (vs 1).

• **15:4** *Honor your father and mother:* Exod 20:12=Deut 5:16. *Honor* is taken to mean "care for."

Those who curse . . .: The second quotation is from Exod 21:17=Lev 20:9.

• **15:5** *If people say to their:* Greek "Whoever says to him." See Introduction, p. 26.

consecrated: In Greek, "given." Set aside for religious purposes, here dishonestly.

• **15:6** *invalidating:* Not just "deviating" from God's word (as in vs 2), but in fact annulling it.

• **15:7** *You phonies:* "Hypocrites," as in 6:5.

depicted you: "Prophesied about you."

• **15:8–9** Isa 29:13.

15 Then Pharisees and scholars from Jerusalem come to Jesus, and say, ²"Why do your disciples deviate from the traditions of the elders? For instance, they don't wash their hands before they eat bread."

³In response he asked them, "Why do you also break God's commandment because of your tradition? ⁴You remember God said, 'Honor your father and mother' and 'Those who curse their father or mother will surely die.' ⁵But you say, 'If people say to their father or mother, "Whatever I might have spent to support you has been consecrated to God," ⁶they don't need to honor their father or mother at all.' So you end up invalidating God's word because of your tradition. ⁷You phonies, how accurately Isaiah depicted you when he said,

⁸This people honors me with their lips,
but their heart strays far away from me.
⁹Their worship of me is empty,
because they insist on teachings that are <merely> human regulations."

¹⁰And he summoned the crowd and said to them, "Listen and try to understand. ¹¹What goes into your mouth doesn't defile you; what comes out of your mouth does."

¹²So the disciples came and said to him, "Don't you realize that the Pharisees who heard this remark were offended by it?"

¹³He responded: "Every plant that my heavenly Father doesn't plant will be rooted out. ¹⁴Never mind them. They are blind guides of blind people! If one blind person guides another, both will end up in a ditch."

- **15:8** *their heart:* That is, their mind.
- **15:9** *empty:* Literally, "in vain."
   they insist on teachings: Greek: "they teach teachings," a Hebrew idiom stressing the verb. Well translated here.
- **15:10** *try to understand:* Greek: "be understanding." The present tense of a verb can express attempt.
- **15:11** Thom 14 is almost identical.
   defile you: Greek: "make you common," that is, in Jewish thinking, unholy, not separate from the secular.
   what comes out of your mouth: Not chiefly speech—see vss 18–19 below.
- **15:12** Jesus' saying (vs 11) contradicts the rules of kosher food. And so *the Pharisees*, who were strict guardians of the Law, would

have been *offended* (or "made to stumble").
   Don't you realize . . .? The Greek has "Do you understand . . .?" SV makes it clearer.
- **15:13** Once an independent saying, perhaps. What does it mean here? Are the Pharisees such a *plant . . .* as the next verse seems to show?
- **15:14** *blind guides:* An oxymoron, of course, and bitingly ironic.
   guides: The Pharisees were strict interpreters of scripture and taught Jews to behave accordingly.
   of blind people: This intensifies the denunciation. Both guides and people are helpless. Some manuscripts lack the phrase, but in any case, the point is made in the rest of the verse.

¹⁵Ἀποκριθεὶς δὲ ὁ Πέτρος εἶπεν αὐτῷ, Φράσον ἡμῖν τὴν παραβολήν.

¹⁶Ὁ δὲ εἶπεν, Ἀκμὴν καὶ ὑμεῖς ἀσύνετοί ἐστε; ¹⁷οὐ νοεῖτε ὅτι πᾶν τὸ εἰσπορευόμενον εἰς τὸ στόμα εἰς τὴν κοιλίαν χωρεῖ καὶ εἰς ἀφεδρῶνα ἐκβάλλεται; ¹⁸τὰ δὲ ἐκπορευόμενα ἐκ τοῦ στόματος ἐκ τῆς καρδίας ἐξέρχεται, κἀκεῖνα κοινοῖ τὸν ἄνθρωπον. ¹⁹ἐκ γὰρ τῆς καρδίας ἐξέρχονται διαλογισμοὶ πονηροί, φόνοι, μοιχεῖαι, πορνεῖαι, κλοπαί, ψευδομαρτυρίαι, βλασφημίαι. ²⁰ταῦτά ἐστιν τὰ κοινοῦντα τὸν ἄνθρωπον, τὸ δὲ ἀνίπτοις χερσὶν φαγεῖν οὐ κοινοῖ τὸν ἄνθρωπον.

Canaanite woman's daughter

²¹Καὶ ἐξελθὼν ἐκεῖθεν ὁ Ἰησοῦς ἀνεχώρησεν εἰς τὰ μέρη Τύρου καὶ Σιδῶνος.

²²Καὶ ἰδοὺ γυνὴ Χαναναία ἀπὸ τῶν ὁρίων ἐκείνων ἐξελθοῦσα ἔκραζεν λέγουσα, Ἐλέησόν με, κύριε υἱὸς Δαυίδ· ἡ θυγάτηρ μου κακῶς δαιμονίζεται.

²³Ὁ δὲ οὐκ ἀπεκρίθη αὐτῇ λόγον. καὶ προσελθόντες οἱ μαθηταὶ αὐτοῦ ἠρώτουν αὐτὸν λέγοντες, Ἀπόλυσον αὐτήν, ὅτι κράζει ὄπισθεν ἡμῶν.

²⁴Ὁ δὲ ἀποκριθεὶς εἶπεν, Οὐκ ἀπεστάλην εἰ μὴ εἰς τὰ πρόβατα τὰ ἀπολωλότα οἴκου Ἰσραήλ.

²⁵Ἡ δὲ ἐλθοῦσα προσεκύνει αὐτῷ λέγουσα, Κύριε, βοήθει μοι.

²⁶Ὁ δὲ ἀποκριθεὶς εἶπεν, Οὐκ ἔξεστιν λαβεῖν τὸν ἄρτον τῶν τέκνων καὶ βαλεῖν τοῖς κυναρίοις.

²⁷Ἡ δὲ εἶπεν, Ναί κύριε, καὶ γὰρ τὰ κυνάρια ἐσθίει ἀπὸ τῶν ψιχίων τῶν πιπτόντων ἀπὸ τῆς τραπέζης τῶν κυρίων αὐτῶν.

²⁸Τότε ἀποκριθεὶς ὁ Ἰησοῦς εἶπεν αὐτῇ, Ὦ γύναι, μεγάλη σου ἡ πίστις· γενηθήτω σοι ὡς θέλεις. καὶ ἰάθη ἡ θυγάτηρ αὐτῆς ἀπὸ τῆς ὥρας ἐκείνης.

15:26 In place of *it's not right,* many MSS read "it's not good," as in Mark 7:27.

• **15:15** As often in this gospel, Peter stands out from the rest. But Jesus' reply is to the disciples generally (2d person plural). The evangelist has introduced Peter.
riddle: "Parable," evidently referring to vs 11.
• **15:16** *are you still as dimwitted as the rest?* "Don't you, at least, understand by now?"
• **15:17** *every thing that goes into the mouth* is inconsequential.
• **15:18** *from the heart:* That is, from the will—called "evil intentions" in vs 19.
• **15:19** It is not food but what is unethical within you that defiles, making you not simply "unclean" but unrighteous, unjust.
sexual immorality: Just what this phrase means isn't clear. It seems not to indicate any specific behavior.

• **15:20** *eating with unwashed hands:* This phrase changes the subject from what has gone just before, the question about eating non-kosher food. It reverts to the Pharisees' objection in vs 2. Here, then, another Rabbinic dictum—washing hands before eating, so as not to defile kosher food—is dismissed.
• **15:21** *the district of Tyre and Sidon:* That is, the region surrounding those Mediterranean port cities just north of Palestine. Gentile territory.
• **15:22** *Canaanite woman:* In the parallel story, Mark 7:24–30, she is called "Syrophoenician," perhaps a more contemporary designation. Our author's term identifies her with the pagan enemies of ancient Israel.
sir: See comment on 8:2.
you son of David: In this gospel, the title is

¹⁵Then Peter replied, "Explain the riddle to us."

¹⁶He said, "Are you still as dim-witted as the rest? ¹⁷Don't you realize that everything that goes into the mouth passes into the stomach and comes out in the outhouse? ¹⁸But the things that come out of the mouth come from the heart, and those things defile a person. ¹⁹For out of the heart emerge evil intentions: murders, adulteries, sexual immorality, thefts, false witnesses, blasphemies. ²⁰These are the things that defile a person. However, eating with unwashed hands doesn't defile anybody."

²¹So Jesus left there, and withdrew to the district of Tyre and Sidon.

Canaanite woman's daughter

²²And this Canaanite woman from those parts appeared and cried out, "Have mercy on me, sir, you son of David. My daughter is severely possessed."

²³When he did not respond at all, his disciples came and began to complain: "Get rid of her, because she is badgering us."

²⁴But in response he said, "I was sent only to the lost sheep of the house of Israel."

²⁵She came and bowed down to him, saying, "Sir, please help me."

²⁶He replied, "It's not right to take bread out of children's mouths and throw it to the dogs."

²⁷She said, "Of course, sir, but even the dogs eat the scraps that fall from their master's table."

²⁸Then in response Jesus said to her, "My good woman, your trust is enormous. Your wish is as good as fulfilled." And her daughter was cured at that moment.

---

used elsewhere in connection with Jesus' healing (9:27, 20:30).

severely possessed: By "demons" and therefore very sick.

- **15:23** *he did not respond at all:* Why, do you suppose . . . at least in our author's understanding?
- **15:24** If this is Jesus' reply to the disciples, it is consonant with his instructions to the disciples when he sent them out (see 10:6). Is the logic here that since he has no responsibility for her, neither have they? Or is he complying with their request and speaking here to the woman, trying to turn aside her urgent appeal, as perhaps in vs 26?
- **15:25** The woman tries a second time to break through the barrier separating Jews and Gentiles.
- **15:26** Is Jesus, tongue in cheek, quoting an expression of Jewish racism? Or does he mean what this says?

right: Or "permitted."

bread: Evidently Jesus' attention and healing power.

dogs: Perhaps a common way of referring to Gentiles—highly insulting.

- **15:27** The woman is either clever or desperate, or both. She answers Jesus' objection (vs 26). Despite its pejorative meaning in Jesus' world, she turns "dogs" into a positive image that reinforces a persuasive riposte.
- **15:28** *trust:* A better translation than "faith," which can be mistaken for mere belief. How has she shown her trust? By somehow recognizing him initially as the Anointed? Or by her persistence? Or a combination of the two?

at that moment: The healing is both instantaneous and done from afar.

²⁹Καὶ μεταβὰς ἐκεῖθεν ὁ Ἰησοῦς ἦλθεν παρὰ τὴν θάλασσαν τῆς Γαλιλαίας, καὶ ἀναβὰς εἰς τὸ ὄρος ἐκάθητο ἐκεῖ. ³⁰καὶ προσῆλθον αὐτῷ ὄχλοι πολλοὶ ἔχοντες μεθ' ἑαυτῶν χωλούς, τυφλούς, κυλλούς, κωφούς, καὶ ἑτέρους πολλοὺς καὶ ἔρριψαν αὐτοὺς παρὰ τοὺς πόδας αὐτοῦ, καὶ ἐθεράπευσεν αὐτούς· ³¹ὥστε τὸν ὄχλον θαυμάσαι βλέποντας κωφοὺς λαλοῦντας, κυλλοὺς ὑγιεῖς καὶ χωλοὺς περιπατοῦντας καὶ τυφλοὺς βλέποντας· καὶ ἐδόξασαν τὸν θεὸν Ἰσραήλ.

Loaves & fish for 4000

³²Ὁ δὲ Ἰησοῦς προσκαλεσάμενος τοὺς μαθητὰς αὐτοῦ εἶπεν, Σπλαγχνίζομαι ἐπὶ τὸν ὄχλον, ὅτι ἤδη ἡμέραι τρεῖς προσμένουσίν μοι καὶ οὐκ ἔχουσιν τί φάγωσιν· καὶ ἀπολῦσαι αὐτοὺς νήστεις οὐ θέλω, μήποτε ἐκλυθῶσιν ἐν τῇ ὁδῷ.

³³Καὶ λέγουσιν αὐτῷ οἱ μαθηταί, Πόθεν ἡμῖν ἐν ἐρημίᾳ ἄρτοι τοσοῦτοι ὥστε χορτάσαι ὄχλον τοσοῦτον;

³⁴Καὶ λέγει αὐτοῖς ὁ Ἰησοῦς, Πόσους ἄρτους ἔχετε;

Οἱ δὲ εἶπαν, Ἑπτὰ καὶ ὀλίγα ἰχθύδια.

³⁵Καὶ παραγγείλας τῷ ὄχλῳ ἀναπεσεῖν ἐπὶ τὴν γῆν.

³⁶Ἔλαβεν τοὺς ἑπτὰ ἄρτους καὶ τοὺς ἰχθύας καὶ εὐχαριστήσας ἔκλασεν καὶ ἐδίδου τοῖς μαθηταῖς, οἱ δὲ μαθηταὶ τοῖς ὄχλοις. ³⁷καὶ ἔφαγον πάντες καὶ ἐχορτάσθησαν. καὶ τὸ περισσεῦον τῶν κλασμάτων ἦραν ἑπτὰ σπυρίδας πλήρεις. ³⁸οἱ δὲ ἐσθίοντες ἦσαν τετρακισχίλιοι ἄνδρες χωρὶς γυναικῶν καὶ παιδίων. ³⁹καὶ ἀπολύσας τοὺς ὄχλους ἐνέβη εἰς τὸ πλοῖον καὶ ἦλθεν εἰς τὰ ὅρια Μαγαδάν.

• **15:29** *went <back> to the sea of Galilee:* In other words he returned from Gentile territory to his own. The story of the 5000 was also set on the shore of the sea (14:14)

  climbed up the mountain: To escape the crowds? If so, not successfully (vs 30a).

• **15:30–31** This account, preceding the miraculous feeling, is very roughly parallel to the healing of the deaf mute in Mark 7:32–37. But it is much briefer and *many others* are healed.

• **15:30** *the lame, the blind, the maimed, the mute, and many others:* A summary of Jesus' healing ministry. Compare his answer to John the Baptist (11:5).

• **15:31** *when they saw … they gave all the credit to the God of Israel:* Only Matthew has this. In Mark 7:37 the credit is given to Jesus. The author's change here seems just the reverse of 19:16, where he avoids Mark 10:18 ("Why do you call me good? No one is good except for God alone.")

  gave all the credit: Often translated "glorified," a bit archaic.

  the God of Israel: In the Greek, simply "the God Israel," a Hebraism, equivalent to our "Israel's God."

• **15:32–39** This account so closely parallels14:15–21—loaves and fish for 5000—that the two stories must be different versions of one tradition. The same duplication appears in Mark 6:35–44 and 8:1–9, but not in Luke.

• **15:32** Here, as in Mark, Jesus is the one taking initiative for the miraculous feeding, in contrast to the 5000 story (14:15), where it was the disciples who are worried.

²⁹Then Jesus left there and went <back> to the Sea of Galilee. And he climbed up the mountain and sat there. ³⁰And huge crowds came to him and brought with them the lame, the blind, the maimed, the mute, and many others, and they laid them at his feet and he healed them. ³¹As a result, the crowd was astonished when they saw the mute now speaking, the maimed made strong, the lame walking, and the blind seeing. And they gave all the credit to the God of Israel.

³²Then Jesus called his disciples aside and said: "I feel sorry for the crowd because they have already spent three days with me and now they've run out of food. And I don't want to send them away hungry, for fear they'll collapse on the road."

Loaves & fish for 4000

³³And the disciples say to him, "How can we get enough bread here in this desolate place to feed so many people?"

³⁴Jesus says to them, "How many loaves do you have?"

They replied, "Seven, plus a few fish."

³⁵And he ordered the crowd to sit down on the ground.

³⁶And he took the seven loaves and the fish and gave thanks and broke them into pieces, and started giving <them> to the disciples, and the disciples <started giving them> to the crowds. ³⁷And everyone had more than enough to eat. Then they picked up seven baskets of leftover scraps. ³⁸Those who had eaten numbered four thousand, not counting women and children. ³⁹And after he sent the crowds away, he got into the boat and went to the Magadan region.

---

they have already spent three days with me: When the story is preceded by vss 30–31 we are to understand that meanwhile time has passed.

- **15:33** The disciples assume it will be their responsibility to solve the problem. Or at least they point out the seeming impossibility.
- **15:35** The crowd is not to go off in search of food but to wait for the miracle. The Greek here is a dependent clause; literally, "Having ordered the crowd to sit down on the ground [36]he took the seven loaves. . . ."
- **15:36** As in 14:19, Jesus' actions here are like those at the last supper (26:26), except for "gave thanks" in place of "gave a blessing" over the loaves—the same idea.
- **15:37** *everyone had more than enough to eat:*

"They ate and were fed," like the Israelites in the wilderness (Exod 16:13–21). The crowd here is in a deserted place too.

they picked up seven baskets of leftover scraps: In 14:20 it was twelve baskets. Do these numbers mean something? See on 16:9–10 below.

- **15:38** *not counting women and children:* The miracle is still greater than in Mark 8:9 ("about four thousand people"). See comment on 14:21
- **15:39** *the Magadan region:* Neither this nor "the Dalmanoutha district" named in the parallel in Mark 8:10 can now be identified. Possibly on the northwest coast of the lake—see below on 27:61.

Interpretive Note: The Nature Miracles

Except for two more healings (the epileptic boy in ch 17 and two blind men in 20) all Jesus' miracles in Matthew have now been recounted. And several of them are what are called nature miracles—not healings (see the Interpretive Note, p. 90) but involving the inanimate: "multiplication" of loaves, walking on water, stilling a storm. How shall we, as moderns, understand Jesus' miracles—literally, his deeds of power *(dynameis)*—when they violate what we know as the laws of nature? For most people with even some scientific knowledge, who believe that the world is self-governing, it is not possible to accept the miracle stories as the original hearers of the gospel did. Yet we can take it for granted that the laws that run the world are an expression of God's creativity and governance.

I believe it is best to focus not on the events themselves but on their theological meaning—much as we deal with mythological elements in the gospels (see the Glossary). In fact, to ask what, if anything, "really happened" is to fail to understand the stories' message, a bit like the disciples who did not understand the symbolism of leaven or the number of baskets of leftovers after the miracle of the loaves (16:5–12).

The two *feeding* stories (of the 5000 and the 4000) have to do with meeting human need, ordinary material need. Jesus enacts what Heaven's domain will be like, when everyone, especially the poor, at last will have enough. And, as we saw, the stories also have a eucharistic dimension, reflecting the church's re-presentation of Jesus' last supper with the disciples.

Stilling the storm (the one nature miracle in chs 8–9, briefly repeated in 14:24, 32), in which Jesus has God's power (it was believed) over weather, is both an expression of the meeting of human need and a christological display. No doubt Jesus' (and Peter's!) *walking on the water* is the most difficult for us to appropriate. It seems to be sheer prodigy on Jesus' part, almost the kind of portent or "sign," as in the Fourth Gospel, which Jesus routinely refused to provide. Still, we can recognize Jesus' coming to his disciples in their fear and isolation, and revealing himself to them in a kind of theophany reminiscent of Psalm 29:3. Likewise the transformation of Jesus on the mountain (17:1–13). These elements are clearest in the version of this story in John 6:16–21.

Some readers understand Jesus' *resurrection* as a nature miracle—in fact the greatest portent of all—since it includes most of the elements we have noted here. See the Interpretive Note, p. 245.

Request for a sign

16 Καὶ προσελθόντες οἱ Φαρισαῖοι καὶ Σαδδουκαῖοι πειράζοντες ἐπηρώτησαν αὐτὸν σημεῖον ἐκ τοῦ οὐρανοῦ ἐπιδεῖξαι αὐτοῖς.

²Ὁ δὲ ἀποκριθεὶς εἶπεν αὐτοῖς, Ὀψίας γενομένης λέγετε, Εὐδία, πυρράζει γὰρ ὁ οὐρανός· ³καὶ πρωΐ, Σήμερον χειμών, πυρράζει γὰρ στυγνάζων ὁ οὐρανός. τὸ μὲν πρόσωπον τοῦ οὐρανοῦ γινώσκετε διακρίνειν, τὰ δὲ σημεῖα τῶν καιρῶν οὐ δύνασθε; ⁴Γενεὰ πονηρὰ καὶ μοιχαλὶς σημεῖον ἐπιζητεῖ, καὶ σημεῖον οὐ δοθήσεται αὐτῇ εἰ μὴ τὸ σημεῖον Ἰωνᾶ. καὶ καταλιπὼν αὐτοὺς ἀπῆλθεν.

Bread & leaven

⁵Καὶ ἐλθόντες οἱ μαθηταὶ εἰς τὸ πέραν ἐπελάθοντο ἄρτους λαβεῖν. ⁶ὁ δὲ Ἰησοῦς εἶπεν αὐτοῖς, Ὁρᾶτε καὶ προσέχετε ἀπὸ τῆς ζύμης τῶν Φαρισαίων καὶ Σαδδουκαίων.

⁷Οἱ δὲ διελογίζοντο ἐν ἑαυτοῖς λέγοντες ὅτι Ἄρτους οὐκ ἐλάβομεν.

⁸Γνοὺς δὲ ὁ Ἰησοῦς εἶπεν, Τί διαλογίζεσθε ἐν ἑαυτοῖς, ὀλιγόπιστοι, ὅτι ἄρτους οὐκ ἔχετε; ⁹οὔπω νοεῖτε; οὐδὲ μνημονεύετε τοὺς πέντε ἄρτους τῶν πεντακισχιλίων καὶ πόσους κοφίνους ἐλάβετε; ¹⁰οὐδὲ τοὺς ἑπτὰ ἄρτους τῶν τετρακισχιλίων καὶ πόσας σπυρίδας ἐλάβετε; ¹¹πῶς οὐ νοεῖτε ὅτι οὐ περὶ ἄρτων εἶπον ὑμῖν; προσέχετε δὲ ἀπὸ τῆς ζύμης τῶν Φαρισαίων καὶ Σαδδουκαίων.

¹²Τότε συνῆκαν ὅτι οὐκ εἶπεν προσέχειν ἀπὸ τῆς ζύμης τῶν ἄρτων ἀλλὰ ἀπὸ τῆς διδαχῆς τῶν Φαρισαίων καὶ Σαδδουκαίων.

What are people saying?

¹³Ἐλθὼν δὲ ὁ Ἰησοῦς εἰς τὰ μέρη Καισαρείας τῆς Φιλίππου ἠρώτα τοὺς μαθητὰς αὐτοῦ λέγων, Τίνα λέγουσιν οἱ ἄνθρωποι εἶναι τὸν υἱὸν τοῦ ἀνθρώπου;

16:2b–3 Some MSS omit this saying and have only vs. 4 as Jesus' reply to the officials' challenge. But the saying is probably original. Possibly the scribal omission occurred in a place such as Egypt, where the climate was different from Palestine's.

16:13 Some MSS insert "me" before *the son of Adam*.

• **16:1–4** In 12:38–40 "scholars and Pharisees" have already asked for a sign from Jesus. Why this duplication? Because the author has two distinct traditions, both probably post-Easter, dealing with Jesus' messianic status. This one is from Mark (8:11–13), the earlier from Q.

• **16:1** Here the request is made *to put [Jesus] to the test:* The intent is hardly friendly.

 Sadducees: See Glossary.

 A sign in the sky: Or, ". . . from heaven," that is, a supernatural demonstration of Jesus' authority.

• **16:2–3** *When it's evening . . . Early in the morning . . . :* Jesus evidently quotes a proverb similar to the modern one, "Red sky at night, sailor's delight; red sky at morning, sailor take warning."

• **16:3** *winter weather:* That is, rain storms.

 you can't discern the signs of the times: The Jewish leaders want a sign when there are signs all around them of what is taking place in Jesus' ministry.

 the times: The present.

• **16:4** *except the sign of Jonah:* Since no such exception is to be found in the Markan parallel, someone who handed on the Jesus tradition, or our author himself, has added this. It comes from Q (see Luke 11:29). Perhaps the reader is expected to remember 12:40, where the cryptic remark was explained.

• **16:5–12** From Mark 8:14–21.

• **16:6** *leaven:* Yeast was a symbol of impurity, and therefore of evil or corruption, evidently since only unleavened bread was considered holy enough to eat during the Passover

16 And the Pharisees and Sadducees came, and to put him to the test they asked him to show them a sign in the sky.

[2]In response he said to them, "When it's evening, you say, 'It'll be fair weather because the sky looks red.' [3]Early in the morning, <you say,> 'The day will bring winter weather because the sky looks red and dark.' You know how to read the face of the sky, but you can't discern the signs of the times. [4]An evil and immoral generation seeks a sign, yet no sign will be given it except the sign of Jonah." And he turned his back on them and walked away.

[5]And the disciples came to the opposite shore, but they forgot to bring any bread. [6]Jesus said to them, "Look, take care and guard against the leaven of the Pharisees and Sadducees."

[7]Now they looked quizzically at each other, saying, "We didn't bring any bread."

[8]Aware of this, Jesus said, "Why are you puzzled that you don't have any bread? You have so little trust! [9]You still aren't using your heads, are you? You don't remember the five loaves for the five thousand and how many baskets you carried away, do you? [10]Nor the seven loaves for four thousand and how many big baskets you filled? [11]How can you possibly think I was talking to you about bread? Just be on guard against the leaven of the Pharisees and Sadducees."

[12]Then they understood that he was not talking about guarding against the leaven in bread but against the teaching of the Pharisees and Sadducees.

[13]When Jesus came to the region of Caesarea Philippi, he started questioning his disciples, asking, "What are people saying about the son of Adam?"

---

celebration. In their haste to escape from slavery in Egypt the Israelites had been able to take along only unleavened dough for bread (Ex 12:34).

- **16:7** *We didn't bring any bread:* They can only take Jesus literally.
- **16:8** *Aware of this:* Jesus knows (supernaturally?) what they are discussing.
- **16:8b–9a** If they are concerned about their lack of bread, they have too *little trust.* They have only to remember Jesus' miraculous feedings of the crowds (14:13–20 and 15:29–39).

  You still aren't using your heads, are you? "Don't you understand yet?"
- **16:9b–10** The disciples also don't understand the meaning of the number of baskets left over—12 and 7 (14:20 and 15:37). Some

have suggested that they represent Jews (the 12 tribes of Israel) and Gentiles (believed to comprise 70 nations). But the modern reader may be just as puzzled as the disciples.

- **16:11b–12** Not in Mark; evidently the evangelist adds this to pick up the theme of vs 6, after the interruption about literal bread.
- **16:12** *the teaching of the Pharisees and Sadducees:* Now the author makes it clear what their *leaven* is. Possibly their seeking a sign from him and so casting doubt on his work (the preceding episode) amounts to such false teaching.
- **16:13–20** In Mark 8, which our author is following, Jesus next heals a blind man at Bethsaida (8:22–26). But both Matthew and Luke omit that story. (In Matthew Bethsaida is mentioned only at 11:21, in a damnation.)

¹⁴Οἱ δὲ εἶπαν, Οἱ μὲν Ἰωάννην τὸν βαπτιστήν, ἄλλοι δὲ Ἠλίαν, ἕτεροι δὲ Ἰερεμίαν ἢ ἕνα τῶν προφητῶν.

¹⁵Λέγει αὐτοῖς, Ὑμεῖς δὲ τίνα με λέγετε εἶναι;

¹⁶Ἀποκριθεὶς δὲ Σίμων Πέτρος εἶπεν, Σὺ εἶ ὁ Χριστὸς ὁ υἱὸς τοῦ θεοῦ τοῦ ζῶντος.

¹⁷Ἀποκριθεὶς δὲ ὁ Ἰησοῦς εἶπεν αὐτῷ, Μακάριος εἶ, Σίμων Βαριωνᾶ, ὅτι σὰρξ καὶ αἷμα οὐκ ἀπεκάλυψέν σοι ἀλλ' ὁ πατήρ μου ὁ ἐν τοῖς οὐρανοῖς. ¹⁸κἀγὼ δέ σοι λέγω ὅτι σὺ εἶ Πέτρος, καὶ ἐπὶ ταύτῃ τῇ πέτρᾳ οἰκοδομήσω μου τὴν ἐκκλησίαν καὶ πύλαι ᾅδου οὐ κατισχύσουσιν αὐτῆς. ¹⁹δώσω σοι τὰς κλεῖδας τῆς βασιλείας τῶν οὐρανῶν, καὶ ὃ ἐὰν δήσῃς ἐπὶ τῆς γῆς ἔσται δεδεμένον ἐν τοῖς οὐρανοῖς, καὶ ὃ ἐὰν λύσῃς ἐπὶ τῆς γῆς ἔσται λελυμένον ἐν τοῖς οὐρανοῖς.

²⁰Τότε διεστείλατο τοῖς μαθηταῖς ἵνα μηδενὶ εἴπωσιν ὅτι αὐτός ἐστιν ὁ Χριστός.

Jesus destined to suffer

²¹Ἀπὸ τότε ἤρξατο ὁ Ἰησοῦς δεικνύειν τοῖς μαθηταῖς αὐτοῦ ὅτι δεῖ αὐτὸν εἰς Ἱεροσόλυμα ἀπελθεῖν καὶ πολλὰ παθεῖν ἀπὸ τῶν

16:21 A few MSS read "the Anointed" after *Jesus*.

If they were following Mark independently of each other, as seems most likely, it's possible that their versions of Mark lacked the story. It is one of a very few complete stories in Mark not paralleled in either Matthew or Luke. (See Introduction, p. 10, on the "Minor Agreements.") But it is so similar to other healings—notably the healing of blind Bartimaeus in Mark 10:46–52 (compare Matt 20:29–34=Luke 18:35–43)—that perhaps our author (and the writer of Luke) thought it redundant. He resumes Mark at 8:27.

• **16:13** *Caesarea Philippi:* A Gentile city just north of Galilee, it had been rebuilt by Herod Philip, half-brother of Herod Antipas, and named both for *Caesar*—the Emperor—and himself. It was famous for its shrine to the god Pan; hence it's modern name Banias, Arabic having no letter P.

The question who or what Jesus is has not arisen explicitly until now. Only Herod Antipas had anticipated it, and he gave an incorrect answer (14:2).

about the son of Adam: In Mark 8:27, "about me." The evangelist changes the pronoun to this title. Why? To lend an air of mystery? Anyway, in vs 15 he makes it clear that Jesus refers to himself.

• **16:14** *John the Baptist:* Raised from the dead, that is, as Herod had believed (14:2).

Elijah: In accordance with Mal 4:5, some expected Elijah to return as the precursor

of God's judging presence. See Jesus' saying about Elijah, 17: 11–12.

The answers to Jesus' question follow Mark, except that *Jeremiah* is singled out as *one of the prophets*, perhaps because our author has special interest in Jeremiah. He alone cites prophecies by Jeremiah—in 2:17 (grief over the murdered babies) and 27:9 (the thirty coins given to Judas as bribe).

• **16:15** The answers are wrong, but what matters is his followers' understanding of Jesus' role and destiny.

• **16:16** *Simon Peter:* Peter is called by this double name only in this passage. See below on vss 17 and 18.

the son of … God: Added to Mark's *the Anointed*, evidently by the evangelist. The titles are synonymous.

the living God: A phrase used by our author alone, here and in 26:63 (the high priest's demand). It is a Biblical phrase: see, for example, Deut 5:26, Ps 42:2, Jer 10:10.

• **16:17–19** These verses have no parallel in the other gospels, though they bear a slight resemblance to John 1:42, noted below on vss 17, 19.

• **16:17** *Congratulations:* Using the same term as in 5:3–11. See Translation Note, p. 63.

Simon son of Jonah: Only here so identified—but in John 1:42 Jesus calls him "John's son," also "Rock" (next verse).

• **16:18** *Rock:* See on 10:2.

¹⁴They said, "Some <say, 'He is> John the Baptist,' but others, 'Elijah,' and others, 'Jeremiah or one of the prophets.'"

¹⁵He says to them, "What about you, who do you say I am?"

¹⁶And Simon Peter responded, "You are the Anointed, the son of the living God!"

¹⁷And in response Jesus said to him, "Congratulations, Simon son of Jonah, because flesh and blood did not reveal this to you, but my Father who is in heaven. ¹⁸Let me tell you, you are Peter, 'the Rock,' and on this very rock I will build my community, and the gates of Hell will not be able to hold out against it. ¹⁹I'm going to give you the keys of Heaven's domain, and whatever you bind on earth will be considered bound in heaven, and whatever you release on earth will be considered released in heaven."

²⁰Then he ordered the disciples to tell no one that he was the Anointed.

²¹From that time on Jesus started to make it clear to his disciples that he was destined to go to Jerusalem, and suffer a great deal at

Jesus destined to suffer

---

on this very rock: A play, of course, on Simon Peter's nickname. Peter is all too fallible, as we see below in vss 22 and 23. Does Jesus mean that even out of rocks (or clods) like Peter he can fashion his new Israel?

community: In all the gospels the Greek word *ekklêsia* occurs only here and at 18:17. Earlier, Paul had used it regularly to identify the Christian congregations he wrote to. It means an assembled group of people and was used in the Septuagint for God's people, Israel. Eventually it was translated "church."

the gates of Hades: What does the image mean? *Hades* is of course Hell, the place of evil. Its gates, then, hold in check all the power of the underworld.

hold out against: There is a common misunderstanding of this saying—as if Hell, or its gates, will storm the church but will fail to succeed. But of course gates don't storm; they are stormed. Does the church then have the commission of storming Hell and overcoming evil? What does this involve? In any case, Jesus promises that it will succeed.

• **16:19** *give you:* Singular pronoun, in other words to Peter himself.

the keys of Heaven's domain: Authority not to bar the entrance but to open the way into the new creation, through the very opposite of "the gates of Hades."

bind . . . release: This is often held to mean forgiving and condemning, that is, decid-

ing who will and will not in the end enter *God's domain.* (That is explicitly the meaning of a similar promise Jesus makes to all the disciples in John 20:23.) But the image is Rabbinic and means, rather, determining what actions are permitted and not permitted. To Peter—and also to the congregation built on that rock (see 18:18)—is given the power and the responsibility to decide which rules or principles apply to followers of Jesus and which do not. It has to do with how, not whether, one can enter the new age. And our author esp. has set out for his church a guidebook to those rules and principles.

in heaven: That is, by God.

• **16:20** Harking back to vs 16, and paralleling Mark 8:30. The silence imposed here stems from the esp. Markan theme of the messianic secret, which our author uses only occasionally. Is its role here secrecy, to keep the fact of Jesus' messiahship from others? Or is it a mystery whose time is beginning to come, but so far only for these few?

• **16:21–23** This is the first of three predictions of Jesus' fate (the second and third in 17:22–23 and 20:18–19; see also 26:2) —following those in Mark 8, 9, and 10. The second half of the gospel, then, will be overshadowed by the path that Jesus now announces lies before him.

I believe it most unlikely that Jesus foresaw this early his eventual arrest and

πρεσβυτέρων καὶ ἀρχιερέων καὶ γραμματέων καὶ ἀποκτανθῆναι καὶ τῇ τρίτῃ ἡμέρᾳ ἐγερθῆναι.

²²Καὶ προσλαβόμενος αὐτὸν ὁ Πέτρος ἤρξατο ἐπιτιμᾶν αὐτῷ λέγων, Ἴλεώς σοι, κύριε· οὐ μὴ ἔσται σοι τοῦτο.

²³Ὁ δὲ στραφεὶς εἶπεν τῷ Πέτρῳ, Ὕπαγε ὀπίσω μου, Σατανᾶ· σκάνδαλον εἶ ἐμοῦ, ὅτι οὐ φρονεῖς τὰ τοῦ θεοῦ ἀλλὰ τὰ τῶν ἀνθρώπων.

Saving &
losing life

²⁴Τότε ὁ Ἰησοῦς εἶπεν τοῖς μαθηταῖς αὐτοῦ, Εἴ τις θέλει ὀπίσω μου ἐλθεῖν, ἀπαρνησάσθω ἑαυτὸν καὶ ἀράτω τὸν σταυρὸν αὐτοῦ καὶ ἀκολουθείτω μοι.

²⁵Ὃς γὰρ ἐὰν θέλῃ τὴν ψυχὴν αὐτοῦ σῶσαι ἀπολέσει αὐτήν· ὃς δ᾽ ἂν ἀπολέσῃ τὴν ψυχὴν αὐτοῦ ἕνεκεν ἐμοῦ εὑρήσει αὐτήν. ²⁶τί γὰρ ὠφεληθήσεται ἄνθρωπος ἐὰν τὸν κόσμον ὅλον κερδήσῃ τὴν δὲ 28υχὴν αὐτοῦ ζημιωθῇ; ἢ τί δώσει ἄνθρωπος ἀντάλλαγμα τῆς 29υχῆς αὐτοῦ;

²⁷Μέλλει γὰρ ὁ υἱὸς τοῦ ἀνθρώπου ἔρχεσθαι ἐν τῇ δόξῃ τοῦ πατρὸς αὐτοῦ μετὰ τῶν ἀγγέλων αὐτοῦ, καὶ τότε ἀποδώσει ἑκάστῳ κατὰ τὴν πρᾶξιν αὐτοῦ. ²⁸ἀμὴν λέγω ὑμῖν ὅτι εἰσίν τινες τῶν ὧδε ἑστώτων οἵτινες οὐ μὴ γεύσωνται θανάτου ἕως ἂν ἴδωσιν τὸν υἱὸν τοῦ ἀνθρώπου ἐρχόμενον ἐν τῇ βασιλείᾳ αὐτοῦ.

---

execution, still less his resurrection, or that he solemnly predicted them to his disciples. Rather, the three episodes were introduced later into the story, perhaps not until the writing of Mark, to justify Jesus' fate: If he had predicted it, it was acceptable, much as Old Testament prophecy made an event inevitable (see comment on 27:27–66).

• **16:21** *From that time on Jesus started to make it clear to his disciples:* As in Mark, our author emphatically enhances the importance of this episode in the gospel's plot. Mark 8:31–32 has "He started teaching them" and "he said this plainly" (no longer in parables, that is.)

that he: In Mark, "that the son of Adam." The author here removes any question about Jesus' prediction.

destined to go to Jerusalem: Only in Matthew is Jerusalem specified at this point as the eventual venue of his fate.

on the third day: In Mark 8:31, "after three days." Our author, like the author of Luke (9:22), has corrected each of the predictions to conform more exactly to the account of Jesus' crucifixion and resurrection. But see above on the sign of Jonah (12:40) and below on 27:63.

be raised: The evangelist here, and elsewhere, changes Mark's "rise." Despite Jesus' divine power, he will be subject to God's raising him.

• **16:22** *lecture:* Or "reprimand."

help you: Strictly, "be merciful to you."

• **16:23** *Get out of my sight, you Satan, you:* Obviously a curse. Go to hell, Peter.

dangerous to me: "A stumbling block [*or* offense] for me." The temptation of avoiding what lies before him is something Jesus must not consider.

the hands of the elders and ranking priests and scholars, and be killed and, on the third day, be raised.

²²And Peter took him aside and began to lecture him, saying, "God help you, master; this will never happen to you!

²³But he turned on Peter and said, "Get out of my sight, you Satan, you. You are dangerous to me because you are not thinking in God's terms, but in human terms."

²⁴Jesus said to his disciples, "If any of you wants to come after me you should deny yourself, pick up your cross, and follow me!

²⁵"Remember, by trying to save your own life, you are going to lose it, but by losing your life for my sake, you are going to find it. ²⁶After all, what good will it do if you acquire the whole world but forfeit your life? Or what will you give in exchange for your life?

²⁷"Remember, the son of Adam is going to come in the glory of his Father with his messengers, and then he will reward all people according to their deeds. ²⁸I swear to you: Some of those standing here won't ever taste death before they see the son of Adam's imperial rule arriving."

*Saving &
losing life*

• **16:24–26** *any of you:* In the Greek the third-person masculine is used—"If anyone ... let him, ..." and so forth. The translators, as elsewhere, have shifted to second person to avoid the use of gender-specific pronouns. See Introduction, p. 26.

• **16:24–25** A rather different version of these two sayings is used at 10:38–39.

• **16:24** *come after me:* As his disciple.
  pick up your cross: How?
  follow me: Imitate him.

• **16:25** *Remember:* Translates the Greek *gar* (conventionally rendered "for").
  for my sake: Like Luke (9:24) omitting "and for the sake of the good news," found in Mark 8:35. Why?

• **16:27** The return of Jesus at the end of the age, as already announced in 10:23. Rather different from Mark 8:38=9:26: "Those who are ashamed of me and my message, ...

of them the son of Adam will likewise be ashamed when he comes...."
  and then he will reward...: Stronger than the merely negative "be ashamed" in Mark and Luke. The wording is similar to Ps 28:4.
  All people according to their deeds: The Greek has "everyone according to his deeds." The plurals avoid non-inclusive language, as in vss 24–26.

• **16:28** An expectation obviously still held in the author's time.
  won't ever: In Greek, an emphatic double negative.
  the son of Adam's imperial rule: A rare wording, instead of "heaven's imperial rule" (Mark 9:1, Luke 9:27). Conventionally translated "the kingdom of the son of Man."

Jesus transformed

17 Καὶ μεθ' ἡμέρας ἓξ παραλαμβάνει ὁ Ἰησοῦς τὸν Πέτρον καὶ Ἰάκωβον καὶ Ἰωάννην τὸν ἀδελφὸν αὐτοῦ καὶ ἀναφέρει αὐτοὺς εἰς ὄρος ὑψηλὸν κατ' ἰδίαν. ²καὶ μετεμορφώθη ἔμπροσθεν αὐτῶν, καὶ ἔλαμψεν τὸ πρόσωπον αὐτοῦ ὡς ὁ ἥλιος, τὰ δὲ ἱμάτια αὐτοῦ ἐγένετο λευκὰ ὡς τὸ φῶς. ³καὶ ἰδοὺ ὤφθη αὐτοῖς Μωϋσῆς καὶ Ἠλίας συλλαλοῦντες μετ' αὐτοῦ.

⁴Ἀποκριθεὶς δὲ ὁ Πέτρος εἶπεν τῷ Ἰησοῦ, Κύριε, καλόν ἐστιν ἡμᾶς ὧδε εἶναι· εἰ θέλεις, ποιήσω ὧδε τρεῖς σκηνάς, σοὶ μίαν καὶ Μωϋσεῖ μίαν καὶ Ἠλίᾳ μίαν.

⁵Ἔτι αὐτοῦ λαλοῦντος ἰδοὺ νεφέλη φωτεινὴ ἐπεσκίασεν αὐτούς, καὶ ἰδοὺ φωνὴ ἐκ τῆς νεφέλης λέγουσα, Οὗτός ἐστιν ὁ υἱός μου ὁ ἀγαπητός, ἐν ᾧ εὐδόκησα· ἀκούετε αὐτοῦ.

⁶Καὶ ἀκούσαντες οἱ μαθηταὶ ἔπεσαν ἐπὶ πρόσωπον αὐτῶν καὶ ἐφοβήθησαν σφόδρα.

⁷Καὶ προσῆλθεν ὁ Ἰησοῦς καὶ ἁψάμενος αὐτῶν εἶπεν, Ἐγέρθητε καὶ μὴ φοβεῖσθε. ⁸ἐπάραντες δὲ τοὺς ὀφθαλμοὺς αὐτῶν οὐδένα εἶδον εἰ μὴ αὐτὸν Ἰησοῦν μόνον.

⁹Καὶ καταβαινόντων αὐτῶν ἐκ τοῦ ὄρους ἐνετείλατο αὐτοῖς ὁ Ἰησοῦς λέγων, Μηδενὶ εἴπητε τὸ ὅραμα ἕως οὗ ὁ υἱὸς τοῦ ἀνθρώπου ἐκ νεκρῶν ἐγερθῇ.

¹⁰Καὶ ἐπηρώτησαν αὐτὸν οἱ μαθηταὶ λέγοντες, Τί οὖν οἱ γραμματεῖς λέγουσιν ὅτι Ἠλίαν δεῖ ἐλθεῖν πρῶτον;

¹¹Ὁ δὲ ἀποκριθεὶς εἶπεν, Ἠλίας μὲν ἔρχεται καὶ ἀποκαταστήσει

• **17:1–13** Continuing to follow Mark 9:2–8.

• **17:1** *Six days later:* As in Mark; Luke has "eight." Counting from when? This recalls Exod 24:16, where after six days God spoke to Moses out of the cloud that covered the mountain. That story is a general model for this one.

Peter ... and James and his brother John: These three seem to form an inner group among the disciples. They were three of the first disciples called by Jesus (4:18–22). And, again with Peter's brother Andrew, they head the list of "the twelve apostles" in 10:2–4.

a lofty mountain: Like the mountain where Moses received the Law.

• **17:2** *He was transformed:* This is probably what is called a divine passive, meaning "God transformed him."

and his face shone like the sun: Not found in Mark 9:2, (and only loosely like Luke 9:29). It may be a reminder of how Moses' face shone when he came down from the mountain of God (Exod 34:29–30).

• **17:3** *Moses and Elijah:* Probably representing the Law and the Prophets, respectively—in the time of this gospel, the two canonical components of Hebrew scripture.

[they] were conversing with Jesus: As equals, presumably.

• **17:4** *Master:* Greek *kyrie;* Mark has "Rabbi" and Luke a different word for "Master." Here the title certainly implies more, at least to the reader, than a human overlord or teacher. Peter gave Jesus a divine title in 16:16, but what he says to Jesus here shows that he has not yet understood it. This revelation will make it plain.

If you want: Only Matthew has this clause. Peter will defer to Jesus' wish.

I'll set up three tents: Peter stands out in this account by offering to do this by himself; Mark and Luke have "we."

tents: The same Greek word is used in LXX for the "tabernacle" that held God's presence while Israel was in the wilderness.

one for you, one for Moses, and one for Elijah: Peter recognizes from the vision, so far, that

17 Six days later, Jesus takes Peter along, and James and his brother John, and he leads them off by themselves to a lofty mountain. ²He was transformed in front of them and his face shone like the sun, and his clothes turned as white as light. ³Then Moses and Elijah appeared to them and were conversing with Jesus.

⁴Peter said to Jesus, "Master, it's a good thing we're here. If you want, I'll set up three tents, one for you, one for Moses, and one for Elijah!"

⁵While he was still speaking, a bright cloud cast a shadow over them, and suddenly a voice spoke from the cloud: "This is my favored son. I fully approve of him. Listen to him!"

⁶And when they heard this, the disciples fell down, frightened out of their wits.

⁷And Jesus came and touched them and said: "Get up; don't be afraid." ⁸Looking up they saw no one except Jesus by himself.

⁹And as they came down from the mountain, Jesus ordered them: "Don't tell anyone about this vision until the son of Adam has been raised from the dead."

¹⁰And the disciples questioned him: "Then why do the scholars claim that Elijah must come first?"

¹¹In response he said, "Elijah is indeed coming and will restore

Jesus transformed

---

the three religious heroes have the same status.

• **17:5** *a bright cloud:* Like the cloud in Exod 13:21 that led the children of Israel in the wilderness by day.

I fully approve of him: Only Matthew has this phrase here. Like the rest of what the voice says, it parallels the divine voice at Jesus' baptism (3:17).

• **17:6–7** Except for the mention of fright—found slightly earlier in the story in Luke (9:34) and earlier still in Mark (9:6)—these two verses are to be found only in Matthew. They express a heightened sense of Jesus' status.

• **17:8** *they saw no one except Jesus by himself:* Jesus is greater than Moses and Elijah. He alone is to be adored.

• **17:9** *vision:* A Greek word found only here among the synoptic gospels. More formal, more memorable than Mark's "what they had seen."

until the son of Adam has been raised from the dead: Only then will the full understanding

of Jesus' divine sonship be possible.

Our author omits the next verse in Mark (9:10): "And they kept it to themselves, puzzling over what this could mean, this 'rising from the dead.'" If the evangelist is a former Pharisee, he takes an understanding of resurrection for granted.

• **17:10** An odd question, since Elijah has just appeared to them. The evangelist simply follows Mark here. It must have been a separate unit of tradition that the author of Mark attached here because of "Elijah." It maybe seeks to refute the Jewish rabbis' objection that Jesus cannot be the Anointed because Elijah has to come first.

the scholars: See Glossary.

Elijah must come: As predicted in Mal 4:5.

• **17:11** Jesus confirms the prediction.

Elijah is indeed coming and will restore everything: An interpretation evidently of Mal 4:6 ("He will turn the hearts of parents to their children and the hearts of children to their parents").

πάντα· ¹²λέγω δὲ ὑμῖν ὅτι Ἠλίας ἤδη ἦλθεν, καὶ οὐκ ἐπέγνωσαν αὐτὸν ἀλλὰ ἐποίησαν ἐν αὐτῷ ὅσα ἠθέλησαν· οὕτως καὶ ὁ υἱὸς τοῦ ἀνθρώπου μέλλει πάσχειν ὑπ' αὐτῶν.

¹³Τότε συνῆκαν οἱ μαθηταὶ ὅτι περὶ Ἰωάννου τοῦ βαπτιστοῦ εἶπεν αὐτοῖς.

The epileptic   ¹⁴Καὶ ἐλθόντων πρὸς τὸν ὄχλον προσῆλθεν αὐτῷ ἄνθρωπος γονυπετῶν αὐτὸν ¹⁵καὶ λέγων, Κύριε, ἐλέησόν μου τὸν υἱόν, ὅτι σεληνιάζεται καὶ κακῶς πάσχει· πολλάκις γὰρ πίπτει εἰς τὸ πῦρ καὶ πολλάκις εἰς τὸ ὕδωρ. ¹⁶καὶ προσήνεγκα αὐτὸν τοῖς μαθηταῖς σου, καὶ οὐκ ἠδυνήθησαν αὐτὸν θεραπεῦσαι.

¹⁷Ἀποκριθεὶς δὲ ὁ Ἰησοῦς εἶπεν, Ὦ γενεὰ ἄπιστος καὶ διεστραμμένη, ἕως πότε μεθ' ὑμῶν ἔσομαι; ἕως πότε ἀνέξομαι ὑμῶν; φέρετέ μοι αὐτὸν ὧδε. ¹⁸καὶ ἐπετίμησεν αὐτῷ ὁ Ἰησοῦς καὶ ἐξῆλθεν ἀπ' αὐτοῦ τὸ δαιμόνιον καὶ ἐθεραπεύθη ὁ παῖς ἀπὸ τῆς ὥρας ἐκείνης.

¹⁹Τότε προσελθόντες οἱ μαθηταὶ τῷ Ἰησοῦ κατ' ἰδίαν εἶπον, Διὰ τί ἡμεῖς οὐκ ἠδυνήθημεν ἐκβαλεῖν αὐτό;

²⁰Ὁ δὲ λέγει αὐτοῖς, Διὰ τὴν ὀλιγοπιστίαν ὑμῶν· ἀμὴν γὰρ λέγω ὑμῖν, ἐὰν ἔχητε πίστιν ὡς κόκκον σινάπεως, ἐρεῖτε τῷ ὄρει τούτῳ, Μετάβα ἔνθεν ἐκεῖ, καὶ μεταβήσεται· καὶ οὐδὲν ἀδυνατήσει ὑμῖν.

Son of Adam will die & be raised   ²²Συστρεφομένων δὲ αὐτῶν ἐν τῇ Γαλιλαίᾳ εἶπεν αὐτοῖς ὁ Ἰησοῦς, Μέλλει ὁ υἱὸς τοῦ ἀνθρώπου παραδίδοσθαι εἰς χεῖρας ἀνθρώπων, ²³καὶ ἀποκτενοῦσιν αὐτόν, καὶ τῇ τρίτῃ ἡμέρᾳ ἐγερθήσεται. καὶ ἐλυπήθησαν σφόδρα.

17:21 Some mss have as vs 21: "The only thing that can drive this kind out is prayer." Very likely it was taken from Mark 9:29 by scribes who copied it in after the gospel was written.
17:22 Some important mss substitute "were living" for *had been reunited*. See the comment on this verse.

• **17:12** *Elijah has already come:* Jesus interprets the prediction. It applies to John the Baptist, as the disciples soon realize (vs 13).

   they . . . had their way with him: John's death, as told in 14:1–12. Elijah has come . . . and has already been taken away.

   So the son of Adam is going to suffer: Jesus will experience what his former mentor did. This reiteration of the prediction in 16:21 is not found in Mark 9:13. And it is almost superfluous with vss 22–23 coming up just below.

• **17:13** Only our author makes this explicit.

• **17:14–21** This is a highly streamlined version of the longer story in Mark 9:14–29. The evangelist compresses the account of the boy's illness and eliminates the question of the man's trust in Jesus' power to heal. Instead, the focus is on the inability of the disciples to heal him.

• **17:14** *a person:* The Greek does not say, as this is usually translated, "a man."

• **17:17** *distrustful:* Or "unbelieving," "faithless."

   lot: Is Jesus speaking of the disciples' lack of trust and their inability to accomplish the healing, as in vss 19–20? Or more generally of the demon-possessed time in which he lived . . . as in 12:39? Probably the latter—the word used here is, literally, "generation."

   how long . . . ? Repeatedly asked by a weary God . . . of Pharaoh, of a faithless Israel, and so forth. Jesus, whose destiny has now been made known, has no patience with this *lot.*

• **17:18** *rebuked the demon:* It is taken for granted, in Jesus' world, that illness is caused by demon-possession.

   right then and there: Greek, "at that hour."

• **17:20** *Because of your lack of trust:* This answer

everything. ¹²But I tell you that Elijah has already come, and they did not recognize him but had their way with him. So the son of Adam is also going to suffer at their hands."

¹³Then the disciples understood that he had been talking to them about John the Baptist.

¹⁴And when they rejoined the crowd, a person approached and knelt before him ¹⁵and said, "Lord, have mercy on my son, because he is epileptic and suffers great <danger>. For instance, he often falls into the fire and just as often into the water. ¹⁶So I brought him to your disciples, but they couldn't heal him."

The epileptic

¹⁷In response Jesus said, "You distrustful and perverted lot, how long must I associate with you? How long must I put up with you? Bring him here to me!" ¹⁸And Jesus rebuked the demon and it came out of him and the child was healed right then and there.

¹⁹Later the disciples came to Jesus privately and asked, "Why couldn't we drive it out?"

²⁰So he says to them, "Because of your lack of trust. I swear to you, even if your trust were no larger than a mustard seed, you would say to this mountain, 'Move from here to there,' and it will move. And nothing will be beyond you."

²²And when they had been reunited in Galilee, Jesus said to them, "The son of Adam is about to be turned over to his enemies, ²³and they will end up killing him, and on the third day he'll be raised." And they were very sad.

Son of Adam will die & be raised

---

is apparently our author's creation. It is not the answer in Mark (9:29). Possibly the time of this gospel's writing was one of diminishing faith within the church.

I swear to you . . .: Except for the evangelist's ending (*And nothing will be beyond you*) this saying is taken from Q (Luke 17:6). Another form of it, from Mark, is used in 21:21.

beyond you: Greek: "impossible for you."

• **17:21** In the best Greek manuscripts there is no vs 21, a late re-insertion of Mark 9:29b ("The only thing that can drive this kind out is prayer"), which our author had omitted. See Introduction, p. 28, and the Text-Critical Note.

• **17:22–23** After 16:21, this is Jesus' second prediction of his death (based on Mark 9:30–32). The third is at 20:18–19.

• **17:22** *had been reunited in Galilee:* Or "were

gathered [again] in Galilee." But when had they been dispersed? This small difficulty perhaps motivated copyists to change the reading to "were living in Galilee," found in some manuscripts.

the son of Adam: It should be clear to the reader by now that the evangelist understands this title to mean simply Jesus.

to his enemies: "Into the hands [that is, the power] of humans." Does the evangelist have the Jewish leaders in mind, or the Romans?

• **17:23** *on the third day:* Mark 9:31 has "three days after he is killed." See on 16:21.

And they were very sad: In Mark (and Luke 9:45) they were instead unable to understand what Jesus was saying and afraid to ask him. Here the disciples clearly understand.

Temple tax

²⁴Ἐλθόντων δὲ αὐτῶν εἰς Καφαρναοὺμ προσῆλθον οἱ τὰ δίδραχμα λαμβάνοντες τῷ Πέτρῳ καὶ εἶπαν, Ὁ διδάσκαλος ὑμῶν οὐ τελεῖ τὰ δίδραχμα; ²⁵λέγει, Ναί.

Καὶ ἐλθόντα εἰς τὴν οἰκίαν προέφθασεν αὐτὸν ὁ Ἰησοῦς λέγων, Τί σοι δοκεῖ, Σίμων; οἱ βασιλεῖς τῆς γῆς ἀπὸ τίνων λαμβάνουσιν τέλη ἢ κῆνσον; ἀπὸ τῶν υἱῶν αὐτῶν ἢ ἀπὸ τῶν ἀλλοτρίων;

²⁶Εἰπόντος δέ, Ἀπὸ τῶν ἀλλοτρίων,

Ἔφη αὐτῷ ὁ Ἰησοῦς, Ἄρα γε ἐλεύθεροί εἰσιν οἱ υἱοί. ²⁷ἵνα δὲ μὴ σκανδαλίσωμεν αὐτούς, πορευθεὶς εἰς θάλασσαν βάλε ἄγκιστρον καὶ τὸν ἀναβάντα πρῶτον ἰχθὺν ἆρον, καὶ ἀνοίξας τὸ στόμα αὐτοῦ εὑρήσεις στατῆρα· ἐκεῖνον λαβὼν δὸς αὐτοῖς ἀντὶ ἐμοῦ καὶ σοῦ.

• **17:24–27** Only Matthew has this story.

• **17:24** *And when they came to Capernaum:* This is how the next episode in Mark begins. Our author uses it to introduce this legend unique to his tradition.

the temple tax: Levied by priests in support of the Jerusalem temple. In Greek, a *didrachmon*, a coin amounting to two denarii or, in Jewish coinage, half a shekel. Perhaps equal to a day's pay for a common laborer.

came to Peter: As often in this gospel, and perhaps in its tradition, Peter is singled out.

• **17:25** *That's right:* Was this true? At least the evangelist, perhaps formerly a devout Pharisee, assumes that Jesus would have paid the tax. But the story that follows raises doubt.

secular rulers: "The kings of the world." Here the Roman rulers must be meant because the Greek word for *tolls* derives from the Latin *census*. A census was taken for the purpose of establishing tax and tolls.

on their own people or on aliens? The answer is "On aliens," as Peter replies. That is, the burden of taxation would be born by those living in occupied territories. That means the Jews in Roman occupied Palestine.

• **17:26a** In Greek a dependent clause, a bare genitive absolute: "When <Peter> said . . . Jesus responded. . . ."

• **17:26b** *Then their own people are exempt:* By analogy, Jews should not have to pay taxes to their own priests who ruled the temple. Vss 25–26 may contain authentic teaching of Jesus, contrary to the Jesus Seminar's consensus (Funk, *Five Gospels*, 212–13). See below on 22:21 and just below on vs 27.

their own people: Literally, "their sons."

• **17:27** This little legend seems to qualify what Jesus has said in vs 26. Here he advises that it is best, after all, to pay the temple tax. With its brief miracle, told almost in passing, it seems to be a story created after

²⁴And when they came to Capernaum, those who collect the temple tax came to Peter and said, "Your teacher pays his temple tax, doesn't he?" ²⁵He said, "That's right."

And when he got home, Jesus anticipated what was on Peter's mind: "What are you thinking, Simon? On whom do secular rulers levy taxes and tolls? Do they levy them on their own people or on aliens?"

²⁶<Peter> said, "On aliens."

Jesus responded to him, "Then their own people are exempt. ²⁷Still, we don't want to get in trouble with them, so go down to the sea, cast your line in, and take the first fish that rises. Open its mouth and you will find a coin. Take it and pay them for both of us."

Jesus' time and used by those who passed on the tradition to keep the peace with Jerusalem leaders. Later still—after the temple's destruction in 70 CE, that is, in the evangelist's time—the Jewish temple tax had been replaced by a Roman tax in support of the pagan temple to Jupiter Capitolinus in Rome. Would Christians have wanted to pay that tax?

get in trouble with them: In the context a good translation for "offend them."

Open its mouth and you will find a coin: Jesus does not himself pay the tax; God, by working the miracle, takes that onus from him.

a coin: In Greek, a "stater," equal to four drachmas, or two didrachmas, and so adequate to pay the tax for both of them (see on vs 24).

The private teaching Jesus next gives his disciples in Mark (beginning at 9:33) sug-

gests the fourth discourse (Chap. 18). It begins almost imperceptibly but concludes clearly enough at 19:1. It has to do chiefly with issues and problems of Christians with one another, and might be considered Instructions for the Administration of the Church. In its present form it probably reflects the situation of the evangelist's church more than that of Jesus' lifetime. And like the other discourses, it is a collection of once separate sayings; the "you" addressed is sometimes singular, sometimes plural.

First, the question of hierarchy in the church, and how "the weaker brothers and sisters," as Paul called them, should be treated by those in authority. The teaching that follows pertains not simply or even primarily to children. They are a metaphor for any of the "little ones" who are the greatest in God's empire.

The fourth
discourse

Like children
in Heaven's
domain

Hand,
foot, & eye

18 Ἐν ἐκείνῃ τῇ ὥρᾳ προσῆλθον οἱ μαθηταὶ τῷ Ἰησοῦ λέγοντες, Τίς ἄρα μείζων ἐστὶν ἐν τῇ βασιλείᾳ τῶν οὐρανῶν;

²Καὶ προσκαλεσάμενος παιδίον ἔστησεν αὐτὸ ἐν μέσῳ αὐτῶν ³καὶ εἶπεν, Ἀμὴν λέγω ὑμῖν, ἐὰν μὴ στραφῆτε καὶ γένησθε ὡς τὰ παιδία, οὐ μὴ εἰσέλθητε εἰς τὴν βασιλείαν τῶν οὐρανῶν. ⁴ὅστις οὖν ταπεινώσει ἑαυτὸν ὡς τὸ παιδίον τοῦτο, οὗτός ἐστιν ὁ μείζων ἐν τῇ βασιλείᾳ τῶν οὐρανῶν. ⁵καὶ ὃς ἐὰν δέξηται ἓν παιδίον τοιοῦτο ἐπὶ τῷ ὀνόματί μου, ἐμὲ δέχεται.

⁶Ὃς δ᾽ ἂν σκανδαλίσῃ ἕνα τῶν μικρῶν τούτων τῶν πιστευόντων εἰς ἐμέ, συμφέρει αὐτῷ ἵνα κρεμασθῇ μύλος ὀνικὸς περὶ τὸν τράχηλον αὐτοῦ καὶ καταποντισθῇ ἐν τῷ πελάγει τῆς θαλάσσης.

⁷Οὐαὶ τῷ κόσμῳ ἀπὸ τῶν σκανδάλων· ἀνάγκη γὰρ ἐλθεῖν τὰ σκάνδαλα, πλὴν οὐαὶ τῷ ἀνθρώπῳ δι᾽ οὗ τὸ σκάνδαλον ἔρχεται. ⁸Εἰ δὲ ἡ χείρ σου ἢ ὁ πούς σου σκανδαλίζει σε, ἔκκοψον αὐτὸν καὶ βάλε ἀπὸ σοῦ· καλόν σοί ἐστιν εἰσελθεῖν εἰς τὴν ζωὴν κυλλὸν ἢ χωλὸν ἢ δύο χεῖρας ἢ δύο πόδας ἔχοντα βληθῆναι εἰς τὸ πῦρ τὸ αἰώνιον. ⁹καὶ εἰ ὁ ὀφθαλμός σου σκανδαλίζει σε, ἔξελε αὐτὸν καὶ βάλε ἀπὸ σοῦ· καλόν σοί ἐστι μονόφθαλμον εἰς τὴν ζωὴν εἰσελθεῖν ἢ δύο ὀφθαλμοὺς ἔχοντα βληθῆναι εἰς τὴν γέενναν τοῦ πυρός.

¹⁰Ὁρᾶτε μὴ καταφρονήσητε ἑνὸς τῶν μικρῶν τούτων· λέγω

• **18:1** *At that moment:* This phrase is not to be taken literally. Our author, like Mark's, could hardly have had in hand an itinerary for Jesus' career. He feels entirely free to rearrange stories and sayings. Rather, the phrase seems to be simply his editorial transition from the preceding story.

the disciples approached Jesus...: This introduces the discourse. The same clause is used to begin the first discourse (5:1) and the fifth (24:3).

Who is greatest in Heaven's domain? In Mark (9:33–34) Jesus knows that the disciples were secretly debating this. Here they broach the issue without any prompting, asking what is at least a useful question. Our author omits a saying from Mark (9:35: "If anyone wants to be 'number one,' that person has to be last of all and servant of all"). He will use it in 20:26–27, where it recurs in Mark.

• **18:2** *her:* The Greek word for *child* used here is neither masculine nor feminine, so the child could be either a girl or a boy. SV has chosen to use *her* instead of the conventional "him."

I swear to you: "Amen, I say to you." Jesus' way of making an important pronouncement.

• **18:3–4** Inserted by the evangelist, vs 3 from a later point in Mark (10:15).

• **18:3** *If you don't:* You plural.

do an about-face: A better translation than the usual "repent."

become like children: What might this mean?

• **18:4** Unique to Matthew. Does the evangelist create it to give explicit answer to the disciples' question in vs 1? There is no such answer in the Markan parallel.

put themselves on a level with: More literally, "humble themselves to be like."

• **18:5–6** The metaphor of becoming like children now shifts to another saying about a child. Here the word evidently means anyone who is fragile, naive, or easily misled. Or someone who has "become like" a child (vs 3).

• **18:5** The appearance of a related saying at 10:40 probably explains the author's omitting Mark 9:37b ("And whoever accepts me is not so much accepting me as the one who sent me").

in my name: See "in the name of" in the Glossary.

is accepting me: In other words, "thereby accepts me."

The evangelist here again omits material from Mark (9:38–41), which focused on Jesus' saying about a non-disciple, exorcising demons in his name: "Whoever is not

18 At that moment the disciples approached Jesus with the question, "Who is greatest in Heaven's domain?"

²And he called a child over, had her stand in front of them, ³and said, "I swear to you, if you don't do an about-face and become like children, you'll never enter Heaven's domain. ⁴Therefore those who put themselves on a level with this child are greatest in Heaven's domain. ⁵And whoever accepts one such child in my name is accepting me.

⁶"Any of you who misleads one of these little ones who trusts me would be better off to have a millstone hung around your neck and be drowned in the deepest part of the sea!

⁷"Damn the world for the snares it sets! And even though snares are inevitable, damn the person who sets them. ⁸If your hand or your foot gets you into trouble, cut it off and throw it away! It's better for you to enter life maimed or lame than to be thrown into the eternal fire with both hands and both feet. ⁹And if your eye gets you into trouble, rip it out and throw it away! After all, it's better for you to enter life one-eyed than to be thrown into Gehenna's fire with both your eyes.

¹⁰"See that you don't disdain one of these little ones. For I tell

---

against us is on our side." It may be that such ecumenical teaching is unacceptable to our author. The contrary view, found in 12:30 ("The one who isn't with me is against me") is more akin to this gospel's point of view.

• **18:6** *Any of you:* Not second person in Greek, but used by the translators to avoid non-inclusive language later in the sentence; see Introduction, p. 26.

misleads: Or "trips up." See below on 18:7–9.

millstone: Strictly, the upper millstone that a donkey usually turned, shaped like a slice of pineapple and 3 ft. or more in diameter. The vividness and exaggeration of Jesus' image is typical of his first-century Jewish mind.

• **18:7–9** Teaching about the "little ones" will resume in vs 10. Following Mark, this little section picks up on *misleads* in vs 6 as a catchword. Each of these four verses contains a form of the root *skandal-*, which means "mislead," "offend," "trip up," "cause to stumble." There seems no adequate way of showing this in English. It is variously translated in vss 6–9: *misleads, sets . . . snares, gets . . . into trouble*

• **18:7** Inserted from Q (Luke 7:1).

Damn: Traditionally, "Woe to," as in 11:21. See Translation Note, p. 63.

snares: Or "traps." In Greek, related to "mis-

leads" (vs 6).

snares are inevitable: The world Christians inhabit can easily trip one up.

• **18:8–9** How are we to understand this double saying? Not literally, one assumes, but then how? Perhaps it enjoins us to act decisively to rid ourselves of those temptations not set for us by *the world* (vs 7) but present in our own makeup.

• **18:8** *If your hand or your foot:* The "your" is singular.

gets . . . into trouble: The same verb again.

enter life . . . be thrown into the eternal fire: In Matthew these terms are apocalyptic. They speak of a last judgment, at the end of the age. However, to "enter life" must originally have meant joining the empire of God in the here and now.

• **18:9** *Gehenna's fire:* See Glossary. The same as "eternal fire" in the preceding verse.

• **18:10** This verse, perhaps a creation of the author, resumes the question how the *little ones* are to be treated.

See that you don't: The "you" is plural.

disdain: "Think little of."

one of these little ones: Not even one of them.

their guardian angels: Greek, "their angels in heaven." In SV the noun here is almost always translated "messengers." But it can

Lost sheep

γὰρ ὑμῖν ὅτι οἱ ἄγγελοι αὐτῶν ἐν οὐρανοῖς διὰ παντὸς βλέπουσι τὸ πρόσωπον τοῦ πατρός μου τοῦ ἐν οὐρανοῖς. [11]

¹²Τί ὑμῖν δοκεῖ;

Ἐὰν γένηταί τινι ἀνθρώπῳ ἑκατὸν πρόβατα καὶ πλανηθῇ
ἓν ἐξ αὐτῶν, οὐχὶ ἀφήσει τὰ ἐνενήκοντα ἐννέα ἐπὶ τὰ ὄρη
καὶ πορευθεὶς ζητεῖ τὸ πλανώμενον; ¹³καὶ ἐὰν γένηται εὑρεῖν
αὐτό, ἀμὴν λέγω ὑμῖν ὅτι χαίρει ἐπ᾽ αὐτῷ μᾶλλον ἢ ἐπὶ τοῖς
ἐνενήκοντα ἐννέα τοῖς μὴ πεπλανημένοις.

¹⁴Οὕτως οὐκ ἔστιν θέλημα ἔμπροσθεν τοῦ πατρὸς ὑμῶν τοῦ ἐν οὐρανοῖς ἵνα ἀπόληται ἓν τῶν μικρῶν τούτων.

Disciples & forgiveness

¹⁵Ἐὰν δὲ ἁμαρτήσῃ ὁ ἀδελφός σου, ὕπαγε ἔλεγξον αὐτὸν μεταξὺ σοῦ καὶ αὐτοῦ μόνου. ἐάν σου ἀκούσῃ, ἐκέρδησας τὸν ἀδελφόν σου· ¹⁶ἐὰν δὲ μὴ ἀκούσῃ, παράλαβε μετὰ σοῦ ἔτι ἕνα ἢ δύο, ἵνα ἐπὶ στόματος δύο μαρτύρων ἢ τριῶν σταθῇ πᾶν ῥῆμα· ¹⁷ἐὰν δὲ παρακούσῃ αὐτῶν, εἰπὲ τῇ ἐκκλησίᾳ· ἐὰν δὲ καὶ τῆς ἐκκλησίας παρακούσῃ, ἔστω σοι ὥσπερ ὁ ἐθνικὸς καὶ ὁ τελώνης.

¹⁸Ἀμὴν λέγω ὑμῖν· ὅσα ἐὰν δήσητε ἐπὶ τῆς γῆς ἔσται δεδεμένα ἐν οὐρανῷ, καὶ ὅσα ἐὰν λύσητε ἐπὶ τῆς γῆς ἔσται λελυμένα ἐν οὐρανῷ. ¹⁹πάλιν λέγω ὑμῖν ὅτι ἐὰν δύο συμφωνήσωσιν ἐξ ὑμῶν ἐπὶ τῆς

18:11 A verse, reading "The Son of Adam came to save what was lost," is missing in the best MSS. Evidently it was inserted to harmonize with Luke 19:10.

18:14 Many MSS read "my" in place of *your*.

18:15 Most MSS read *does wrong against you* but the latter two words are lacking in the earliest MSS. They may have been "imported" from what Peter asks in vs 21.

---

also mean God's agents delegated to watch over certain people, particularly those needing special care, like the *little ones*.

constantly gaze on the face of my Father in heaven: That is, have God's special attention.

• **18:11** See the Text-Critical Note.

• **18:12–14** An analogy; see below on vs 14. The author extends the teaching session borrowed from Mark 9:42–50 (omitting its last two verses on salt, used earlier in 5:13), first of all with this little passage from Q (Luke 15:3–5), in which the issue of the "little ones" in the community is further dealt with. Thom 107 has:

The <Father's> empire is like a shepherd who had a hundred sheep. ²One of them, the largest, went astray. He left the ninety-nine and looked for the one until he found it. ³After he had toiled, he said to the sheep, 'I love you more than the ninety-nine.

• **18:12** *What do you think about this?* Engaging the reader's attention. Like "Listen . . ." in 21:33. The "you" is plural.

wanders off: Or "goes astray." In Luke, "is lost." Our author knows this latter phrase (end of vs 14) but perhaps has in mind for the moment not children but errant church members.

• **18:13** *you can bet:* A colloquial equivalent of "Amen I tell you." See Translation Note (p. 63) on "I swear to you." The "you" is plural.

• **18:14** This ending is mostly the evangelist's. In Luke, the shepherd calls his friends to help him celebrate finding his lost sheep.

In the same way: An explicit analogy, not a parable or an allegory.

your Father: The "your" is plural.

not . . . lost: Does this mean "saved," the usual understanding? If so, from what? Perhaps instead it means not rejected or abandoned by society.

• **18:15** A briefer saying is in Luke 17:3b: "If your companion does wrong, scold that person; if there is a change of heart, forgive the person."

some companion: Greek, "your brother/

you, their guardian angels constantly gaze on the face of my Father in heaven.

¹²"What do you think about this?

> If someone has a hundred sheep and one of them wanders off, won't he leave the ninety-nine in the hills and go look for the one that wandered off? ¹³And if he should find it, you can bet he'll rejoice over it more than over the ninety-nine that didn't wander off.

¹⁴"In the same way it is the intention of your Father in heaven that not one of these little ones be lost.

¹⁵"And if some companion does wrong, go try to have it out between the two of privately. If that person listens to you, you have won your companion over. ¹⁶But if not, take one or two others with you so that 'every fact may be supported by two or three witnesses.' ¹⁷Then if the person refuses to listen to them, report it to the congregation. If someone refuses to listen even to the congregation, treat that one like a pagan or toll collector.

¹⁸"I swear to you, whatever you bind on earth will be considered bound in heaven, and whatever you release on earth will be considered released in heaven. ¹⁹Again I assure you, if two of you

---

sister." Probably not just a friend but a fellow Christian. "Your" is singular.

does wrong: Without "against you"(see the Text-Critical Note) the teaching seems to apply to the church, and not interpersonal relations; it means "sins." The instruction is about keeping your fellow Christian in line.

try to have it out: The present tense suggests "try to."

you have won your companion over: Strictly the verb here means "regained," so the meaning is apparently not so much "won over to your side of the argument" as held on to a fellow Christian. The "your" is singular.

• **18:16–17** Here the evangelist has broadened vs 15 into an ecclesiastical process, but the "you" continues to be singular.

• **18:16** *so that every fact may be supported by two or three witnesses:* This seems to be a paraphrase of Deut 19:15.

• **18:17** *congregation:* See on 16:18.

a pagan or toll collector: That is, an alien, a

stranger, or at the least a Jew not loyal to other Jews.

• **18:18** The possibility of wrongdoing by a community member, vss 15–17, raises the question of the church's role as to ethics. The same words are spoken to Peter in 16:19, except that there the "you" is singular.

bind . . . release: Does this have to do with determining what and what not is permissible behavior? Or with conveying and withholding forgiveness? The former, it seems; see above on 16:19

you: Plural, apparently the congregation as a body.

in heaven: That is, "by God."

• **18:19–20** Another uniquely Matthean saying, and yet another, having to do with the church as community and probably suggested by the catch-phrase "two or three" in vs 16.

• **18:19** *if two of you on earth agree:* Or "agree on earth"; it makes no difference.

γῆς περὶ παντὸς πράγματος οὗ ἐὰν αἰτήσωνται, γενήσεται αὐτοῖς παρὰ τοῦ πατρός μου τοῦ ἐν οὐρανοῖς. ²⁰οὗ γάρ εἰσιν δύο ἢ τρεῖς συνηγμένοι εἰς τὸ ἐμὸν ὄνομα, ἐκεῖ εἰμι ἐν μέσῳ αὐτῶν.

²¹Τότε προσελθὼν ὁ Πέτρος εἶπεν αὐτῷ, Κύριε, ποσάκις ἁμαρτήσει εἰς ἐμὲ ὁ ἀδελφός μου καὶ ἀφήσω αὐτῷ; ἕως ἑπτάκις;

²²Λέγει αὐτῷ ὁ Ἰησοῦς, Οὐ λέγω σοι ἕως ἑπτάκις ἀλλὰ ἕως ἑβδομηκοντάκις ἑπτά.

The unforgiving slave

²³Διὰ τοῦτο ὡμοιώθη ἡ βασιλεία τῶν οὐρανῶν ἀνθρώπῳ βασιλεῖ, ὃς ἠθέλησεν συνᾶραι λόγον μετὰ τῶν δούλων αὐτοῦ. ²⁴ἀρξαμένου δὲ αὐτοῦ συναίρειν προσηνέχθη αὐτῷ εἷς ὀφειλέτης μυρίων ταλάντων. ²⁵μὴ ἔχοντος δὲ αὐτοῦ ἀποδοῦναι ἐκέλευσεν αὐτὸν ὁ κύριος πραθῆναι καὶ τὴν γυναῖκα καὶ τὰ τέκνα καὶ πάντα ὅσα ἔχει, καὶ ἀποδοθῆναι.

²⁶Πεσὼν οὖν ὁ δοῦλος προσεκύνει αὐτῷ λέγων, Μακροθύμησον ἐπ' ἐμοί, καὶ πάντα ἀποδώσω σοι. ²⁷σπλαγχνισθεὶς δὲ ὁ κύριος τοῦ δούλου ἐκείνου ἀπέλυσεν αὐτὸν καὶ τὸ δάνειον ἀφῆκεν αὐτῷ.

²⁸Ἐξελθὼν δὲ ὁ δοῦλος ἐκεῖνος εὗρεν ἕνα τῶν συνδούλων αὐτοῦ, ὃς ὤφειλεν αὐτῷ ἑκατὸν δηνάρια, καὶ κρατήσας αὐτὸν ἔπνιγεν λέγων, Ἀπόδος εἴ τι ὀφείλεις.

²⁹Πεσὼν οὖν ὁ σύνδουλος αὐτοῦ παρεκάλει αὐτὸν λέγων, Μακροθύμησον ἐπ' ἐμοί, καὶ ἀποδώσω σοι. ³⁰Ὁ δὲ οὐκ ἤθελεν ἀλλὰ ἀπελθὼν ἔβαλεν αὐτὸν εἰς φυλακὴν ἕως ἀποδῷ τὸ ὀφειλόμενον.

³¹Ἰδόντες οὖν οἱ σύνδουλοι αὐτοῦ τὰ γενόμενα ἐλυπήθησαν σφόδρα καὶ ἐλθόντες διεσάφησαν τῷ κυρίῳ ἑαυτῶν πάντα τὰ γενόμενα.

• **18:20** Perhaps more believable than vs 19.

• **18:21–22** The author seems to pick up Q again, after vs 15. For there is something like this in the corresponding verse in Luke (17:4), perhaps in the form to be found in Q: "If someone wrongs you seven times a day, and seven times turns around and says to you, 'I'm sorry,' you should forgive that person." Our evangelist has left out the repentance of the sinner, and so upped the ante for Jesus' follower. That he has omitted "a day" doesn't of course help, since Jesus is not speaking literally.

• **18:21** Peter again appears onstage to ask the question that Jesus will answer in the following verse.

Master: Or "Lord."

companion: Greek, "brother." Not so much friend as fellow-Christian.

and still expect my forgiveness: Literally, "and I must forgive" that one.

seven times: The seemingly exaggerated number comes from Q; it serves to "set up" the outlandish reply.

• **18:22** *seventy-seven:* Or even "seventy times seven"; the Greek is ambiguous. But of course in either case the answer means "without limit."

• **18:23–35** A parable unique to Matthew. No doubt placed here for its lesson of forgiveness. Possibly authentic to Jesus, in some form (as the exaggeration in vs 24—ten million dollars—suggests), but certainly not as an allegory of God's forgiveness. And Jesus' parables did not usually have an obvious ethical moral.

• **18:23** *This is why:* Usually translated "Therefore." The phrase is simply connective, and the connection to the preceding is the matter of forgiveness.

secular ruler: Greek, "a man [who was] a king," an odd construction. Perhaps "a king"

on earth agree on anything you ask for, it will be done for you by my Father in heaven. ²⁰In fact, wherever two or three are gathered together in my name, I will be there among them."

²¹Then Peter came up and asked him, "Master, how many times can a companion wrong me and still expect my forgiveness? As many as seven times?"

²²Jesus replies to him, "I don't say to you seven times, but as many as seventy-seven times.

²³This is why Heaven's imperial rule should be compared to a secular ruler who decided to settle accounts with his slaves. ²⁴When the settling began, this one debtor was brought in who owed ten million dollars. ²⁵Since he couldn't pay it back, his master ordered him sold, along with his wife and children and everything he had, in order to recover the debt.

The unforgiving slave

²⁶At this prospect, the slave fell down and groveled before him: 'Be patient with me, and I'll repay every cent.' ²⁷Because he was compassionate, the master let the slave go and canceled the debt.

²⁸As soon as he got out, that same fellow collared one of his fellow slaves who owed him a hundred dollars, and grabbed him by the neck and demanded: 'Pay back what you owe!'

²⁹His fellow slave fell down and begged him: 'Be patient with me and I'll pay you back.'

³⁰But he wasn't interested; instead, he went out and had the man thrown in prison until he paid the debt.

³¹When his fellow slaves realized what had happened, they were terribly distressed, and they went and reported to their master everything that had taken place.

---

is the evangelist's addition. This would make him stand for God, as in vs 35. Elsewhere in the story he is called simply a master.

settle accounts with his slaves: A number of a rich man's (or a king's) slaves would have high standing, responsible for a major part of his affairs, including financial ones. The same is true in the parable of the entrusted money (25:14–30); see also 24:45–47.

• **18:24** *this one debtor:* Such slaves could evidently borrow from their owner for their own use.

ten million dollars: Greek: 10,000 talents. No factor can realistically translate this amount into contemporary terms, but it was obviously vast, in fact unimaginably so. The exaggeration for effect, no doubt, to contrast outlandishly with the amount in vs 28.

• **18:25** *sold:* As of course slaves could be.

to recover the debt: The story is hardly realistic.

• **18:26** *At this prospect:* Usually, "Therefore."

I'll repay every cent: If he could, by recalling the debts owed him. Not very likely.

• **18:27** *canceled the debt:* Or "forgave him the loan," with the same verb as in vs 35: "forgive each other." His forgiveness is lavish, again to contrast with vss 28–30.

• **18:28** *got out:* Out of trouble, evidently.

one of his fellow slaves: An ironic turn of events.

a hundred dollars: In Greek, "100 denarii." Whatever the precise modern equivalent, an infinitesimal fraction of the 10,000 talents he owed the master.

• **18:29** *Be patient with me and I'll pay you back:* As the first slave had begged his master (vs 26).

• **18:30** *he wasn't interested:* "He wouldn't."

• **18:31–34** While the original parable may have included these verses, it more likely ended with vs 30 (like the earliest form of

³²Τότε προσκαλεσάμενος αὐτὸν ὁ κύριος αὐτοῦ λέγει αὐτῷ, Δοῦλε πονηρέ, πᾶσαν τὴν ὀφειλὴν ἐκείνην ἀφῆκά σοι, ἐπεὶ παρεκάλεσάς με· ³³οὐκ ἔδει καὶ σὲ ἐλεῆσαι τὸν σύνδουλόν σου, ὡς κἀγὼ σὲ ἠλέησα; ³⁴καὶ ὀργισθεὶς ὁ κύριος αὐτοῦ παρέδωκεν αὐτὸν τοῖς βασανισταῖς ἕως οὗ ἀποδῷ πᾶν τὸ ὀφειλόμενον.

³⁵Οὕτως καὶ ὁ πατήρ μου ὁ οὐράνιος ποιήσει ὑμῖν, ἐὰν μὴ ἀφῆτε ἕκαστος τῷ ἀδελφῷ αὐτοῦ ἀπὸ τῶν καρδιῶν ὑμῶν.

---

the leased vineyard—see below on 21:40–43). If so, this block was added to provide a scene of judgment, with its moral for those who don't forgive (vs 35).

• **18:32** *canceled:* See vs 27.
• **18:33** *treat . . . with . . . consideration:* The Greek is a bit more specific, "show mercy [*or* pity] toward," just as the master "was compas-

³²And so in the end his master summoned him: 'You wicked slave,' he says to him, 'I canceled your entire debt because you begged me. ³³Wasn't it only fair for you to treat your fellow slave with the same consideration as I treated you?' ³⁴And the master was so angry he handed him over to those in charge of punishment until he paid back everything he owed.

³⁵"That's what my heavenly Father will do to you, unless you each find it in your hearts to forgive your brother and sister."

---

sionate" in vs 27.

• **18:34** *punishment:* Perhaps "torture."

• **18:35** Not part of the parable, but an allegorical moral, no doubt added by the evangelist, the master standing for God and "you" (plural) for the members of the church. This warning is similar to 6:15, only more threatening. See above on 6:14–15.

**Jesus
leaves Galilee**

19 Καὶ ἐγένετο ὅτε ἐτέλεσεν ὁ Ἰησοῦς τοὺς λόγους τούτους, μετῆρεν ἀπὸ τῆς Γαλιλαίας καὶ ἦλθεν εἰς τὰ ὅρια τῆς Ἰουδαίας πέραν τοῦ Ἰορδάνου. ²καὶ ἠκολούθησαν αὐτῷ ὄχλοι πολλοί, καὶ ἐθεράπευσεν αὐτοὺς ἐκεῖ.

**Created
male & female**

³Καὶ προσῆλθον αὐτῷ Φαρισαῖοι πειράζοντες αὐτὸν καὶ λέγοντες, Εἰ ἔξεστιν ἀνθρώπῳ ἀπολῦσαι τὴν γυναῖκα αὐτοῦ κατὰ πᾶσαν αἰτίαν;

⁴Ὁ δὲ ἀποκριθεὶς εἶπεν, Οὐκ ἀνέγνωτε ὅτι ὁ κτίσας ἀπ' ἀρχῆς ἄρσεν καὶ θῆλυ ἐποίησεν αὐτούς; ⁵καὶ εἶπεν, Ἕνεκα τούτου καταλείψει ἄνθρωπος τὸν πατέρα καὶ τὴν μητέρα καὶ κολληθήσεται τῇ γυναικὶ αὐτοῦ, καὶ ἔσονται οἱ δύο εἰς σάρκα μίαν. ⁶ὥστε οὐκέτι εἰσὶν δύο ἀλλὰ σὰρξ μία. ὃ οὖν ὁ θεὸς συνέζευξεν ἄνθρωπος μὴ χωριζέτω.

⁷Λέγουσιν αὐτῷ, Τί οὖν Μωϋσῆς ἐνετείλατο δοῦναι βιβλίον ἀποστασίου καὶ ἀπολῦσαι αὐτήν;

⁸Λέγει αὐτοῖς ὅτι Μωϋσῆς πρὸς τὴν σκληροκαρδίαν ὑμῶν ἐπέτρεψεν ὑμῖν ἀπολῦσαι τὰς γυναῖκας ὑμῶν, ἀπ' ἀρχῆς δὲ οὐ γέγονεν οὕτως. ⁹λέγω δὲ ὑμῖν ὅτι ὃς ἂν ἀπολύσῃ τὴν γυναῖκα αὐτοῦ μὴ ἐπὶ πορνείᾳ καὶ γαμήσῃ ἄλλην μοιχᾶται.

Celibacy

¹⁰Λέγουσιν αὐτῷ οἱ μαθηταί, Εἰ οὕτως ἐστὶν ἡ αἰτία τοῦ ἀνθρώπου μετὰ τῆς γυναικός, οὐ συμφέρει γαμῆσαι.

¹¹Ὁ δὲ εἶπεν αὐτοῖς, Οὐ πάντες χωροῦσιν τὸν λόγον τοῦτον ἀλλ' οἷς δέδοται. ¹²εἰσὶν γὰρ εὐνοῦχοι οἵτινες ἐκ κοιλίας μητρὸς ἐγεννήθησαν οὕτως, καὶ εἰσὶν εὐνοῦχοι οἵτινες εὐνουχίσθησαν ὑπὸ

• **Chaps. 19–20** For Jesus' journey up to Jerusalem (he enters the city at the beginning of chap. 21) the evangelist follows Mark rather closely, with only one major insertion (20:1–16).

• **19:1** *when Jesus had finished this instruction:* The formula by which the evangelist concludes each of the five blocks of uninterrupted teaching he has assembled, this fourth one having begun at 18:1–2 and giving *Instructions for the Church.* If the gospel as a whole can be thought of as a Manual of Discipline (see Introduction, p. 9), that is true especially of this chapter at the heart of Matthew.

he took leave of Galilee: In Mark 10:1 this is simply one of a number of shifts from place to place. Our author has made it Jesus' final departure from his home territory. He is on his way to Jerusalem. (See above on 16:21).

to the territory of Judea across the Jordan: Mark has "Judea and across the Jordan." It's not clear how this journey in Matthew should be envisioned. In the first century

no part of Judea was east of the Jordan. Possibly we should understand "to the territory of Judea, [by traveling] east of the Jordan," so as to avoid Samaria (note his instruction in 10:5).

• **19:2** *and he healed them there:* The author's addition, as several times earlier in the gospel.

• **19:3** *for any reason:* Does this mean "for whatever reason [he pleases]"? The question is a trap (*the Pharisees* are seeking *to test him*), since first-century Judaism allowed a man to divorce his wife, as we would say, unilaterally.

• **19:4** Gen 1:27.

• **19:5** Gen 2:24.
  wife: In Greek, "woman."
  body: A better rendering than "flesh." Also in vs 6.

• **19:7** The quotation is from Deut 24:1.

• **19:8** *obstinate:* "Hardhearted."

• **19:9** This essentially repeats Jesus' teaching in 5:31–32.
  Now, I tell you: In contrast to Moses.

19 And when Jesus had finished this instruction, he took leave of Galilee and went to the territory of Judea across the Jordan. ²And large crowds followed him and he healed them there.

³And the Pharisees approached him and, to test him, they ask, "Is <a husband> permitted to divorce his wife for any reason?"

⁴In response he puts a question to them: "Haven't you read that in the beginning the Creator 'made them male and female,' ⁵and <that further on> it says, 'for this reason, a man will leave his father and mother and be united with his wife, and the two will be one body'? ⁶Consequently, from then on they are one body instead of two. Therefore those God has coupled together, no one should separate."

⁷They say to him, "Then why did Moses order to give her 'a writ of divorce and send her away'?"

⁸He says to them, "Because you are obstinate Moses permitted you to divorce your wives, but it wasn't like that originally. ⁹Now, I tell you, whoever divorces his wife, except for infidelity, and marries another commits adultery."

¹⁰The disciples say to him, "If this is how it is in the case of a man and his wife, it's better not to marry."

¹¹Then he said to them, "Not everyone will be able to accept this advice, only those for whom it was intended. ¹²In fact, there are castrated men who were born that way, and those who were castrated by others, and those who castrated themselves because

---

except for infidelity: See above on 5:32. The phrase is absent in the parallels at Mark 10:11 and Luke 16:18. Since it also contradicts vs 8 and what precedes it, this must be an addition either by the evangelist or his tradition.

commits adultery: The author is following Mark 10:2–12 here. But he omits "against her" (in Mark's vs 11) after these words, as well as Mark's vs 12: "and if she divorces her husband and marries another, she commits adultery." The focus is entirely on the husband.

• **19:10–12** There is nothing like this in the other gospels.

• **19:11** *Not everyone will be able to accept this advice:* Jesus, or a later transmitter of the tradition, acknowledges the difficulty the saying presents.

this advice: "This saying," expectation. Presumably the prohibition of divorce, not the disciples' suggestion that marriage itself is ruled out. For that, see end of vs 12.

only those for whom it was intended: Together

with the "except for infidelity " in vs 9, a further limitation of the divorce prohibition.

• **19:12** This follows on vs 10, if self-castration means choosing celibacy. But see the third comment below.

In fact: Greek *gar.*

castrated men: Greek, "eunuchs."

castrated themselves because of the Heaven's imperial rule: This is perhaps not meant literally. (But so the third-century theologian Origen of Alexandria chillingly understood it.) One possibility is that the saying does not advocate celibacy but recognizes that renouncing a culturally endemic masculine dominance in order to become worthy of God's empire would be seen by others as self-emasculation.

because of: Or "for the sake of."

If you are able to accept <this advice>: Again, a limitation on the extent to which this teaching applies. The Greek is very terse: "Let the one who can accept accept."

τῶν ἀνθρώπων, καὶ εἰσὶν εὐνοῦχοι οἵτινες εὐνούχισαν ἑαυτοὺς διὰ τὴν βασιλείαν τῶν οὐρανῶν. ὁ δυνάμενος χωρεῖν χωρείτω.

Like children in heaven's domain

¹³Τότε προσηνέχθησαν αὐτῷ παιδία ἵνα τὰς χεῖρας ἐπιθῇ αὐτοῖς καὶ προσεύξηται· οἱ δὲ μαθηταὶ ἐπετίμησαν αὐτοῖς.

¹⁴Ὁ δὲ Ἰησοῦς εἶπεν, Ἄφετε τὰ παιδία καὶ μὴ κωλύετε αὐτὰ ἐλθεῖν πρός με, τῶν γὰρ τοιούτων ἐστὶν ἡ βασιλεία τῶν οὐρανῶν. ¹⁵καὶ ἐπιθεὶς τὰς χεῖρας αὐτοῖς ἐπορεύθη ἐκεῖθεν.

Man with money

¹⁶Καὶ ἰδοὺ εἷς προσελθὼν αὐτῷ εἶπεν, Διδάσκαλε, τί ἀγαθὸν ποιήσω ἵνα σχῶ ζωὴν αἰώνιον;

¹⁷Ὁ δὲ εἶπεν αὐτῷ, Τί με ἐρωτᾷς περὶ τοῦ ἀγαθοῦ; εἷς ἐστιν ὁ ἀγαθός· εἰ δὲ θέλεις εἰς τὴν ζωὴν εἰσελθεῖν, τήρησον τὰς ἐντολάς.

¹⁸Λέγει αὐτῷ, Ποίας;

Ὁ δὲ Ἰησοῦς εἶπεν, Τὸ Οὐ φονεύσεις, Οὐ μοιχεύσεις, Οὐ κλέψεις, Οὐ ψευδομαρτυρήσεις, ¹⁹Τίμα τὸν πατέρα καὶ τὴν μητέρα, καί, Ἀγαπήσεις τὸν πλησίον σου ὡς σεαυτόν.

²⁰Λέγει αὐτῷ ὁ νεανίσκος· Πάντα ταῦτα ἐφύλαξα· τί ἔτι ὑστερῶ;

²¹Ἔφη αὐτῷ ὁ Ἰησοῦς, Εἰ θέλεις τέλειος εἶναι, ὕπαγε πώλησόν σου τὰ ὑπάρχοντα καὶ δὸς τοῖς πτωχοῖς, καὶ ἕξεις θησαυρὸν ἐν οὐρανοῖς, καὶ δεῦρο ἀκολούθει μοι.

²²Ἀκούσας δὲ ὁ νεανίσκος τὸν λόγον ἀπῆλθεν λυπούμενος· ἦν γὰρ ἔχων κτήματα πολλά.

Needle's eye

²³Ὁ δὲ Ἰησοῦς εἶπεν τοῖς μαθηταῖς αὐτοῦ, Ἀμὴν λέγω ὑμῖν ὅτι πλούσιος δυσκόλως εἰσελεύσεται εἰς τὴν βασιλείαν τῶν οὐρανῶν.

• **19:13–15** Similar to 18:1–5.

• **19:13** *lay his hands on them:* To bless? In Mark and Luke, "touch them."

and pray: Not in the parallel in Mark or Luke, so apparently added by the evangelist. Together with the change in "lay hands on them," this perhaps reflects practice in the Matthean church.

• **19:14** *Heaven's domain belongs to people like that:* Traditionally "Of such is the Kingdom of Heaven." The SV wording is apt.

people like that: The passage has to do not just with children but any of the "little ones" of 18:3–6.

The evangelist omits Mark 10:15 ("I swear to you, if you don't do an about-face and become like children, you'll never enter God's domain"), having inserted it at 18:3 into the Markan text he followed there.

• **19:16–17** Subtly but significantly changed from Mark 10:17–18, which reads, "'Good teacher, what do I have to do to inherit eternal life?' Jesus said to him, 'Why do you call me good? No one is good except for God

alone.'"

• **19:16** *Teacher, what good . . . :* The word *good* has moved from where Mark had it. It's no longer an epithet for Jesus ("Good Teacher"). Now it fills out the person's question: *What good do I have to do . . . ?*

eternal life: A phrase used rarely in the synoptic gospels, but common in the Gospel of John.

• **19:17** *Why do you ask me about the good?* Instead of Mark's "Why do you call me good?" Our author would perhaps be comfortable with calling Jesus "Good" but wants the question asked to contain the adjective

There is only One who is good: Essentially the same as Mark's "no one is good except for God alone." God is good and therefore the source of all good.

If you want to enter life, observe the commandments: The original question is now answered explicitly, unlike Mark (10:19—"You know the commandments"). God, who is good, has told us what is good.

enter life: The evangelist changed Mark's

of Heaven's imperial rule. If you are able to accept <this advice>, accept it."

¹³Then little children were brought to him so he could lay his hands on them and pray, but the disciples scolded them.

Like children in heaven's domain

¹⁴Jesus said, "Let the children alone. Don't try to stop them from coming up to me. After all, Heaven's domain belongs to people like that." ¹⁵And when he had laid his hands on them, he left that place.

¹⁶And then someone came and asked him, "Teacher, what good do I have to do to have eternal life?"

Man with money

¹⁷He said to him, "Why do you ask me about the good? There is only One who is good. If you want to enter life, observe the commandments."

¹⁸He says to him, "Which ones?"

Jesus replied, "'You must not murder, you are not to commit adultery, you are not to steal, you are not to give false testimony, ¹⁹you are to honor your father and mother, and you are to love your neighbor as yourself.'"

²⁰The young man says to him, "I have observed all these; what am I missing?"

²¹Jesus said to him, "If you want to be perfect, then go for it: Sell your belongings and give <the proceeds> to the poor and you will have treasure in heaven. And then come, follow me!"

²²When the young man heard this advice, he went away dejected, since he had a fortune.

²³Jesus said to his disciples, "I swear to you, it's difficult for the

Needle's eye

"inherit" eternal life to "have" in vs 16 and here uses another synonym; probably not significant changes.

• **19:18–19** Jesus' answer to the man's further question (*Which* [commandments]?) follows Mark 10:19 closely. It cites what we would call the ethical commandments, against *murder, adultery, steal[ing], false testimony,* and for respect of *father and mother.* Not the cultic ones, such as, "You are to make no idol for yourself." The evangelist omits Mark's "you are not to defraud" probably only to save space, in view of his adding love of neighbor in vs 19.

• **19:19** *and you are to love your neighbor as yourself:* To Mark's list our evangelist has added this commandment, which comes from Lev 19:18; it is found also at Matt 22:39, where Jesus summarizes the whole Law. The question is answered.

• **19:20** *The young man:* He has not been described as young till now, and in Mark and Luke he is not so called. In those accounts he says that he has done all these things *since*

his youth. Why the change? Is his youth important to the evangelist?

• **19:21** *If you want to be perfect:* Added by our author, since it is not in Mark or Luke. A literal and obviously impossible perfection can hardly be intended. Can the directive to sell all and come follow Jesus be seen as a "counsel of perfection," for those few who can accept it? Or does it apply to all who would be Jesus' disciples? Very soon (vs 27) Peter, speaking for all the disciples, will say "we left everything to follow you." Presumably that is meant to be the model of discipleship. How can modern middle-class Christians call themselves disciples?

then go for it: In Greek, simply "Go." The SV translation captures in modern idiom the note of decisive action Jesus calls for.

• **19:22** *the young man . . . had a fortune:* As in Mark this leads into the next section about riches and poverty.

²⁴πάλιν δὲ λέγω ὑμῖν, εὐκοπώτερόν ἐστιν κάμηλον διὰ τρυπήματος ῥαφίδος διελθεῖν ἢ πλούσιον εἰσελθεῖν εἰς τὴν βασιλείαν τοῦ θεοῦ.

²⁵Ἀκούσαντες δὲ οἱ μαθηταὶ ἐξεπλήσσοντο σφόδρα λέγοντες, Τίς ἄρα δύναται σωθῆναι;

²⁶Ἐμβλέψας δὲ ὁ Ἰησοῦς εἶπεν αὐτοῖς, Παρὰ ἀνθρώποις τοῦτο ἀδύνατόν ἐστιν, παρὰ δὲ θεῷ πάντα δυνατά.

Leaving everything

²⁷Τότε ἀποκριθεὶς ὁ Πέτρος εἶπεν αὐτῷ, Ἰδοὺ ἡμεῖς ἀφήκαμεν πάντα καὶ ἠκολουθήσαμέν σοι· τί ἄρα ἔσται ἡμῖν;

²⁸Ὁ δὲ Ἰησοῦς εἶπεν αὐτοῖς, Ἀμὴν λέγω ὑμῖν ὅτι ὑμεῖς οἱ ἀκολουθήσαντές μοι ἐν τῇ παλιγγενεσίᾳ, ὅταν καθίσῃ ὁ υἱὸς τοῦ ἀνθρώπου ἐπὶ θρόνου δόξης αὐτοῦ, καθήσεσθε καὶ ὑμεῖς ἐπὶ δώδεκα θρόνους κρίνοντες τὰς δώδεκα φυλὰς τοῦ Ἰσραήλ. ²⁹καὶ πᾶς ὅστις ἀφῆκεν οἰκίας ἢ ἀδελφοὺς ἢ ἀδελφὰς ἢ πατέρα ἢ μητέρα ἢ τέκνα ἢ ἀγροὺς ἕνεκεν τοῦ ὀνόματός μου, ἑκατονταπλασίονα λήμψεται καὶ ζωὴν αἰώνιον κληρονομήσει.

³⁰Πολλοὶ δὲ ἔσονται πρῶτοι ἔσχατοι καὶ ἔσχατοι πρῶτοι.

• **19:24** *Let me put it this way:* Greek: "And again I tell you." The doubling of a saying that was in the first instance (vs 23) a kind of summary, emphasizes it.

squeeze through a needle's eye: A deliberately ridiculous image. (Another outlandish saying about a camel, a big and ungainly animal, is at 23:24: "gulp down a camel.") Contrary to a widespread belief, there is no evidence of a gate in Jerusalem that was called the Needle's Eye, which it was difficult, but not impossible, for a camel to squeeze through.

God's domain: This is one of a very few instances where the phrase is not "heaven's domain," otherwise characteristic of Matthew. (Besides this one, 12:22; 21:22, 43.) Did the evangelist forget to change it in these places? See Translation Note p. 46.

• **19:25** *who can be saved?:* That is, evidently, "have eternal life" (vs16).

• **19:26** *for God everything's possible:* This ending of the discussion about riches and the new age is found also in Mark and Luke. Is it an easing of the rigor of Jesus' teaching for a church that now includes some who are rich?

• **19:27** *What do we get out of it?:* A curious question. Jesus has said that they will "enter life."

• **19:28** Our author has inserted this saying into the text of Mark he is following. Those who leave everything to follow Jesus (vs 27) will gain, besides the reward promised in vs 30, this more worldly one.

rich to enter Heaven's domain. ²⁴Let me put it this way: It's easier for a camel to squeeze through a needle's eye than for a wealthy person to get into God's domain."

²⁵When the disciples heard this, they were quite perplexed and said, "Well then, who can be saved?"

²⁶Jesus looked them in the eye, and said to them, "For mortals this is impossible; for God everything's possible."

²⁷In response Peter said to him, "Look at us, we left everything to follow you! What do we get out of it?"

Leaving everything

²⁸Jesus told them, "I swear to you, you who have followed me, when the son of Adam is seated on his throne of glory in the renewal <of creation>, you also will be seated on twelve thrones and sit in judgment on the twelve tribes of Israel. ²⁹And everyone who on my account has left homes or brothers or sisters or father or mother or children or farms will receive a hundred times as much, and inherit eternal life.

³⁰"Many of the first will be last, and of the last many will be first.

---

when the son of Adam is seated on his throne of glory in the renewal <of creation>: A common imagining of the last judgment, which will mark the end of this age and the beginning of another; *the son of Adam* takes the place of God.

the renewal <of creation>: The rare Greek word (*palingenesia*) means more than a renovation, but a beginning again.

sit in judgment on the twelve tribes of Israel: Jesus' "twelve" will constitute the new Israel. The image is like the divine council that is sometimes portrayed in the OT, for example Ps 82:1. The twelve will be justices and God the chief justice.

• **19:29** Jesus' closest followers are those who have done what the rich young man in vss

20–22 could not do. And far more. They have given up not only wealth but *homes or brothers or sisters or father or mother or children or farms.*

will receive a hundred times as much and inherit eternal life: Mark has "will receive a hundred times as much *in this age* and *in the age to come* eternal life" (10:30)

• **19:30** This saying, from Mark 10:31, acts like a coda also at 20:16 (and at Luke 13:30). It may once have been an independent saying, but was attached here by Mark's author. It gives a somewhat different image of the last judgment: the new age of God brings a 180-degree reversal of human hierarchies of wealth, prestige, and power.

20 Ὁμοία γάρ ἐστιν ἡ βασιλεία τῶν οὐρανῶν ἀνθρώπῳ οἰκοδεσπότῃ, ὅστις ἐξῆλθεν ἅμα πρωῒ μισθώσασθαι ἐργάτας εἰς τὸν ἀμπελῶνα αὐτοῦ. ²συμφωνήσας δὲ μετὰ τῶν ἐργατῶν ἐκ δηναρίου τὴν ἡμέραν ἀπέστειλεν αὐτοὺς εἰς τὸν ἀμπελῶνα αὐτοῦ.

³Καὶ ἐξελθὼν περὶ τρίτην ὥραν εἶδεν ἄλλους ἑστῶτας ἐν τῇ ἀγορᾷ ἀργούς ⁴καὶ ἐκείνοις εἶπεν, Ὑπάγετε καὶ ὑμεῖς εἰς τὸν ἀμπελῶνα, καὶ ὃ ἐὰν ᾖ δίκαιον δώσω ὑμῖν. ⁵οἱ δὲ ἀπῆλθον. Πάλιν ἐξελθὼν περὶ ἕκτην καὶ ἐνάτην ὥραν ἐποίησεν ὡσαύτως. ⁶Περὶ δὲ τὴν ἑνδεκάτην ἐξελθὼν εὗρεν ἄλλους ἑστῶτας καὶ λέγει αὐτοῖς, Τί ὧδε ἑστήκατε ὅλην τὴν ἡμέραν ἀργοί;

⁷Λέγουσιν αὐτῷ, Ὅτι οὐδεὶς ἡμᾶς ἐμισθώσατο.

Λέγει αὐτοῖς, Ὑπάγετε καὶ ὑμεῖς εἰς τὸν ἀμπελῶνα.

⁸Ὀψίας δὲ γενομένης λέγει ὁ κύριος τοῦ ἀμπελῶνος τῷ ἐπιτρόπῳ αὐτοῦ, Κάλεσον τοὺς ἐργάτας καὶ ἀπόδος αὐτοῖς τὸν μισθὸν ἀρξάμενος ἀπὸ τῶν ἐσχάτων ἕως τῶν πρώτων.

⁹Καὶ ἐλθόντες οἱ περὶ τὴν ἑνδεκάτην ὥραν ἔλαβον ἀνὰ δηνάριον. ¹⁰καὶ ἐλθόντες οἱ πρῶτοι ἐνόμισαν ὅτι πλεῖον λήμψονται· καὶ ἔλαβον ἀνὰ δηνάριον καὶ αὐτοί. ¹¹λαβόντες δὲ ἐγόγγυζον κατὰ τοῦ οἰκοδεσπότου ¹²λέγοντες, Οὗτοι οἱ ἔσχατοι μίαν ὥραν ἐποίησαν, καὶ ἴσους ἡμῖν αὐτοὺς ἐποίησας τοῖς βαστάσασι τὸ βάρος τῆς ἡμέρας καὶ τὸν καύσωνα.

¹³Ὁ δὲ ἀποκριθεὶς ἑνὶ αὐτῶν εἶπεν, Ἑταῖρε, οὐκ ἀδικῶ σε· οὐχὶ δηναρίου συνεφώνησάς μοι; ¹⁴ἆρον τὸ σὸν καὶ ὕπαγε. θέλω δὲ τούτῳ τῷ ἐσχάτῳ δοῦναι ὡς καὶ σοί· ¹⁵οὐκ ἔξεστίν μοι ὃ θέλω ποιῆσαι ἐν τοῖς ἐμοῖς; ἢ ὁ ὀφθαλμός σου πονηρός ἐστιν ὅτι ἐγὼ ἀγαθός εἰμι;

¹⁶Οὕτως ἔσονται οἱ ἔσχατοι πρῶτοι καὶ οἱ πρῶτοι ἔσχατοι.

• **20:1–16** This parable is unique to Matthew. Why is it placed here, do you suppose? It is the author's only major insertion into the Markan text he is following. It is one of Jesus' most striking parables, certainly authentic to him.

• **20:1** *For Heaven's imperial rule is like . . .:* This evangelist, esp., introduces parables as similes for the new age.

proprietor: Or perhaps "landowner." See below on vs 8.

went out . . . to hire workers for his vineyard: Into town, to hire day laborers. The grape harvest is labor-intensive and cannot be delayed.

the first thing in the morning: About 6 a.m.

• **20:2** *a silver coin a day:* The Roman *denarius*, probably the common daily wage for a day laborer. At least those hired *agreed* to it.

• **20:3** *9 a.m.:* "The third hour."

idle: Probably not lazy, but out of work (vs 7).

• **20:5** *noon . . . 3 p.m.:* The sixth and the ninth hour.

• **20:6** *5 p.m.:* The eleventh hour, probably one hour before quitting time at sunset.

• **20:7** *no one hired us:* So they are jobless, not lazy. But today's prejudice against the unemployed may have been current then

• **20:8** *the owner of the vineyard tells his foreman:* Is "the owner" the person mentioned in vs 1, or was that the foreman, there called "proprietor"? Anyway, it makes no real difference to the meaning of the parable.

starting with those hired last and ending with those hired first: This detail is essential to the

20 For Heaven's imperial rule is like a proprietor who went out the first thing in the morning to hire workers for his vineyard. ²After agreeing with the workers for a silver coin a day, he sent them into his vineyard.

³And going out around 9 a.m., he saw others idle in the marketplace ⁴and he said to them, 'You go into the vineyard too, and I'll pay you whatever is fair.' ⁵So they went. Around noon he went out again, and at 3 p.m., and did the same. ⁶About 5 p.m. he went out and found others idle and says to them, 'Why did you stand around here idle the whole day?'

⁷They reply, 'Because no one hired us.'

He tells them, 'You go into the vineyard as well.'

⁸When evening came, the owner of the vineyard tells his foreman, 'Call the workers and pay them their wages, starting with those hired last and ending with those hired first.'

⁹Those hired at 5 p.m. came up and received a silver coin each. ¹⁰Those hired first came, thinking they would receive more. But they also got a silver coin apiece. ¹¹They took it and began to grumble against the proprietor:

¹²'These guys hired last worked only an hour, but you've made them equal to us who did most of the work during the heat of the day.'

¹³In response he said to one of them, 'Look, my friend, did I wrong you? You agreed with me for a silver coin, didn't you? ¹⁴Take your wage and go on! I intend to treat the one hired last the same way I treat you. ¹⁵Is there some law forbidding me to do as I please with my money? Or is your eye envious because I am generous?'

¹⁶The last will be first and the first last.'

Vineyard laborers

---

story's drama.

- **20:9** *a silver coin each:* The amount promised those hired at 6 a.m. See comment on vs 2.
- **20:11** *grumble:* Or "gripe."
- **20:12** *you've made them equal to us:* The objection seems to be based not on the discrepancy in hours worked, that is, the apparent unfairness, but rather on the matter of status, as if those who were hired first were somehow superior to those who had been "idle" part or most of the day, and esp. *during the heat of the day.* But of course we are meant to understand their objection as based on the discrepancy in pay. See further my essay, " 'You have made them equal to us' (Mt 20:1–16)."
- **20:14** *I intend to treat the one hired last the same way I treat you:* Not a principle to be

applied to labor relations, but he gives the going daily wage because one could barely survive and feed one's family on it, and certainly not on less.

- **20:15** *to do as I please with my money:* He sounds ruthless but in fact he is generous, a generosity that infuriates those who worked all day.

  envious because I am generous: Greek, "evil because I am good."
- **20:16** This saying forms another coda at 19:30, but though it more or less fits there (see comment), it doesn't here. At first it may seem to, since the workers hired last are paid first, but of course the story's point is not the order they are paid in, but that they receive equal pay.

Son of Adam will die & be raised

¹⁷Καὶ ἀναβαίνων ὁ Ἰησοῦς εἰς Ἱεροσόλυμα παρέλαβεν τοὺς δώδεκα κατ' ἰδίαν καὶ ἐν τῇ ὁδῷ εἶπεν αὐτοῖς, ¹⁸Ἰδοὺ ἀναβαίνομεν εἰς Ἱεροσόλυμα, καὶ ὁ υἱὸς τοῦ ἀνθρώπου παραδοθήσεται τοῖς ἀρχιερεῦσιν καὶ γραμματεῦσιν, καὶ κατακρινοῦσιν αὐτὸν θανάτῳ ¹⁹καὶ παραδώσουσιν αὐτὸν τοῖς ἔθνεσιν εἰς τὸ ἐμπαῖξαι καὶ μαστιγῶσαι καὶ σταυρῶσαι, καὶ τῇ τρίτῃ ἡμέρᾳ ἐγερθήσεται.

Jesus' cup

²⁰Τότε προσῆλθεν αὐτῷ ἡ μήτηρ τῶν υἱῶν Ζεβεδαίου μετὰ τῶν υἱῶν αὐτῆς προσκυνοῦσα καὶ αἰτοῦσά τι ἀπ' αὐτοῦ.

²¹Ὁ δὲ εἶπεν αὐτῇ, Τί θέλεις;

Λέγει αὐτῷ, Εἰπὲ ἵνα καθίσωσιν οὗτοι οἱ δύο υἱοί μου εἷς ἐκ δεξιῶν σου καὶ εἷς ἐξ εὐωνύμων σου ἐν τῇ βασιλείᾳ σου.

²²Ἀποκριθεὶς δὲ ὁ Ἰησοῦς εἶπεν, Οὐκ οἴδατε τί αἰτεῖσθε. δύνασθε πιεῖν τὸ ποτήριον ὃ ἐγὼ μέλλω πίνειν;

Λέγουσιν αὐτῷ, Δυνάμεθα.

²³Λέγει αὐτοῖς, Τὸ μὲν ποτήριόν μου πίεσθε, τὸ δὲ καθίσαι ἐκ δεξιῶν μου καὶ ἐξ εὐωνύμων οὐκ ἔστιν ἐμὸν τοῦτο δοῦναι, ἀλλ' οἷς ἡτοίμασται ὑπὸ τοῦ πατρός μου.

"Number one" is slave

²⁴Καὶ ἀκούσαντες οἱ δέκα ἠγανάκτησαν περὶ τῶν δύο ἀδελφῶν. ²⁵ὁ δὲ Ἰησοῦς προσκαλεσάμενος αὐτοὺς εἶπεν, Οἴδατε ὅτι οἱ ἄρχοντες τῶν ἐθνῶν κατακυριεύουσιν αὐτῶν καὶ οἱ μεγάλοι κατεξουσιάζουσιν αὐτῶν. ²⁶οὐχ οὕτως ἔσται ἐν ὑμῖν, ἀλλ' ὃς ἐὰν θέλῃ ἐν ὑμῖν μέγας γενέσθαι ἔσται ὑμῶν διάκονος, ²⁷καὶ ὃς ἂν θέλῃ ἐν ὑμῖν εἶναι πρῶτος ἔσται ὑμῶν δοῦλος· ²⁸ὥσπερ ὁ υἱὸς τοῦ ἀνθρώπου οὐκ ἦλθεν διακονηθῆναι ἀλλὰ διακονῆσαι καὶ δοῦναι τὴν ψυχὴν αὐτοῦ λύτρον ἀντὶ πολλῶν.

Two blind men

²⁹Καὶ ἐκπορευομένων αὐτῶν ἀπὸ Ἰεριχὼ ἠκολούθησεν αὐτῷ ὄχλος πολύς. ³⁰καὶ ἰδοὺ δύο τυφλοὶ καθήμενοι παρὰ τὴν ὁδὸν

20:30 Some mss omit *Lord*, and a few have "Jesus" instead.

• **20:17–34** The rest of the chapter follows Mark 10 closely.

• **20:17–19** This is the third such prediction Jesus makes, following Mark 10:32–34. The others are at 16:21 and 17:22–23.

• **20:17** *On the way up to Jerusalem:* A journey that began at 16:21 and was reinforced at 19:1 by Jesus' formal departure from Galilee. See below, vs 29 and 21:1.

• **20:18** *Listen:* Or "Look." Traditionally rendered "Behold!"

• **20:19** *to ridicule:* As in 27:27–31. This detail is in Mark, and also "spit upon," which our evangelist omits.

on the third day he will be raised: See above on 16:21.

• **20:20** *the mother of the sons of Zebedee:* In Mark (Luke lacks this story) it is James and John themselves who make the request. The

change has been made also in the next verse, but not in vs 22. Has the evangelist shifted the inappropriate request from the disciples to their mother, to protect their reputation?

the sons of Zebedee: Named James and John; see 4:21.

• **20:21** *sit one at your right hand and one at your left:* In the places of honor, in other words, above the other disciples.

in your domain: Assuming that Jesus will preside as a kind of potentate over "God's empire."

• **20:22** The forms of "you" in this verse are all plural, showing that the story was originally, as in Mark, of the two men themselves asking the favor from Jesus. The response to his question (*We can!*) is a further indication.

the cup that I'm about to drink?: What does this mean? Many think it refers to Jesus'

¹⁷On the way up to Jerusalem Jesus took the twelve aside privately and said to them as they walked along, ¹⁸"Listen, we're going up to Jerusalem, and the son of Adam will be turned over to the ranking priests and scholars, and they will sentence him to death, ¹⁹and turn him over to foreigners to ridicule, and flog, and crucify. Yet on the third day he will be raised."

²⁰Then the mother of the sons of Zebedee came up to him with her sons, bowed down before him, and asked him for a favor.

²¹He said to her, "What do you want?"

She said to him, "Give me your word that these two sons of mine may sit one at your right hand and one at your left in your domain."

²²In response Jesus said, "You have no idea what you're asking for. Can you drink the cup that I'm about to drink?"

They said to him, "We can!"

²³He says to them, "You'll be drinking my cup, but as for sitting at my right or my left, that's not mine to grant; it belongs to those for whom my Father has reserved it."

²⁴And when they learned of it, the ten became annoyed with the two brothers. ²⁵And calling them aside, Jesus said, "You know how foreign rulers lord it over their subjects, and how their strong men tyrannize them. ²⁶It's not going to be like that with you! With you, whoever wants to become great will be your servant, ²⁷and whoever among you wants to be 'number one' is to be your slave. ²⁸After all, the son of Adam didn't come to be served but to serve, even to give his life as a ransom for many."

²⁹And as they were leaving Jericho, a huge crowd followed him. ³⁰There were two blind men sitting beside the road. When they

Son of Adam will die & be raised

Jesus' cup

"Number one" is slave

Two blind men

---

death. As evidently in his prayer in Gethsemane (26:39). The evangelist leaves out a second question in Mark (10:38): "or undergo the baptism I'm undergoing?"

• **20:23** *You'll be drinking my cup:* Perhaps reflecting the author's knowledge, after the fact, that some of the disciples would be martyred.

my Father: Lacking in Mark, but probably implied there.

• **20:24–28** Jesus corrects the misunderstanding of the disciples—both the sons of Zebedee and the other ten—about what it means to be great in God's empire.

• **20:24** *the ten:* The rest of "the twelve."

• **20:25** *foreign:* Gentile.

• **20:27** *number one:* Greek, "first."

• **20:28** *a ransom for many:* Perhaps a reference to Isa 53:12. This brief part-verse is the only

reference in Matthew to the idea that Jesus' death was atoning, a central element in Paul's developed theology (Rom 3:24–26).

ransom: Freeing those held hostage, whether by sin or oppression.

20:29 *leaving Jericho:* This is curious, since we have not been told of their arrival. At last report (19:1) they had gone to Transjordan. (It is even stranger in Mark 10:46: "Then they come to Jericho. As he was leaving Jericho. . . .") No doubt the author is simply preparing for Jesus' approach to Jerusalem in 21:1. Jericho is deep in the Jordan valley, almost 4000 feet below Jerusalem but only about sixteen miles distant.

• **20:30** *two blind men:* As also in 9:27–31, which is perhaps a variant of this story. In both Mark and Luke there is only one blind man (in Mark alone he is named, "Bartimae-

ἀκούσαντες ὅτι Ἰησοῦς παράγει, ἔκραξαν λέγοντες, Ἐλέησον ἡμᾶς, κύριε, υἱὸς Δαυίδ.

³¹Ὁ δὲ ὄχλος ἐπετίμησεν αὐτοῖς ἵνα σιωπήσωσιν· οἱ δὲ μεῖζον ἔκραξαν λέγοντες, Ἐλέησον ἡμᾶς, κύριε, υἱὸς Δαυίδ.

³²Καὶ στὰς ὁ Ἰησοῦς ἐφώνησεν αὐτοὺς καὶ εἶπεν, Τί θέλετε ποιήσω ὑμῖν;

³³Λέγουσιν αὐτῷ, Κύριε, ἵνα ἀνοιγῶσιν οἱ ὀφθαλμοὶ ἡμῶν.

³⁴Σπλαγχνισθεὶς δὲ ὁ Ἰησοῦς ἥψατο τῶν ὀμμάτων αὐτῶν, καὶ εὐθέως ἀνέβλεψαν καὶ ἠκολούθησαν αὐτῷ.

---

us"). And in those two gospels he is a beggar; *beside the road* is an obvious place to beg, but here we are not told that the blind men were begging. Assuming that the evangelist had the same traditions as Mark and Luke, why these changes?

    son of David: That is, the Anointed/the Messiah.

• **20:31** *The crowd yelled at them to shut up:* Because yelling was unseemly? Or unsuitable

learned that Jesus was going by, they shouted, "Have mercy on us, Lord, you son of David."

³¹The crowd yelled at them to shut up, but they shouted all the louder, "Have mercy on us, Lord, you son of David."

³²Jesus paused and called out to them, "What do you want me to do for you?"

³³They said to him, "Lord, open our eyes!"

³⁴Then Jesus took pity on them, touched their eyes, and right away they regained their sight and followed him.

---

for lowly beggars?

• **20:34** *Jesus took pity on them [and] touched their eyes:* The evangelist changes Mark, where Jesus simply tells them to go, and that their trust has cured them.

followed him: Simply joining the growing crowd that has been following him throughout the gospel, or becoming disciples?

Jesus enters
Jerusalem

21 Καὶ ὅτε ἤγγισαν εἰς Ἱεροσόλυμα καὶ ἦλθον εἰς Βηθφαγὴ εἰς τὸ Ὄρος τῶν Ἐλαιῶν, τότε Ἰησοῦς ἀπέστειλεν δύο μαθητὰς ²λέγων αὐτοῖς, Πορεύεσθε εἰς τὴν κώμην τὴν κατέναντι ὑμῶν, καὶ εὐθέως εὑρήσετε ὄνον δεδεμένην καὶ πῶλον μετ' αὐτῆς· λύσαντες ἀγάγετέ μοι. ³καὶ ἐάν τις ὑμῖν εἴπῃ τι, ἐρεῖτε ὅτι Ὁ κύριος αὐτῶν χρείαν ἔχει· εὐθὺς δὲ ἀποστελεῖ αὐτούς. ⁴Τοῦτο δὲ γέγονεν ἵνα πληρωθῇ τὸ ῥηθὲν διὰ τοῦ προφήτου λέγοντος,

⁵Εἴπατε τῇ θυγατρὶ Σιών·
Ἰδοὺ ὁ βασιλεύς σου ἔρχεταί σοι πραῢς
καὶ ἐπιβεβηκὼς ἐπὶ ὄνον
καὶ ἐπὶ πῶλον υἱὸν ὑποζυγίου.

⁶Πορευθέντες δὲ οἱ μαθηταὶ καὶ ποιήσαντες καθὼς συνέταξεν αὐτοῖς ὁ Ἰησοῦς ⁷ἤγαγον τὴν ὄνον καὶ τὸν πῶλον καὶ ἐπέθηκαν ἐπ' αὐτῶν τὰ ἱμάτια, καὶ ἐπεκάθισεν ἐπάνω αὐτῶν. ⁸ὁ δὲ πλεῖστος ὄχλος ἔστρωσαν ἑαυτῶν τὰ ἱμάτια ἐν τῇ ὁδῷ, ἄλλοι δὲ ἔκοπτον κλάδους ἀπὸ τῶν δένδρων καὶ ἐστρώννυον ἐν τῇ ὁδῷ. ⁹οἱ δὲ ὄχλοι οἱ προάγοντες αὐτὸν καὶ οἱ ἀκολουθοῦντες ἔκραζον λέγοντες,

Ὡσαννὰ τῷ υἱῷ Δαυίδ·
Εὐλογημένος ὁ ἐρχόμενος ἐν ὀνόματι κυρίου·
Ὡσαννὰ ἐν τοῖς ὑψίστοις.

21:7 Some important mss have "on it" in place of the first *on them*, probably trying to correct our author's overly literal use of Zechariah 9:9. Then the cloaks are put on only the donkey, and Jesus sits on them (the cloaks) and rides on only one animal. But that is probably not original.

• **21:1** *When they got close to Jerusalem:* See on 20:17.

Bethphage at the Mount of Olives: A little-known village, evidently somewhere on the side of the Mount, probably near Bethany (see vs 17 below). Mark and Luke have "Bethphage and Bethany," which reflects a vague grasp of Judean geography. But our evangelist's simplification doesn't necessarily mean greater precision, perhaps only the wish for a leaner text.

the Mount of Olives: Overlooking Jerusalem from the east, part of the central ridge that runs from north to south in Palestine, dropping off sharply to the east into the Rift Valley and the Jordan River.

• **21:2** *just inside:* Strictly, "right away" (*eutheôs*).

a donkey . . . and a colt alongside her: In Mark and Luke Jesus says they'll find simply "a colt." We'll see just below why this gospel speaks of two animals.

• **21:3** *Their master:* Many versions translate as "the Lord" for all three gospels. This ignores the possessive pronoun, which could refer to the owner of the animal[s], not Jesus as the Master or Lord in an absolute sense. Does the Greek, and SV's more correct rendering, suggest deceit on Jesus' part? Or does our author mean "Their Lord," that is, their creator? That seems unlikely to me.

• **21:4–5** The typically Matthean citation of prophecy fulfillment (see Introduction, p. 19), not found in Mark or Luke even though this passage lies behind both their accounts. The quotation is a bit premature, since Jesus has not yet ridden on the animals.

• **21:4** *the prophet:* Unnamed. Perhaps because the evangelist doesn't know that the passage quoted is from Zech (9:9).

• **21:5** *in all modesty mounted on a donkey:* That is, not on a magnificent steed.

and on a colt, the foal of a donkey: In Hebrew, this is simply poetic parallelism, saying the

21 When they got close to Jerusalem, and came to Bethphage at the Mount of Olives, Jesus sent two disciples ahead ²with these instructions: "Go into the village across the way, and just inside you will find a donkey tied up, and a colt alongside her. Untie <them> and bring <them> to me. ³And if anyone says anything to you, you are to say, 'Their master has need of them and he will send them back right away.'" ⁴This happened so the word spoken through the prophet would come true:

> ⁵Tell the daughter of Zion,
> Look, your king comes to you in all modesty
> mounted on a donkey
> and on a colt, the foal of a donkey.

⁶Then the disciples went and did as Jesus instructed them, ⁷and brought the donkey and colt and they placed their cloaks on them, and he sat on them. ⁸The enormous crowd spread their cloaks on the road, and others cut branches from the trees and spread them on the road. ⁹The crowds leading the way and those following kept shouting,

> Hosanna to the son of David!
> Blessed is the one who comes in the name of the Lord!
> Hosanna in the highest!

---

same thing twice in slightly different words: "On a donkey . . . [that is,] a colt, the foal of a beast of burden." But although Mark and Luke got it right, our evangelist has chosen to understand this to mean two animals, with *and* between the parallel phrases. He therefore will show the prophecy literally fulfilled in vs 7.

• **21:7** *they placed their cloaks on them, and he sat on them:* This is the more difficult reading (see the Text-Critical Note) and hence most probably the original. How this was to be managed is not clear. It only matters to the evangelist that scripture, which he takes at face value, be fulfilled. In some medieval depictions, Jesus rides on the donkey and her colt walks along beneath her.

• **21:8** *the enormous crowd:* Those who have followed Jesus from early in his ministry, perhaps as much from curiosity as conviction.

spread their cloaks on the road, . . . and spread [branches] on the road: Evidently by way of

recognizing and honoring a king, as for Jehu in 2 Kgs 9:13. The branches are identified as palms only in John 12:13.

• **21:9** The author gives a somewhat neater form of the crowd's shout than in Mark 11:9–10, omitting "Blessed is the coming kingdom of our father David." Our evangelist recognizes that *the son of David,* the messianic title he inserts, is not simply a restorer of the political golden age of Israelite memory.

Hosanna: Evidently the corruption of a Hebrew phrase ("Save now" or "Save we pray"). It has come to mean "Praise," just as the Greek *Kyrie eleison,* which means "Lord have mercy," is used in Eastern Christianity as an expression of adoration.

Blessed is the one who comes in the name of the Lord! Ps 118:26, traditionally welcoming the pilgrim to Jerusalem by greeting in God's name. Here of course it's an acclamation of Jesus' coming as *the Lord.*

¹⁰Καὶ εἰσελθόντος αὐτοῦ εἰς Ἱεροσόλυμα ἐσείσθη πᾶσα ἡ πόλις λέγουσα, Τίς ἐστιν οὗτος; ¹¹οἱ δὲ ὄχλοι ἔλεγον, Οὗτός ἐστιν ὁ προφήτης Ἰησοῦς ὁ ἀπὸ Ναζαρὲθ τῆς Γαλιλαίας.

Temple as hideout

¹²Καὶ εἰσῆλθεν Ἰησοῦς εἰς τὸ ἱερὸν καὶ ἐξέβαλεν πάντας τοὺς πωλοῦντας καὶ ἀγοράζοντας ἐν τῷ ἱερῷ, καὶ τὰς τραπέζας τῶν κολλυβιστῶν κατέστρεψεν καὶ τὰς καθέδρας τῶν πωλούντων τὰς περιστεράς,

¹³Καὶ λέγει αὐτοῖς, Γέγραπται,

Ὁ οἶκός μου οἶκος προσευχῆς κληθήσεται,
ὑμεῖς δὲ αὐτὸν ποιεῖτε σπήλαιον λῃστῶν.

Children cheer Jesus

¹⁴Καὶ προσῆλθον αὐτῷ τυφλοὶ καὶ χωλοὶ ἐν τῷ ἱερῷ, καὶ ἐθεράπευσεν αὐτούς. ¹⁵ἰδόντες δὲ οἱ ἀρχιερεῖς καὶ οἱ γραμματεῖς τὰ θαυμάσια ἃ ἐποίησεν καὶ τοὺς παῖδας τοὺς κράζοντας ἐν τῷ ἱερῷ καὶ λέγοντας, Ὡσαννὰ τῷ υἱῷ Δαυίδ, ἠγανάκτησαν ¹⁶καὶ εἶπαν αὐτῷ, Ἀκούεις τί οὗτοι λέγουσιν;

Ὁ δὲ Ἰησοῦς λέγει αὐτοῖς, Ναί. οὐδέποτε ἀνέγνωτε ὅτι Ἐκ στόματος νηπίων καὶ θηλαζόντων κατηρτίσω αἶνον;

¹⁷Καὶ καταλιπὼν αὐτοὺς ἐξῆλθεν ἔξω τῆς πόλεως εἰς Βηθανίαν καὶ ηὐλίσθη ἐκεῖ.

Fig tree without figs

¹⁸Πρωῒ δὲ ἐπανάγων εἰς τὴν πόλιν ἐπείνασεν. ¹⁹καὶ ἰδὼν συκῆν μίαν ἐπὶ τῆς ὁδοῦ ἦλθεν ἐπ' αὐτὴν καὶ οὐδὲν εὗρεν ἐν αὐτῇ εἰ μὴ φύλλα μόνον, καὶ λέγει αὐτῇ, Μηκέτι ἐκ σοῦ καρπὸς γένηται εἰς τὸν αἰῶνα. καὶ ἐξηράνθη παραχρῆμα ἡ συκῆ.

²⁰Καὶ ἰδόντες οἱ μαθηταὶ ἐθαύμασαν λέγοντες, Πῶς παραχρῆμα ἐξηράνθη ἡ συκῆ;

21:12 *God's temple:* An unusual way of designating the temple. Some MSS lack *God's.*

• **21:10b–11** The city's excited response is unique to Matthew.

• **21:11** *The crowds:* Who are these people? Presumably the crowd of vss 8–9, who had come with Jesus to the city.

the prophet Jesus: An explicit identification not used till now, except that in 13:57 Jesus implied that it applies to himself. It reappears below in vs 46.

• **21:12–13** At this point in Mark (11:11) Jesus goes to the temple, looks around, and goes out to Bethany for the night. Only next day does he purify the temple. Our author simplifies this, moving the temple incident here, and drastically abbreviates it.

• **21:12** *the temple area:* Evidently the outer court of the temple, open to the public. It was allowable to conduct business that provided what was needed to worship in the temple—that is, animals for sacrifice.

the bankers: Who would change Roman money into Jewish, as was required to buy sacrificial victims.

pigeon merchants: For the poor it was impossible to pay for a larger animal.

• **21:13** *It is written:* In Isa 56:7. The quotation is copied from Mark (11:17), but the evangelist has omitted the final phrase there—"for all peoples." Why? He certainly believes that Gentiles have a place in the Christian church. Does he perhaps think that the temple in Jerusalem—destroyed by his time—has no relevance for latter day converts?

a hideout for crooks: A better translation than the usual "den of thieves." The phrase is from Jer 7:11.

¹⁰And when he entered into Jerusalem the whole city trembled, saying, "Who is this?" ¹¹The crowds said, "This is the prophet Jesus, from Nazareth in Galilee!"

¹²And Jesus went into God's temple and chased all the vendors and shoppers out of the temple area and he turned the bankers' tables upside down, along with the chairs of the pigeon merchants.

Temple as hideout

¹³Then he says to them, "It is written,

My house is to be regarded as a house of prayer,
but you're turning it into 'a hideout for crooks.'"

¹⁴And some blind and lame people came to him in the temple area, and he healed them. ¹⁵Then the ranking priests and scholars saw the remarkable feats he performed, and the children who kept cheering in the temple area, shouting, "Hosanna to the son of David," and they were infuriated. ¹⁶And they said to him, "Do you hear what these children are saying?"

Children cheer Jesus

Jesus says to them, "Of course. Have you never read 'You have produced praise for yourself out of the mouths of babies and nursing infants'?"

¹⁷And leaving them behind, he went outside the city to Bethany and spent the night there.

¹⁸Early in the morning, as he was returning to the city, he got hungry. ¹⁹And so when he spotted a single fig tree on the way, he went up to it, and found nothing on it except some leaves, and he says to it, "You are never to bear fruit again!" And the fig tree withered instantly.

Fig tree without figs

²⁰And when the disciples saw this, they said in amazement, "How could the fig tree wither up so quickly?"

• **21:14–17** Except for the last verse, nothing here has a parallel in the other gospels.

• **21:14** *and he healed them:* A transitional notice that our author uses more than once.

• **21:15** *remarkable feats:* Greek, "wonders," not the same word usually translated "miracles," but overlapping in meaning.

Hosanna to the son of David: Reiterating the phrase used by the crowd in vs 9.

• **21:16** The quotation is an adaptation of Ps 8:2. There "you" refers to God, but in this gospel any phrase referring to God can equally be applied to Jesus.

• **21:17** *went outside the city to Bethany:* At this point, deviating from Mark. See on vss 12–13.

Bethany: A village not far outside Jerusalem to the southeast, on the road to Jericho.

• **21:19** *You are never to bear fruit again!* Jesus' natural human anger, presumably. But there is no mention as in Mark that "it wasn't [the] time for figs," a circumstance that would make Jesus' act not only spiteful but irrational.

withered instantly: Instead of sometime during the ensuing day or night, as in Mark (11:12–14, 20–21). The point of the story is not Jesus' anger but his miraculous ability, as the disciples' reaction in the next verse shows. Since the fig tree was sometimes a symbol for Israel or Jerusalem, this act has also been understood as a prophetic act of judgment on Jesus' part

²¹Ἀποκριθεὶς δὲ ὁ Ἰησοῦς εἶπεν αὐτοῖς, Ἀμὴν λέγω ὑμῖν, ἐὰν ἔχητε πίστιν καὶ μὴ διακριθῆτε, οὐ μόνον τὸ τῆς συκῆς ποιήσετε, ἀλλὰ κἂν τῷ ὄρει τούτῳ εἴπητε, Ἄρθητι καὶ βλήθητι εἰς τὴν θάλασσαν, γενήσεται· ²²καὶ πάντα ὅσα ἂν αἰτήσητε ἐν τῇ προσευχῇ πιστεύοντες λήμψεσθε.

On whose authority?

²³Καὶ ἐλθόντος αὐτοῦ εἰς τὸ ἱερὸν προσῆλθον αὐτῷ διδάσκοντι οἱ ἀρχιερεῖς καὶ οἱ πρεσβύτεροι τοῦ λαοῦ λέγοντες, Ἐν ποίᾳ ἐξουσίᾳ ταῦτα ποιεῖς; καὶ τίς σοι ἔδωκεν τὴν ἐξουσίαν ταύτην;

²⁴Ἀποκριθεὶς δὲ ὁ Ἰησοῦς εἶπεν αὐτοῖς, Ἐρωτήσω ὑμᾶς κἀγὼ λόγον ἕνα, ὃν ἐὰν εἴπητέ μοι κἀγὼ ὑμῖν ἐρῶ ἐν ποίᾳ ἐξουσίᾳ ταῦτα ποιῶ· ²⁵τὸ βάπτισμα τὸ Ἰωάννου πόθεν ἦν; ἐξ οὐρανοῦ ἢ ἐξ ἀνθρώπων;

Οἱ δὲ διελογίζοντο ἐν ἑαυτοῖς λέγοντες, Ἐὰν εἴπωμεν, Ἐξ οὐρανοῦ, ἐρεῖ ἡμῖν, Διὰ τί οὖν οὐκ ἐπιστεύσατε αὐτῷ; ²⁶ἐὰν δὲ εἴπωμεν, Ἐξ ἀνθρώπων, φοβούμεθα τὸν ὄχλον, πάντες γὰρ ὡς προφήτην ἔχουσιν τὸν Ἰωάννην. ²⁷καὶ ἀποκριθέντες τῷ Ἰησοῦ εἶπαν, Οὐκ οἴδαμεν.

Ἔφη αὐτοῖς καὶ αὐτός, Οὐδὲ ἐγὼ λέγω ὑμῖν ἐν ποίᾳ ἐξουσίᾳ ταῦτα ποιῶ.

Two sons

²⁸Τί δὲ ὑμῖν δοκεῖ;

Ἄνθρωπος εἶχεν τέκνα δύο. καὶ προσελθὼν τῷ πρώτῳ εἶπεν, Τέκνον, ὕπαγε σήμερον ἐργάζου ἐν τῷ ἀμπελῶνι.

21:28–31 Some MSS reverse the order of the sons' responses, the first saying No and then changing his mind, etc. And the answer of the listeners is "The first." (But a few of those MSS retain *The second.* Puzzling.) If the original text had the initially refusing son first, the order might have been reversed in order to make the story into an allegory, so that the initially willing son would stand for Israel, and the refusing one for the Gentiles. It would be harder to account for a change in the opposite direction.

• **21:21** *if you have trust:* Not primarily a matter of faith—that is, belief—but of confidence in God. Yet belief is not altogether absent.

if you do not doubt: That is, if you don't fail to trust what God can do.

but you can even say to this mountain . . .: While this passage comes from Mark 11:22–24, a similar saying appears in 17:20, and Thom 48 has a somewhat different version: "If two make peace with each other in a single house, they will say to this mountain, 'Move from here!' and it will move."

Our author omits the saying about forgiveness that concludes the scene in Mark (11:25). It appears there only because of the catchword "prayer," and in a slightly different form it has already been used in Matthew at 6:14.

• **21:23–27** A slight abbreviation of Mark

(11:27–33).

• **21:23** *the ranking priests and elders of the people:* Mark also lists "scholars." Is it significant that they are omitted?

while he was teaching: Added to Mark.

right . . . authority: Two slightly varying translations for the same Greek word *exousia*. The leaders are asking, Is it God's authority? Isn't it Satan's? And this is a trap. If he answers what he believes to be true, that it is by God's authority, he will be accused of blasphemy—and it is not yet the appointed time for him to be so accused and condemned (26:65–66). Instead he puts a shrewd question to his questioners, placing them in a similar dilemma—vss 24–26.

doing these things: It's not clear what this means: Teaching, or also purifying the temple and healing people there? But of course

²¹In response Jesus said to them, "I swear to you, if you have trust and do not doubt, not only can you do this to a fig tree but you can even say to this mountain, 'Up with you and into the sea!' and that's what will happen; ²²and everything you ask for in prayer you'll get if you trust."

²³And when he came to the temple area, the ranking priests and elders of the people approached him while he was teaching, and asked, "By what right are you doing these things?" and "Who gave you this authority?"

On whose authority?

²⁴In response Jesus said to them, "I also have one question for you. If you answer me, I'll tell you by what authority I do these things. ²⁵The baptism of John, what was its origin? Was it heaven-sent or was it of human origin?"

And they conferred among themselves, saying, "If we say 'heaven-sent,' he'll say to us, 'Then why didn't you trust him?'

²⁶ And if we say 'Of human origin' we're being afraid of the crowd, since everybody considers John a prophet." ²⁷And they answered Jesus by saying, "We can't tell."

And he in turn replied to them: "Neither am I going to tell you by what authority I do these things.

²⁸"Now what do you think?

Two sons

A man had two sons. He went to the first, and said, 'Son, go and work in the vineyard today.'

---

the point is the question of Jesus' authority in general.

• **21:24–25** Jesus' counter-question is also a kind of trap, but it is more. If the authorities understood who *John* was, and what he was doing, they would not have needed to ask their question of Jesus, whose work is in part a continuation of John's and was inaugurated by the latter-day Elijah, who had come to introduce the new age (11:14, 17:11–12).

• **21:25** *God-sent or . . . of human origin?:* Literally, "from heaven or from humans?"

• **21:26** *we're being afraid of the crowd:* In fact they were afraid of the crowd (see vs 46) but didn't want to show it or admit to themselves that they were.

• **21:27** *We can't tell:* Literally, "We don't know." A nice translation, playing on the word "tell" (vs 24) in English—they claim that they can't

decide but in fact they're not willing to *say* what they believe to be true, that the Baptist did not have divine authority.

And he in turn: The Greek is emphatic (*kai autos*).

• **21:28–32** This saying is found only in Matthew. The original order of the two sons' responses is hard to discern, since manuscripts differ so much (see the Text-Critical Note). But the meaning is probably not dependent on it.

• **21:28** *Now what do you think?* In other words, What do you make of this story? The parable of lost sheep begins in the same way, at 18:12, but as Jesus told them parables rarely ended in questions—as in vs 31a here. (On the question in 21:40, following the parable of the leased vineyard, see comment there.) And at first sight, at least, there seems to us

²⁹Ὁ δὲ ἀποκριθεὶς εἶπεν, Ἐγώ, κύριε, καὶ οὐκ ἀπῆλθεν.
³⁰Προσελθὼν δὲ τῷ ἑτέρῳ εἶπεν ὡσαύτως.
Ὁ δὲ ἀποκριθεὶς εἶπεν, Οὐ θέλω, ὕστερον δὲ μεταμεληθεὶς
ἀπῆλθεν.

³¹ Τίς ἐκ τῶν δύο ἐποίησεν τὸ θέλημα τοῦ πατρός;

Λέγουσιν, Ὁ δεύτερος.

Λέγει αὐτοῖς ὁ Ἰησοῦς, Ἀμὴν λέγω ὑμῖν ὅτι οἱ τελῶναι καὶ
αἱ πόρναι προάγουσιν ὑμᾶς εἰς τὴν βασιλείαν τοῦ θεοῦ. ³²ἦλθεν
γὰρ Ἰωάννης πρὸς ὑμᾶς ἐν ὁδῷ δικαιοσύνης, καὶ οὐκ ἐπιστεύσατε
αὐτῷ, οἱ δὲ τελῶναι καὶ αἱ πόρναι ἐπίστευσαν αὐτῷ· ὑμεῖς δὲ
ἰδόντες οὐδὲ μετεμελήθητε ὕστερον τοῦ πιστεῦσαι αὐτῷ.

Leased vineyard

³³Ἄλλην παραβολὴν ἀκούσατε.

Ἄνθρωπος ἦν οἰκοδεσπότης ὅστις ἐφύτευσεν ἀμπελῶνα
καὶ φραγμὸν αὐτῷ περιέθηκεν καὶ ὤρυξεν ἐν αὐτῷ ληνὸν
καὶ ᾠκοδόμησεν πύργον καὶ ἐξέδετο αὐτὸν γεωργοῖς καὶ
ἀπεδήμησεν. ³⁴ὅτε δὲ ἤγγισεν ὁ καιρὸς τῶν καρπῶν, ἀπέστειλεν
τοὺς δούλους αὐτοῦ πρὸς τοὺς γεωργοὺς λαβεῖν τοὺς καρποὺς
αὐτοῦ. ³⁵καὶ λαβόντες οἱ γεωργοὶ τοὺς δούλους αὐτοῦ ὃν μὲν
ἔδειραν, ὃν δὲ ἀπέκτειναν, ὃν δὲ ἐλιθοβόλησαν.

---

moderns to be nothing startling about the story, as we have learned to expect of Jesus' parables. On the contrary, it appears to be obvious—the second son does right and the first does not.

Son: Or "My boy"; the Greek uses the familial word for a child, *teknon,* which suggests a good relation between fathers and sons

• **21:29–31** The story would be startling, perhaps shocking, to its original hearers. By first-century CE Jewish standards, both brothers bring shame on their father. To fail to do what your father commands, and esp. after agreeing, disgraces him. But to say "No" to your father, even if you obey in the end, also disgraces him. Can it be that Jesus, who according to our author is speaking to the Jewish leaders of vs 23, is seeking to trick his hearers with the apparently straightforward question, *Which of the two …?* Dr. Tom Thatcher points out that this very brief story, if authentic to Jesus, would have circulated without evidence of its original audience. It may have been not a parable but a kind of riddle, to which the concluding question (vs 31a) is basic, esp. if the answer is not at all clear.

• **21:29** *Yes sir, I will!:* Very terse in Greek, but emphatic (*Egô, kyrie*).

sir: See comment on 8:2.

• **21:31** *They say.… Jesus says:* Two historic presents, relatively rare in Matthew, compared to Mark.

toll collectors and prostitutes will get into God's domain: For our author, the point of the story is an allegory about the Jewish leaders, "the ranking priests and elders of the people." They neither said "Yes" originally, nor first said "No" and later obeyed. Each of the sons had both disobeyed and obeyed; the leaders only disobeyed.

toll collectors and prostitutes: On the former, see Glossary. They are often coupled with "sinners."

• **21:32** This verse may seem not quite to fit the story of the two sons, which had to do with obedience, not belief. But of course the Baptist's advocacy was in the name of God and called for obedience.

advocating justice: In Greek, "in the road [or way] of justice."

justice: A better translation than the usual "righteousness." The latter can have a purely religious sense, not the ethical one intended here.

believe: In this case the more common translation of *pisteuein* is better than "trust."

Even when you observed <this>…: Under-

²⁹He responded, 'Yes sir, I will!'…but he didn't go.

³⁰Then he went to the second and said the same thing. He responded, 'I won't!'…but later on he thought better of it and went.

³¹"Which of the two did what the father wanted?" They say, "The second."

Jesus says to them,

I swear to you, the toll collectors and prostitutes will get into God's domain, but you will not. ³²After all, John came to you advocating justice, but you didn't believe him; yet the toll collectors and prostitutes believed him. Even when you observed <this>, you didn't think better of it later on and believe him.

³³"Listen to another parable:

Leased vineyard

There once was a landlord who 'planted a vineyard, put a hedge around it, dug a winepress in it, built a tower,' leased it out to some farmers, and went abroad. ³⁴Now when it was about harvest time, he sent his slaves to the farmers to collect his crop. ³⁵And the farmers grabbed his slaves, and one they beat and another they killed, and another they stoned.

---

standably, the self-appointed spiritual leaders of the people wouldn't have followed the example of *toll collectors and prostitutes,* but they should have.

then think better of it later on: Like the second son in Jesus' story.

• **21:33–46** As to SV's title for the parable, see below on vs 41. Our author retains the Markan context of Jesus' approaching death. In Mark it had already become an allegory—quite a different kind of story from a parable—about Jews (all Jews!) killing the son of God. The author of Mark, or whoever inserted the quotation from Isaiah into vs 33, accomplished this allegorizing. The insertion is not found in Thom 65:

A […] person owned a vineyard and rented it to some farmers, so they could work it and he could collect its crop from them. ²He sent his slave so the farmers would give him the vineyard's crop. ³They grabbed him, beat him, and almost killed him, and the slave returned and told his master. ⁴His master said, "Perhaps he didn't know them." ⁵He sent another slave, and the farmers beat that one as well. ⁶Then the master sent his son and said, "Perhaps they'll show my son some respect." ⁷Because the farmers knew that he

was the heir to the vineyard, they grabbed him and killed him.

The story was allegorized, of course, because of the parallel between the owner's son and Jesus as God's son, once that view of Jesus had been established.

• **21:33** The quoted words are from Isa 5, the "Song of the Vineyard," where they are a condemnation of sinful Israel's disobedience. The original parable was simply about an absentee landlord and some tenant farmers. Jesus' hearers would identify with the tenants, and the landlord—far from representing God—would be seen in a negative light. But with the insertion of the Isaiah quote into the story, it became a condemnation of non-Christian Jews, indeed of all Jews. The tenants, representing Israel, are now villains from the start. As in vs 41 they are the "wicked tenants," the usual name for this story.

As allegory the landlord is of course God, who has entrusted his vineyard to Israel. The slaves he sends to reap benefit (justice and righteousness) from the vineyard are the prophets that Israel rejected and even killed.

• **21:34–36** Mark 12:2–5 has a single slave sent each time and a third killed. Our author

³⁶Πάλιν ἀπέστειλεν ἄλλους δούλους πλείονας τῶν πρώτων, καὶ ἐποίησαν αὐτοῖς ὡσαύτως.

³⁷Ὕστερον δὲ ἀπέστειλεν πρὸς αὐτοὺς τὸν υἱὸν αὐτοῦ λέγων, Ἐντραπήσονται τὸν υἱόν μου.

³⁸Οἱ δὲ γεωργοὶ ἰδόντες τὸν υἱὸν εἶπον ἐν ἑαυτοῖς, Οὗτός ἐστιν ὁ κληρονόμος· δεῦτε ἀποκτείνωμεν αὐτὸν καὶ σχῶμεν τὴν κληρονομίαν αὐτοῦ, ³⁹καὶ λαβόντες αὐτὸν ἐξέβαλον ἔξω τοῦ ἀμπελῶνος καὶ ἀπέκτειναν.

⁴⁰Ὅταν οὖν ἔλθῃ ὁ κύριος τοῦ ἀμπελῶνος, τί ποιήσει τοῖς γεωργοῖς ἐκείνοις;

⁴¹Λέγουσιν αὐτῷ, Κακοὺς κακῶς ἀπολέσει αὐτοὺς καὶ τὸν ἀμπελῶνα ἐκδώσεται ἄλλοις γεωργοῖς, οἵτινες ἀποδώσουσιν αὐτῷ τοὺς καρποὺς ἐν τοῖς καιροῖς αὐτῶν.

⁴²Λέγει αὐτοῖς ὁ Ἰησοῦς, Οὐδέποτε ἀνέγνωτε ἐν ταῖς γραφαῖς,

Λίθον ὃν ἀπεδοκίμασαν οἱ οἰκοδομοῦντες,
οὗτος ἐγενήθη εἰς κεφαλὴν γωνίας·
παρὰ κυρίου ἐγένετο αὕτη
καὶ ἔστιν θαυμαστὴ ἐν ὀφθαλμοῖς ἡμῶν;

⁴³Διὰ τοῦτο λέγω ὑμῖν ὅτι ἀρθήσεται ἀφ' ὑμῶν ἡ βασιλεία τοῦ θεοῦ καὶ δοθήσεται ἔθνει ποιοῦντι τοὺς καρποὺς αὐτῆς.

⁴⁵Καὶ ἀκούσαντες οἱ ἀρχιερεῖς καὶ οἱ Φαρισαῖοι τὰς παραβολὰς αὐτοῦ ἔγνωσαν ὅτι περὶ αὐτῶν λέγει· ⁴⁶καὶ ζητοῦντες αὐτὸν κρατῆσαι ἐφοβήθησαν τοὺς ὄχλους, ἐπεὶ εἰς προφήτην αὐτὸν εἶχον.

21:44 Some important MSS have as vs 44 "Everyone who falls over that stone will be smashed to bits, and anyone on whom it falls will be crushed." Probably some scribes copied it in from Luke 20:18.

---

perhaps wanted to parallel more closely Israel's treatment of God's many prophets.

• **21:37** The landlord's son of course now stands for Jesus, son of God.

• **21:38** ...*the heir! Come on, let's kill him and we'll have his inheritance!* This makes no sense in the allegory. But in the original parable the land may once have belonged to those now reduced by forfeiture to tenants of an absentee landlord. The story as Jesus told it might have suggested to its hearers that even in desperate economic circumstances the oppressed are not helpless. That they kill the owner's son is of course not intended as a directive to be followed (since we know Jesus' teaching about violence—5:39a, for instance). Parables do not simply give moral advice.

• **21:39** *dragged him outside the vineyard, and killed him:* This reverses the order of these two acts found in Mark 15:20, 22. There the son is killed, then his body thrown out

of the vineyard. With our author's reversal the story more closely reflects Jesus' crucifixion outside the walls of Jerusalem. Luke (20:9–19) has made the same change.

• **21:40–43** The parable itself, the plot of the story, ends with vs 39, as in the Gospel of Thomas. What follows is later interpretation, emphasizing the allegorical meaning.

• **21:40** *When the owner of the vineyard comes, then what will he do to those farmers?:* A parable needs no interpretation added to it. And, so far as we know, Jesus did not originally quiz his hearers at the end of a parable. But now the allegory must be driven home. God will come at the end of the age and punish those who killed his son.

• **21:41** In Mark 12:9 Jesus answers his own question. The scene is a bit less artificial here.

He'll bring the villains to a miserable end: Mark has only "do away with those farmers." In the year 70 CE, the Jewish revolt

³⁶Again he sent other slaves, more than the first group, and they did the same thing to them.

³⁷Then finally he sent his son to them, with the thought, 'They will show this son of mine some respect.'

³⁸But when the farmers recognized the son they said to one another, 'This fellow's the heir. Come on, let's kill him and we'll have his inheritance!' ³⁹And they grabbed him, dragged him outside the vineyard, and killed him.

⁴⁰"When the owner of the vineyard comes, then, what will he do to those farmers?"

⁴¹They say to him, "He'll bring the villains to a miserable end and lease the vineyard out to other farmers who will deliver their produce to him at the proper time."

⁴²Jesus says to them, "Haven't you read in the scriptures,

A stone that the builders rejected
has ended up as the keystone.
It was the Lord's doing
and is something for us to admire . . .?

⁴³"Therefore I say to you, God's domain will be taken away from you and given to a people who <will> make it productive."

⁴⁵And when the ranking priests and Pharisees heard his parable, they realized that he was talking about them. ⁴⁶They wanted to seize him, but were afraid of the crowds, because everyone regarded him as a prophet.

---

failed, the temple was destroyed, and great numbers of Jews were driven into exile. For the allegorical interpreter of this parable, writing after that time, all that happened to Israel was seen as God's punishment for the death of Jesus.

villains: See above on vs 33. The traditional title for the parable, the wicked tenants, is correct for the evangelist, but it is not appropriate to Jesus' original parable. So SV's more neutral title is better.

and lease the vineyard out to other farmers: God has transferred his covenant of Israel to Christians and their church.

• **21:42** The quotation is from Ps 118:22–23. It celebrates the restoration of the crucified Jesus and has been interjected, since it breaks the connection between vss 41 and 43, and 43 negates its affirmation.

something for us to admire: Or "wonderful in our eyes."

• **21:43** *Therefore:* The connection is with vs 41.

God's domain will be taken away from you: This explicit and condemning moral occurs only in Matthew. It drives home the anti-Jewish burden of the allegory.

from you: Jesus is speaking again to the Jewish teachers of vs 27, as vs 45 shows.

a people who <will> make it productive: Christians, evidently, whether Jewish or Gentile.

Doubtless an allusion to Isa 5—esp. vss 2, 4, and 7.

• **[21:44]** If this verse was part of the original text of Matthew (see the Text-Critical Note), it further turns the affirmation in the Psalm quotation of vs 42 into a threat.

• **21:45** *they realized that he was talking about them:* They stand self-condemned, in our author's eyes.

• **21:46** *because everyone regarded him as a prophet:* Evidently added by the evangelist, reiterating Jesus' public acceptance, as in vs 11 above.

**Royal
wedding feast**

22 Καὶ ἀποκριθεὶς ὁ Ἰησοῦς πάλιν εἶπεν ἐν παραβολαῖς αὐτοῖς λέγων,

[2]Ὡμοιώθη ἡ βασιλεία τῶν οὐρανῶν ἀνθρώπῳ βασιλεῖ, ὅστις ἐποίησεν γάμους τῷ υἱῷ αὐτοῦ. [3]καὶ ἀπέστειλεν τοὺς δούλους αὐτοῦ καλέσαι τοὺς κεκλημένους εἰς τοὺς γάμους, καὶ οὐκ ἤθελον ἐλθεῖν.

[4]Πάλιν ἀπέστειλεν ἄλλους δούλους λέγων, Εἴπατε τοῖς κεκλημένοις, Ἰδοὺ τὸ ἄριστόν μου ἡτοίμακα, οἱ ταῦροί μου καὶ τὰ σιτιστὰ τεθυμένα καὶ πάντα ἕτοιμα· δεῦτε εἰς τοὺς γάμους.

[5]Οἱ δὲ ἀμελήσαντες ἀπῆλθον, ὃς μὲν εἰς τὸν ἴδιον ἀγρόν, ὃς δὲ ἐπὶ τὴν ἐμπορίαν αὐτοῦ· [6]οἱ δὲ λοιποὶ κρατήσαντες τοὺς δούλους αὐτοῦ ὕβρισαν καὶ ἀπέκτειναν.

[7]Ὁ δὲ βασιλεὺς ὠργίσθη καὶ πέμψας τὰ στρατεύματα αὐτοῦ ἀπώλεσεν τοὺς φονεῖς ἐκείνους καὶ τὴν πόλιν αὐτῶν ἐνέπρησεν. [8]τότε λέγει τοῖς δούλοις αὐτοῦ, Ὁ μὲν γάμος ἕτοιμός ἐστιν, οἱ δὲ κεκλημένοι οὐκ ἦσαν ἄξιοι· [9]πορεύεσθε οὖν ἐπὶ τὰς διεξόδους τῶν ὁδῶν καὶ ὅσους ἐὰν εὕρητε καλέσατε εἰς τοὺς γάμους.

[10]Καὶ ἐξελθόντες οἱ δοῦλοι ἐκεῖνοι εἰς τὰς ὁδοὺς συνήγαγον πάντας οὓς εὗρον, πονηρούς τε καὶ ἀγαθούς· καὶ ἐπλήσθη ὁ γάμος ἀνακειμένων.

[11]Εἰσελθὼν δὲ ὁ βασιλεὺς θεάσασθαι τοὺς ἀνακειμένους εἶδεν

• **22:1–14** A roughly similar parable appears in Luke 14:16–24 and Thom 64. This one is more clearly allegorical. The Thomas version:

Someone was receiving guests. When he had prepared the dinner, he sent his slave to invite the guests. [2]The slave went to the first and said, "My master invites you." The first replied, [3]"Some merchants owe me money; they are coming to me tonight. I have to go and give them instructions. Please excuse me from dinner." [4] The slave went to another and said, "My master has invited you." [5]The second said to the slave, "I have bought a house, and I have been called away for a day. I shall have no time." [6]The slave went to another and said, "My master invites you." [7]The third said to the slave, "My friend is to be married, and I am to arrange the banquet. I shall not be able to come. Please excuse me from dinner." [8]The slave went to another and said, "My master invites you." [9]The fourth said to the slave, "I have bought an estate, and I am going to collect the rent. I shall not be able

to come. Please excuse me." [10]The slave returned and said to his master, "Those whom you invited to dinner have asked to be excused." [11]The master said to his slave, "Go out on the streets and bring back whomever you find to have dinner."

• **22:1** *responded to them, again in parables:* As just now with the leased vineyard, 21:33–42.

in parables: In fact there are no parables after this one till the two in chap. 25, since the evangelist treats the story about the person not properly dressed for a wedding (vss 11–13)—originally separate, no doubt—as part of this parable.

• **22:2** *a secular ruler:* Who clearly stands for the divine ruler of *Heaven's imperial rule.*

a . . . ruler who gave a wedding celebration for his son: In Luke's story the host is not a king, the meal is not a marriage feast and not given for a special guest. These details make the parable at once allegorical: A marriage feast was a common way of imagining the messianic age, when God's son would appear.

gave: That is, planned to give, inviting guests to come when summoned. See on the

22 Jesus responded to them, again in parables:

²Heaven's imperial rule is like a secular ruler who gave a wedding celebration for his son. ³He sent his slaves to summon those who had been invited to the wedding, but they declined to attend.

⁴He sent additional slaves with these instructions: "Tell those invited, 'Look, my feast is ready, my oxen and fat calves have been slaughtered, and everything is set. Come to the wedding!'"

⁵But they couldn't have cared less, and they went off, one to his own farm, one to his business, ⁶while the rest seized his slaves, beat them up and killed them.

⁷Now the king got angry and sent his armies to destroy those murderers and burn their city. ⁸Then he tells his slaves: "The wedding celebration is ready but those we've invited didn't prove deserving. ⁹So go to the city gates and invite anybody you find to the wedding."

¹⁰Those slaves then went out into the streets and collected everybody they could find, the good and bad alike. And the wedding hall was full of guests.

¹¹The king came in to see the guests for himself and noticed

---

next verse.

- **22:3** *to summon those who had been invited:* In ancient Jewish practice, apparently, the original invitation was simply preliminary. Inconvenient as it seems to us, the specific time of the party would be made known only when the meal was in preparation (see vs 4).

  but they declined to attend: In Luke there is no such advance summary of the guests' response. This blanket refusal seems meant to suggest Israel's rejection of the messianic idea altogether . . . like the portrayal of the crowd in John 19:15 shouting back to Pilate, "We have no king but the emperor."

- **22:4** *my oxen and fat calves have been slaughtered:* The scale of preparation fits a royal wedding. There is nothing parallel to this in either Luke or Thomas.

- **22:5** *one to his own farm, one to his business:* Summarizing the list of excuses in the parallel versions of the story

- **22:6** *seized his slaves, beat them up and killed them:* Emblematic of Israel's reception of God's prophets, as in the leased vineyard

(21:35–39).

- **22:7** Altogether out of proportion with the plot of the story. This insertion obviously alludes to the destruction of Jerusalem in 70 CE, interpreted as divine retribution for Israel's rejection of God's messiah.

- **22:8** *those we've invited didn't prove deserving:* Israel, called to the messianic banquet, has forfeited its right to take part.

- **22:9** *the city gates:* Where common people would congregate.

- **22:10** *the good and bad alike:* Not found in Luke. As with the parable of the sabotage of weeds (13:24–30), this description perhaps reflects our evangelist's Christian community, with a morally mixed membership.

- **22:11–13** The parable of the banquet is complete with vs 10 (*And the wedding hall was full of guests*). What follows is a different one, but becomes part of the main parable. It is unique to Matthew and has been appended by our author, or by some earlier caretaker of the Jesus tradition.

ἐκεῖ ἄνθρωπον οὐκ ἐνδεδυμένον ἔνδυμα γάμου, ¹²καὶ λέγει
αὐτῷ, Ἑταῖρε, πῶς εἰσῆλθες ὧδε μὴ ἔχων ἔνδυμα γάμου;
Ὁ δὲ ἐφιμώθη.

¹³Τότε ὁ βασιλεὺς εἶπεν τοῖς διακόνοις, Δήσαντες αὐτοῦ
πόδας καὶ χεῖρας ἐκβάλετε αὐτὸν εἰς τὸ σκότος τὸ ἐξώτερον· ἐκεῖ
ἔσται ὁ κλαυθμὸς καὶ ὁ βρυγμὸς τῶν ὀδόντων.

¹⁴Πολλοὶ γάρ εἰσιν κλητοί, ὀλίγοι δὲ ἐκλεκτοί.

The emperor
& God

¹⁵Τότε πορευθέντες οἱ Φαρισαῖοι συμβούλιον ἔλαβον ὅπως αὐτὸν
παγιδεύσωσιν ἐν λόγῳ. ¹⁶καὶ ἀποστέλλουσιν αὐτῷ τοὺς μαθητὰς
αὐτῶν μετὰ τῶν Ἡρῳδιανῶν λέγοντες, Διδάσκαλε, οἴδαμεν ὅτι
ἀληθὴς εἶ καὶ τὴν ὁδὸν τοῦ θεοῦ ἐν ἀληθείᾳ διδάσκεις, καὶ οὐ μέλει
σοι περὶ οὐδενός· οὐ γὰρ βλέπεις εἰς πρόσωπον ἀνθρώπων. ¹⁷εἰπὲ οὖν
ἡμῖν τί σοι δοκεῖ· ἔξεστιν δοῦναι κῆνσον Καίσαρι ἢ οὔ;

¹⁸Γνοὺς δὲ ὁ Ἰησοῦς τὴν πονηρίαν αὐτῶν εἶπεν, Τί με πειράζετε,
ὑποκριταί; ¹⁹ἐπιδείξατέ μοι τὸ νόμισμα τοῦ κήνσου.

Οἱ δὲ προσήνεγκαν αὐτῷ δηνάριον.

²⁰Καὶ λέγει αὐτοῖς, Τίνος ἡ εἰκὼν αὕτη καὶ ἡ ἐπιγραφή;

²¹Λέγουσιν αὐτῷ, Καίσαρος.

Τότε λέγει αὐτοῖς, Ἀπόδοτε οὖν τὰ Καίσαρος Καίσαρι καὶ τὰ τοῦ
θεοῦ τῷ θεῷ.

22:23 Many ᴍss show the Sadducees beginning to challenge Jesus by stating
their denial of resurrection: "... some Sadducees came up to him and said
'There is no resurrection.'"

• **22:12** *And the man was speechless:* Understandably, since according to the foregoing he was ushered into the wedding at the last minute and without advance notice. Evidently two once separate stories have been merged, both dealing with improper response to God's call.

• **22:14** A moral probably separate originally from either parable, and perhaps the evangelist's creation. It can very roughly summarize the first of the two stories. But what is the fundamental difference between *called* and *chosen*?

• **22:15** The leaders react to Jesus' condemnation of them, overt or implied.

the Pharisees: Singled out here, without mention of the ranking priests or elders of chap. 21. In The author's day, it was the Pharisees primarily who were in authority. But there seems no particular reason for his variation in naming Jesus' opponents from one episode to the next.

with a riddle: Strictly, only "with a word." But they seek to *trap* (literally "ensnare")

him and hope his reply to their question in the next verse will catch him out.

• **22:16** *they send their disciples:* The Pharisees play the dominant role; in Mark 12:13 they and the Herodians (see the next comment) act only as emissaries of the ranking priests and scholars and elders (Mark 11:27). Here it is the Pharisees' *disciples* who are sent. Is this intended to mean the latter-day Pharisees of the author's own time?

the Herodians: Mentioned only here in Matthew (twice in Mark; not in Luke). It's not known just who these were, or what connection they had to Herod Antipas, who during Jesus' time was ruler of Galilee with Rome's consent. Evidently they had a stake in cooperating with the emperor.

we know that...: Their flattery is devious (as Jesus recognizes—vs 18). The evangelist and reader, of course, know it to be true.

• **22:17** The questioners pretend to consult Jesus on what is *permissible* under Jewish law, and whether obeying Roman law transgresses it. (See just below on "poll tax.") After the

this man not properly attired.¹²And he says to him, "You! What are you doing here not dressed right?"

And the man was speechless.

¹³Then the king ordered his waiters: "Bind him hand and foot and throw him where it is utterly dark. They'll weep and grind their teeth out there."

¹⁴"After all, many are called but few are chosen."

¹⁵Then the Pharisees went and conferred on how to trap him with a riddle. ¹⁶And they send their disciples to him along with the Herodians to say, "Teacher, we know that you are honest and that you teach God's way forthrightly, and are impartial, because you pay no attention to appearances. ¹⁷So tell us what you think: Is it permissible to pay the poll tax to the <Roman> emperor or not?"

The emperor & God

¹⁸Jesus knew how devious they were, and said, "Why do you provoke me, you pious frauds? ¹⁹Let me see the coin used to pay the poll tax."

And they handed him a silver coin.

²⁰And he says to them, "Whose picture is this? Whose name is on it?"

²¹They say to him, "The emperor's."

Then he says to them, "Pay the emperor what belongs to the emperor, and God what belongs to God!"

---

failure of the Jewish revolt in 70 CE most Jews would probably be inclined to submit to Roman demands, but the question must have been a matter of debate. Where did Jesus stand on the issue? Like the challenge posed to him in 21:23, this is a dangerous question, as he obviously recognizes.

poll tax: Greek *kênsos,* from the Latin *census.* There were no polls, of course, no democracy. On the contrary, this *tax* was no doubt used to pay for the oppressive Roman army of occupation in Palestine, not representative government. The modern connotation of "poll tax" is apt here. See comment on 17:25.

• **22:18** *provoke:* Strictly, "test."

pious frauds: A vernacular translation of the plural of *hypokritês.*

• **22:19–21** Jesus is canny but doesn't evade the question.

• **22:19** *silver coin:* The *denarius,* a coin in the Roman currency. Jewish coins were probably not acceptable for paying the tax.

• **22:20** Is Jesus shrewdly involving his hostile questioners in answering the question?

• **22:21** *Pay the emperor what belongs to the emperor, and God what belongs to God!* Almost identical in Thom 100 (except that there, at the end, Jesus adds: "and give me what is mine.") People have almost always taken this to suggest the "separation of church and state." But what does not belong to God? Jesus does not say an outright "No" to the Pharisees' question. That would immediately invite political notice. But he implies the negative answer. So he skillfully lays upon his hearers the decision whether or not to pay the tax. (In like manner some of the stories Jesus told were not the obvious allegories they appear to be in Matthew but parables that force the hearer to decide how to understand and respond.) The saying here is very likely to be authentic to Jesus.

the emperor: Greek, "Caesar," but no longer a name, like Julius Caesar's. Rather, the title used by his successors. (From which "Kaiser" and "Czar" derive.)

**Wife of
seven brothers**

²²Καὶ ἀκούσαντες ἐθαύμασαν, καὶ ἀφέντες αὐτὸν ἀπῆλθαν.

²³Ἐν ἐκείνῃ τῇ ἡμέρᾳ προσῆλθον αὐτῷ Σαδδουκαῖοι, λέγοντες μὴ εἶναι ἀνάστασιν, καὶ ἐπηρώτησαν αὐτὸν ²⁴λέγοντες, Διδάσκαλε, Μωϋσῆς εἶπεν, Ἐάν τις ἀποθάνῃ μὴ ἔχων τέκνα, ἐπιγαμβρεύσει ὁ ἀδελφὸς αὐτοῦ τὴν γυναῖκα αὐτοῦ καὶ ἀναστήσει σπέρμα τῷ ἀδελφῷ αὐτοῦ. ²⁵ἦσαν δὲ παρ' ἡμῖν ἑπτὰ ἀδελφοί· καὶ ὁ πρῶτος γήμας ἐτελεύτησεν, καὶ μὴ ἔχων σπέρμα ἀφῆκεν τὴν γυναῖκα αὐτοῦ τῷ ἀδελφῷ αὐτοῦ· ²⁶ὁμοίως καὶ ὁ δεύτερος καὶ ὁ τρίτος ἕως τῶν ἑπτά. ²⁷ὕστερον δὲ πάντων ἀπέθανεν ἡ γυνή. ²⁸ἐν τῇ ἀναστάσει οὖν τίνος τῶν ἑπτὰ ἔσται γυνή; πάντες γὰρ ἔσχον αὐτήν·

²⁹Ἀποκριθεὶς δὲ ὁ Ἰησοῦς εἶπεν αὐτοῖς, Πλανᾶσθε μὴ εἰδότες τὰς γραφὰς μηδὲ τὴν δύναμιν τοῦ θεοῦ· ³⁰ἐν γὰρ τῇ ἀναστάσει οὔτε γαμοῦσιν οὔτε γαμίζονται, ἀλλ' ὡς ἄγγελοι ἐν τῷ οὐρανῷ εἰσιν. ³¹περὶ δὲ τῆς ἀναστάσεως τῶν νεκρῶν οὐκ ἀνέγνωτε τὸ ῥηθὲν ὑμῖν ὑπὸ τοῦ θεοῦ λέγοντος, ³²Ἐγώ εἰμι ὁ θεὸς Ἀβραὰμ καὶ ὁ θεὸς Ἰσαὰκ καὶ ὁ θεὸς Ἰακώβ; οὐκ ἔστιν ὁ θεὸς νεκρῶν ἀλλὰ ζώντων.

³³Καὶ ἀκούσαντες οἱ ὄχλοι ἐξεπλήσσοντο ἐπὶ τῇ διδαχῇ αὐτοῦ.

**The greatest
commandment**

³⁴Οἱ δὲ Φαρισαῖοι ἀκούσαντες ὅτι ἐφίμωσεν τοὺς Σαδδουκαίους συνήχθησαν ἐπὶ τὸ αὐτό, ³⁵καὶ ἐπηρώτησεν εἷς ἐξ αὐτῶν νομικὸς πειράζων αὐτόν, ³⁶Διδάσκαλε, ποία ἐντολὴ μεγάλη ἐν τῷ νόμῳ;

³⁷Ὁ δὲ ἔφη αὐτῷ, Ἀγαπήσεις κύριον τὸν θεόν σου ἐν ὅλῃ τῇ καρδίᾳ σου καὶ ἐν ὅλῃ τῇ ψυχῇ σου καὶ ἐν ὅλῃ τῇ διανοίᾳ σου· ³⁸αὕτη ἐστὶν ἡ μεγάλη καὶ πρώτη ἐντολή. ³⁹δευτέρα δὲ ὁμοία αὐτῇ, Ἀγαπήσεις τὸν

• **22:22** *dumbfounded:* Whatever he meant, they cannot contradict him.

• **22:23–33** Following 21:23–27 (On whose authority?) and the preceding story, this is the third time Jesus' opponents put a provocative question to him.

• **22:23** *no resurrection:* See Glossary. This was a subject of disagreement between Pharisees and the theologically more conservative Sadducees, who found no warrant for the idea in the scriptures.

• **22:24** *Teacher:* Less fulsome than the Pharisees' flattery in vs 16 above. But while this title pretends to indicate a genuine solicitation of Jesus' opinion, the exaggerated and ludicrous scenario leading up to the question makes ridiculous any answer but that approved by the askers.

If someone dies . . .: The quotation is a summary of the so-called Levirate law in Deut 25:5–6.

• **22:25–28** A fanciful story, driving the idea of resurrection to absurdity.

• **22:25** *we knew:* "Among us."

• **22:28b** Here the Greek particle *gar* indicates a parenthetical remark by the evangelist.

• **22:29–32** Jesus' reply perhaps reflects not so much what he taught, but Christian answers to questions like these.

• **22:29** *You have missed the point again:* Greek, "You keep straying [from the truth]."

you underestimate . . .: Or "you don't understand. . . ."

• **22:30** *heaven's messengers:* In the past usually translated "angels in heaven."

• **22:31** *God's word to you:* What God has said

²²Upon hearing his reply, they were dumbfounded. And they withdrew from him and went away.

²³That same day, some Sadducees—who maintain there is no resurrection—came up to him and questioned him: ²⁴"Teacher," they said, "Moses said, 'If someone dies without children, his brother is obligated to marry the widow and produce offspring for his brother.' ²⁵Now there were seven brothers we knew; the first married and died. And since he left no children, he left his widow to his brother. ²⁶The second brother did the same thing, and the third, and so on, through the seventh brother. ²⁷Finally the wife died. ²⁸In the resurrection, then, whose wife, of the seven, will she be?" (They had all married her.)

Wife of seven brothers

²⁹In response Jesus said to them, "You have missed the point again, all because you underestimate both the scriptures and the power of God. ³⁰After all, at the resurrection people do not marry but resemble heaven's messengers. ³¹As for the resurrection of the dead, haven't you read God's word to you: ³²'I am the God of Abraham and the God of Isaac and the God of Jacob.' This is not the God of the dead, rather of the living."

³³And when the crowd heard, they were stunned by his teaching.

³⁴When the Pharisees learned that he had silenced the Sadducees, they got together <to conspire> against him. ³⁵And one of them, a legal expert, put him to the test: ³⁶"Teacher, which commandment in the Law is the greatest?"

The greatest commandment

³⁷<Jesus> replied, "'You are to love the Lord your God with all your heart and all your soul and all your mind.' ³⁸This commandment is the chief, the foremost. ³⁹And the second is like it: 'You are to love

---

for your benefit.
- **22:32** *I am the God of Abraham . . .:* Exod 3:6.
  the living: The patriarchs are alive in their descendants.
- **22:33** Why *stunned?* The theme of Jesus' impressing the crowds runs through most of the gospel. This particular teaching is no more radical or astonishing than others. An exaggeration for dramatic effect, perhaps. The evangelist pictures Jesus, who before long will be condemned and executed, as increasingly perceived to be a uniquely good and wise and powerful person.
- **22:36–38** Another a provocative question put to Jesus. According to one view, all the commandments were of equal authority and importance, but legal experts in Jesus'

time often considered the question of the greatest commandment. For example, Rabbi Hillel was asked how to sum up the whole Law while standing on one leg. He replied by citing Deut 6:4, like Jesus' first response here.
- **22:37** Curiously, the evangelist omits from the text he is following (Mark 12:29) the famous introduction to the great commandment, the *Shema:* "Hear, Israel, the Lord your God, the Lord is one. You are to love. . . ."
- **22:39** As in Mark, Lev 19:18 is described as a near equivalent and added. Thus Jesus gives a compound yet single answer to the question. Thom 25 reads: "Love your friends [or brother and sister] like your own soul, protect them like the pupil of your eye."

πλησίον σου ὡς σεαυτόν. ⁴⁰ἐν ταύταις ταῖς δυσὶν ἐντολαῖς ὅλος ὁ νόμος κρέμαται καὶ οἱ προφῆται.

David's lord and son

⁴¹Συνηγμένων δὲ τῶν Φαρισαίων ἐπηρώτησεν αὐτοὺς ὁ Ἰησοῦς ⁴²λέγων, Τί ὑμῖν δοκεῖ περὶ τοῦ Χριστοῦ; τίνος υἱός ἐστιν;

Λέγουσιν αὐτῷ, Τοῦ Δαυίδ.

⁴³Λέγει αὐτοῖς, Πῶς οὖν Δαυὶδ ἐν πνεύματι καλεῖ αὐτὸν κύριον λέγων,

⁴⁴Εἶπεν κύριος τῷ κυρίῳ μου·
Κάθου ἐκ δεξιῶν μου,
ἕως ἂν θῶ τοὺς ἐχθρούς σου ὑποκάτω τῶν ποδῶν σου;

⁴⁵Εἰ οὖν Δαυὶδ καλεῖ αὐτὸν κύριον, πῶς υἱὸς αὐτοῦ ἐστιν;

⁴⁶Καὶ οὐδεὶς ἐδύνατο ἀποκριθῆναι αὐτῷ λόγον οὐδὲ ἐτόλμησέν τις ἀπ᾽ ἐκείνης τῆς ἡμέρας ἐπερωτῆσαι αὐτὸν οὐκέτι.

• **22:40** This extends Mark 12:31b ("There is no other commandment greater than these"). Not simply the greatest commandment but what is sometimes called the Summary of the Law, it is parallel to 7:12, the so-called Golden Rule.

Next in Mark (12:32–34) is a little passage in which one of the scholars commends Jesus for his summation of the Law and in turn is commended by Jesus. Omitted for brevity. Or because of the evangelist's animus against the scholars (note the next chapter)?

• **22:41–46** Finally, another question, the fifth, is raised: the question of Messiahship (of *the Anointed*). This time Jesus puts the question, perhaps knowing that it was an issue for the Pharisees.

• **22:42** *Whose son is he?* That is, what kind of

your neighbor as yourself.' ⁴⁰On these two commandments depends everything in the Law and the Prophets."

⁴¹When the Pharisees gathered around, Jesus asked them, ⁴²"What do you think about the Anointed? Whose son is he?"

They said to him, "David's."

⁴³He said to them, "Then how can David call him 'lord,' while speaking under the influence of the spirit:

**David's
lord and son**

⁴⁴The Lord said to my lord,
'Sit here at my right,
until I make your enemies grovel at your feet'?

⁴⁵"If David actually called him 'lord,' how can he be his son?"

⁴⁶And no one could come up with an answer to his riddle. After that no one dared ask him a question.

---

messiah?

David's: They give the expected reply. The Anointed is to be political, perhaps a military victor, like David.

• **22:43–46** Jesus takes for granted that David wrote the Psalms and that Ps 110:1 is a prediction of the messiah. So he is not to be like David. Jesus states this as a question and the authorities can dispute it.

• **22:43** *while speaking under the influence of the spirit:* For Jesus, as for the evangelist, all scripture is taken to be inspired.

• **22:44** *The Lord said to my lord:* That is, God said to the [future] messiah.

• **22:46** *come up with an answer to his riddle:* Or simply "answer him a word."

After that: In Greek, "from that day."

23 Τότε ὁ Ἰησοῦς ἐλάλησεν τοῖς ὄχλοις καὶ τοῖς μαθηταῖς αὐτοῦ
²λέγων, Ἐπὶ τῆς Μωϋσέως καθέδρας ἐκάθισαν οἱ γραμματεῖς καὶ οἱ
Φαρισαῖοι. ³πάντα οὖν ὅσα ἐὰν εἴπωσιν ὑμῖν ποιήσατε καὶ τηρεῖτε,
κατὰ δὲ τὰ ἔργα αὐτῶν μὴ ποιεῖτε· λέγουσιν γὰρ καὶ οὐ ποιοῦσιν.
⁴δεσμεύουσιν δὲ φορτία βαρέα καὶ ἐπιτιθέασιν ἐπὶ τοὺς ὤμους τῶν
ἀνθρώπων, αὐτοὶ δὲ τῷ δακτύλῳ αὐτῶν οὐ θέλουσιν κινῆσαι αὐτά.
⁵πάντα δὲ τὰ ἔργα αὐτῶν ποιοῦσιν πρὸς τὸ θεαθῆναι τοῖς ἀνθρώποις·
πλατύνουσιν γὰρ τὰ φυλακτήρια αὐτῶν καὶ μεγαλύνουσιν τὰ
κράσπεδα, ⁶φιλοῦσιν δὲ τὴν πρωτοκλισίαν ἐν τοῖς δείπνοις καὶ
τὰς πρωτοκαθεδρίας ἐν ταῖς συναγωγαῖς ⁷καὶ τοὺς ἀσπασμοὺς ἐν
ταῖς ἀγοραῖς καὶ καλεῖσθαι ὑπὸ τῶν ἀνθρώπων, Ῥαββί. ⁸ὑμεῖς δὲ
μὴ κληθῆτε, Ῥαββί· εἷς γάρ ἐστιν ὑμῶν ὁ διδάσκαλος, πάντες δὲ
ὑμεῖς ἀδελφοί ἐστε. ⁹καὶ πατέρα μὴ καλέσητε ὑμῶν ἐπὶ τῆς γῆς,
εἷς γάρ ἐστιν ὑμῶν ὁ πατὴρ ὁ οὐράνιος. ¹⁰μηδὲ κληθῆτε καθηγηταί,
ὅτι καθηγητὴς ὑμῶν ἐστιν εἷς ὁ Χριστός. ¹¹ὁ δὲ μείζων ὑμῶν ἔσται
ὑμῶν διάκονος. ¹²ὅστις δὲ ὑψώσει ἑαυτὸν ταπεινωθήσεται καὶ ὅστις
ταπεινώσει ἑαυτὸν ὑψωθήσεται.

23:4 Many mss have "hard to bear" after *heavy burdens,* probably to read like
Luke 11:46.

• **23:1–36** Up till now our author has portrayed Jesus frequently confronted by antagonistic Jewish leaders. In each case Jesus has confounded his adversaries (for example, 22:46), but always as the object of criticism. Now Jesus mounts a direct and sustained attack upon them, taking as his cue a very brief warning about them in Mark 12:38–40. The Pharisees, together with their associates, the scholars are the targets of this assault.

In Jesus' time Pharisees and scholars probably had little prominence or power as religious leaders. They belonged to a relatively small sect, a movement, within Judaism. But after the disastrous end to the Jewish revolt, and the destruction of the Jerusalem temple, in 70 CE, it was the Pharisees and scholars who emerged as the surviving leaders. And by then, the part of the Christian movement that remained within Judaism was increasingly under fire from those leaders. The severity of Jesus' offensive against them here reflects the increasing disaffection of Christian Jews of the evangelist's church. That is, the debates depicted here reflect little if at all issues that arose in Jesus' lifetime, rather the hostile confrontations mounted by the synagogue against the evangelist's church in the late first century CE. (To an even greater degree, the same is true of the community portrayed in the Gospel of John.) Some have

suggested that, like Paul, the evangelist had been a Pharisee and after his conversion condemned his former brothers in faith. Further, that the authorities' decision in about 85 CE to expel Christians from the synagogue has enhanced this polemic.

In short, the following diatribe, which has blackened the name of the Pharisees over the centuries, is an expression of late first-century Christian prejudice.

• **23:1–12** This first section of the chapter has parallels in both Mark and Luke, as does what follows in vss 13–36. But the message is not yet scathing. It lays bare what our author sees as the insincerity and false piety of the Jewish teachers. To say the least they abuse their "privileges."

• **23:1** Is this the beginning of the last great discourse ("sermon"), which concludes at 26:1? Or does it begin only in chap. 24? See below, comment on 24:4.

• **23:2** *scholars and Pharisees:* The former usually and misleadingly called simply scribes. They dealt with text of scripture, but they were no mere copyists. See Glossary.

occupy the chair of Moses: Is this meant ironically? Perhaps not, in view of what immediately follows. They evidently had, or assumed, the role of interpreting the Law.

• **23:3** *you're supposed to observe and follow everything they tell you.* On the other hand, their hypocrisy may invalidate their authority.

23 Then Jesus said to the crowds and to his disciples, ²"The scholars and Pharisees occupy the chair of Moses. ³This means you're supposed to observe and follow everything they tell you. But don't do what they do; after all, they're all talk and no action. ⁴They invent heavy burdens to lay on people's shoulders, but they won't lift a finger to do anything themselves. ⁵Everything they do, they do for show. So they widen their phylacteries and enlarge their tassels. ⁶They love the best couches at banquets and prominent seats in synagogues ⁷and respectful greetings in marketplaces, and they like to be called 'Rabbi' by everyone. ⁸But you are not to be called 'Rabbi'; after all, you have only one teacher, and all of you belong to the same family. ⁹And don't call anyone on earth 'father,' since you have only one Father, and he is in heaven. ¹⁰You are not to be called 'instructors,' because you have only one instructor, the Anointed. ¹¹Remember, whoever is greater than you will be your servant: ¹²those who promote themselves will be demoted and those who demote themselves will be promoted.

Jesus denounces the Jerusalem leaders / Scholars' privileges

---

they're all talk and no action: A close rendering of the Greek. It means, of course, that they don't "practice what they preach."

• **23:4** *invent:* Greek, "tie on."

heavy burdens: Evidently strenuous rules of religious and moral observance.

• **23:5** *phylacteries:* Texts from the Law, in black leather boxes, wrapped with straps on the forehead and the arm, in literal observance of Deut 6:8.

tassels: Or fringes, on garments. See Num 15:38–39.

• **23:6** An abbreviation of Mark 12:38b–39 and Luke 20:46. For some reason (can it be accidental?) the evangelist does not make use of the next verse in Mark (12:40—"They are the ones who prey on widows and their families, and recite long prayers just to put on airs. These people will get a stiff sentence!") Nor does he insert the story of the widow's gift—Mark 12:41–44—the last episode in Mark before the apocalyptic discourse that will be the model for Matthew's chaps. 24–25

couches at banquets: In Greek and Roman culture, formal meals were eaten while reclining, usually on the left elbow.

• **23:7** *Rabbi:* Meaning "My great one," a title for religious teachers.

• **23:8** *you are not to be called Rabbi:* The disciples (esp. in the author's time) are to have a teaching role with respect to what God requires—but not the usual teacher's title.

you have only one teacher: Does this refer to Jesus, as in vs 10, or to God (vs 9)?

all of you belong to the same family: In Greek, you are all "brothers." A rabbi's disciples thought of themselves as a family, as brothers and sisters, often traveling with their master.

• **23:9** *don't call anyone on earth Father:* Was it Jesus, or the evangelist in his Christian community, who issued this polemic against traditional patriarchialism?

• **23:10** *the Anointed:* Perhaps Jesus did not refer to himself as the Anointed. But after the resurrection, he was assumed to have been, and to be, the Messiah. Certainly the evangelist intends this as Jesus' reference to himself here.

• **23:11–12** These two statements make the same point in different ways. They express a common theme in this gospel. Vs 11 is found also at 20:26 (in the same context as Mark 10:43), and vs 12 is akin to the idea that the first will be last, and the last first (19:30, 20:16). This perspective is subversive of the Jewish religious hierarchy, and of all hierarchy, whether in the family (see on vs 9) or in the structure of the Roman Empire. And in the church?

• **23:12** *promote . . . demote:* Traditionally translated "exalt . . . humble."

¹³Οὐαὶ δὲ ὑμῖν, γραμματεῖς καὶ Φαρισαῖοι ὑποκριταί, ὅτι κλείετε τὴν βασιλείαν τῶν οὐρανῶν ἔμπροσθεν τῶν ἀνθρώπων· ὑμεῖς γὰρ οὐκ εἰσέρχεσθε οὐδὲ τοὺς εἰσερχομένους ἀφίετε εἰσελθεῖν.

¹⁵Οὐαὶ ὑμῖν, γραμματεῖς καὶ Φαρισαῖοι ὑποκριταί, ὅτι περιάγετε τὴν θάλασσαν καὶ τὴν ξηρὰν ποιῆσαι ἕνα προσήλυτον, καὶ ὅταν γένηται ποιεῖτε αὐτὸν υἱὸν γεέννης διπλότερον ὑμῶν.

¹⁶Οὐαὶ ὑμῖν, ὁδηγοὶ τυφλοὶ οἱ λέγοντες, Ὃς ἂν ὀμόσῃ ἐν τῷ ναῷ, οὐδέν ἐστιν· ὃς δ' ἂν ὀμόσῃ ἐν τῷ χρυσῷ τοῦ ναοῦ, ὀφείλει. ¹⁷μωροὶ καὶ τυφλοί, τίς γὰρ μείζων ἐστίν, ὁ χρυσὸς ἢ ὁ ναὸς ὁ ἁγιάσας τὸν χρυσόν; ¹⁸καί, Ὃς ἂν ὀμόσῃ ἐν τῷ θυσιαστηρίῳ, οὐδέν ἐστιν· ὃς δ' ἂν ὀμόσῃ ἐν τῷ δώρῳ τῷ ἐπάνω αὐτοῦ, ὀφείλει. ¹⁹τυφλοί, τί γὰρ μεῖζον, τὸ δῶρον ἢ τὸ θυσιαστήριον τὸ ἁγιάζον τὸ δῶρον; ²⁰ὁ οὖν ὀμόσας ἐν τῷ θυσιαστηρίῳ ὀμνύει ἐν αὐτῷ καὶ ἐν πᾶσι τοῖς ἐπάνω αὐτοῦ· ²¹καὶ ὁ ὀμόσας ἐν τῷ ναῷ ὀμνύει ἐν αὐτῷ καὶ ἐν τῷ κατοικοῦντι αὐτόν, ²²καὶ ὁ ὀμόσας ἐν τῷ οὐρανῷ ὀμνύει ἐν τῷ θρόνῳ τοῦ θεοῦ καὶ ἐν τῷ καθημένῳ ἐπάνω αὐτοῦ.

²³Οὐαὶ ὑμῖν, γραμματεῖς καὶ Φαρισαῖοι ὑποκριταί, ὅτι ἀποδεκατοῦτε τὸ ἡδύοσμον καὶ τὸ ἄνηθον καὶ τὸ κύμινον καὶ ἀφήκατε τὰ βαρύτερα τοῦ νόμου, τὴν κρίσιν καὶ τὸ ἔλεος καὶ τὴν πίστιν· ταῦτα ἔδει ποιῆσαι κἀκεῖνα μὴ ἀφιέναι. ²⁴ὁδηγοὶ τυφλοί, οἱ διϋλίζοντες τὸν κώνωπα, τὴν δὲ κάμηλον καταπίνοντες.

23:14 Some MSS include as vs 14, "Damn you, you scholars and Pharisees, you impostors! You prey on widows and their families, and recite long prayers just for the sake of appearances. Therefore you will get a stiff sentence." This follows, but has not simply been copied from Mark 12:40 (cf. Luke 20: 47), which the evangelist evidently omitted. (Why else would major MSS of Matthew lack it?) A few MSS put this after vs 12.

• **23:13–36** Jesus now directly condemns the religious leaders, seven times. Perhaps that number, common in Jewish thought, was deliberate in the assembling of this tirade.
• **23:13** This is parallel to Luke 11:52 (Q); similarly, most of vss 23–36. Thom 39 reads: "The Pharisees and the scholars have taken the keys of knowledge and have hidden them. ² They have not entered, nor have they allowed those who want to enter to do so."
You scholars and Pharisees, you impostors! *Damn you!* This outcry opens all the denunciations (vss 15, 16, 23, 25, 27, 29).
scholars and Pharisees: See comment on 23:1–36.
impostors: In Greek, hypocrites, sometimes also translated "phonies."
Damn you: See Translation Note p. 63.
slam the door of Heaven's domain: How do they do this? By attempting to decide who

can and cannot enter? By placing ritual observances beyond the financial means of the poor?
You yourselves don't enter: Even if they could.
• **23:14** See the Text-Critical Note.
• **23:15** The second invective.
more: In the Greek, "doubly." How was this so?
child of Hell: A Hebraism, meaning destined for Hell, because the way into God's empire is blocked (vs 13).
Hell: In Greek "Gehenna," a Hebrew name (see Glossary). In 11:23, it was "Hades."
• **23:16–22** The third condemnation.
• **23:16** *blind guides:* A damning image, used already in 15:14.
swear by the temple … swear by the treasure in the temple: There is no evidence of this particular distinction in the Rabbinic debates

¹³"You scholars and Pharisees, you impostors! Damn you! You slam the door of Heaven's domain in people's faces. You yourselves don't enter, and you block the way of those trying to enter.

¹⁵"You scholars and Pharisees, you impostors! Damn you! You scour land and sea to make one convert, and when you do, you make that person more a child of Hell than you are.

¹⁶"Damn you, you blind guides who claim: 'When you swear by the temple, it doesn't matter, but when you swear by the treasure in the temple, it is binding.' ¹⁷You blind fools, which is greater, the treasure or the temple that makes the gold sacred? ¹⁸You go on: 'When you swear by the altar, it doesn't matter, but when you swear by the offering that lies on the altar, it is binding.' ¹⁹You sightless souls, which is greater, the offering or the altar that makes the offering sacred? ²⁰So when you swear by the altar, you swear by the altar and everything on it. ²¹And anyone who swears by the temple, swears by the temple and the one who makes it home, ²²and anyone who swears by heaven swears by the throne of God and the one who occupies it.

²³"You scholars and Pharisees, you impostors! Damn you! You pay tithes on mint and dill and cumin too, but ignore the really important matters of the Law, such as justice and mercy and trust. You should have attended to the last without ignoring the first. ²⁴You blind leaders! You strain out a gnat and gulp down a camel.

Damn you, scholars & Pharisees

---

over oaths. Perhaps this is a parody.

swear by: Meaning, of course, take an oath on the basis of.

- **23:17** To swear by part of something is to swear by all of it. So to make distinction between part and whole, as in the previous verse, is meaningless

- **23:21** *and the one who makes it home:* After vs 20 you'd expect "and everything in it," referring to vs 16. But Jesus is moving toward the idea (in vss 21 and 22) that all oaths are in fact oaths "by God." The temple is God's *home.*

- **23:22** *the throne of God* is in *heaven.*

- **23:23–36** Most of this is from Q (see Luke 11:39–51).

- **23:23–26** The fourth and fifth condemnations, again of the Pharisees for their trivial rules.

- **23:23** Like Luke 11:42.

pay tithes: Offer a tenth of any food, or its value, for sacrifice in the temple.

mint and dill and cumin: All foods, even seasonings, were to be tithed, according to Rabbinic regulations.

really important: "Weightier."

matters of the Law, such as justice and mercy and trust: The closest parallel in the Hebrew scriptures is Mic 6:8 ("do justice and love kindness and walk humbly with your God"). Jesus, or the evangelist, evidently considers ethical teaching in the prophets as equivalent to the Law itself.

- **23:24** Another outrageous, comical saying about the camel, unique to Matthew but like the one from Mark about the eye of the needle—19:24. For the gist of this verse, see 7:3: "the sliver in your friend's eye . . . the timber in your own."

²⁵Οὐαὶ ὑμῖν, γραμματεῖς καὶ Φαρισαῖοι ὑποκριταί, ὅτι καθαρίζετε τὸ ἔξωθεν τοῦ ποτηρίου καὶ τῆς παροψίδος, ἔσωθεν δὲ γέμουσιν ἐξ ἁρπαγῆς καὶ ἀκρασίας. ²⁶Φαρισαῖε τυφλέ, καθάρισον πρῶτον τὸ ἐντὸς τοῦ ποτηρίου, ἵνα γένηται καὶ τὸ ἐκτὸς αὐτοῦ καθαρόν.

²⁷Οὐαὶ ὑμῖν, γραμματεῖς καὶ Φαρισαῖοι ὑποκριταί, ὅτι παρομοιάζετε τάφοις κεκονιαμένοις, οἵτινες ἔξωθεν μὲν φαίνονται ὡραῖοι, ἔσωθεν δὲ γέμουσιν ὀστέων νεκρῶν καὶ πάσης ἀκαθαρσίας. ²⁸οὕτως καὶ ὑμεῖς ἔξωθεν μὲν φαίνεσθε τοῖς ἀνθρώποις δίκαιοι, ἔσωθεν δέ ἐστε μεστοὶ ὑποκρίσεως καὶ ἀνομίας.

²⁹Οὐαὶ ὑμῖν, γραμματεῖς καὶ Φαρισαῖοι ὑποκριταί, ὅτι οἰκοδομεῖτε τοὺς τάφους τῶν προφητῶν καὶ κοσμεῖτε τὰ μνημεῖα τῶν δικαίων, ³⁰καὶ λέγετε, Εἰ ἤμεθα ἐν ταῖς ἡμέραις τῶν πατέρων ἡμῶν, οὐκ ἂν ἤμεθα αὐτῶν κοινωνοὶ ἐν τῷ αἵματι τῶν προφητῶν. ³¹ὥστε μαρτυρεῖτε ἑαυτοῖς ὅτι υἱοί ἐστε τῶν φονευσάντων τοὺς προφήτας. ³²καὶ ὑμεῖς πληρώσατε τὸ μέτρον τῶν πατέρων ὑμῶν. ³³ὄφεις, γεννήματα ἐχιδνῶν, πῶς φύγητε ἀπὸ τῆς κρίσεως τῆς γεέννης; ³⁴διὰ τοῦτο ἰδοὺ ἐγὼ ἀποστέλλω πρὸς ὑμᾶς προφήτας καὶ σοφοὺς καὶ γραμματεῖς· ἐξ αὐτῶν ἀποκτενεῖτε καὶ σταυρώσετε καὶ ἐξ αὐτῶν μαστιγώσετε ἐν ταῖς συναγωγαῖς ὑμῶν καὶ διώξετε ἀπὸ πόλεως εἰς πόλιν· ³⁵ὅπως ἔλθῃ ἐφ᾽ ὑμᾶς πᾶν αἷμα δίκαιον ἐκχυννόμενον ἐπὶ τῆς γῆς ἀπὸ τοῦ αἵματος Ἄβελ τοῦ δικαίου ἕως τοῦ αἵματος Ζαχαρίου υἱοῦ Βαραχίου, ὃν ἐφονεύσατε μεταξὺ τοῦ ναοῦ καὶ τοῦ

• **23:25–26** Compare Luke 11:39–40
• **23:25** *cups and plates:* No doubt rules of cleanliness. But even more, metaphors for the "scholars and Pharisees" themselves.
  full of greed and dissipation: The leaders, in their eating and drinking.
• **23:27–28** The sixth damning is similar to Luke 11:39. Here the leaders are condemned not so much for their practices as for their very character (*You are like . . .*).
• **23:27** Only loosely parallel to Luke 11:44.
  tombs . . . dead bones and every kind of decay: Death was viewed as unclean and therefore defiling, and *whitewash[ing] tombs* on the outside could not change this.
• **23:28** A paraphrase of vs. 25., not found in Q
  decent: Better than the usual "righteous."
  doing nothing but posturing and disregarding the Law: "Full of hypocrisy and lawlessness." On the latter, see above on 7:23.
• **23:29–36** The seventh and last condemnation. This is by far the longest. The indictment proper runs up to 34.
• **23:29–31** A bit like Luke 11:47–48.
• **23:29** Their honoring of the righteous dead is a meaningless gesture.
• **23:30** Not in Q. Perhaps the evangelist's creation.

joined them in spilling the prophets' blood: "Been their partners in blood."
• **23:31** You claim that you would not have killed the prophets. But in fact *You are the descendants* of those who did. So you would have done the same.
• **23:32** The evangelist has added this sarcasm.
• **23:33** *spawn of Satan:* As in 3:7 (John the Baptist's phrase) and 12:34.
  Hell's: Greek, "Gehenna's."
• **23:34–36** Luke 11:49–51 is much like this.
  Some see these three verses as introduction to the Lament over Jerusalem that ends the chapter (23:37–39), but those addressed here are still, it seems, the Jewish leaders.
• **23:34** *that is why I send you prophets . . .:* As if God provides the victims in order to demonstrate their guilt.
  I send you . . .: God speaks, with Jesus acting as prophet. In the Hebrew Scriptures a prophet often begins his message, "Thus says the Lord."
  The present tense ("send") can be understood as a reference to the present ("I am now sending . . ."). Or to the future "I am going to send . . ."). Even to the past ("All this time I have been sending . . .") In any

²⁵"You scholars and Pharisees, you impostors! Damn you! You wash the outside of cups and plates, but inside they are full of greed and dissipation. ²⁶You blind Pharisee, first clean the inside of the cup and then the outside will be clean too.

²⁷"You scholars and Pharisees, you impostors! Damn you! You are like whitewashed tombs: on the outside they look beautiful, but inside they are full of dead bones and every kind of decay. ²⁸So you too look like decent people on the outside, but on the inside you are doing nothing but posturing and disregarding the Law.

²⁹"You scholars and Pharisees, you impostors! Damn you! You erect tombs to the prophets and decorate the graves of the righteous ³⁰and claim: 'If we had lived in the days of our ancestors, we wouldn't have joined them in spilling the prophets' blood.' ³¹Thus you witness against yourselves: You are descendants of those who murdered the prophets. ³²Go ahead, finish off what your ancestors left undone! ³³You serpents! You spawn of Satan! How are you going to escape Hell's judgment? ³⁴Look, that is why I send you prophets and sages and scholars. Some you're going to kill and crucify, and some you're going to beat in your synagogues and hound from town to town. ³⁵As a result there will be on your heads all the innocent blood that has been shed on the earth, from the blood of innocent Abel to the blood of Zechariah, son of Baruch, whom you murdered

---

case the continued or repeated action is emphasized. Perhaps it is meant chiefly as a future, like the futures in the second half of the verse (*you're going to kill . . . you're going to beat*) and refers to Christian leaders who have been or will be persecuted by the late first-century Jewish leaders.

prophets and sages and scholars: Clearly Christians with special roles. Luke has "prophets and apostles." Has the evangelist inserted "and scholars" because he had been a scholar (a "scribe") himself (13:52)? But if Q had "and apostles," would he have omitted that, or changed it to *sages*? Perhaps "and apostles" is the Lukan author's addition to Q (which would then have read simply "prophets"), and our evangelist has added the second and third nouns.

prophets: It's not clear what their role in the church would have been—perhaps not to foretell the future but, in the more classical sense, to be spokespersons for God.

sages: The same Greek word as "the wise" in 11:25. Together with the parallel to that saying in Luke, these are the only uses of the word in any of the gospels. We simply don't know what role such people would have played.

scholars: Serving, no doubt, much the same role in the church as Jewish scholars in Judaism, but interpreting the Hebrew scriptures in a Christian way, for example drawing up lists of *testimonia*; see Introduction, p. 19.

kill and crucify: A Hebraism. It means "kill by crucifying," something that could take place only in collaboration with Rome. Is Jesus' crucifixion in mind here? Apparently not, since the prediction involves a number of people (*some*). Or does this speak of what his disciples can expect later on, in the time of this gospel's writing? Perhaps the latter, in the light of what follows: *beat in your synagogues and hound from town to town.* This is not in Luke, nor do we have any evidence that Jesus' followers were so persecuted during his lifetime.

• **23:35** A dense verse.

on your heads: As your responsibility. Not on "this generation" as a whole, as in Luke 11:50. And see on vs 36, just below.

all the innocent blood: A massive indictment.

from the blood of innocent Abel to the blood of Zechariah, son of Baruch: From the earliest to what perhaps was the most recent instance of the murder of God's emissaries.

θυσιαστηρίου. ³⁶ἀμὴν λέγω ὑμῖν, ἥξει ταῦτα πάντα ἐπὶ τὴν γενεὰν ταύτην.

Lament over Jerusalem

³⁷Ἰερουσαλὴμ Ἰερουσαλήμ, ἡ ἀποκτείνουσα τοὺς προφήτας καὶ λιθοβολοῦσα τοὺς ἀπεσταλμένους πρὸς αὐτήν, ποσάκις ἠθέλησα ἐπισυναγαγεῖν τὰ τέκνα σου, ὃν τρόπον ὄρνις ἐπισυνάγει τὰ νοσσία αὐτῆς ὑπὸ τὰς πτέρυγας, καὶ οὐκ ἠθελήσατε. ³⁸ἰδοὺ ἀφίεται ὑμῖν ὁ οἶκος ὑμῶν ἔρημος. ³⁹λέγω γὰρ ὑμῖν, οὐ μή με ἴδητε ἀπ' ἄρτι ἕως ἂν εἴπητε, Εὐλογημένος ὁ ἐρχόμενος ἐν ὀνόματι κυρίου.

24:36 *nor even the son* is lacking in many MSS. Did scribes omit it because it contradicted the later orthodox Christian view of Jesus' divinity?

---

innocent Abel: Gen. 4:8. Regarded as a prophet?

Zechariah, son of Baruch: Perhaps the prophet of the Book of Zechariah, who in the book's first verse is designated "son of Berechaiah" (Greek *Barachios*). But according to 2 Chr 24:20–21 the Zechariah who was "stoned . . . to death in the court of the house of the Lord" was "son of the priest Jehoiada." Probably this confusion cannot be adequately sorted out; at any rate it doesn't matter. The original audience would know the Zechariah in question.

whom you murdered: Your ancestors did, and so you did. Note how the author portrays Jesus speaking as if not such a descen-

dant himself. The actual context is more likely about 85 CE, when the church was in bitter conflict with Jewish leaders.

between the temple and the altar: A curious phrase. But see Ezek 8:16 and Joel 2:17.

"Temple" here is *naos* ("sanctuary"), not the more general *hieron*, which consisted of three concentric courts. We are probably to think of the innermost court, that of the priests. Maybe the stoning to death occurred as Zechariah was going up to make sacrifice, after he had condemned Israel and foretold that God would destroy it.

• **23:36** A concluding solemn oath. On *I swear to you,* see Translation Note p. 61.

rain down on this generation: Luke 11:51b

Interpretive Note: The Pharisees

How shall we understand this chapter, whether or not it is part of Jesus' last discourse (see on 24:4)? It has given rise to the image of the Pharisees as evil, while in fact in Jesus' lifetime they represented perhaps the most responsible and ethical movement within Judaism, even though Jesus did not ally himself with them. The picture painted here reflects the time of the evangelist, when Pharisees had succeeded to the place of leadership in Judaism following the catastrophe of the year 70. And even more it reflects the fact that those Jews—including the Pharisees who had not become believers in Jesus as the Anointed—

between the temple and the altar. ³⁶I swear to you, all these things are going to rain down on this generation.

³⁷"Jerusalem, Jerusalem, you murder the prophets and stone those sent to you! How often I wanted to gather your children as a hen gathers her chicks under her wings, but you wouldn't let me. ³⁸Can't you see, your house is being abandoned as a ruin? ³⁹I tell you, you certainly won't see me from now on until you say, 'Blessed is the one who comes in the name of the Lord.'"

Lament over Jerusalem

---

has "this generation will have to answer for it." But here it seems to be the leaders who are responsible not only for their own destruction but for what will happen to *this generation.*

• **23:37–39** Parallel to Luke 13:34–35. Why does our evangelist place this lament here? To show Jesus' compassion alongside his angry condemnation? In any case, like a prophet Jesus speaks for God.

• **23:37** *Jerusalem, Jerusalem:* The holy city represented the soul of Israel, of Judaism.

gather your children as a hen gathers her chicks under her wings: A disarming simile. The rage of the condemning of Pharisees and scholars gives way to this wonderful imagining of protecting love.

but you wouldn't let me: The tone is not anger, but sadness—for the people at least, if not their leaders.

• **23:38** A prediction of the destruction of the Jerusalem temple.

is being abandoned: Greek, "is being emptied out for you."

as a ruin: The author adds this.

• **23:39** *until you say, Blessed is the one who comes . . .:* That is, until Jesus is hailed on his return to earth, in contrast to these same words that were spoken in false greeting (21:9).

---

who were not Christians, were from time to time pressuring, even persecuting their Christian neighbors. (In fact, that is what the perhaps overly zealous Pharisee Paul had done long before 70). So they had become the enemy of the church and therefore could be depicted as the enemy of Jesus, so that his condemnation of them—virtually none of it going back to Jesus himself—satisfied the beleaguered church's regrettable but understandable animosity toward them. Tragically, it has contributed to the anti-Jewish tone of the gospel and to the monstrous fact of Christian hatred of Jews through the centuries ever since. It is reassuring that the chapter ends not with venom but with lament.

**The fifth
discourse**

24 Καὶ ἐξελθὼν ὁ Ἰησοῦς ἀπὸ τοῦ ἱεροῦ ἐπορεύετο, καὶ προσῆλθον οἱ μαθηταὶ αὐτοῦ ἐπιδεῖξαι αὐτῷ τὰς οἰκοδομὰς τοῦ ἱεροῦ.

²Ὁ δὲ ἀποκριθεὶς εἶπεν αὐτοῖς, Οὐ βλέπετε ταῦτα πάντα; ἀμὴν λέγω ὑμῖν, οὐ μὴ ἀφεθῇ ὧδε λίθος ἐπὶ λίθον ὃς οὐ καταλυθήσεται.

**Signs of
final agonies**

³Καθημένου δὲ αὐτοῦ ἐπὶ τοῦ Ὄρους τῶν Ἐλαιῶν προσῆλθον αὐτῷ οἱ μαθηταὶ κατ' ἰδίαν λέγοντες, Εἰπὲ ἡμῖν πότε ταῦτα ἔσται καὶ τί τὸ σημεῖον τῆς σῆς παρουσίας καὶ συντελείας τοῦ αἰῶνος;

⁴Καὶ ἀποκριθεὶς ὁ Ἰησοῦς εἶπεν αὐτοῖς, Βλέπετε μή τις ὑμᾶς πλανήσῃ· ⁵πολλοὶ γὰρ ἐλεύσονται ἐπὶ τῷ ὀνόματί μου λέγοντες, Ἐγώ εἰμι ὁ Χριστός, καὶ πολλοὺς πλανήσουσιν. ⁶μελλήσετε δὲ ἀκούειν πολέμους καὶ ἀκοὰς πολέμων· ὁρᾶτε μὴ θροεῖσθε· δεῖ γὰρ γενέσθαι, ἀλλ' οὔπω ἐστὶν τὸ τέλος. ⁷ἐγερθήσεται γὰρ ἔθνος ἐπὶ ἔθνος καὶ βασιλεία ἐπὶ βασιλείαν καὶ ἔσονται λιμοὶ καὶ σεισμοὶ κατὰ τόπους· ⁸πάντα δὲ ταῦτα ἀρχὴ ὠδίνων.

⁹Τότε παραδώσουσιν ὑμᾶς εἰς θλῖψιν καὶ ἀποκτενοῦσιν ὑμᾶς, καὶ

• **Chaps. 24–25** The fifth discourse. (Or did the sermon begin with chap. 23? See below on 24:4 and 26:1.) They represent this gospel's Apocalyptic Discourse, much of it parallel to Mark 13 and Luke 21. A vivid scenario for the end of the age and a collection of various images and predictions, it is often more specific than Mark's. Our author writes later than Mark . . . well after the destruction of the temple in Jerusalem, in 70 CE. That event now serves not as the end in itself but as a kind of model for the cataclysm still expected at the end of the age. I doubt whether much or any of this teaching goes back to Jesus himself; rather, it was imagined after his death and the rise of his followers' belief in his resurrection, which for them showed him to be the Anointed. Since he had not seemed during his lifetime to be the Anointed they had expected, his return was projected, to occur at the end of the age. Paul, the earliest Christian writer, played a major role in this projection.

The discourse begins informally, with Jesus' prediction of the coming destruction of the Jerusalem temple buildings (24:1–2).

• **24:1** *leaving the temple area:* Where he had been, evidently, since 21:23.

sacred buildings: That is, of the temple, the sacred precinct, as a whole—including the inner shrine and the surrounding courts of priests, of [male] Israel, of women, and of Gentiles.

• **24:2** *take a good look at:* In Greek, "Don't you see . . . ?"

you can be sure: Two brief words in Greek, called particles (*ou mê*), make the saying emphatic. A more vernacular translation: "No way will one stone. . . ."

not one of these stones will be left on top of another!: An exaggeration, of course. But it would have seemed like that to those who had seen the Roman assault on the temple or the resulting demolition.

• **24:3** *the Mount of Olives:* The ridge of hills beyond the steep Valley Kidron to the east of Jerusalem and directly overlooking the temple.

the disciples came to him: Mark (13:3) names four only ("Peter, James, John, and Andrew"). Our author, while maintaining the Markan privacy of this teaching, addresses it to all the disciples.

the sign: The visual indication, a public one.

your coming and the end of the age: Mark (13:4) and Luke (21:7) do not name these particular expectations.

your coming: Jesus' return to earth after his death and resurrection. (Sometimes called "the Second Coming," but that is incorrect except for the Fourth Gospel, according to which Jesus "came down from heaven" in the first place—6:38.) The noun means simply "presence," and therefore "arrival." Jesus' return, or the Son of Man's coming, is

24 And as Jesus was leaving the temple area his disciples came to him and called his attention to the sacred buildings.

²In response he said to them, "Yes, take a good look at all this! I swear to you, you can be sure not one of these stones will be left on top of another. Every last one will certainly be knocked down."

³As he was sitting on the Mount of Olives, the disciples came to him privately, and said, "Tell us, when are these things going to happen, and what will be the sign of your coming and the end of the age?"

⁴And in response Jesus said to them: "Stay alert, otherwise someone might delude you. ⁵You know, many will come using my name, and claim, 'I am the Anointed!' and they will delude many people. ⁶You are going to hear about wars and rumors of wars. See that you are not afraid. For these are inevitable, but it is not yet the end. ⁷For nation will rise up against nation and empire against empire; and there will be famines and earthquakes everywhere. ⁸Now all these things mark the beginning of the final agonies.

⁹"At that time they will turn you over for torture, and will kill

---

not spoken of until this chapter.

the end of the age: Not the so-called end of the world, but the beginning of God's empire.

• **24:4** This discourse is initiated not by Jesus, as at 5:2, 10:5, and 13:3, but by the disciples (as at 18:1). Still, there is reason to see chap. 23 as the start of this "sermon." For one thing, that would make the last discourse roughly equal in length to the first, chaps. 5–7. It's true that the audience changes here, but that is true in the midst of the third discourse (see 13:10). There is no concluding formula ("When Jesus had finished . . .") at the end of chap. 23. And the idea of final judgment that runs through chaps. 24–25 comes to expression already in chap. 23 (for example vs 36: "All these things are going to rain down on this generation"). And the beginning of the sermons is generally less defined than the endings. To be sure, the fact that only chaps. 24–25 are conveyed "privately" may argue against considering chap. 23 part of the discourse. On the other hand, the third discourse is presented partly in public, partly to the disciples alone (see 13:36).

The author now closely follows Mark 13, known as the Little Apocalypse (to distinguish it from the book of Revelation, called simply The Apocalypse—the major one). On "Apocalypse" see Glossary.

Stay alert: Or "Watch out." Usually rendered

"Beware."

otherwise someone might: Or, "lest someone."

delude you: Strictly, "lead you astray." Mark uses this word once, in 13:22, which is paralleled in vs 24 below. Our evangelist introduces it here early in the discourse, and again in vs 11. Apparently the problems of falling into error and even defection from the church were acute in his time.

• **24:5** People will pretend to be Jesus come back to life. Did this happen in our author's time?

• **24:6** *hear about wars:* Or "hear <the noise> of battle." Does the author mean wars on earth, or in the sky?

• **24:7** *nation will rise up against nation:* Or "people . . . against people."

everywhere: Or "almost anywhere."

• **24:8** *the beginning of the final agonies:* Many translations have "only the beginning. . . ." But "only" is not found in the Greek. Is the meaning, then, not one of discouragement (much more to come) but rather the opposite (the end is near)?

final agonies: Greek, "labor pains."

• **24:9** *Torture* is mentioned only by this author. Very likely some in the Matthean community had experienced it.

and will kill you: Martyrdom will be more widespread than predicted in Mark 13:12 (murder of family members) and in Luke 21:16 ("some of you").

ἔσεσθε μισούμενοι ὑπὸ πάντων τῶν ἐθνῶν διὰ τὸ ὄνομά μου. ¹⁰καὶ τότε σκανδαλισθήσονται πολλοὶ καὶ ἀλλήλους παραδώσουσιν καὶ μισήσουσιν ἀλλήλους· ¹¹καὶ πολλοὶ ψευδοπροφῆται ἐγερθήσονται καὶ πλανήσουσιν πολλούς· ¹²καὶ διὰ τὸ πληθυνθῆναι τὴν ἀνομίαν ψυγήσεται ἡ ἀγάπη τῶν πολλῶν. ¹³ὁ δὲ ὑπομείνας εἰς τέλος οὗτος σωθήσεται. ¹⁴καὶ κηρυχθήσεται τοῦτο τὸ εὐαγγέλιον τῆς βασιλείας ἐν ὅλῃ τῇ οἰκουμένῃ εἰς μαρτύριον πᾶσιν τοῖς ἔθνεσιν, καὶ τότε ἥξει τὸ τέλος.

Days of distress

¹⁵Ὅταν οὖν ἴδητε τὸ βδέλυγμα τῆς ἐρημώσεως τὸ ῥηθὲν διὰ Δανιὴλ τοῦ προφήτου ἑστὸς ἐν τόπῳ ἁγίῳ, ὁ ἀναγινώσκων νοείτω, ¹⁶τότε οἱ ἐν τῇ Ἰουδαίᾳ φευγέτωσαν εἰς τὰ ὄρη, ¹⁷ὁ ἐπὶ τοῦ δώματος μὴ καταβάτω ἆραι τὰ ἐκ τῆς οἰκίας αὐτοῦ, ¹⁸καὶ ὁ ἐν τῷ ἀγρῷ μὴ ἐπιστρεψάτω ὀπίσω ἆραι τὸ ἱμάτιον αὐτοῦ. ¹⁹οὐαὶ δὲ ταῖς ἐν γαστρὶ ἐχούσαις καὶ ταῖς θηλαζούσαις ἐν ἐκείναις ταῖς ἡμέραις. ²⁰προσεύχεσθε δὲ ἵνα μὴ γένηται ἡ φυγὴ ὑμῶν χειμῶνος μηδὲ σαββάτῳ. ²¹ἔσται γὰρ τότε θλῖψις μεγάλη οἵα οὐ γέγονεν ἀπ᾿ ἀρχῆς κόσμου ἕως τοῦ νῦν οὐδ᾿ οὐ μὴ γένηται. ²²καὶ εἰ μὴ ἐκολοβώθησαν αἱ ἡμέραι ἐκεῖναι, οὐκ ἂν ἐσώθη πᾶσα σάρξ· διὰ δὲ τοὺς ἐκλεκτοὺς κολοβωθήσονται αἱ ἡμέραι ἐκεῖναι.

²³Τότε ἐάν τις ὑμῖν εἴπῃ, Ἰδοὺ ὧδε ὁ Χριστός, ἤ, Ὧδε, μὴ πιστεύσητε· ²⁴ἐγερθήσονται γὰρ ψευδόχριστοι καὶ ψευδοπροφῆται καὶ δώσουσιν σημεῖα μεγάλα καὶ τέρατα ὥστε πλανῆσαι, εἰ δυνατόν,

---

• **24:10–12** Here the author, departing from Mark 13:9–12, does not repeat the troubles enumerated earlier in chap. 10 (vss 17–23). According to this gospel, they will not happen only at the end of the age. Disciples can expect them as part of their normal experience. Instead the author "predicts" troubles that perhaps his church has experienced, so that the gospel's readers can understand that the end has begun! See on vs 8 above. Neither Mark nor Luke has a any parallel to these verses foretelling chaos within the church.

• **24:10** *lose faith:* Or "fall away," "stumble." The result will be treachery (*betray[al] of one another*) and dissension (*hat[red] of one another*) within the Christian community.

• **24:11** Very similar to vs 5.

• **24:12** *lawlessness:* The work of the "phony prophets," evidently.

• **24:13** Despite the chaos, it will be possible to *hold out to the end [and] be saved:* The same promise was made in 10:22.

• **24:14** The need for a universal preaching of the new age before the end of the old, evil age is mentioned only in this gospel. The end has begun and *will come . . .* but there is much to do first.

this good news: Ironic after all the outlined woes. But see on vs 8.

the . . . inhabited world: The *ecumenê* in Greek.

• **24:15** *the devastating desecration (as described by Daniel the prophet) standing in the holy place:* In Dan 9:27, for example. There the prophet alluded, in veiled language, to the fact that the Gentile Syrian king, Antiochus Epiphanes, had recently set up his own statue as a god in the Jerusalem temple. This happened in 167 BCE. That, of course, desecrated the temple. Here either some such horrifying idea is to be imagined for the future, or the author is referring to some similar occurrence that took place at the time of the destruction of the temple in 70 CE.

devastating desecration: The sacrilege (an idol) that is "devastating" to Jewish religious sensibility. In 165 BCE, after the Maccabees' successful revolt, the temple had to undergo reconsecration (*Hanukkah*).

as described by Daniel the prophet: Only our author refers to a prophecy in Daniel.

(the reader had better figure out what this means): In apocalyptic literature, things are

you, and you will be universally hated because of me. ¹⁰And then many will lose faith, and they will betray one another and hate each other. ¹¹And many phony prophets will appear and will delude many. ¹²And as lawlessness spreads, mutual love will grow cool. ¹³Those who hold out to the end will be saved! ¹⁴And this good news of <Heaven's> imperial rule will have been proclaimed in the whole inhabited world, for evidence to all peoples. And then the end will come.

¹⁵"So when you see the 'devastating desecration' (as described by Daniel the prophet) standing 'in the holy place' (the reader had better figure out what this means), ¹⁶then the people in Judea should head for the hills. ¹⁷No one on the roof should go downstairs to retrieve anything; ¹⁸and no one in the field should turn back to get a coat. ¹⁹It'll be too bad for pregnant women and nursing mothers in those days! ²⁰Pray that you don't have to flee during the winter or on the sabbath day. ²¹For there will be utter distress, the likes of which has not occurred since the world began until now, and will never occur again. ²²And if those days had not been cut short, no human being would have survived. But for the sake of the chosen people, those days will be cut short.

²³"Then if someone says to you, 'Look, here is the Anointed' or 'over here,' don't count on it! ²⁴After all, counterfeit messiahs and phony prophets will show up, and they'll offer great portents and

Days of distress

---

often coded to hide them from the enemy, in this case the Roman empire.

• **24:16–22** Christians in Jerusalem in fact fled the Roman takeover of the city. It is not clear whether vss 17–18 describe what actually took place. The evangelist mainly repeats what he finds in Mark, who may have imagined what would happen. Or was Mark written just after this crisis—and therefore gives a factual report? In any case, for our evangelist this is still to come; it will be like what happened in the year 70 . . . only worse.

• **24:19** It'll be too bad for: Often translated "Woe to" but here with a different meaning from what in SV is translated "Damn you").

• **24:20** to flee during the winter or on the sabbath day: Respectively, difficult or a violation of Jewish law (which according to this gospel to some degree still governed Christians: 5:17–18).

• **24:21** Not even the flood in the time of Noah (Gen 7–9) was so dreadful. But like the flood this catastrophe will never occur again.

• **24:22** If those days had not been cut short: Mark 13:20 reads "if the Lord had not cut short. . . ." The same is meant here. The

construction is called a "divine passive," intending God as the agent of the action but choosing not to speak explicitly of God—a practice of Jewish piety sometimes used by our author.

the chosen people: Not the people of Israel, evidently, but Christians.

those days will be cut short: The nearly impossible test is still to come, but soon.

• **24:23** Look, here is the Anointed or Over here: False hopes that Jesus' expected return has occurred. Compare vs 5. In contrast to this, Thom 113:2–3 has:

It will not come by watching for it. ³It will not be said, "Look, here!" or "Look, there!" Rather, the Father's imperial rule is spread out upon the earth, and people don't see it.

• **24:24** they'll offer great portents and miracles: In the Greek: ". . . portents and miracles will be offered." If this is a divine passive, such as in vs 22, God will offer them. So as to deceive? SV attributes their appearance not to God but to the counterfeit messiahs and phony prophets.

the chosen people: As in vs 22.

καὶ τοὺς ἐκλεκτούς· ²⁵ἰδοὺ προείρηκα ὑμῖν. ²⁶ἐὰν οὖν εἴπωσιν
ὑμῖν, Ἰδοὺ ἐν τῇ ἐρήμῳ ἐστίν, μὴ ἐξέλθητε· Ἰδοὺ ἐν τοῖς ταμείοις,
μὴ πιστεύσητε· ²⁷ὥσπερ γὰρ ἡ ἀστραπὴ ἐξέρχεται ἀπὸ ἀνατολῶν
καὶ φαίνεται ἕως δυσμῶν, οὕτως ἔσται ἡ παρουσία τοῦ υἱοῦ τοῦ
ἀνθρώπου· ²⁸ὅπου ἐὰν ᾖ τὸ πτῶμα, ἐκεῖ συναχθήσονται οἱ ἀετοί.

²⁹Εὐθέως δὲ μετὰ τὴν θλῖψιν τῶν ἡμερῶν ἐκείνων

**Son
of Adam
comes on clouds**

ὁ ἥλιος σκοτισθήσεται,
καὶ ἡ σελήνη οὐ δώσει τὸ φέγγος αὐτῆς,
καὶ οἱ ἀστέρες πεσοῦνται ἀπὸ τοῦ οὐρανοῦ,
καὶ αἱ δυνάμεις τῶν οὐρανῶν σαλευθήσονται.

³⁰Καὶ τότε φανήσεται τὸ σημεῖον τοῦ υἱοῦ τοῦ ἀνθρώπου ἐν
οὐρανῷ, καὶ τότε κόψονται πᾶσαι αἱ φυλαὶ τῆς γῆς καὶ ὄψονται τὸν
υἱὸν τοῦ ἀνθρώπου ἐρχόμενον ἐπὶ τῶν νεφελῶν τοῦ οὐρανοῦ μετὰ
δυνάμεως καὶ δόξης πολλῆς· ³¹καὶ ἀποστελεῖ τοὺς ἀγγέλους αὐτοῦ
μετὰ σάλπιγγος μεγάλης, καὶ ἐπισυνάξουσιν τοὺς ἐκλεκτοὺς αὐτοῦ
ἐκ τῶν τεσσάρων ἀνέμων ἀπ' ἄκρων οὐρανῶν ἕως ἄκρων αὐτῶν.

³²Ἀπὸ δὲ τῆς συκῆς μάθετε τὴν παραβολήν· ὅταν ἤδη ὁ κλάδος
αὐτῆς γένηται ἁπαλὸς καὶ τὰ φύλλα ἐκφύῃ, γινώσκετε ὅτι ἐγγὺς
τὸ θέρος· ³³οὕτως καὶ ὑμεῖς, ὅταν ἴδητε πάντα ταῦτα, γινώσκετε
ὅτι ἐγγύς ἐστιν ἐπὶ θύραις. ³⁴ἀμὴν λέγω ὑμῖν ὅτι οὐ μὴ παρέλθῃ
ἡ γενεὰ αὕτη ἕως ἂν πάντα ταῦτα γένηται. ³⁵ὁ οὐρανὸς καὶ ἡ γῆ
παρελεύσεται, οἱ δὲ λόγοι μου οὐ μὴ παρέλθωσιν.

• **24:25** Apocalyptic discloses to those who can understand it what will happen, so that they not be misled.

• **24:26–28** This block is paralleled in Luke 17:23–24, 37, but not in Mark. It fits nicely after verses 23–25, and it introduces the theme of the coming of the son of Adam (the rest of the chapter).

• **24:26** Another version of the saying in vs 23.

he's in the wilderness: Like John the Baptist, evidently.

one of the secret rooms: What does this mean?

• **24:27** *just as lightning:* Does this mean that the appearing of *the son of Adam* will be unmistakable? Or sudden? Perhaps both. In either case, he will not need to be searched for.

• **24:28** A popular proverb? Possibly it means that these things will be unmistakable (see the preceding comment).

• **24:29** These portents would be the fulfillment of what had been predicted in Isa 13:10, 34:4 and other prophets, signifying the end of the age. The Greek wording here is identical to LXX.

tribulation: It was taken for granted that the end could not come without an enormous struggle, without "final agonies" (vs 8).

the stars will fall from the sky: Like the sun and moon, according to Gen 1:17, these were attached to the underside of the dome that was called sky.

the heavenly forces: Often translated as "the powers." Having determining power over human life, like the planets in astrological belief. Their hold on earthly events will be broken.

• **24:30** *And then the son of Adam's sign will appear in the sky, and every tribe of the earth will lament:* The evangelist has inserted this half of the verse into Mark's words. The same prediction appears in Rev 1:7.

miracles to delude, if possible, even the chosen people. ²⁵Look, I have warned you in advance. ²⁶In fact, if they should say to you, 'Look, he's in the wilderness,' don't go out there; 'Look, he's in one of the secret rooms,' don't count on it. ²⁷For just as lightning comes out of the east and is visible all the way to the west, that's what the coming of the son of Adam will be like. ²⁸For wherever there's a corpse, that's where vultures gather.

²⁹"Immediately after the tribulation of those days

the sun will be darkened,
and the moon will not give off her glow,
and the stars will fall from the sky,
and the heavenly forces will be shaken!

Son of Adam comes on clouds

³⁰"And then the son of Adam's sign will appear in the sky, and every tribe of the earth will lament, and they'll see the son of Adam coming on the clouds of the sky with great power and splendor. ³¹And he'll send out his messengers with a blast on the trumpet, and they'll gather his chosen people from the four winds, from one end of the sky to the other!

³²"Take a cue from the fig tree. When its branch is already in bud and leaves come out, you know that summer is near. ³³So, when you see all these things, you ought to realize that he is near, just outside your door. ³⁴I swear to God, this generation certainly won't pass into oblivion before all these things take place! ³⁵The earth will pass into oblivion and so will the sky, but my words will never be obliterated!

---

the son of Adam's sign will appear in the sky: What is this sign? In any case, it will be unmistakable.

every tribe of the earth will lament: In repentance or despair?

the son of Adam coming on the clouds of the sky: An enactment of the vision in Dan 7:13. There, however, "one like a son of Adam" travels not to earth from heaven but just the reverse, to appear before God's throne. and it represents the righteous of Israel.

• **24:31** *his messengers:* See Glossary.

with a blast on the trumpet: Like others of these predictions, this is akin to Paul's in 1 Thess 4:16–17.

the four winds: The four points of the compass, as we would say.

from one end of the sky to the other: On a flat and finite earth, the sky—which is the upper story of the three-level universe—must have ends.

• **24:32** *take a cue:* Strictly, "learn the parable,"

treated as a simile.

[the fig tree's] branch is already in bud and leaves come out: In Palestine a sign of the sudden change of seasons.

• **24:33** *he is near:* Or "it [the end] is near."

just outside your door: It couldn't be nearer. In Greek, "at the gates [of the city]." So *your* is plural.

• **24:34** How does this relate to the delay expected in vs 14 (till the good news is universally made known)? It seems that the evangelist both seeks to energize the mission (see 28:19–20a) and expects that in the near future the end will come.

I swear to God: What follows is an imposing declaration.

pass into oblivion: Or simply "disappear."

• **24:35** Reassurance that, like the Jewish Torah, the revelation conveyed in Jesus' *words* will survive the eschaton.

³⁶Περὶ δὲ τῆς ἡμέρας ἐκείνης καὶ ὥρας οὐδεὶς οἶδεν, οὐδὲ οἱ ἄγγελοι τῶν οὐρανῶν οὐδὲ ὁ υἱός, εἰ μὴ ὁ πατὴρ μόνος.

³⁷Ὥσπερ γὰρ αἱ ἡμέραι τοῦ Νῶε, οὕτως ἔσται ἡ παρουσία τοῦ υἱοῦ τοῦ ἀνθρώπου. ³⁸ὡς γὰρ ἦσαν ἐν ταῖς ἡμέραις ταῖς πρὸ τοῦ κατακλυσμοῦ τρώγοντες καὶ πίνοντες, γαμοῦντες καὶ γαμίζοντες, ἄχρι ἧς ἡμέρας εἰσῆλθεν Νῶε εἰς τὴν κιβωτόν, ³⁹καὶ οὐκ ἔγνωσαν ἕως ἦλθεν ὁ κατακλυσμὸς καὶ ἦρεν ἅπαντας, οὕτως ἔσται ἡ παρουσία τοῦ υἱοῦ τοῦ ἀνθρώπου. ⁴⁰τότε δύο ἔσονται ἐν τῷ ἀγρῷ, εἷς παραλαμβάνεται καὶ εἷς ἀφίεται· ⁴¹δύο ἀλήθουσαι ἐν τῷ μύλῳ, μία παραλαμβάνεται καὶ μία ἀφίεται. ⁴²γρηγορεῖτε οὖν, ὅτι οὐκ οἴδατε ποίᾳ ἡμέρᾳ ὁ κύριος ὑμῶν ἔρχεται.

⁴³Ἐκεῖνο δὲ γινώσκετε ὅτι εἰ ᾔδει ὁ οἰκοδεσπότης ποίᾳ φυλακῇ ὁ κλέπτης ἔρχεται, ἐγρηγόρησεν ἂν καὶ οὐκ ἂν εἴασεν διορυχθῆναι τὴν οἰκίαν αὐτοῦ. ⁴⁴διὰ τοῦτο καὶ ὑμεῖς γίνεσθε ἕτοιμοι, ὅτι ᾗ οὐ δοκεῖτε ὥρᾳ ὁ υἱὸς τοῦ ἀνθρώπου ἔρχεται.

⁴⁵Τίς ἄρα ἐστὶν ὁ πιστὸς δοῦλος καὶ φρόνιμος ὃν κατέστησεν ὁ κύριος ἐπὶ τῆς οἰκετείας αὐτοῦ τοῦ δοῦναι αὐτοῖς τὴν τροφὴν ἐν καιρῷ; ⁴⁶μακάριος ὁ δοῦλος ἐκεῖνος ὃν ἐλθὼν ὁ κύριος αὐτοῦ εὑρήσει οὕτως ποιοῦντα· ⁴⁷ἀμὴν λέγω ὑμῖν ὅτι ἐπὶ πᾶσιν τοῖς ὑπάρχουσιν αὐτοῦ καταστήσει αὐτόν. ⁴⁸ἐὰν δὲ εἴπῃ ὁ κακὸς δοῦλος ἐκεῖνος ἐν

• **24:36–51** The end will come during the present generation (vs 34), but no one knows when.
• **24:36** *minute:* Greek "hour."
   nor even the son: Jesus' knowledge is as limited as everyone's even though he is *the son.*
   With this verse, and the teaching on watchfulness used elsewhere in the discourse by Matthew, the Markan apocalypse comes to an end. But not in Matthew, where three blocks of material from Q continue the theme of being ready, and then another chapter altogether is added.
• **24:37–41** The first block of Q material, more extensive in Luke 17:26–35.
• **24:37** The end of the age will be like its beginning, the flood (Gen 6–8).
• **24:38** *flood:* The Greek word is "cataclysm."
   they ate and drank, married and were given in marriage: Is this said in criticism (as in vs 49 below) or does it simply mean normal daily life?
   married and were given in marriage: It was held that only a man could marry; a woman was *given in marriage* by her father or other male relative. She was in a sense a man's

property.
   Noah boarded the ark: A quotation of Gen 7:7.
• **24:39** *they were oblivious:* Should they have been more aware? Or is the point rather the unexpectedness of the cataclysm? The evangelist omits a second example from this passage in Q, the story of Lot and his wife (Luke 17:28–31).
• **24:40–41** This, understood literally (together with 1 Thess 4:17), is the basis for what fundamentalists call the Rapture, from the Latin for being *taken.* It's usually assumed that being *taken* is the desirable alternative.
• **24:40** *two men will be in the field:* Luke (17:34) has "two will be in one bed," or "on one couch."
• **24:41** *grinding at the mill:* Making meal from grain, probably by crushing between flat stones. See on 18:6.
• **24:42** An injunction not found in Luke's version. But it has little meaning in the light of vss 40–41. That is, how would it have helped the man or the woman left? Or does it belong with vs 43?

³⁶"As for that exact day and minute: no one knows, not even heaven's messengers, nor even the son—no one, except the Father alone.

³⁷"The son of Adam's coming will be just like the days of Noah. ³⁸This is how people behaved then before the flood came: they ate and drank, married and were given in marriage, until the day 'Noah boarded the ark,' ³⁹and they were oblivious until the flood came and swept them all away. This is how it will be when the son of Adam comes. ⁴⁰Then two men will be in the field; one will be taken and one will be left. ⁴¹Two women will be grinding at the mill; one will be taken and one left. ⁴²So stay alert! You never know on what day your Lord comes.

⁴³"Mark this well: if the homeowner had known when the burglar was coming, he would have been on guard and not have allowed anyone to break into his house. ⁴⁴By the same token, you too should be prepared. Remember, the son of Adam is coming when you least expect it.

⁴⁵"Who then is the reliable and shrewd slave to whom the master assigns responsibility for his household, to provide them with food at the right time? ⁴⁶Congratulations to the slave who's on the job when his master arrives. ⁴⁷I swear to you, the master will put him in charge of all his property. ⁴⁸But suppose that slave <is> worthless

---

stay alert: Or "keep awake." The ending of Mark's apocalypse (13:37).

your Lord: An unusual phrase.

comes: A present tense referring, of course, to the future.

• **24:43–44** A brief metaphor (from Q—Luke 12:39–40), with explicit moral. It drives home the point that the eschaton will be completely unexpected.

• **24:43** *when:* In Greek, "at what watch [= division of the night]."

been on guard: Or "stayed awake."

break into: Greek, "dig through [a house made of adobe]"

• **24:44** *is coming:* See on vs 42.

when you least expect it: Literally, "at an hour you don't imagine."

• **24:45–51** Continuing to follow Q, a kind of double parable, with built-in morals (vss 46, 51).

• **24:45** *Who then is...?* Does the question expect an answer? Perhaps it is no more pointed than "What do you think...?" (18:12, 21:28).

• **24:46** *Congratulations to:* Better than the traditional version, "Blessed is."

the slave who's on the job when his master arrives: This is "the reliable and shrewd slave" of the question in the previous verse.

on the job: "Doing this."

• **24:47** *in charge of all his property:* The highest possible promotion of a reliable slave.

• **24:48–51** The injunction of watchfulness now turns to a negative example, not only carelessness but even moral and ethical dissolution. The penalty is worse than simply being taken by surprise.

• **24:48** *suppose that slave <is> worthless <and> says:* The Greek, in a too condensed way, has "suppose that worthless slave says," the opposite of the slave of vss 46–47. Here he is more "shrewd" than "reliable" (see vs 45).

to himself: "In his heart."

My master is taking his time: The so-called delay of the parousia, of the risen Jesus' return to end the age, was increasingly a problem for the late first-century church.

taking his time: A nice rendering of *chronizei.*

τῇ καρδίᾳ αὐτοῦ, Χρονίζει μου ὁ κύριος, ⁴⁹καὶ ἄρξηται τύπτειν τοὺς συνδούλους αὐτοῦ, ἐσθίῃ δὲ καὶ πίνῃ μετὰ τῶν μεθυόντων, ⁵⁰ἥξει ὁ κύριος τοῦ δούλου ἐκείνου ἐν ἡμέρᾳ ᾗ οὐ προσδοκᾷ καὶ ἐν ὥρᾳ ᾗ οὐ γινώσκει, ⁵¹καὶ διχοτομήσει αὐτὸν καὶ τὸ μέρος αὐτοῦ μετὰ τῶν ὑποκριτῶν θήσει· ἐκεῖ ἔσται ὁ κλαυθμὸς καὶ ὁ βρυγμὸς τῶν ὀδόντων.

• **24:51** *cut him to pieces:* Or "cut him off."

fate with <other> impostors, where they will moan and grind their teeth: Punishment in hell.

impostors: In Greek, "hypocrites."

<and> says to himself, 'My master is taking his time,' ⁴⁹and begins to beat his fellow slaves, and starts eating and drinking with drunkards. ⁵⁰That slave's master will show up on the day he least expects and at an hour he doesn't suspect, ⁵¹will cut him to pieces, and assign him a fate with <other> impostors, where they will moan and grind their teeth.

Ten maidens

25 Τότε ὁμοιωθήσεται ἡ βασιλεία τῶν οὐρανῶν δέκα παρθένοις, αἵτινες λαβοῦσαι τὰς λαμπάδας ἑαυτῶν ἐξῆλθον εἰς ὑπάντησιν τοῦ νυμφίου. ²πέντε δὲ ἐξ αὐτῶν ἦσαν μωραὶ καὶ πέντε φρόνιμοι. ³αἱ γὰρ μωραὶ λαβοῦσαι τὰς λαμπάδας αὐτῶν οὐκ ἔλαβον μεθ᾽ ἑαυτῶν ἔλαιον. ⁴αἱ δὲ φρόνιμοι ἔλαβον ἔλαιον ἐν τοῖς ἀγγείοις μετὰ τῶν λαμπάδων ἑαυτῶν. ⁵χρονίζοντος δὲ τοῦ νυμφίου ἐνύσταξαν πᾶσαι καὶ ἐκάθευδον.

⁶Μέσης δὲ νυκτὸς κραυγὴ γέγονεν, Ἰδοὺ ὁ νυμφίος, ἐξέρχεσθε εἰς ἀπάντησιν αὐτοῦ. ⁷τότε ἠγέρθησαν πᾶσαι αἱ παρθένοι ἐκεῖναι καὶ ἐκόσμησαν τὰς λαμπάδας ἑαυτῶν.

⁸Αἱ δὲ μωραὶ ταῖς φρονίμοις εἶπαν, Δότε ἡμῖν ἐκ τοῦ ἐλαίου ὑμῶν, ὅτι αἱ λαμπάδες ἡμῶν σβέννυνται.

⁹Ἀπεκρίθησαν δὲ αἱ φρόνιμοι λέγουσαι, Μήποτε οὐ μὴ ἀρκέσῃ ἡμῖν καὶ ὑμῖν· πορεύεσθε μᾶλλον πρὸς τοὺς πωλοῦντας καὶ ἀγοράσατε ἑαυταῖς.

¹⁰Ἀπερχομένων δὲ αὐτῶν ἀγοράσαι ἦλθεν ὁ νυμφίος, καὶ αἱ ἕτοιμοι εἰσῆλθον μετ᾽ αὐτοῦ εἰς τοὺς γάμους καὶ ἐκλείσθη ἡ θύρα.

¹¹Ὕστερον δὲ ἔρχονται καὶ αἱ λοιπαὶ παρθένοι λέγουσαι, Κύριε κύριε, ἄνοιξον ἡμῖν.

¹²Ὁ δὲ ἀποκριθεὶς εἶπεν, Ἀμὴν λέγω ὑμῖν, οὐκ οἶδα ὑμᾶς.

¹³Γρηγορεῖτε οὖν, ὅτι οὐκ οἴδατε τὴν ἡμέραν οὐδὲ τὴν ὥραν.

The entrusted money

¹⁴Ὥσπερ γὰρ ἄνθρωπος ἀποδημῶν ἐκάλεσεν τοὺς ἰδίους δούλους καὶ παρέδωκεν αὐτοῖς τὰ ὑπάρχοντα αὐτοῦ, ¹⁵καὶ ᾧ

25:1 A few MSS read "the bridegroom and the bride," which perhaps accords more closely with some wedding customs.

• **Chap. 25** Three major parables complete the discourse, each presented as an allegory describing the last judgment.

• **25:1–13** This parable is to be found only in Matthew. But in Luke 12:35–37 there is a briefer saying with some interesting similarities: "Keep . . . your lamps lighted. Imitate those who are waiting for their master to come home from a wedding, ready to open the door for him as soon as he arrives and knocks. Those slaves the master finds alert when he arrives are to be congratulated."

• **25:1** *When the time comes:* Greek, simply "Then." Evidently referring to the coming of the son of Adam (24:44).

maidens who took their lamps and went out to meet the bridegroom: Perhaps a custom in the wedding rite . . .: young women going from the bride's household to the groom's, waiting to escort him to the wedding, presum-

ably at night. The messianic age was often thought of as a wedding celebration (see, for example, the parable in 22:1–10).

lamps: In first-century Palestine these would have been shallow clay dishes, with two sides closed over the top and a wick protruding from a kind of spout at one end—a very rudimentary form of what we think of as Aladdin's lamp. They would have held relatively little oil, enough to burn for a few hours at most.

• **25:6** *Look, the bridegroom is coming!:* Literally, "Behold the bridegroom!"

25:7 *trimmed their lamps:* That is, the wicks, which were like short pieces of loosely woven rope. The lamps had been left burning as they slept.

• **25:9** *go to the shopkeeper:* This is obviously a fictional story; that the shop would hardly be open "in the middle of the night" (vs 6) is

25 When the time comes, Heaven's imperial rule will be like ten maidens who took their lamps and went out to meet the bridegroom. ²Five of them were foolish and five were sensible. ³Now the foolish maidens had taken their lamps but failed to take oil with them, ⁴while the sensible ones took flasks of oil along with their lamps. ⁵When the bridegroom didn't come, they all dozed off and fell asleep.

Ten maidens

⁶But in the middle of the night there was a shout: 'Look, the bridegroom is coming! Let's go out to meet him.' ⁷Then the maidens all got up and trimmed their lamps.

⁸The foolish said to the sensible ones, 'Let us have some of your oil because our lamps are going out.'

⁹But the prudent maidens responded, 'We can't do that in case there isn't enough for both you and us. Instead, you had better go to the shopkeeper and buy some for yourselves.'

¹⁰While they were gone to get some, the bridegroom arrived and those who had come prepared accompanied him to the wedding; then the door was closed.

¹¹The other maidens finally come and say, 'Lord, lord, open the door for us.'

¹²He responded, 'I swear to you, I don't recognize you.'

¹³"So stay alert because you don't know either the day or the hour.

¹⁴You know, it's like a man going on a trip, who called his slaves and turned his wealth over to them. ¹⁵To the first he gave

The entrusted money

---

beside the point.
- **25:10c–12** *then the door was closed . . . I don't recognize you:* Notice similarities to Luke 13:25: "Once the master of the house gets up and bars the door, you'll be left standing outside and knocking at the door: 'Sir, open up for us.' But he'll answer you, 'I don't know where you come from.'" The latter portion also resembles Matt 7:23.
- **25:11** *Lord, lord:* Within the story, this would be translated "Master, master," but for the allegorical application of the parable to Jesus' return this is better.
- **25:12** *He responded:* The bridegroom stands for the Son of Adam on his return.
- **25:13** A moral added to the once independent parable to apply it to this apocalyptic context. Or perhaps the parable always had the coming of the messiah in mind. Especially if that is the case, it is not authentic to the historical Jesus, at least in its present form and extent. The verse is almost identical to 24:42a, and to Mark 13:35.

- **25:14–30** Another once independent parable, usually called the parable of the talents. There is a somewhat different version of the story in Luke 19:12–27 (Pounds).
- **25:14** *it's like:* Describing the end of the age—that is, apparently, the last judgment, at least in the author's view. In an earlier form the parable was no doubt simply about the new age of God, "God's empire," with no apocalyptic expectation.
  his slaves: Clearly his trusted servants, the hierarchy of his household staff. See comment on 18:23–24.
- **25:15** *thirty thousand silver coins:* In Greek, "five *talanta*." A *talanton* was originally a gold weight, and then a coin, worth an enormous amount, equal to six thousand *silver coins* ("denarii"; see on 20:2). It can be very estimated that the value of the 5 "talents" entrusted to the first slave was equal to about a hundred year's wages for a common laborer. (When speaking of wages it would be meaningless to translate this amount into a

μὲν ἔδωκεν πέντε τάλαντα, ᾧ δὲ δύο, ᾧ δὲ ἕν, ἑκάστῳ κατὰ τὴν ἰδίαν δύναμιν, καὶ ἀπεδήμησεν.

Εὐθέως ¹⁶πορευθεὶς ὁ τὰ πέντε τάλαντα λαβὼν ἠργάσατο ἐν αὐτοῖς καὶ ἐκέρδησεν ἄλλα πέντε·

¹⁷Ὡσαύτως ὁ τὰ δύο ἐκέρδησεν ἄλλα δύο.

¹⁸Ὁ δὲ τὸ ἓν λαβὼν ἀπελθὼν ὤρυξεν γῆν καὶ ἔκρυψεν τὸ ἀργύριον τοῦ κυρίου αὐτοῦ.

¹⁹Μετὰ δὲ πολὺν χρόνον ἔρχεται ὁ κύριος τῶν δούλων ἐκείνων καὶ συναίρει λόγον μετ' αὐτῶν. ²⁰καὶ προσελθὼν ὁ τὰ πέντε τάλαντα λαβὼν προσήνεγκεν ἄλλα πέντε τάλαντα λέγων, Κύριε, πέντε τάλαντά μοι παρέδωκας· ἴδε ἄλλα πέντε τάλαντα ἐκέρδησα.

²¹Ἔφη αὐτῷ ὁ κύριος αὐτοῦ, Εὖ, δοῦλε ἀγαθὲ καὶ πιστέ, ἐπὶ ὀλίγα ἧς πιστός, ἐπὶ πολλῶν σε καταστήσω· εἴσελθε εἰς τὴν χαρὰν τοῦ κυρίου σου.

²²Προσελθὼν δὲ καὶ ὁ τὰ δύο τάλαντα εἶπεν, Κύριε, δύο τάλαντά μοι παρέδωκας· ἴδε ἄλλα δύο τάλαντα ἐκέρδησα.

²³Ἔφη αὐτῷ ὁ κύριος αὐτοῦ, Εὖ, δοῦλε ἀγαθὲ καὶ πιστέ, ἐπὶ ὀλίγα ἧς πιστός, ἐπὶ πολλῶν σε καταστήσω· εἴσελθε εἰς τὴν χαρὰν τοῦ κυρίου σου.

²⁴Προσελθὼν δὲ καὶ ὁ τὸ ἓν τάλαντον εἰληφὼς εἶπεν, Κύριε, ἔγνων σε ὅτι σκληρὸς εἶ ἄνθρωπος, θερίζων ὅπου οὐκ ἔσπειρας καὶ συνάγων ὅθεν οὐ διεσκόρπισας, ²⁵καὶ φοβηθεὶς ἀπελθὼν ἔκρυψα τὸ τάλαντόν σου ἐν τῇ γῇ· ἴδε ἔχεις τὸ σόν.

---

contemporary currency.) Our word "talent" arose from this story, partly because of the words *to each in relation to his ability*. Once the parable was allegorized, "talent" came to be understood not as money but symbolically, as the God-given ability each person has. But its original meaning had to do simply with money.

put the money to work: Greek, "worked with it."

twelve thousand . . . six thousand: Respectively two *talanta* and one *talanton*.

• **25:16** *right away*: The Greek has the word underlying this (*eutheôs*) at the end of vs 15, but it is highly unlikely at the end of a sentence; instead, like most editors, we take it with vs 16.

made another thirty thousand: Perhaps not by investing but as a swindler (like his owner—vs 24).

• **25:17** Here and in vss 22–23 the *second* slave ("the one who [had received] the two [*talanta*]") is simply a pale version of the first.

• **25:18** This slave contrasts sharply with the first two and originally was the focus of the story, the one Jesus' hearers would identify with.

dug a hole, and hid his master's silver: In that culture, the safest way to protect the money.

• **25:19** *After a long absence*: Not found in Luke's version of the story (19:15). Has it come into this text, once it became allegory, because of Jesus' long delayed return? It makes less

thirty thousand silver coins, to the second twelve thousand, and to the third six thousand—to each in relation to his ability—and he left.

¹⁶The one who had received the thirty thousand went out right away and put the money to work; he made another thirty thousand. .

¹⁷The second also doubled his money.

¹⁸But the third, who had received the smallest amount, went out, dug a hole, and hid his master's silver.

¹⁹After a long absence, the slaves' master returned to settle accounts with them. ²⁰The first, who had received thirty thousand, came and produced an additional thirty thousand, with this report: 'Master, you handed me thirty thousand silver coins; as you can see, I have made you another thirty thousand.'

²¹His master commended him: 'Well done, you competent and reliable slave! You have been trustworthy in small amounts; I'll put you in charge of large amounts. Come celebrate with your master.'

²²The one with twelve thousand also came and reported: 'Master, you handed me twelve thousand silver coins; as you can see, I have made you another twelve thousand.'

²³His master commended him: 'Well done, you competent and reliable slave! You have been trustworthy in small amounts; I'll put you in charge of large amounts. Come celebrate with your master.'

²⁴The one who had received six thousand also came and reported: 'Master, I know that you are ruthless, reaping where you didn't sow and gathering where you didn't scatter. ²⁵Since I was afraid, I went out and buried your money in the ground. Here, you <can> have what belongs to you!'

---

sense if the master is supposed to stand for God—and in either case, the third slave's description of him in vs 24 hardly fits!

• **25:21, 23** I'll put you in charge of large amounts: Rather like the "the reliable and shrewd slave" of 24:45, 47.

• **25:24** reaping where you didn't sow and gathering where you didn't scatter: In other words, defrauding others.

• **25:25** Here, you <can> have what belongs to you: He refuses to enter into the corrupt dealings of the master. But he does not defraud him. In the original version of this parable (that is, as Jesus might have taught it) was this third slave the villain, or was his owner? (His master doesn't deny the way he has been described—vs 26.) Was the slave right about the master's ethics? Was he a whistle-blower? That would make him the hero, and a martyr, in the eyes of Jesus' mostly underclass audience. See Appendix. (In a version of this parable that evidently appeared in the second-century Gospel of the Nazoreans—according the fourth-century writer Eusebius; see Miller, Complete Gospels, 445–46—the third slave is the one commended.)

Clearly, however, despite this and what we noted on vs 19, in the evangelist's eyes the master stands for God. And that justifies his condemnation of the slave who has not put his God-given potential to good use.

²⁶Ἀποκριθεὶς δὲ ὁ κύριος αὐτοῦ εἶπεν αὐτῷ, Πονηρὲ δοῦλε καὶ ὀκνηρέ, ᾔδεις ὅτι θερίζω ὅπου οὐκ ἔσπειρα καὶ συνάγω ὅθεν οὐ διεσκόρπισα; ²⁷ἔδει σε οὖν βαλεῖν τὰ ἀργύριά μου τοῖς τραπεζίταις, καὶ ἐλθὼν ἐγὼ ἐκομισάμην ἂν τὸ ἐμὸν σὺν τόκῳ. ²⁸ἄρατε οὖν ἀπ' αὐτοῦ τὸ τάλαντον καὶ δότε τῷ ἔχοντι τὰ δέκα τάλαντα· ²⁹τῷ γὰρ ἔχοντι παντὶ δοθήσεται καὶ περισσευθήσεται, τοῦ δὲ μὴ ἔχοντος καὶ ὃ ἔχει ἀρθήσεται ἀπ' αὐτοῦ. ³⁰καὶ τὸν ἀχρεῖον δοῦλον ἐκβάλετε εἰς τὸ σκότος τὸ ἐξώτερον· ἐκεῖ ἔσται ὁ κλαυθμὸς καὶ ὁ βρυγμὸς τῶν ὀδόντων.

Sheep and goats

³¹Ὅταν δὲ ἔλθῃ ὁ υἱὸς τοῦ ἀνθρώπου ἐν τῇ δόξῃ αὐτοῦ καὶ πάντες οἱ ἄγγελοι μετ' αὐτοῦ, τότε καθίσει ἐπὶ θρόνου δόξης αὐτοῦ· ³²καὶ συναχθήσονται ἔμπροσθεν αὐτοῦ πάντα τὰ ἔθνη, καὶ ἀφορίσει αὐτοὺς ἀπ' ἀλλήλων, ὥσπερ ὁ ποιμὴν ἀφορίζει τὰ πρόβατα ἀπὸ τῶν ἐρίφων, ³³καὶ στήσει τὰ μὲν πρόβατα ἐκ δεξιῶν αὐτοῦ, τὰ δὲ ἐρίφια ἐξ εὐωνύμων. ³⁴τότε ἐρεῖ ὁ βασιλεὺς τοῖς ἐκ δεξιῶν αὐτοῦ, Δεῦτε οἱ εὐλογημένοι τοῦ πατρός μου, κληρονομήσατε τὴν ἡτοιμασμένην ὑμῖν βασιλείαν ἀπὸ καταβολῆς κόσμου. ³⁵ἐπείνασα γὰρ καὶ ἐδώκατέ μοι φαγεῖν, ἐδίψησα καὶ ἐποτίσατέ με, ξένος ἤμην καὶ συνηγάγετέ με, ³⁶γυμνὸς καὶ περιεβάλετέ με, ἠσθένησα καὶ ἐπεσκέψασθέ με, ἐν φυλακῇ ἤμην καὶ ἤλθατε πρός με.

³⁷Τότε ἀποκριθήσονται αὐτῷ οἱ δίκαιοι λέγοντες, Κύριε, πότε σε εἴδομεν πεινῶντα καὶ ἐθρέψαμεν, ἢ διψῶντα καὶ ἐποτίσαμεν; ³⁸πότε δέ σε εἴδομεν ξένον καὶ συνηγάγομεν, ἢ γυμνὸν καὶ περιεβάλομεν; ³⁹πότε δέ σε εἴδομεν ἀσθενοῦντα ἢ ἐν φυλακῇ καὶ ἤλθομεν πρός σε;

⁴⁰Καὶ ἀποκριθεὶς ὁ βασιλεὺς ἐρεῖ αὐτοῖς, Ἀμὴν λέγω ὑμῖν, ἐφ' ὅσον ἐποιήσατε ἑνὶ τούτων τῶν ἀδελφῶν μου τῶν ἐλαχίστων, ἐμοὶ ἐποιήσατε.

• **25:26** *cowardly:* Or "lazy."

• **25:28** *the greatest sum:* Greek, "the ten talents," that is, the original five plus the five more he earned.

• **25:29** A very similar form of this saying is found at 13:12, and also Mark 4:25, Luke 8:18, and Thom 41. It has been inserted into the story, which isn't quite over yet, as a moral.

   those who don't have: Translated as plural to avoid "he/she." See Introduction, p. 26.

• **25:30** *where it is utterly dark:* "Into the outermost darkness," farthest from the light.

   Out there they'll weep and grind their teeth: A warning used in this gospel six times in all. See comment on 8:12. Perhaps originally it referred not to a place of eternal torment but to a dungeon—whatever the difference.

• **25:31–46** This extraordinary story, unique to Matthew, is not strictly a parable. The last judgment will be like (*much as*—vs 32) a shepherd sorting his flock into *sheep and goats*. The story is a simile about the mixed church, like that of the weeds among the wheat (13:24–30). It explains how the church is allowed by God to include both righteous and sinners ... until the end. But far more, it brings the elaborate apocalyptic drama to the fundamental and prophetic ethic of Jesus' ministry down to the level of the least, "the most inconspicuous" members of society (vs 40).

• **25:31** The coming of the *Son of Adam* has already been spoken of a number of times. In what follows there is, at last, a detailed portrayal of what it will be like.

   he will occupy his glorious throne: Like a king

²⁶But his master replied to him, 'You incompetent, cowardly slave! So you knew that I reap where I didn't sow and gather where I didn't scatter, did you? ²⁷Then you should have taken my money to the bankers. When I returned I would have received my capital with interest. ²⁸So take the money away from this fellow and give it to the one who has the greatest sum. ²⁹In fact, to everyone who has, more will be given and then some; and from those who don't have, even what they do have will be taken away. ³⁰And throw this worthless slave where it is utterly dark. Out there they'll weep and grind their teeth.'

³¹When the son of Adam comes in his glory, accompanied by all his messengers, then he will occupy his glorious throne. ³²And all peoples will be assembled before him, and he will separate them into groups, much as a shepherd segregates sheep from goats. ³³He'll place the sheep to his right and the goats to his left. ³⁴Then the king will say to those at his right, 'Come, you who have the blessing of my Father, inherit the domain prepared for you from the foundation of the world. ³⁵As you may remember, I was hungry and you gave me something to eat; I was thirsty and you gave me something to drink; I was a foreigner and you took me in. ³⁶I was naked and you clothed me; I was ill and you visited me; I was in prison and you came to see me.'

Sheep and goats

³⁷Then the virtuous will say to him, 'Lord, when did we see you hungry and feed you or thirsty and give you a drink? ³⁸When did we notice that you were a foreigner and take you in? Or naked and clothe you? ³⁹When did we find you ill or in prison and come to visit you?'

⁴⁰And the king will respond to them: 'I swear to you, whatever you did for the most inconspicuous members of my family, you did for me as well.'

---

sitting in judgment, not simply to receive adoration. He is called "king" from this point forward in the story (vss 34, 40). He presides in God's place, of course.

- **25:32** *all peoples:* All nations, not in a political but an ethnic sense.

  into groups: "From one another."

- **25:33** *to his right:* The place of honor—from the point of view of the right-handed majority of this world.

- **25:34** *the domain prepared for you from the foundation of the world:* The "sheep" are not themselves predestined for salvation. But their reward has been ready from the beginning of time. It is their love for the neighbor that will give them entry into God's empire (vss 35–36).

- **25:35–36** *I was...* (six times): The austere

and holy judge, sitting upon his splendid throne, speaks of himself as an impoverished, luckless outcast! This mixing of grandiloquent Christian apocalyptic with the lowliness of the man Jesus is extraordinary.

- **25:36** *visited me:* "Looked in on me."

- **25:37** *the virtuous:* Anticipating what they will be shown to be.

  Lord, when...? Their astonishment is understandable.

- **25:40** *my family:* "My brothers."

  most inconspicuous: In the context, an esp. apt interpretation of "least."

  for me as well: The son of Adam lives in his people.

⁴¹Τότε ἐρεῖ καὶ τοῖς ἐξ εὐωνύμων, Πορεύεσθε ἀπ' ἐμοῦ οἱ κατηραμένοι εἰς τὸ πῦρ τὸ αἰώνιον τὸ ἡτοιμασμένον τῷ διαβόλῳ καὶ τοῖς ἀγγέλοις αὐτοῦ. ⁴²ἐπείνασα γὰρ καὶ οὐκ ἐδώκατέ μοι φαγεῖν, ἐδίψησα καὶ οὐκ ἐποτίσατέ με, ⁴³ξένος ἤμην καὶ οὐ συνηγάγετέ με, γυμνὸς καὶ οὐ περιεβάλετέ με, ἀσθενὴς καὶ ἐν φυλακῇ καὶ οὐκ ἐπεσκέψασθέ με.

⁴⁴Τότε ἀποκριθήσονται καὶ αὐτοὶ λέγοντες, Κύριε, πότε σε εἴδομεν πεινῶντα ἢ διψῶντα ἢ ξένον ἢ γυμνὸν ἢ ἀσθενῆ ἢ ἐν φυλακῇ καὶ οὐ διηκονήσαμέν σοι;

⁴⁵Τότε ἀποκριθήσεται αὐτοῖς λέγων, Ἀμὴν λέγω ὑμῖν, ἐφ' ὅσον οὐκ ἐποιήσατε ἑνὶ τούτων τῶν ἐλαχίστων, οὐδὲ ἐμοὶ ἐποιήσατε.

⁴⁶Καὶ ἀπελεύσονται οὗτοι εἰς κόλασιν αἰώνιον, οἱ δὲ δίκαιοι εἰς ζωὴν αἰώνιον.

• **25:41–46** Parallel to vss 34–40.
• **25:41** *everlasting:* "Agelong."
  his messengers: It was believed that Satan, *the devil*, was a fallen angel [*messenger*], origi-

nally one of God's messengers. So Satan's messengers would have fallen with him.
• **25:44** *help you:* More exactly, "take care of you."

Interpretive Note: Apocalyptic

What are we to make of these two chapters of apocalyptic, especially if Jesus himself did not use that kind of theology, did not announce that he would return? The material is evidently the imaginative creation of the earliest Christians (from Paul onward), to compensate for the disillusionment caused by Jesus' premature death. It uses categories and symbols already present in much Jewish thought of Jesus' time, particularly that of the Pharisees. I find it to be powerful mythology, coming to its fullest expression in the Book of Revelation. But to take it as a factual prediction of the future is as misguided as treating the creation stories in Genesis 1–3 as reports of historical fact. And we are helped in making use of all this by the tendency in our evangelist's 25th chapter, where the *ethical* dimension is uppermost, even in the parable of the Money in trust, but especially in the vision of the Sheep and goats.

⁴¹Next, he will say to those at his left, 'Get away from me! You are condemned to the everlasting fire prepared for the devil and his messengers!' ⁴²As you too may remember, I was hungry and you didn't give me anything to eat; I was thirsty and you refused me a drink; ⁴³I was a foreigner and you failed to offer me hospitality; naked and you didn't clothe me; ill and in prison and you didn't visit me.'

⁴⁴Then they will give him a similar reply: 'Lord, when did we notice that you were hungry or thirsty or a foreigner or naked or ill or in prison and did not attempt to help you?'

⁴⁵He will then respond: 'I swear to you, whatever you didn't do for the most inconspicuous members of my family, you didn't do for me.'

⁴⁶The second group will then head for everlasting punishment, but the virtuous for everlasting life."

26 Καὶ ἐγένετο ὅτε ἐτέλεσεν ὁ Ἰησοῦς πάντας τοὺς λόγους τούτους, εἶπεν τοῖς μαθηταῖς αὐτοῦ, ²Οἴδατε ὅτι μετὰ δύο ἡμέρας τὸ πάσχα γίνεται, καὶ ὁ υἱὸς τοῦ ἀνθρώπου παραδίδοται εἰς τὸ σταυρωθῆναι.

³Τότε συνήχθησαν οἱ ἀρχιερεῖς καὶ οἱ πρεσβύτεροι τοῦ λαοῦ εἰς τὴν αὐλὴν τοῦ ἀρχιερέως τοῦ λεγομένου Καϊάφα ⁴καὶ συνεβουλεύσαντο ἵνα τὸν Ἰησοῦν δόλῳ κρατήσωσιν καὶ ἀποκτείνωσιν· ⁵ἔλεγον δέ, Μὴ ἐν τῇ ἑορτῇ, ἵνα μὴ θόρυβος γένηται ἐν τῷ λαῷ.

Woman anoints Jesus

⁶Τοῦ δὲ Ἰησοῦ γενομένου ἐν Βηθανίᾳ ἐν οἰκίᾳ Σίμωνος τοῦ λεπροῦ, ⁷προσῆλθεν αὐτῷ γυνὴ ἔχουσα ἀλάβαστρον μύρου βαρυτίμου καὶ κατέχεεν ἐπὶ τῆς κεφαλῆς αὐτοῦ ἀνακειμένου. ⁸ἰδόντες δὲ οἱ μαθηταὶ ἠγανάκτησαν λέγοντες, Εἰς τί ἡ ἀπώλεια αὕτη; ⁹ἐδύνατο γὰρ τοῦτο πραθῆναι πολλοῦ καὶ δοθῆναι πτωχοῖς.

¹⁰Γνοὺς δὲ ὁ Ἰησοῦς εἶπεν αὐτοῖς, Τί κόπους παρέχετε τῇ γυναικί; ἔργον γὰρ καλὸν ἠργάσατο εἰς ἐμέ· ¹¹πάντοτε γὰρ τοὺς πτωχοὺς ἔχετε μεθ᾽ ἑαυτῶν, ἐμὲ δὲ οὐ πάντοτε ἔχετε· ¹²βαλοῦσα γὰρ αὕτη τὸ μύρον τοῦτο ἐπὶ τοῦ σώματός μου πρὸς τὸ ἐνταφιάσαι με ἐποίησεν. ¹³ἀμὴν λέγω ὑμῖν, ὅπου ἐὰν κηρυχθῇ τὸ εὐαγγέλιον τοῦτο ἐν ὅλῳ τῷ κόσμῳ, λαληθήσεται καὶ ὃ ἐποίησεν αὕτη εἰς μνημόσυνον αὐτῆς.

Priests promise to pay

¹⁴Τότε πορευθεὶς εἷς τῶν δώδεκα, ὁ λεγόμενος Ἰούδας Ἰσκαριώτης, πρὸς τοὺς ἀρχιερεῖς ¹⁵εἶπεν, Τί θέλετέ μοι δοῦναι, κἀγὼ

• **Chaps. 26–27** The account of Jesus' last days—his arrest, trial, and execution—is often called the Passion Narrative, from the Latin *passio,* suffering. The author follows Mark very closely. In a few places he introduces material not found in the other gospels. Neither here nor in Luke is there anything from Q.

• **26:1** *concluded his discourse:* Greek "finished all these words." This verse belongs with chaps. 24–25. The fifth and final of Jesus' so-called sermons is now over. But where did it begin? See on 24:4. In any case, it is Jesus' teaching about *The Time of the End.*

• **26:2** Our author puts this opening of the account of the passion into Jesus' mouth.

Passover comes in two days: The point of this datum, from Mark 14:1, is unclear.

the son of Adam will be turned over to be crucified: What the gospel portrays as Jesus' earlier predictions (at 16:21, 17:22–23, 20:18–19) are now about to come true. Our author adds this reminder to the Markan text he is following (Mark 14:1). It has the effect of Jesus' accepting and allowing what is going to happen.

• **26:3** *gathered in the courtyard:* A formal meeting of sorts, with a decision taken. Unlike Mark 14:1, where we hear that the leaders kept looking for a way to arrest Jesus but not that they gathered. Such a night meeting, evidently of the Sanhedrin, was irregular and very likely illegal.

elders of the people: In place of "scholars" in Mark 14:1. Does "of the people" intend to involve the Jews generally in accountability for what follows? That will appallingly be the case at 27:25.

Caiaphas: The name is unknown in Mark and at this point in Luke (where it appears only at 3:2). It is well known to the fourth evangelist, author of the gospel of John.

• **26:4** *conspired:* The author makes explicit what is only implied in Mark 14:1, perhaps to emphasize Jewish responsibility.

trickery: Or stealth, as the next verse explains.

• **26:5** *Not during the festival . . .:* Yet Jesus' arrest and crucifixion did take place during the Passover festival. Is the author (and Mark's too) suggesting incompetence or helplessness on the part of the leaders? Or only the high popular approval of Jesus?

a riot among the people: Passover time, one

26 And so when Jesus had concluded his discourse, he told his disciples, [2]"You know that Passover comes in two days, and the son of Adam will be turned over to be crucified."

[3]Then the ranking priests and elders of the people gathered in the courtyard of the high priest, whose name was Caiaphas, [4]and they conspired to seize Jesus by trickery and kill him. [5]But they kept saying: "Not during the festival, so there won't be a riot among the people."

[6]While Jesus was in Bethany at the house of Simon the leper, [7]a woman who had an alabaster jar of very expensive myrrh came up to him and poured it over his head while he was reclining <at table>. [8]When they saw this, the disciples were annoyed, and said, "What good purpose is served by this waste? [9]After all, she could have sold it for a good price and given <the money> to the poor."

Woman anoints Jesus

[10]But Jesus saw through <what they were saying> and said to them, "Why are you bothering this woman? After all, she has done me a courtesy. [11]There will always be poor around; but I won't always be around. [12]By pouring this myrrh on my body she has made me ready for burial. [13]I swear to you, wherever this good news is announced in all the world, what she has done will be told in memory of her."

[14]Then one of the twelve, Judas Iscariot by name, went to the ranking priests [15]and said, "What are you willing to pay me if I turn

Priests promise to pay

---

of the major festivals of Judaism, when crowds filled the city, was a time of nationalist fervor in opposition to the ruthless Roman occupation. The Jewish leaders are collaborators with Roman rule and will do anything to forestall or curtail such a demonstration.

• **26:6–13** Based on Mark 14:3–9. Luke 7:36–50 tells a similar story about a woman who bathes and anoints Jesus' feet.

• **26:6** *Bethany:* See above on 21:17.

at the house of Simon the leper: As in the Markan parallel story. The Lukan story takes place in the house of "a Pharisee" whom Jesus calls by the name of Simon. (See also John 12:1–8.)

• **26:7** *myrrh:* An aromatic substance, usually combined with oil, as apparently here.

• **26:10** *courtesy:* Greek: "good deed."

• **26:11** *There will always be poor around:* A paraphrase of Deut 15:11. That this story shows Jesus using it has often been the excuse for complacency about poverty, hardly what he would have meant by it.

• **26:12** *made me ready for burial:* As in Mark 14:8, John 12:7. It's extraordinary that none of the evangelists even hint at understand-

ing this act as Jesus' anointing to be messiah ("the Anointed").

• **26:13** *this good news:* Mark 14:9 has simply "the good news." Does the phrase here mean this evangelist's version of the good news as a whole? Or this particular story?

what she has done will be told in memory of her: An obligation that, ironically, has scarcely ever been fulfilled. Not even her name has been kept. In John 12:3 she is identified as Mary, sister of Martha and Lazarus, but this is probably not factual.

• **26:14–16** This little passage sets the stage for Judas' eventual betrayal of Jesus to the Jewish authorities. We can only speculate why Judas did this—for gain only? from disillusionment that Jesus was not the Messiah he counted on? in order to instigate the conflict between the authorities and Jesus that would begin the battle for justice that he expected Jesus would fight and win?

• **26:15** Judas's agreeing to betray Jesus means that he will actually *turn him over* to them.

What are you willing to pay me? Unlike Mark 14:10; here Judas bargains. The legend of the traitorous Judas has grown.

ὑμῖν παραδώσω αὐτόν; οἱ δὲ ἔστησαν αὐτῷ τριάκοντα ἀργύρια. ¹⁶καὶ ἀπὸ τότε ἐζήτει εὐκαιρίαν ἵνα αὐτὸν παραδῷ.

Jesus celebrates Passover

¹⁷Τῇ δὲ πρώτῃ τῶν ἀζύμων προσῆλθον οἱ μαθηταὶ τῷ Ἰησοῦ λέγοντες, Ποῦ θέλεις ἑτοιμάσωμέν σοι φαγεῖν τὸ πάσχα; ¹⁸Ὁ δὲ εἶπεν, Ὑπάγετε εἰς τὴν πόλιν πρὸς τὸν δεῖνα καὶ εἴπατε αὐτῷ, Ὁ διδάσκαλος λέγει, Ὁ καιρός μου ἐγγύς ἐστιν, πρὸς σὲ ποιῶ τὸ πάσχα μετὰ τῶν μαθητῶν μου. ¹⁹καὶ ἐποίησαν οἱ μαθηταὶ ὡς συνέταξεν αὐτοῖς ὁ Ἰησοῦς καὶ ἡτοίμασαν τὸ πάσχα.

²⁰Ὀψίας δὲ γενομένης ἀνέκειτο μετὰ τῶν δώδεκα. ²¹καὶ ἐσθιόντων αὐτῶν εἶπεν, Ἀμὴν λέγω ὑμῖν ὅτι εἷς ἐξ ὑμῶν παραδώσει με.

²²Καὶ λυπούμενοι σφόδρα ἤρξαντο λέγειν αὐτῷ εἷς ἕκαστος, Μήτι ἐγώ εἰμι, κύριε;

²³Ὁ δὲ ἀποκριθεὶς εἶπεν, Ὁ ἐμβάψας μετ' ἐμοῦ τὴν χεῖρα ἐν τῷ τρυβλίῳ οὗτός με παραδώσει. ²⁴ὁ μὲν υἱὸς τοῦ ἀνθρώπου ὑπάγει καθὼς γέγραπται περὶ αὐτοῦ, οὐαὶ δὲ τῷ ἀνθρώπῳ ἐκείνῳ δι' οὗ ὁ υἱὸς τοῦ ἀνθρώπου παραδίδοται· καλὸν ἦν αὐτῷ εἰ οὐκ ἐγεννήθη ὁ ἄνθρωπος ἐκεῖνος.

²⁵Ἀποκριθεὶς δὲ Ἰούδας ὁ παραδιδοὺς αὐτὸν εἶπεν, Μήτι ἐγώ εἰμι, ῥαββί;

Λέγει αὐτῷ, Σὺ εἶπας.

²⁶Ἐσθιόντων δὲ αὐτῶν λαβὼν ὁ Ἰησοῦς ἄρτον καὶ εὐλογήσας ἔκλασεν καὶ δοὺς τοῖς μαθηταῖς εἶπεν, Λάβετε φάγετε, τοῦτό ἐστιν τὸ σῶμά μου.

²⁷Καὶ λαβὼν ποτήριον καὶ εὐχαριστήσας ἔδωκεν αὐτοῖς λέγων, Πίετε ἐξ αὐτοῦ πάντες, ²⁸τοῦτο γάρ ἐστιν τὸ αἷμά μου τῆς διαθήκης

26:28 Some MSS have "the new covenant." That is undoubtedly meant but was probably added later, to jibe with Luke 22:20.

---

thirty silver coins: In Zech 11:12 this is the paltry amount the ministry of God's prophet is valued at. There may be a reference also to Exod 21:32 (the amount a slave is worth). The word here is not the *denarius* of 20:2 (the wage promised the vineyard laborers) but perhaps a coin worth much less

• **26:17** *the first <day> of Unleavened Bread:* When the weeklong celebration of Passover begins.

• **26:18–19** In Mark this scene is longer and demonstrates Jesus' foreknowledge. Why has the evangelist removed that here? For brevity only?

• **26:18** *so-and-so:* NRSV has "a certain man." The Greek is more vague. Presumably the disciples would have known whom Jesus meant; but not the evangelist.

My time: In Greek, "my *kairos*," the time appointed for me. Elsewhere it is usually called

Jesus' *hôra*, his hour.

at your place: In Greek, "with you," an idiom like the French *chez vous*.

• **26:20** *the twelve:* See on 10:1.

• **26:21** *one of you is going to turn me in:* Mark identifies the betrayer as "one of you eating with me," a quotation from Ps 41:9 that we might expect the evangelist to include. Possibly the reader is expected to recognize the reference.

• **26:22** *upset:* A better translation than the usual "sad."

I'm not the one, am I? A "No" is clearly expected. Another translation: "It can't be me, can it?"

• **26:23** *The one who dips his hand in the bowl with me:* That is, who shares the common bowl. This could apply to any of the twelve, eating with Jesus. But vs 25 shows that it was Judas, who apparently at that moment was

him over to you?" They agreed on thirty silver coins. ¹⁶And from that moment he started looking for the right occasion to turn him in.

¹⁷On the first <day> of Unleavened Bread the disciples came to Jesus, and said, "Where do you want us to get things ready for you to celebrate Passover?"

Jesus celebrates Passover

¹⁸He said, "Go into the city to so-and-so and say to him, 'The teacher says, "My time is near, I will observe Passover at your place with my disciples."'" ¹⁹And the disciples did as Jesus instructed them and they got things ready for Passover.

²⁰When it was evening, he was reclining <at table> with the twelve. ²¹And as they were eating, he said, "I swear to you, one of you is going to turn me in."

²²And they were very upset and each one said to him in turn, "I'm not the one, am I, Lord?"

²³In response he said, "The one who dips his hand in the bowl with me—that's who's going to turn me in. ²⁴The son of Adam departs just as the scriptures predict, but damn the one responsible for turning the son of Adam in. It would be better for that man if he'd never been born."

²⁵Judas, who was to turn him in, responded, "You can't mean me, can you, Rabbi?"

He says to him, "You have said it."

²⁶As they were eating, Jesus took a loaf, gave a blessing, and broke it apart. And he gave it to the disciples, and said, "Take some and eat; this is my body."

²⁷He also took a cup and gave thanks and offered it to them, saying, "Drink from it, all of you, ²⁸for this is my blood of the covenant, which has been poured out for many for the forgiveness

---

taking from the bowl.

• **26:24** This saying reflects the church's understanding that what happened was necessary and even acceptable, since it fulfilled scripture—but also its condemnation of the disciple who betrayed his own master. Compare 18:7.

as the scriptures predict: Strictly, "as it is written about him."

• **26:25** *You can't mean me . . .?:* More strictly, "I'm not [that one], am I, rabbi?"

You have said it: Jesus' explicit identification of Judas as the betrayer is unique to Matthew.

• **26:26–27** Bread (*loaf*) and cup of wine (*fruit of the vine*—vs 29) are the elements of any meal, and are not esp. characteristic of the Passover seder. Yet in Mark 14:12, followed by Matthew and Luke, that meal is identified as a celebration of Passover. John 13:1,

perhaps more accurately, places Jesus' last supper "before the Passover celebration." The identification/confusion of last supper and seder was further complicated when the meal—commemorated from very early times in the eucharist—became a Christian Passover.

my body . . . my blood: How are we to understand these phrases, which are at the least shocking to Jewish sensibilities? Symbolically, at the very least. From early times, also eucharistically; but Jesus here issues no directive to repeat the meal.

• **26:28** *blood of the covenant:* In Exod 24:8 this accomplishes the contract between Israel and God. See also Zech 9:11. In Luke 22:20 and 1 Cor 11:25 it is called the "new" covenant. Does our author assume that? Or does he see this in a way to be the same blood as in Exodus?

τὸ περὶ πολλῶν ἐκχυννόμενον εἰς ἄφεσιν ἁμαρτιῶν. ²⁹λέγω δὲ ὑμῖν, οὐ μὴ πίω ἀπ’ ἄρτι ἐκ τούτου τοῦ γενήματος τῆς ἀμπέλου ἕως τῆς ἡμέρας ἐκείνης ὅταν αὐτὸ πίνω μεθ’ ὑμῶν καινὸν ἐν τῇ βασιλείᾳ τοῦ πατρός μου.

³⁰Καὶ ὑμνήσαντες ἐξῆλθον εἰς τὸ Ὄρος τῶν Ἐλαιῶν.

Peter takes an oath

³¹Τότε λέγει αὐτοῖς ὁ Ἰησοῦς, Πάντες ὑμεῖς σκανδαλισθήσεσθε ἐν ἐμοὶ ἐν τῇ νυκτὶ ταύτῃ, γέγραπται γάρ,

Πατάξω τὸν ποιμένα,
καὶ διασκορπισθήσονται τὰ πρόβατα τῆς ποίμνης.

³²μετὰ δὲ τὸ ἐγερθῆναί με προάξω ὑμᾶς εἰς τὴν Γαλιλαίαν.

³³Ἀποκριθεὶς δὲ ὁ Πέτρος εἶπεν αὐτῷ, Εἰ πάντες σκανδαλισθήσονται ἐν σοί, ἐγὼ οὐδέποτε σκανδαλισθήσομαι.

³⁴Ἔφη αὐτῷ ὁ Ἰησοῦς, Ἀμὴν λέγω σοι ὅτι ἐν ταύτῃ τῇ νυκτὶ πρὶν ἀλέκτορα φωνῆσαι τρὶς ἀπαρνήσῃ με.

³⁵Λέγει αὐτῷ ὁ Πέτρος, Κἂν δέῃ με σὺν σοὶ ἀποθανεῖν, οὐ μή σε ἀπαρνήσομαι. ὁμοίως καὶ πάντες οἱ μαθηταὶ εἶπαν.

Jesus in Gethsemane

³⁶Τότε ἔρχεται μετ’ αὐτῶν ὁ Ἰησοῦς εἰς χωρίον λεγόμενον Γεθσημανί καὶ λέγει τοῖς μαθηταῖς, Καθίσατε αὐτοῦ ἕως ἀπελθὼν ἐκεῖ προσεύξωμαι.

³⁷Καὶ παραλαβὼν τὸν Πέτρον καὶ τοὺς δύο υἱοὺς Ζεβεδαίου ἤρξατο λυπεῖσθαι καὶ ἀδημονεῖν. ³⁸τότε λέγει αὐτοῖς, Περίλυπός ἐστιν ἡ ψυχή μου ἕως θανάτου· μείνατε ὧδε καὶ γρηγορεῖτε μετ’ ἐμοῦ.

³⁹Καὶ προελθὼν μικρὸν ἔπεσεν ἐπὶ πρόσωπον αὐτοῦ προσευχόμενος καὶ λέγων, Πάτερ μου, εἰ δυνατόν ἐστιν, παρελθάτω ἀπ’ ἐμοῦ τὸ ποτήριον τοῦτο· πλὴν οὐχ ὡς ἐγὼ θέλω ἀλλ’ ὡς σύ.

⁴⁰Καὶ ἔρχεται πρὸς τοὺς μαθητὰς καὶ εὑρίσκει αὐτοὺς καθεύδοντας, καὶ λέγει τῷ Πέτρῳ, Οὕτως οὐκ ἰσχύσατε μίαν ὥραν γρηγορῆσαι μετ’ ἐμοῦ; ⁴¹γρηγορεῖτε καὶ προσεύχεσθε, ἵνα μὴ εἰσέλθητε εἰς πειρασμόν· τὸ μὲν πνεῦμα πρόθυμον ἡ δὲ σὰρξ ἀσθενής.

---

my blood . . . which has been poured out: The temporal perspective is that of the church, looking back and conflating Jesus' words with what had soon happened to him. But a crucifixion involved very little shedding of blood, and no breaking of a body (like the bread). If these sayings go back in some form to Jesus, as seems likely to me, they suggest that he expected not a crucifixion but to be stoned to death—killed by the Jewish authorities, not by Rome.

• **26:29** *for the first time:* Probably the correct interpretation of what is, literally, "new"; certainly better than the usual "again."

• **26:30** *sang a hymn:* Perhaps assumed to be one of the Psalms usually sung at the Pass-over meal. Some versions translate "sang the hymn."

left for the Mount of Olives: Why? Because that is where David went when he had been betrayed by his trusted counselor Ahitophel (2 Sam 15:30), who has a parallel in Judas, and, as the following little episode begins to show, even in Peter and the other disciples.

• **26:31** *take offense at me:* Literally, "be scandalized/caused to stumble. . . ."And so "desert" me (vs 56) or *be scattered* as in the following quotation.

I will strike the shepherd . . .: From Zech 13:7.

• **26:32** This verse, important later on, is intrusive here—unless it hints that after the resurrection the scattered followers will

of sins. ²⁹Now I tell you, I certainly won't drink any of this fruit of the vine from now on, until that day when I drink it for the first time with you in my Father's domain!"

³⁰And they sang a hymn and left for the Mount of Olives.

³¹Then Jesus says to them, "All of you will take offense at me this night. Remember, it is written,

Peter takes
an oath

I will strike the shepherd
and the sheep of his flock will be scattered!

³²"But after I'm raised, I'll go ahead of you to Galilee."

³³In response Peter said to him, "If everyone else takes offense at you, I never will."

³⁴Jesus said to him, "I swear to you, tonight before the rooster crows you will disown me three times!"

³⁵Peter says to him, "Even if they condemn me to die with you, I will never disown you!" And all of the disciples took the same oath—all of them.

³⁶Then Jesus goes with them to a place called Gethsemane, and he says to the disciples, "Sit down here while I go over there and pray."

Jesus in
Gethsemane

³⁷And taking Peter and the two sons of Zebedee, he began to feel dejected and full of anguish. ³⁸He says to them, "I'm so grieved I want to die. Stay here with me and be alert."

³⁹And he went a little farther, lay face down, and prayed, "My Father, if it is possible, take this cup away from me! Yet it's not what I want <that matters>, but what you want."

⁴⁰And he returns to the disciples and finds them sleeping, and says to Peter, "So you couldn't stay awake with me for one hour? ⁴¹Be alert, and pray that you won't be put to the test. Though the spirit is willing, the flesh is weak."

---

be united.

• **26:34** *disown me:* Or "deny [that you know] me."

• **26:35** *they condemn me to die:* "I must die."
took the same oath: "Said the same."
all of them: "All" is emphatic in the Greek—ironically, considering what will happen.

• **26:36** *Gethsemane:* Meaning <a place where there was an> "olive oil press," probably on the Mount of Olives or its slopes. In John the place of arrest (vss 47–53) is an unnamed "garden." That datum and the name Gethsemane have been combined in tradition, "the Garden of Gethsemane," but nowhere in the gospels is that phrase used.

• **26:37** *Peter and the two sons of Zebedee:* The same disciples Jesus took with him to the mountaintop where he was transformed (17:1).
sons of Zebedee: James and John (4:21).
dejected: Or "upset." Like the disciples in vs 22.

• **26:38** *I'm so grieved I want to die:* More literally "My soul is sad to [the point of] death," almost a quote of Ps 42:6 and Jonah 4:9.
be alert: Or "stay awake. Also in vs 41.

• **26:39** *this cup:* A metaphor of the fate that awaits him.

• **26:41** *put to the test:* Like Jesus.
the spirit . . . the flesh: Not soul versus body so much as intention versus action.

⁴²Πάλιν ἐκ δευτέρου ἀπελθὼν προσηύξατο λέγων, Πάτερ μου, εἰ οὐ δύναται τοῦτο παρελθεῖν ἐὰν μὴ αὐτὸ πίω, γενηθήτω τὸ θέλημά σου.

⁴³Καὶ ἐλθὼν πάλιν εὗρεν αὐτοὺς καθεύδοντας, ἦσαν γὰρ αὐτῶν οἱ ὀφθαλμοὶ βεβαρημένοι. ⁴⁴καὶ ἀφεὶς αὐτοὺς πάλιν ἀπελθὼν προσηύξατο ἐκ τρίτου τὸν αὐτὸν λόγον εἰπὼν πάλιν.

⁴⁵Τότε ἔρχεται πρὸς τοὺς μαθητὰς καὶ λέγει αὐτοῖς, Καθεύδετε τὸ λοιπὸν καὶ ἀναπαύεσθε· ἰδοὺ ἤγγικεν ἡ ὥρα καὶ ὁ υἱὸς τοῦ ἀνθρώπου παραδίδοται εἰς χεῖρας ἁμαρτωλῶν. ⁴⁶ἐγείρεσθε ἄγωμεν· ἰδοὺ ἤγγικεν ὁ παραδιδούς με.

Judas turns Jesus in

⁴⁷Καὶ ἔτι αὐτοῦ λαλοῦντος ἰδοὺ Ἰούδας εἷς τῶν δώδεκα ἦλθεν καὶ μετ' αὐτοῦ ὄχλος πολὺς μετὰ μαχαιρῶν καὶ ξύλων ἀπὸ τῶν ἀρχιερέων καὶ πρεσβυτέρων τοῦ λαοῦ.

⁴⁸Ὁ δὲ παραδιδοὺς αὐτὸν ἔδωκεν αὐτοῖς σημεῖον λέγων, Ὃν ἂν φιλήσω αὐτός ἐστιν, κρατήσατε αὐτόν.

⁴⁹Καὶ εὐθέως προσελθὼν τῷ Ἰησοῦ εἶπεν, Χαῖρε, ῥαββί, καὶ κατεφίλησεν αὐτόν.

⁵⁰Ὁ δὲ Ἰησοῦς εἶπεν αὐτῷ, Ἑταῖρε, ἐφ' ὃ πάρει;

Τότε προσελθόντες ἐπέβαλον τὰς χεῖρας ἐπὶ τὸν Ἰησοῦν καὶ ἐκράτησαν αὐτόν. ⁵¹καὶ ἰδοὺ εἷς τῶν μετὰ Ἰησοῦ ἐκτείνας τὴν χεῖρα ἀπέσπασεν τὴν μάχαιραν αὐτοῦ καὶ πατάξας τὸν δοῦλον τοῦ ἀρχιερέως ἀφεῖλεν αὐτοῦ τὸ ὠτίον.

⁵²Τότε λέγει αὐτῷ ὁ Ἰησοῦς, Ἀπόστρεψον τὴν μάχαιράν σου εἰς τὸν τόπον αὐτῆς· πάντες γὰρ οἱ λαβόντες μάχαιραν ἐν μαχαίρῃ ἀπολοῦνται. ⁵³ἢ δοκεῖς ὅτι οὐ δύναμαι παρακαλέσαι τὸν πατέρα μου, καὶ παραστήσει μοι ἄρτι πλείω δώδεκα λεγιῶνας ἀγγέλων; ⁵⁴πῶς οὖν πληρωθῶσιν αἱ γραφαὶ ὅτι οὕτως δεῖ γενέσθαι;

⁵⁵Ἐν ἐκείνῃ τῇ ὥρᾳ εἶπεν ὁ Ἰησοῦς τοῖς ὄχλοις, Ὡς ἐπὶ λῃστὴν ἐξήλθατε μετὰ μαχαιρῶν καὶ ξύλων συλλαβεῖν με; καθ' ἡμέραν ἐν τῷ ἱερῷ ἐκαθεζόμην διδάσκων καὶ οὐκ ἐκρατήσατέ με.

• **26:42** *My Father, if it's inevitable . . . your will prevails:* The evangelist adds these words, echoing vs 39. Jesus resigns himself to his inexorable suffering.

if it's inevitable that I drink this< cup>: A paraphrase of slightly ambiguous Greek, which probably says "if this <cup> can't go away unless I drink it." Another translation: "if it is not possible for this to pass by me unless I drink <the cup>. . . ."

your will prevails: Strictly, "let your will prevail."

• **26:45** *time:* In Greek "hour."

foreigners: Greek, "sinners." (See Gal 2:15, where "Gentiles" are assumed to be "sinners.") Another meaning might be the Jew-ish leaders, but it is in fact to the Romans that Jesus is ultimately turned over.

• **26:46** *who is going to turn me in:* Strictly, "who turns me in," "my betrayer."

• **26:47** *a great crowd:* The evangelist exaggerates the size of the arresting party.

the ranking priests and elders of the people: As in 26:3.

• **26:48–49** The kiss was a normal way of greeting a close friend, but of course here it is the disingenuous act that has ever since been known as the Judas-kiss.

• **26:50** *what are you doing here?* The Greek is so terse that it's difficult to translate. Another possibility: "Do what you're here for." Jesus' word to Judas is not paralleled in Mark

⁴²Again for a second time he went away and prayed, "My Father, if it's inevitable that I drink this <cup>, your will prevails."

⁴³And once again he came and found them sleeping, since their eyes had grown heavy. ⁴⁴And leaving them again, he went away and prayed, repeating the same words for a third time.

⁴⁵Then he comes to the disciples and says to them, "Are you still sleeping, still taking your rest? Look, the time is at hand! The son of Adam is being turned over to foreigners. ⁴⁶Get up, let's go. See for yourselves. Here comes the one who is going to turn me in."

⁴⁷And as he was speaking, suddenly Judas, one of the twelve, arrived and with him a great crowd wielding swords and clubs, dispatched by the ranking priests and elders of the people.

Judas turns Jesus in

⁴⁸Now the one who was to turn him in had arranged a sign with them, saying, "The one I'm going to kiss is the one you want. Arrest him!"

⁴⁹And he came right up to Jesus, and said, "Hello, Rabbi," and kissed him.

⁵⁰But Jesus said to him, "Friend, what are you doing here?"

Then they came and grabbed him and put him under arrest. ⁵¹At that moment one of those with Jesus lifted his hand, drew his sword, struck the high priest's slave, and cut off his ear.

⁵²Jesus says to him, "Put your sword back where it belongs. For everyone who takes up the sword will be done in by the sword. ⁵³Or do you suppose I am not able to call on my Father, who would put more than twelve divisions of heavenly messengers at my disposal? ⁵⁴<But> then how would the scriptures come true that say these things are inevitable?"

⁵⁵At that moment Jesus said to the crowds, "Have you come out to take me with swords and clubs as you would a rebel? I used to sit there in the temple area day after day teaching, and you didn't lift a hand against me."

14:45. Luke 22:48 has the ironic question "Judas, would you turn in the son of Adam with a kiss?"

• **26:52–54** Not found in Mark or Luke. Luke 22:51a has simply "Stop. That will do."

• **26:52** *Put your sword back where it belongs:* Similar to John 18:11a.

For everyone who takes up the sword will be done in by the sword: Consistent with many other probably authentic sayings of Jesus. It is contradicted by the highly christological—that is, late—vss 53–54.

• **26:53** An assertion of the Son's privilege of divine protection.

divisions: Greek, "legions," a Roman military term.

• **26:54** This wording of the formula for prophecy fulfillment (see Introduction, p. 19) is unique. No specific prophecies are needed here, given all the earlier citations. Similarly vs 56.

are inevitable: Or "must take place."

• **26:55** *At that moment:* The Greek (literally, "at that hour") is puzzling. As in 18:1 it may be simply a phrase of transition.

rebel: In Greek, *lēstēs;* not just an "armed robber" or "bandit," as usually translated. The Jewish leaders had a stake in putting down any anti-Roman activity.

I used to sit there in the temple area day after day teaching: Typified in 21:23. Compare John 18:20.

⁵⁶Τοῦτο δὲ ὅλον γέγονεν ἵνα πληρωθῶσιν αἱ γραφαὶ τῶν προφητῶν. Τότε οἱ μαθηταὶ πάντες ἀφέντες αὐτὸν ἔφυγον.

⁵⁷Οἱ δὲ κρατήσαντες τὸν Ἰησοῦν ἀπήγαγον πρὸς Καϊάφαν τὸν ἀρχιερέα, ὅπου οἱ γραμματεῖς καὶ οἱ πρεσβύτεροι συνήχθησαν. ⁵⁸ὁ δὲ Πέτρος ἠκολούθει αὐτῷ ἀπὸ μακρόθεν ἕως τῆς αὐλῆς τοῦ ἀρχιερέως καὶ εἰσελθὼν ἔσω ἐκάθητο μετὰ τῶν ὑπηρετῶν ἰδεῖν τὸ τέλος.

⁵⁹Οἱ δὲ ἀρχιερεῖς καὶ τὸ συνέδριον ὅλον ἐζήτουν ψευδομαρτυρίαν κατὰ τοῦ Ἰησοῦ ὅπως αὐτὸν θανατώσωσιν, ⁶⁰καὶ οὐχ εὗρον πολλῶν προσελθόντων ψευδομαρτύρων. ὕστερον δὲ προσελθόντες δύο ⁶¹εἶπαν, Οὗτος ἔφη, Δύναμαι καταλῦσαι τὸν ναὸν τοῦ θεοῦ καὶ διὰ τριῶν ἡμερῶν οἰκοδομῆσαι.

⁶²Καὶ ἀναστὰς ὁ ἀρχιερεὺς εἶπεν αὐτῷ, Οὐδὲν ἀποκρίνῃ τί οὗτοί σου καταμαρτυροῦσιν;

⁶³Ὁ δὲ Ἰησοῦς ἐσιώπα.

Καὶ ὁ ἀρχιερεὺς εἶπεν αὐτῷ, Ἐξορκίζω σε κατὰ τοῦ θεοῦ τοῦ ζῶντος ἵνα ἡμῖν εἴπῃς εἰ σὺ εἶ ὁ Χριστὸς ὁ υἱὸς τοῦ θεοῦ.

⁶⁴Λέγει αὐτῷ ὁ Ἰησοῦς, Σὺ εἶπας· πλὴν λέγω ὑμῖν,

Ἀπ' ἄρτι ὄψεσθε τὸν υἱὸν τοῦ ἀνθρώπου
καθήμενον ἐκ δεξιῶν τῆς δυνάμεως
καὶ ἐρχόμενον ἐπὶ τῶν νεφελῶν τοῦ οὐρανοῦ.

• **26:56** *All of this happened so the writings of the prophets would come true:* As implied in Jesus' word, vs 54. Divine necessity explains what is taking place.

all the disciples deserted him and ran away: As the prophet Jesus had predicted in vs 31. At this point in our copies of Mark (14:51–52) there is a brief, puzzling notice of a young follower of Jesus, scantily dressed, who was caught hold of by the arresting party, but who ran off naked. In the so-called and fragmentary Secret Gospel of Mark (Miller, 408–411) there is more about evidently the same young man. Did our evangelist's copy of Mark lack this strange incident, or did he simply omit it as unnecessary?

• **26:57–68** The historicity of this scene is problematic, since presumably none of the disciples witnessed it. It is, at least, a portrayal of the Jewish leaders intent on killing Jesus and of his messianic composure in the face of that.

• **26:57** *before Caiaphas the high priest, where the scholars and elders had assembled:* See on 26:3.

• **26:58** *Peter:* Who evidently had not fled with "all the disciples," vs 56. This brief notice sets up Peter's rejection of Jesus (vss 69–75).

• **26:59** *the . . . Council:* The Sanhedrin—see Glossary. Its makeup is unclear; did the "scholars and elders" of vs 57 belong to it?

looking for false testimony: Mark 14:55 has only "looking for testimony." The evangelist's slight change here attributes to the Council, probably unhistorically, both evil intent and illegal action.

issue a death sentence: Greek, "kill him." If they could convict him, for example, of blasphemy. It is greatly debated whether they had the power to carry it out, or would have had to hand him over to the Romans.

• **26:60** *and they couldn't find <any>:* That is, any testimony sufficient to convict Jesus of capital crime.

perjurers: False witnesses.

• **26:61** *This fellow said, 'I'm able to destroy the temple of God' . . . :* The Council sees this as defaming the temple, evidently a form of blasphemy. Nowhere does Matthew show Jesus making such a statement. Nor does Mark or Luke. It appears in John 2:19 and Thom 71 ("I will destroy [this] house, and no one will be able to build it [. . .].")

I'm able: Mark has "I will." Does our author's change heighten the christology?

⁵⁶All of this happened so the writings of the prophets would come true. Then all the disciples deserted him and ran away.

⁵⁷Those who had arrested Jesus brought him before Caiaphas the high priest, where the scholars and elders had assembled. ⁵⁸But Peter followed him at a distance as far as the <gate to the> courtyard of the high priest. He went in and sat with the attendants to see how things would turn out.

⁵⁹The ranking priests and the whole Council were looking for false testimony against Jesus so they might issue a death sentence; ⁶⁰and they couldn't find <any> even though many perjurers came forward. Finally, two people did come forward ⁶¹and they said, "This fellow said, 'I'm able to destroy the temple of God and rebuild it within three days.'"

⁶²Then the high priest got up and questioned him: "Don't you have something to say? Why do these people testify against you?"

⁶³But Jesus was silent.

And the high priest said to him, "I order you by the living God: Tell us under oath if you are the Anointed, the son of God!"

⁶⁴Jesus says to him, "If you say so. But I tell you,

From now on you will see the son of Adam
sitting at the right hand of Power
and coming on the clouds of the sky."

**Trial before
the Council**

Or is it only because by his time Rome, not Jesus, has destroyed the temple?

. . . and rebuild it within three days': A curious charge, evidently increasing Jesus' blasphemy, since only God could rebuild the temple. Nothing is made here of this alleged boast. In John 2:21 it is understood as Jesus' cryptic assertion that he will accomplish his resurrection.

• **26:62** *the high priest got up:* Perhaps this heightens the portrait of his malice.

• **26:63** *Jesus was silent:* He could have defended himself against this charge. But it would have been futile in the long run. And his silence perhaps depicts his refusing to engage the Council on their level.

I order you . . . under oath: In technical language, "I adjure you." Only Matthew gives the high priest this solemn, juridical way of asking Jesus the question.

if you are the Anointed, the son of God: The high priest makes nothing of his alleged claim about the temple (vs 61), unless that is taken to imply that he considers himself the messiah. The irony, of course, is that he is the Anointed. That is the gospel's message. But for Jesus to say so would be understood

by his accusers as blasphemy. And he is never depicted as claiming that title; at most he acknowledges it when Peter gives it to him (16:16) . . . and then enjoins silence.

if: "Whether" would be better English, but in the Lukan parallel (22:67) this clause comes first and must begin with "If." SV has carefully translated so as to show such parallels.

• **26:64** *If you say so:* Jesus is clever. (In Mark 14:62, he acknowledges that he is.) But in any case the next statement makes it clear enough to the reader.

from now on: Not to recognize Jesus' messiahship, his divine sonship, when he is standing on earth, is therewith to become liable to judgment at the end of the age, as Jesus implies. The phrase is not in Mark, but in Luke 22:69, with slightly different wording in what follows. Are our evangelist and the author of Luke using both Mark and a Q saying here?

you will see the son of Adam sitting at the right hand of Power and coming on the clouds of the sky: Imagery, and the description itself, taken from Dan 7:13 and Ps 110:1. Something very similar appeared earlier in the

⁶⁵Τότε ὁ ἀρχιερεὺς διέρρηξεν τὰ ἱμάτια αὐτοῦ λέγων, Ἐβλασφήμησεν· τί ἔτι χρείαν ἔχομεν μαρτύρων; ἴδε νῦν ἠκούσατε τὴν βλασφημίαν· ⁶⁶τί ὑμῖν δοκεῖ;

Οἱ δὲ ἀποκριθέντες εἶπαν, Ἔνοχος θανάτου ἐστίν. ⁶⁷Τότε ἐνέπτυσαν εἰς τὸ πρόσωπον αὐτοῦ καὶ ἐκολάφισαν αὐτόν, οἱ δὲ ἐράπισαν ⁶⁸λέγοντες, Προφήτευσον ἡμῖν, Χριστέ, τίς ἐστιν ὁ παίσας σε;

A rooster crows

⁶⁹Ὁ δὲ Πέτρος ἐκάθητο ἔξω ἐν τῇ αὐλῇ· καὶ προσῆλθεν αὐτῷ μία παιδίσκη λέγουσα, Καὶ σὺ ἦσθα μετὰ Ἰησοῦ τοῦ Γαλιλαίου.

⁷⁰Ὁ δὲ ἠρνήσατο ἔμπροσθεν πάντων λέγων, Οὐκ οἶδα τί λέγεις.

⁷¹Ἐξελθόντα δὲ εἰς τὸν πυλῶνα εἶδεν αὐτὸν ἄλλη καὶ λέγει τοῖς ἐκεῖ, Οὗτος ἦν μετὰ Ἰησοῦ τοῦ Ναζωραίου.

⁷²Καὶ πάλιν ἠρνήσατο μετὰ ὅρκου ὅτι Οὐκ οἶδα τὸν ἄνθρωπον.

⁷³Μετὰ μικρὸν δὲ προσελθόντες οἱ ἑστῶτες εἶπον τῷ Πέτρῳ, Ἀληθῶς καὶ σὺ ἐξ αὐτῶν εἶ, καὶ γὰρ ἡ λαλιά σου δῆλόν σε ποιεῖ.

⁷⁴Τότε ἤρξατο καταθεματίζειν καὶ ὀμνύειν ὅτι Οὐκ οἶδα τὸν ἄνθρωπον.

Καὶ εὐθέως ἀλέκτωρ ἐφώνησεν. ⁷⁵καὶ ἐμνήσθη ὁ Πέτρος τοῦ ῥήματος Ἰησοῦ εἰρηκότος ὅτι Πρὶν ἀλέκτορα φωνῆσαι τρὶς ἀπαρνήσῃ με· καὶ ἐξελθὼν ἔξω ἔκλαυσεν πικρῶς.

26:71 Some mss read "Nazarene" for *Nazorean.* The latter is the "harder reading."

Apocalyptic discourse (at 24:30).

Power: God, of course.

coming on the clouds of heaven: In Daniel the son of Adam is going from earth to God's throne in heaven. But detaching the text from its Biblical context, as was common in the evangelist's time, better suits his purpose.

• **26:65** *tore his vestment:* A gesture of shock and outrage at Jesus' blasphemy.

He has blasphemed!: The author adds this to the Markan account, where it is only implied.

• **26:66** *What do you think?* What is your verdict?

He deserves to die! Guilt of blasphemy carries automatically the sentence of death (Lev 24:16).

• **26:67** Here it is Council members themselves who administer the abuse, or begin to. In Mark 14:65 only an indefinite "some." But in fact soldiers must have carried out this brutal manhandling, perhaps customary for capital crimes. Our evangelist omits Mark's statement that next the guards hit him as they took him into custody. For brevity? or

⁶⁵Then the high priest tore his vestment, and said, "He has blasphemed! Why do we still need witnesses? See, now you have heard the blasphemy. ⁶⁶What do you think?"

In response they said, "He deserves to die!" ⁶⁷Then they spat in his face, and punched him and slapped him, ⁶⁸saying, "Prophesy for us, you Anointed, you! Who hit you?"

⁶⁹Meanwhile Peter was sitting outside in the courtyard, and a slave woman came up to him, and said, "You too were with Jesus the Galilean."

A rooster crows

⁷⁰But he denied it in front of everyone: "I don't know what you're talking about!"

⁷¹He went out to the entrance, and another <slave woman> saw him and says to the people there, "This fellow was with that Nazorean Jesus."

⁷²And again he denied it and swore: "I don't know the guy!"

⁷³A little later those standing about came and said to Peter, "You really are one of them; even the way you talk gives you away!"

⁷⁴Then he began to curse and swear: "I don't know him!"

And just then a rooster crowed. ⁷⁵And Peter remembered what Jesus had said: "Before the rooster crows you will disown me three times." And he went outside and wept bitterly.

---

to leave the Jewish leaders guilty alone of abusing Jesus?

• **26:68** *Prophesy . . . Who hit you?*: The author, carelessly perhaps, omits the detail in Mark that they had blindfolded Jesus.

Prophesy: Here, with mockery, meaning only "Tell us."

• **26:69** *You too were with Jesus the Galilean:* Guilt by association, which Peter is all too eager to deny (vs 70).

the Galilean: In Jerusalem an outsider. Just as Peter's speech will show him up (vs 73). The evangelist has changed from Mark's

"that Nazarene."

• **26:71** *Nazorean:* No doubt she means simply "from Nazareth." But it may have deeper meaning for our author. See comment on 2:23.

• **26:72** *I don't know the guy!:* In Mark Peter makes this overt rejection of Jesus only once, in Matthew, twice.

• **26:74** *a rooster crowed:* Mark has the rooster crowing twice (14:68, 72) and Jesus predicting that. Why has our author simplified it?

**Trial before
Pilate begins**

27 Πρωΐας δὲ γενομένης συμβούλιον ἔλαβον πάντες οἱ ἀρχιερεῖς καὶ οἱ πρεσβύτεροι τοῦ λαοῦ κατὰ τοῦ Ἰησοῦ ὥστε θανατῶσαι αὐτόν· ²καὶ δήσαντες αὐτὸν ἀπήγαγον καὶ παρέδωκαν Πιλάτῳ τῷ ἡγεμόνι.

Judas repents

³Τότε ἰδὼν Ἰούδας ὁ παραδιδοὺς αὐτὸν ὅτι κατεκρίθη, μεταμεληθεὶς ἔστρεψεν τὰ τριάκοντα ἀργύρια τοῖς ἀρχιερεῦσιν καὶ πρεσβυτέροις ⁴λέγων, Ἥμαρτον παραδοὺς αἷμα ἀθῷον.

Οἱ δὲ εἶπαν, Τί πρὸς ἡμᾶς; σὺ ὄψῃ.

⁵Καὶ ῥίψας τὰ ἀργύρια εἰς τὸν ναὸν ἀνεχώρησεν, καὶ ἀπελθὼν ἀπήγξατο.

⁶Οἱ δὲ ἀρχιερεῖς λαβόντες τὰ ἀργύρια εἶπαν, Οὐκ ἔξεστιν βαλεῖν αὐτὰ εἰς τὸν κορβανᾶν, ἐπεὶ τιμὴ αἵματός ἐστιν.

⁷Συμβούλιον δὲ λαβόντες ἠγόρασαν ἐξ αὐτῶν τὸν Ἀγρὸν τοῦ Κεραμέως εἰς ταφὴν τοῖς ξένοις. ⁸διὸ ἐκλήθη ὁ ἀγρὸς ἐκεῖνος Ἀγρὸς Αἵματος ἕως τῆς σήμερον. ⁹τότε ἐπληρώθη τὸ ῥηθὲν διὰ Ἰερεμίου τοῦ προφήτου λέγοντος, Καὶ ἔλαβον τὰ τριάκοντα ἀργύρια, τὴν τιμὴν τοῦ τετιμημένου ὃν ἐτιμήσαντο ἀπὸ υἱῶν Ἰσραήλ, ¹⁰καὶ ἔδωκαν αὐτὰ εἰς τὸν ἀγρὸν τοῦ κεραμέως, καθὰ συνέταξέν μοι κύριος.

**Trial
before Pilate
continues**

¹¹Ὁ δὲ Ἰησοῦς ἐστάθη ἔμπροσθεν τοῦ ἡγεμόνος· καὶ ἐπηρώτησεν αὐτὸν ὁ ἡγεμὼν λέγων, Σὺ εἶ ὁ βασιλεὺς τῶν Ἰουδαίων;

Ὁ δὲ Ἰησοῦς ἔφη, Σὺ λέγεις.

¹²Καὶ ἐν τῷ κατηγορεῖσθαι αὐτὸν ὑπὸ τῶν ἀρχιερέων καὶ πρεσβυτέρων οὐδὲν ἀπεκρίνατο.

27:4 Some ancient texts read "righteous" instead of *blameless*. It matters very little which is the original.

- **27:1–2** The Jewish trial comes to an end, after the interlude of Peter's denials.
- **27:1** *When morning came:* As the rooster's crow in the preceding verses signaled.

   elders of the people: As usual the evangelist adds the last three words, involving in a way all the Jews.

   formed a plan: Based on their judgment the previous night (26:66).
- **27:2** *turned him over to Pilate the <Roman> governor:* Either because Pilate alone could impose the death sentence (if that were so—it's debatable). Or because their charge against Jesus was the political one of claiming to be Jewish king. By that claim he would have challenged Roman rule over all Jews.

   Pilate: Pontius Pilate, governor of the Roman province of Syria, which included Judea, 26–36 BCE.
- **27:3–10** This episode is found only in Matthew. It reflects the growing legend of Judas, who by the late first century CE had been made a negative model to Christians to lessen their temptation to defect from the

church. His futile attempt to take back his act is portrayed as a pathetic lesson in the entail of sin.
- **27:3** *realizing that he had been condemned:* Which, somehow, he had not anticipated?

   was overcome with remorse: "Had a change of heart."
- **27:4** *this blameless man:* In Greek, "innocent blood."

   That's your problem! More literally, " See to it yourself," which of course is ironic—as if he could now change anything.
- **27:5** *hurling the silver into the temple:* With "the temple treasury" in the next verse this is a vivid reminder of Zech 11:13.

   hanged himself: Thereby forever laying a curse on himself.
- **27:6** *blood money:* Whether because of Judas' death or, more likely, the death of Jesus that the money bought. In Greek, "the price of blood"; compare vs 4.
- **27:7** *buy the . . . the Potter's field:* In Jer 32 the prophet is ordered by God to buy a field. Also perhaps Jer 19:1, where God tells him to buy

27 When morning came, all the ranking priests and elders of the people formed a plan to have Jesus put to death. ²And they bound him and led him away and turned him over to Pilate the <Roman> governor.

Trial before Pilate begins

³Then Judas, who had turned <Jesus> in, realizing that he had been condemned, was overcome with remorse and returned the thirty silver coins to the ranking priests and elders ⁴with this remark, "I have made the grave mistake of turning in this blameless man."

Judas repents

But they said, "What's that to us? That's your problem!"

⁵And hurling the silver into the temple he slunk off, and went out and hanged himself.

⁶The ranking priests took the silver and said, "It wouldn't be right to put this into the temple treasury, since it's blood money."

⁷So they decided to take the money and buy the Potter's Field as a burial ground for foreigners. ⁸As a result, that field has been known as the Bloody Field even to this day. ⁹So the prediction Jeremiah the prophet made came true: "And they took the thirty silver coins, the price some of the Israelites put on a man's head, ¹⁰and they donated it for the Potter's Field, as my Lord commanded me."

¹¹Jesus stood before the governor, and he questioned him: "So you're 'the King of the Judeans,' are you?"

Trial before Pilate continues

Jesus said, "If you say so."

¹²And while he was being accused by the ranking priests and elders, he said absolutely nothing.

---

a potter's jug.

Potter's Field: Was there an actual field by that name? In any case, this is a direct allusion to Zech 11:12-13, but in its Hebrew (not Greek) form. See below on vss 9–10. The mention of "potter" also has resonance with the menacing image in Jer 18:11: "Thus says the Lord, 'I am a potter shaping evil against you . . .'."

a burial ground for foreigners: An act of charity, perhaps, but nevertheless an unclean place where the unclean are buried.

• **27:8** *the Bloody Field:* In Acts 1:18-19 there is a different explanation for this name: by accident Judas was bloodily disemboweled.

even to this day: Would this have been true after the Roman destruction of Jerusalem in the year 70? Perhaps true at least when this story was at first being passed on.

• **27:9–10** *the prediction Jeremiah the prophet made:* The quotation, or rather paraphrase, comes not from Jeremiah but Zechariah (11:12-13). But we have just seen in vs 7 two or three reminders of Jeremiah. And in vss 3,

5, and 7 there have been hints of Zechariah's "prediction." Evidently an intermingling of the two prophets' stories, what is called "intertextuality," has in some way inspired the entire story.

• **27:9** *thirty silver coins:* See on 26:15. The insulting wage of 30 shekels given to Zechariah—"this lordly price," he sarcastically comments.

• **27:11–26** Matthew is now again parallel to Mark and Luke.

• **27:11** *So you're 'the King of the Judeans,' are you?* The question is a dangerous one for Jesus, and he is shown giving a clever answer, in fact making Pilate proclaim his messiahship.

you're 'the King of the Judeans': The "you" is emphasized. "It's you, is it, not someone else?" Pilate isn't shocked, just intent on determining whether Jesus is the one Rome should get rid of.

Judeans: See Translation Note p. 41.

If you say so: Greek, "*You* say so [not me]."

¹³Τότε λέγει αὐτῷ ὁ Πιλᾶτος, Οὐκ ἀκούεις πόσα σου καταμαρτυροῦσιν; ¹⁴καὶ οὐκ ἀπεκρίθη αὐτῷ πρὸς οὐδὲ ἓν ῥῆμα, ὥστε θαυμάζειν τὸν ἡγεμόνα λίαν.

¹⁵Κατὰ δὲ ἑορτὴν εἰώθει ὁ ἡγεμὼν ἀπολύειν ἕνα τῷ ὄχλῳ δέσμιον ὃν ἤθελον. ¹⁶εἶχον δὲ τότε δέσμιον ἐπίσημον λεγόμενον Ἰησοῦν Βαραββᾶν. ¹⁷συνηγμένων οὖν αὐτῶν εἶπεν αὐτοῖς ὁ Πιλᾶτος, Τίνα θέλετε ἀπολύσω ὑμῖν, Ἰησοῦν τὸν Βαραββᾶν ἢ Ἰησοῦν τὸν λεγόμενον Χριστόν; ¹⁸ᾔδει γὰρ ὅτι διὰ φθόνον παρέδωκαν αὐτόν.

¹⁹Καθημένου δὲ αὐτοῦ ἐπὶ τοῦ βήματος ἀπέστειλεν πρὸς αὐτὸν ἡ γυνὴ αὐτοῦ λέγουσα, Μηδὲν σοὶ καὶ τῷ δικαίῳ ἐκείνῳ· πολλὰ γὰρ ἔπαθον σήμερον κατ’ ὄναρ δι’ αὐτόν.

²⁰Οἱ δὲ ἀρχιερεῖς καὶ οἱ πρεσβύτεροι ἔπεισαν τοὺς ὄχλους ἵνα αἰτήσωνται τὸν Βαραββᾶν, τὸν δὲ Ἰησοῦν ἀπολέσωσιν. ²¹ἀποκριθεὶς δὲ ὁ ἡγεμὼν εἶπεν αὐτοῖς, Τίνα θέλετε ἀπὸ τῶν δύο ἀπολύσω ὑμῖν;

Οἱ δὲ εἶπαν, Τὸν Βαραββᾶν.

²²Λέγει αὐτοῖς ὁ Πιλᾶτος, Τί οὖν ποιήσω Ἰησοῦν τὸν λεγόμενον Χριστόν;

Λέγουσιν πάντες, Σταυρωθήτω.

²³Ὁ δὲ ἔφη, Τί γὰρ κακὸν ἐποίησεν;

Οἱ δὲ περισσῶς ἔκραζον λέγοντες, Σταυρωθήτω.

²⁴Ἰδὼν δὲ ὁ Πιλᾶτος ὅτι οὐδὲν ὠφελεῖ ἀλλὰ μᾶλλον θόρυβος γίνεται, λαβὼν ὕδωρ ἀπενίψατο τὰς χεῖρας ἀπέναντι τοῦ ὄχλου λέγων, Ἀθῷός εἰμι ἀπὸ τοῦ αἵματος τούτου· ὑμεῖς ὄψεσθε.

27:16, 17 Many MSS omit *Jesus* as Barabbas's first name, perhaps out of reverence, or thinking it to be a mistake.

27:24 A number of important MSS read "this blameless fellow's blood." Scribal insertion of the word is easier to explain than its deletion.

• **27:13** *Don't you have something to say to . . .:* In Greek, "Don't you hear . . .?"—as the high priest had said to him.

• **27:15** *At each festival it was the custom for the governor to set one prisoner free:* If that was true, it would have been an act of amnesty, no doubt in order to placate the crowd at the highly nationalistic times of festival.

At each festival: Usually mistranslated simply "At the festival." The Greek is idiomatic, *kata heortên*, "At festival time."

whichever one they wanted: Who is this "they"?

• **27:16** *Jesus Barabbas:* Mark 15:7 (and similarly Luke 23:19) describes him as a violent guerrilla fighter against Rome (one of "the insurgents who had committed murder during the uprising"). Our author omits that information. Why?

Jesus: Only in Matthew do we have the

man's first name, a common one, a form of Joshua. Whether or not the evangelist had accurate historical information about him, the irony of the crowd's choosing between two men named Jesus is clear.

• **27:17** *Jesus < known as> Barabbas:* The Greek here has "Jesus the Barabbas," perhaps to balance with "Jesus known as the Anointed."

known as the Anointed: Mark 15:9 has simply "the King of the Judeans." Why this change?

• **27:18** *they had turned him in out of envy:* Again, who are *they?* And why are they envious?

• **27:19** This verse is unique to Matthew. Pilates' wife, like Pilate himself a bit later, appears as a friend of Jesus, trying to save him from execution.

sitting on the judgment seat: That is, as in court.

¹³Then Pilate says to him, "Don't you have something to say to the long list of charges they bring against you?" ¹⁴But he did not respond to him, not to a single charge, so the governor was baffled.

¹⁵At each festival it was the custom for the governor to set one prisoner free for the crowd, whichever one they wanted. ¹⁶<The Romans> were then holding a notorious prisoner named Jesus Barabbas. ¹⁷So when the crowd had gathered, Pilate said to them, "Do you want me to free Jesus <known as> Barabbas for you or Jesus known as 'the Anointed'?" ¹⁸He knew that they had turned him in out of envy.

¹⁹While he was sitting on the judgment seat, his wife sent a message to him: "Don't have anything to do with that innocent man, because I have agonized greatly today on account of a dream about him."

²⁰The ranking priests and the elders induced the crowds to ask for Barabbas but to execute Jesus. ²¹In response <to their request> the governor <again> said to them, "Which of the two do you want me to set free for you?"

They said, "Barabbas!"

²²Pilate says to them, "What should I do with Jesus known as 'the Anointed'?"

Everyone responds, "Have him crucified!"

²³But he said, "Why? What has he done wrong?"

But they began to shout all the louder, "Have him crucified!"

²⁴Now when Pilate could see that he was getting nowhere, but rather that a riot was starting, he took water and washed his hands in full view of the crowd, and said, "Don't blame me for this fellow's blood. Now it's your problem!"

Don't have anything to do with that innocent man: The Greek can express this idea only by saying "Don't let there be anything to you and to [him]," that is, "between you."

that innocent man: Only this author says it explicitly.

on account of a dream about him: Like the dreams in the story of Jesus' birth; but here, though it is apparently God's intent for Jesus not to be killed, that intent is thwarted. It's as if Jesus had been slaughtered with the other young children of Bethlehem after all!

• **27:20** If Barabbas was in fact a freedom fighter against Rome, the Jewish leaders, needing to stay in Rome's favor, would probably have preferred to keep Barabbas locked up. But many in the crowds would be supporters of Barabbas's cause. Besides, the leaders as well as the crowd are portrayed as fundamentally enemies of Jesus.

• **27:21–23** The leaders' choice is clear. And now the whole crowd calls for Jesus' death.

• **27:21** *Which of the two do you want me to set free for you?* They have just called for Barabbas. By asking again (added to Mark) is Pilate to be seen as hoping to save Jesus? See below on vs 24.

• **27:23** *began to shout:* Or "kept shouting." See Introduction, p. 27.

• **27:24** *washed his hands:* Disclaiming all responsibility for Jesus' fate. This appears only in Matthew and is very likely a late first-century creation, seeking to appease Rome by absolving it of responsibility for Jesus' death.

Don't blame me for: Greek, "I'm innocent of."

Now it's your problem: As the leaders said to Judas, vs 4. Greek: "You'll [have to] see [to that]."

²⁵Καὶ ἀποκριθεὶς πᾶς ὁ λαὸς εἶπεν, Τὸ αἷμα αὐτοῦ ἐφ' ἡμᾶς καὶ ἐπὶ τὰ τέκνα ἡμῶν.

²⁶Τότε ἀπέλυσεν αὐτοῖς τὸν Βαραββᾶν, τὸν δὲ Ἰησοῦν φραγελλώσας παρέδωκεν ἵνα σταυρωθῇ.

Soldiers make sport of Jesus

²⁷Τότε οἱ στρατιῶται τοῦ ἡγεμόνος παραλαβόντες τὸν Ἰησοῦν εἰς τὸ πραιτώριον συνήγαγον ἐπ' αὐτὸν ὅλην τὴν σπεῖραν. ²⁸καὶ ἐκδύσαντες αὐτὸν χλαμύδα κοκκίνην περιέθηκαν αὐτῷ, ²⁹καὶ πλέξαντες στέφανον ἐξ ἀκανθῶν ἐπέθηκαν ἐπὶ τῆς κεφαλῆς αὐτοῦ καὶ κάλαμον ἐν τῇ δεξιᾷ αὐτοῦ, καὶ γονυπετήσαντες ἔμπροσθεν αὐτοῦ ἐνέπαιξαν αὐτῷ λέγοντες, Χαῖρε, βασιλεῦ τῶν Ἰουδαίων, ³⁰καὶ ἐμπτύσαντες εἰς αὐτὸν ἔλαβον τὸν κάλαμον καὶ ἔτυπτον εἰς τὴν κεφαλὴν αὐτοῦ. ³¹καὶ ὅτε ἐνέπαιξαν αὐτῷ, ἐξέδυσαν αὐτὸν τὴν χλαμύδα καὶ ἐνέδυσαν αὐτὸν τὰ ἱμάτια αὐτοῦ καὶ ἀπήγαγον αὐτὸν εἰς τὸ σταυρῶσαι.

Soldiers crucify Jesus

³²Ἐξερχόμενοι δὲ εὗρον ἄνθρωπον Κυρηναῖον ὀνόματι Σίμωνα, τοῦτον ἠγγάρευσαν ἵνα ἄρῃ τὸν σταυρὸν αὐτοῦ.

³³Καὶ ἐλθόντες εἰς τόπον λεγόμενον Γολγοθᾶ, ὅ ἐστιν Κρανίου Τόπος λεγόμενος, ³⁴ἔδωκαν αὐτῷ πιεῖν οἶνον μετὰ χολῆς μεμιγμένον· καὶ γευσάμενος οὐκ ἠθέλησεν πιεῖν. ³⁵σταυρώσαντες δὲ αὐτὸν διεμερίσαντο τὰ ἱμάτια αὐτοῦ βάλλοντες κλῆρον, ³⁶καὶ καθήμενοι ἐτήρουν αὐτὸν ἐκεῖ. ³⁷καὶ ἐπέθηκαν ἐπάνω τῆς κεφαλῆς αὐτοῦ τὴν αἰτίαν αὐτοῦ γεγραμμένην· Οὗτός ἐστιν Ἰησοῦς ὁ βασιλεῦς τῶν Ἰουδαίων.

³⁸Τότε σταυροῦνται σὺν αὐτῷ δύο λῃσταί, εἷς ἐκ δεξιῶν καὶ εἷς ἐξ εὐωνύμων.

• **27:25** Only in Matthew. The entire crowd (*all the people*) readily accepts the problem.

blame his blood on us: We take full responsibility. This cannot be factual. It represents Matthean anti-Judaism and has led to monstrous Christian persecution of Jews ever since.

and on our children: That is, "and on all our descendants." On the basis of this, all Jews ever since have been subject to being called Christ-killers.

• **27:26** *had Jesus flogged:* Perhaps the usual public treatment of a condemned person.

• **27:27–66** From this point the story is studded with implicit allusions to passages in the Hebrew Scriptures that are evidently understood as prophecies of what Jesus now endures, explaining it as necessary and therefore acceptable. Many of those passages are from Pss 22 and 69 or Isa 50 and 53. It's curious that these are never direct quotations, nor are they used with the common

Matthean formula, "This happened so as to fulfill. . . ."

• **27:27–31** This is perhaps simply traditional horseplay. But the cruel irony is poignant.

• **27:27** *into the governor's residence:* Evidently from his public (and outdoor?) *judgment seat* (vs 19). It's not clear just where this building was, near the Temple or at the western edge of the city. It was used mainly at festival time, when the governor would be in Jerusalem to quell the nationalist fervor that would run high. Ordinarily the governor stayed in Caesarea Maritima, on the Mediterranean coast.

surrounded him: In Greek, almost "ganged up on him."

company: Technically a "cohort"—usually of 600 men, but often fewer.

• **27:28** *crimson cloak:* In Mark 15:17, purple (designating him as mock emperor). Here it is a *cloak* such as soldiers wore, readily available. Together with a *crown* and *staff* (vs 29)

²⁵In response all the people said, "So blame his blood on us and on our children."

²⁶Then he set Barabbas free for them, but had Jesus flogged, and then turned him over to be crucified.

²⁷Then the governor's soldiers took Jesus into the governor's residence and surrounded him with the whole company <of his troops>. ²⁸They stripped him and dressed him in a crimson cloak, ²⁹and they wove a crown out of thorns and put it on his head. They placed a staff in his right hand, and bowing down before him, they made fun of him, saying, "Greetings, 'King of the Judeans'!" ³⁰And spitting on him, the soldiers took the staff and hit him on the head. ³¹And when they had made sport of him, they stripped off the cloak and put his own clothes back on him and led him out to crucify him.

Soldiers make sport of Jesus

³²As they were going out, they came across a Cyrenian named Simon. This fellow they conscripted to carry his cross.

Soldiers crucify Jesus

³³And when <the soldiers> reached the place known as Golgotha (which means "Place of the Skull"), ³⁴they gave him a drink of wine mixed with something bitter, and once he tasted it, he wouldn't drink it. ³⁵After crucifying him, the Romans divided up his garments by throwing dice ³⁶And they sat down there and kept guard over him. ³⁷And over his head they put his crime, which read: "This is Jesus the King of the Judeans."

³⁸Then the soldiers crucified two rebels with him, one on his right and one on his left.

---

the mocking regalia of a *king*.
- **27:29** *crown:* Like a royal wreath.
  staff: Mark lacks this detail
- **27:30** *spitting on him . . . hit him:* In Isa 50:6, the sufferings of God's servant
- **27:32** *a Cyrenian named Simon:* Clearly a Jew. Simon is a form of Simeon, one of Jacob's twelve sons. From Cyrene, a city of North Africa (now Libya), he would have been in Jerusalem for Passover. The evangelist omits Mark's detail that he was the father of Alexander and Rufus, presumably known to the readers of Mark.
  carry his cross: Or perhaps only the cross beam, the upright post being one of many planted on the roads outside Jerusalem, as warning to Jews against challenging Rome's occupation of Judea.
- **27:33** *Golgotha (which means "Place of the Skull"):* The word is Aramaic simply for "skull." Called this because of earlier crucifixions there, and nearby open graves?

- **27:34** *wine mixed with something bitter:* Ps 69:21.
- **27:35** *After crucifying him:* That is, hanging him on a cross. Death came only gradually, from exposure, or exhaustion and so suffocation—a deliberately slow and agonizing means of execution.
  divided up his garments by throwing dice: As in Ps 22:18.
- **27:36** Only in Matthew. See below on vss 62–66.
- **27:38** Perhaps an allusion to Isa 53:12 ("he . . . was numbered with the transgressors").
  rebels: The Greek term is again *lêstês*. They were almost certainly part of an underground organization to free Palestine from Rome's control. Jesus, as supposed "King of Judeans," would equally be seen as a subversive.

³⁹Οἱ δὲ παραπορευόμενοι ἐβλασφήμουν αὐτὸν κινοῦντες τὰς κεφαλὰς αὐτῶν ⁴⁰καὶ λέγοντες, Ὁ καταλύων τὸν ναὸν καὶ ἐν τρισὶν ἡμέραις οἰκοδομῶν, σῶσον σεαυτόν, εἰ υἱὸς εἶ τοῦ θεοῦ, κατάβηθι ἀπὸ τοῦ σταυροῦ.

⁴¹Ὁμοίως καὶ οἱ ἀρχιερεῖς ἐμπαίζοντες μετὰ τῶν γραμματέων καὶ πρεσβυτέρων ἔλεγον, ⁴²Ἄλλους ἔσωσεν, ἑαυτὸν οὐ δύναται σῶσαι· βασιλεὺς Ἰσραήλ ἐστιν, καταβάτω νῦν ἀπὸ τοῦ σταυροῦ καὶ πιστεύσομεν ἐπ' αὐτόν. ⁴³πέποιθεν ἐπὶ τὸν θεόν, ῥυσάσθω νῦν εἰ θέλει αὐτόν· εἶπεν γὰρ ὅτι Θεοῦ εἰμι υἱός.

⁴⁴Τὸ δ' αὐτὸ καὶ οἱ λῃσταὶ οἱ συσταυρωθέντες σὺν αὐτῷ ὠνείδιζον αὐτόν.

The death of Jesus

⁴⁵Ἀπὸ δὲ ἕκτης ὥρας σκότος ἐγένετο ἐπὶ πᾶσαν τὴν γῆν ἕως ὥρας ἐνάτης. ⁴⁶περὶ δὲ τὴν ἐνάτην ὥραν ἀνεβόησεν ὁ Ἰησοῦς φωνῇ μεγάλῃ λέγων, Ηλι ηλι λεμα σαβαχθανι; τοῦτ' ἔστιν, Θεέ μου θεέ μου, ἱνατί με ἐγκατέλιπες;

⁴⁷Τινὲς δὲ τῶν ἐκεῖ ἑστηκότων ἀκούσαντες ἔλεγον ὅτι Ἠλίαν φωνεῖ οὗτος. ⁴⁸καὶ εὐθέως δραμὼν εἷς ἐξ αὐτῶν καὶ λαβὼν σπόγγον πλήσας τε ὄξους καὶ περιθεὶς καλάμῳ ἐπότιζεν αὐτόν.

⁴⁹Οἱ δὲ λοιποὶ ἔλεγον, Ἄφες ἴδωμεν εἰ ἔρχεται Ἠλίας σώσων αὐτόν.

⁵⁰Ὁ δὲ Ἰησοῦς πάλιν κράξας φωνῇ μεγάλῃ ἀφῆκεν τὸ πνεῦμα.

⁵¹Καὶ ἰδοὺ τὸ καταπέτασμα τοῦ ναοῦ ἐσχίσθη ἀπ' ἄνωθεν ἕως

• **27:39** *taunting him, wagging their heads:* Almost verbatim from Ps 22:7. See also Ps 109:25.

• **27:40** *You were going to destroy the temple:* See on 26:61.

• **27:42** *the King of Israel:* Mark 15:32 has "The Anointed, the King of Israel" and Luke 23:35, "God's Anointed, the Chosen One." Maybe the evangelist doesn't include "the Anointed" as redundant with "the King of Israel."

• **27:43** The quote is directly from Ps 22:8.

he said, 'I'm God's son': Not strictly true, but neither the evangelist nor his reader would deny it.

• **27:44** *the rebels who were crucified with him:* If their presence is factual (see above on vs 38) they clearly didn't see him as a comrade in their cause.

• **27:45** *Beginning at noon, darkness:* As Amos threatened (8:9).

Noon . . . mid-afternoon: In Greek "the sixth hour" and "the ninth hour." The latter in the next verse also.

The whole land: Does this mean all of Palestine, or the Roman province of Syria, or the whole world? For people there, of course, it would all be the same.

• **27:46** *Eli, Eli, lema sabachthani:* From Ps 22:1. The author has changed Mark's "Eloi, Eloi," (Aramaic, the common language), to conform to the Hebrew of the psalm, and maybe to make the words less shocking, in their Biblical context. Or perhaps to account better than in Mark 15: 34 for the misunderstanding in the next verse.

Is this cry only a devout recital of the psalm, or more? (Luke omits this part of the narrative. Perhaps he found it incredible.) Unwittingly it demonstrates Paul's statement in 2 Cor 5:21—"For our sake [God] made him who knew no sin to be sin" . . . if sin is understood as experiencing the absence of God.

• **27:47** *This fellow's calling Elijah!* Should we take this to mean that those standing there couldn't believe Jesus would say to God

³⁹Those passing by kept taunting him, wagging their heads, and saying, ⁴⁰"You were going to destroy the temple and rebuild it in three days—save yourself. If you're God's son, come down from the cross!"

⁴¹Likewise the ranking priests made sport of him along with the scholars and elders; they kept saying, ⁴²"He saved others, but he can't even save himself! He's 'the King of Israel'; he should come down from the cross here and now and we'll believe him. ⁴³He trusted God, so God should 'rescue him now if he cares about him.' After all, he said, 'I'm God's son.'"

⁴⁴In the same way the rebels who were crucified with him began to abuse him.

⁴⁵Beginning at noon darkness blanketed the entire land until mid-afternoon. ⁴⁶And about 3 o'clock in the afternoon Jesus shouted at the top of his voice, "Eli, Eli, lema sabachthani" (which means, "My God, my God, why did you abandon me?")

The death of Jesus

⁴⁷When some of those standing there heard, they said, "This fellow's calling Elijah!" ⁴⁸And immediately one of them ran and took a sponge filled with sour wine and stuck it on a pole and offered him a drink.

⁴⁹But the rest were saying, "Wait! Let's see if Elijah comes to rescue him."

⁵⁰Jesus again shouted at the top of his voice . . . and stopped breathing.

⁵¹And suddenly the curtain of the temple was torn in two from

---

"Why did you abandon me"? Or only that they misunderstood the Hebrew?

• **27:48** Reminiscent of Ps 69:21, as in vs 34. Purely as plot, it's not clear why this would take place.

• **27:50** *again:* As in vs 46.

stopped breathing: "Let go his breath." The Greek word for "breath" is *pneuma*, and that word has several meanings. Some would translate "gave up his spirit," that is, his life. In any case of course the point is simply that Jesus dies.

• **27:51a** *the curtain of the temple:* There were two curtains in the temple. The first was huge and hid the entrance to the sanctuary, which was the only enclosed building in the main temple area. The second curtain was inside the sanctuary and smaller. It hid the "holy of holies" and no one could go behind it, except the high priest and only on Yom Kippur.

the curtain . . . was torn in two from top to bottom There is no way of knowing exactly what

was supposed to have occurred, and still less what the author understands by that occurrence. Perhaps it doesn't matter very much which curtain was suddenly and miraculously torn down the middle. But what does it mean? That the destruction of the temple, as Jesus had predicted in 24:2, was now foreshadowed or even beginning to occur? Or that the inner truth of Judaism was now thrown open for all to see? Or what? In any case, the evangelist gives a hint of this event's import by calling it a *sign* (vs 54), a portent from God that with Jesus' death something momentous was taking place.

• **27:51b–53** The report of these events is unique to this gospel. It heightens the significance of Jesus' death by using apocalyptic images, that is, by describing events that were to occur only at the end of the age. This little legend is presumably the insertion, even the creation, of the evangelist. In the context it violates the unity of time, jumping briefly to the following Sunday.

κάτω εἰς δύο καὶ ἡ γῆ ἐσείσθη καὶ αἱ πέτραι ἐσχίσθησαν, ⁵²καὶ τὰ
μνημεῖα ἀνεῴχθησαν καὶ πολλὰ σώματα τῶν κεκοιμημένων ἁγίων
ἠγέρθησαν, ⁵³καὶ ἐξελθόντες ἐκ τῶν μνημείων μετὰ τὴν ἔγερσιν
αὐτοῦ εἰσῆλθον εἰς τὴν ἁγίαν πόλιν καὶ ἐνεφανίσθησαν πολλοῖς. ⁵⁴Ὁ
δὲ ἑκατόνταρχος καὶ οἱ μετ᾽ αὐτοῦ τηροῦντες τὸν Ἰησοῦν ἰδόντες τὸν
σεισμὸν καὶ τὰ γενόμενα ἐφοβήθησαν σφόδρα, λέγοντες, Ἀληθῶς
θεοῦ υἱὸς ἦν οὗτος.

⁵⁵Ἦσαν δὲ ἐκεῖ γυναῖκες πολλαὶ ἀπὸ μακρόθεν θεωροῦσαι,
αἵτινες ἠκολούθησαν τῷ Ἰησοῦ ἀπὸ τῆς Γαλιλαίας διακονοῦσαι
αὐτῷ· ⁵⁶ἐν αἷς ἦν Μαρία ἡ Μαγδαληνὴ καὶ Μαρία ἡ τοῦ Ἰακώβου καὶ
Ἰωσὴφ μήτηρ καὶ ἡ μήτηρ τῶν υἱῶν Ζεβεδαίου.

Joseph buries Jesus

⁵⁷Ὀψίας δὲ γενομένης ἦλθεν ἄνθρωπος πλούσιος ἀπὸ Ἀριμαθαίας,
τοὔνομα Ἰωσήφ, ὃς καὶ αὐτὸς ἐμαθητεύθη τῷ Ἰησοῦ· ⁵⁸οὗτος
προσελθὼν τῷ Πιλάτῳ ᾐτήσατο τὸ σῶμα τοῦ Ἰησοῦ. τότε ὁ Πιλᾶτος
ἐκέλευσεν ἀποδοθῆναι. ⁵⁹καὶ λαβὼν τὸ σῶμα ὁ Ἰωσὴφ ἐνετύλιξεν
αὐτὸ [ἐν] σινδόνι καθαρᾷ ⁶⁰καὶ ἔθηκεν αὐτὸ ἐν τῷ καινῷ αὐτοῦ
μνημείῳ ὃ ἐλατόμησεν ἐν τῇ πέτρᾳ καὶ προσκυλίσας λίθον μέγαν τῇ
θύρᾳ τοῦ μνημείου ἀπῆλθεν. ⁶¹ἦν δὲ ἐκεῖ Μαριὰμ ἡ Μαγδαληνὴ καὶ
ἡ ἄλλη Μαρία καθήμεναι ἀπέναντι τοῦ τάφου.

The tomb is secured

⁶²Τῇ δὲ ἐπαύριον, ἥτις ἐστὶν μετὰ τὴν παρασκευήν, συνήχθησαν
οἱ ἀρχιερεῖς καὶ οἱ Φαρισαῖοι πρὸς Πιλᾶτον ⁶³λέγοντες, Κύριε,
ἐμνήσθημεν ὅτι ἐκεῖνος ὁ πλάνος εἶπεν ἔτι ζῶν, Μετὰ τρεῖς ἡμέρας
ἐγείρομαι. ⁶⁴κέλευσον οὖν ἀσφαλισθῆναι τὸν τάφον ἕως τῆς τρίτης

27:53 A very few MSS lack *after his resurrection*. Did scribes omit it since it
causes confusion in the timing? Or add it, followed then by the majority of
copyists, so as to keep Jesus' resurrection the first to occur?

• **27:52–53** *sleeping saints:* Presumably dead
heroes of Israel—perhaps Abraham, Moses,
Elijah, and so forth.
  came back to life: That is, "were raised," And
before Jesus' resurrection! But they appear
in Jerusalem only *after his resurrection*.
• **27:53** *the holy city:* Jerusalem.
• **27:54** *The Roman officer and those . . . with
him . . . said, "This man really was God's son":*
In Mark (15:39) this follows immediately
after the death of Jesus and the ripping of
the temple curtain. And there it is because
of seeing Jesus' dying that the officer alone,
a Gentile, makes this so-called confession
of faith. Here instead it is *the earthquake
and what had happened*—the tearing of the
curtain and the events of vss 51b–53—that
affected him and all those present. And with
terror. Only then were they led to understand who Jesus was.
  Roman officer: Centurion. See comment
on 8:5.

those keeping watch over Jesus: Does this
mean the other Roman soldiers of vs 36?
Or the women, followers of Jesus, who were
present (vs 55)? In either case, the author
has heightened the effect of Jesus' death on
those present.
• **27:55** *Many women were there:* The male disciples had deserted him (26:56). The evangelist moves a list of the women's names (Mark
15:40) to the next verse.
  assist him: Or "provide for him."
• **27:56** Mark 15:40 has a slightly different list
of women.
• **27:57–60** Crucifixion was considered a form
of hanging. According to Jewish law (Deut
21:22–23) the body of one hanged was under
a curse and had to be buried before nightfall.
Otherwise, the whole land would be defiled.
• **27:57** *Arimathea:* Perhaps ancient Ramah
or Ramathaim, on the western slope of the
hill country of Ephraim, Samuel's birthplace
(1 Sam 1:1). Not to be confused with the

top to bottom, and the earth quaked, rocks were split apart, ⁵²and tombs were opened and many bodies of sleeping saints came back to life. ⁵³And they came out of the tombs after his resurrection and went into the holy city, where they appeared to many. ⁵⁴The <Roman> officer and those keeping watch over Jesus with him witnessed the earthquake and what had happened, and were terrified, and said, "This man really was God's son."

⁵⁵Many women were there observing this from a distance—those who had followed Jesus from Galilee to assist him. ⁵⁶Among them were Mary of Magdala, and Mary the mother of James and Joseph, and the mother of the sons of Zebedee.

⁵⁷When it had grown dark, a rich man from Arimathea named Joseph, who himself was a follower of Jesus, appeared on the scene, ⁵⁸and went to Pilate and requested the body of Jesus. Then Pilate ordered it to be turned over <to him>. ⁵⁹And taking the body, Joseph wrapped it in a clean linen shroud ⁶⁰and put it in his own new tomb, which had been cut in the rock. He rolled a huge stone across the opening of the tomb and went away. ⁶¹But Mary of Magdala and the other Mary stayed there, sitting opposite the tomb.

Joseph buries Jesus

⁶²On the next day, which is the day after Preparation, the ranking priests and the Pharisees met with Pilate ⁶³to tell him: "Your Excellency, we remember what that impostor said while he was still alive: 'After three days I am going to be raised up.' ⁶⁴So order the tomb sealed for three days so his disciples won't come and steal his

The tomb is secured

Ramah of 2:28.

This evangelist differs from Mark and Luke by describing *Joseph* as *a follower of Jesus* and not as "a member of the Council."

- **27:60** *his own new tomb:* In Mark 15:46 simply "a tomb." Luke 23:53 has "a tomb . . . where no one had ever been buried." What is the significance of this? That Jesus' burial was appropriately special?

  rolled a huge stone: Perhaps a flat circular stone, the shape of a millstone, but bigger. It would have sat in a track cut out for it to roll in. Tombs of this sort from the first century CE have been found in Jerusalem.

- **27:61** *Mary of Magdala:* Often called Mary Magdalene. *Magdala* is perhaps at the westernmost point of the Sea of Galilee, maybe also called Magadan.

  the other Mary: Perhaps "Mary the mother of . . . Joseph," as in vs 56. But why doesn't the author say that, when Mark 15:47 has something very close to it?

- **27:62–66** These verses, like vs 36, are to be found only in Matthew. This seems to be a late legend (or the evangelist's invention), seeking to counter the Jewish claim that Jesus' disciples stole his body. The little section prepares for 28:11–15.

- **27:62** *the day after Preparation:* Evidently Saturday, if preparation for the sabbath is meant, as Mark 15:42 says.

  impostor: Or deceiver, one who leads astray.

  After three days I am going to be raised up: Elsewhere in Matthew (see 16:21) Jesus predicts that he'll be raised "on the third day," correcting Mark's "after three days." The other exception (in 12:40) is the saying that, comparable to Jonah's ordeal, "the son of Adam will be in the bowels of the earth for three days and three nights."

- **27:64** *his disciples [will] come and steal his body:* Evidently a belief held by non-Christian Jews, or at least a rumor they spread.

ἡμέρας, μήποτε ἐλθόντες οἱ μαθηταὶ αὐτοῦ κλέψωσιν αὐτὸν καὶ εἴπωσιν τῷ λαῷ, Ἠγέρθη ἀπὸ τῶν νεκρῶν, καὶ ἔσται ἡ ἐσχάτη πλάνη χείρων τῆς πρώτης.

⁶⁵Ἔφη αὐτοῖς ὁ Πιλᾶτος, Ἔχετε κουστωδίαν· ὑπάγετε ἀσφαλίσασθε ὡς οἴδατε.

⁶⁶Οἱ δὲ πορευθέντες ἠσφαλίσαντο τὸν τάφον σφραγίσαντες τὸν λίθον μετὰ τῆς κουστωδίας.

---

deception: About Jesus as deceiver, "impostor" (vs 63).

• **27:65** *the best way you know how:* Does the author suggest that they don't know how very well, since they can't prevent Jesus' resurrection?

• **27:66** *sealing it with a stone:* This is curious, since Joseph had already rolled a stone to close the tomb (vs 60). It suggests that this incident is a late insertion into the account of the burial.

body and tell everyone, 'He has been raised from the dead,' in which case, the last deception will be worse than the first."

⁶⁵Pilate replied to them, "You have a guard; go and secure it the best way you know how."

⁶⁶They went and secured the tomb by sealing it with a stone <and posting> the guard.

28 ᾿Οψὲ δὲ σαββάτων, τῇ ἐπιφωσκούσῃ εἰς μίαν σαββάτων ἦλθεν Μαριὰμ ἡ Μαγδαληνὴ καὶ ἡ ἄλλη Μαρία θεωρῆσαι τὸν τάφον. ²καὶ ἰδοὺ σεισμὸς ἐγένετο μέγας· ἄγγελος γὰρ κυρίου καταβὰς ἐξ οὐρανοῦ καὶ προσελθὼν ἀπεκύλισεν τὸν λίθον καὶ ἐκάθητο ἐπάνω αὐτοῦ. ³ν δὲ ἡ εἰδέα αὐτοῦ ὡς ἀστραπὴ καὶ τὸ ἔνδυμα αὐτοῦ λευκὸν ὡς χιών. ⁴ἀπὸ δὲ τοῦ φόβου αὐτοῦ ἐσείσθησαν οἱ τηροῦντες καὶ ἐγενήθησαν ὡς νεκροί.

⁵᾿Αποκριθεὶς δὲ ὁ ἄγγελος εἶπεν ταῖς γυναιξίν, Μὴ φοβεῖσθε ὑμεῖς, οἶδα γὰρ ὅτι ᾿Ιησοῦν τὸν ἐσταυρωμένον ζητεῖτε· ⁶οὐκ ἔστιν ὧδε, ἠγέρθη γὰρ καθὼς εἶπεν· δεῦτε ἴδετε τὸν τόπον ὅπου ἔκειτο. ⁷καὶ ταχὺ πορευθεῖσαι εἴπατε τοῖς μαθηταῖς αὐτοῦ ὅτι ᾿Ηγέρθη ἀπὸ τῶν νεκρῶν, καὶ ἰδοὺ προάγει ὑμᾶς εἰς τὴν Γαλιλαίαν, ἐκεῖ αὐτὸν ὄψεσθε· ἰδοὺ εἶπον ὑμῖν.

⁸Καὶ ἀπελθοῦσαι ταχὺ ἀπὸ τοῦ μνημείου μετὰ φόβου καὶ χαρᾶς μεγάλης ἔδραμον ἀπαγγεῖλαι τοῖς μαθηταῖς αὐτοῦ.

⁹Καὶ ἰδοὺ ᾿Ιησοῦς ὑπήντησεν αὐταῖς λέγων, Χαίρετε.

Αἱ δὲ προσελθοῦσαι ἐκράτησαν αὐτοῦ τοὺς πόδας καὶ προσεκύνησαν αὐτῷ.

¹⁰Τότε λέγει αὐταῖς ὁ ᾿Ιησοῦς, Μὴ φοβεῖσθε· ὑπάγετε ἀπαγγείλατε τοῖς ἀδελφοῖς μου ἵνα ἀπέλθωσιν εἰς τὴν Γαλιλαίαν, κἀκεῖ με ὄψονται.

¹¹Πορευομένων δὲ αὐτῶν ἰδού τινες τῆς κουστωδίας ἐλθόντες εἰς τὴν πόλιν ἀπήγγειλαν τοῖς ἀρχιερεῦσιν ἅπαντα τὰ γενόμενα. ¹²καὶ συναχθέντες μετὰ τῶν πρεσβυτέρων συμβούλιόν τε λαβόντες ἀργύρια ἱκανὰ ἔδωκαν τοῖς στρατιώταις ¹³λέγοντες, Εἴπατε ὅτι Οἱ μαθηταὶ αὐτοῦ νυκτὸς ἐλθόντες ἔκλεψαν αὐτὸν ἡμῶν κοιμωμένων.

• **Chap. 28** The story shifts now from Friday afternoon to early Sunday morning, from what we call Good Friday to Easter.

• **28:1–7** Parallel to Mark 16:1–7, but with a number of changes.

• **28:1** *Mary of Magdala and the other Mary:* The same women as at Jesus' burial in 27:61.

came to inspect the tomb: In Mark 16:1 the women come to give Jesus a proper burial. Evidently our evangelist considers that the woman who anointed Jesus in Bethany had already done everything necessary, as Jesus had said (26:12).

• **28:2** *there was a strong earthquake:* As before, in 27:51, the evangelist adds this apocalyptic detail.

messenger: In other translations of Matthew usually transliterated as "angel." In Mark 16:5 it is only "a young man."

rolled away the stone: Explaining how it was that the women would find it open and empty.

and was sitting on it: Rather than in the tomb as in Mark.

• **28:3** *The messenger gave off a dazzling light:* In Greek, "his appearance was like lightning." Mark's young man was "wearing a white robe." Matthew's version of the story, as often, has grown taller.

• **28:4** *those who kept watch:* Only in Matthew; the guard posted in 27:66.

• **28:5** *Don't be frightened!* In Greek the "you" is emphasized—"Don't you too be frightened . . ." like the guards (vs 4).

• **28:6** *just as he said:* The evangelist moves this phrase here; in Mark it comes at the end of this unit.

• **28:7** *tell his disciples:* Mark adds, "and Peter," perhaps because they had left the scene separately.

he is going ahead of you to Galilee: As Jesus had promised in 26:32.

Now I have told you: A curious statement. The evangelist evidently has retained Mark's

28 After the sabbath day, at first light on Sunday, Mary of Magdala and the other Mary came to inspect the tomb. ²And just then there was a strong earthquake—a messenger of the Lord had come down from the sky, arrived <at the tomb>, rolled away the stone, and was sitting on it. ³The messenger gave off a dazzling light and wore clothes as white as snow. ⁴But those who kept watch were paralyzed with fear and looked like corpses themselves.

⁵In response the messenger said to the women, "Don't be frightened. I know you are looking for Jesus who was crucified. ⁶He is not here. You see he was raised, just as he said. Come, look at the spot where he was lying. ⁷And run, tell his disciples that he has been raised from the dead. Don't forget, he is going ahead of you to Galilee. There you will see him. Now I have told you."

⁸And they hurried away from the tomb, full of fear and an overpowering joy, and ran to tell his disciples.

⁹And suddenly Jesus met them saying, "Hello!"

They came up and took hold of his feet and worshipped him.

¹⁰Then Jesus says to them, "Don't be afraid. Go tell my companions so they can leave for Galilee, where they will see me."

¹¹While they were on their way, some of the guards returned to the city and reported to the ranking priests everything that had happened. ¹²They met with the elders and hatched a plan: they bribed the soldiers with an adequate amount of money ¹³and ordered them: "Tell everybody that his disciples came at night and

Two Marys at the tomb

Jesus meets the two women

Priests and elders bribe the guard

"[as] he told you," but changed the subject. See on vs 6.

• **28:8** Mark breaks off here (16:8), telling us only that the women "didn't breathe a word of it to anyone because they were afraid." Our story has been considerably changed, so that the women have *fear* but also *an overpowering joy.* More important, they *ran to tell his disciples.*

• **28:9–10** From this point on Matthew reports the resurrection altogether differently from Luke. The two later evangelists were drawing on different traditions, and maybe creating some of the story. They obviously did not have a now-lost ending to Mark.

• **28:9** Only here (and in a different way, in John 20:14-16) does Jesus appear at the tomb.

Hello: The best modern, colloquial translation. More stiffly, "Hail" or "Greetings." Similar to the Hebrew *Shalom,* though that means literally "Peace."

took hold of his feet: In John 20:17 Jesus orders Mary of Magdala not to touch him.

worshipped him: Or does it mean only "honored him"? In Greek, "knelt to him."

• **28:10** Repeating what the messenger had said in vss 5 and 7. So this little section is probably not based on separate tradition.

• **28:11–15** This section has been prepared for in 27:62-66, where the Jewish leaders posted a guard at Jesus' tomb lest his disciples "come and steal his body."

• **28:11–12** *everything that had happened:* That is, that despite their vigil, Jesus' body was missing.

But the leaders *bribed* the guards to tell a different story. They would be protected from punishment (vs 14).

• **28:13** *Tell everybody that his disciples came at night and stole his body:* In other words, the precautions (27:64) had failed.

On a mountain in Galilee

¹⁴καὶ ἐὰν ἀκουσθῇ τοῦτο ἐπὶ τοῦ ἡγεμόνος, ἡμεῖς πείσομεν [αὐτὸν] καὶ ὑμᾶς ἀμερίμνους ποιήσομεν. ¹⁵οἱ δὲ λαβόντες τὰ ἀργύρια ἐποίησαν ὡς ἐδιδάχθησαν. Καὶ διεφημίσθη ὁ λόγος οὗτος παρὰ Ἰουδαίοις μέχρι τῆς σήμερον ἡμέρας.

¹⁶Οἱ δὲ ἔνδεκα μαθηταὶ ἐπορεύθησαν εἰς τὴν Γαλιλαίαν εἰς τὸ ὄρος οὗ ἐτάξατο αὐτοῖς ὁ Ἰησοῦς, ¹⁷καὶ ἰδόντες αὐτὸν προσεκύνησαν, οἱ δὲ ἐδίστασαν.

¹⁸Καὶ προσελθὼν ὁ Ἰησοῦς ἐλάλησεν αὐτοῖς λέγων, Ἐδόθη μοι πᾶσα ἐξουσία ἐν οὐρανῷ καὶ ἐπὶ γῆς. ¹⁹πορευθέντες οὖν μαθητεύσατε πάντα τὰ ἔθνη, βαπτίζοντες αὐτοὺς εἰς τὸ ὄνομα τοῦ πατρὸς καὶ τοῦ υἱοῦ καὶ τοῦ ἁγίου πνεύματος, ²⁰διδάσκοντες αὐτοὺς τηρεῖν πάντα ὅσα ἐνετειλάμην ὑμῖν· καὶ ἰδοὺ ἐγὼ μεθ' ὑμῶν εἰμι πάσας τὰς ἡμέρας ἕως τῆς συντελείας τοῦ αἰῶνος.

• **28:15** *this story has been passed around among Jews until this very day:* One assumes it is this fact that has occasioned the story the evangelist has inserted into Mark, his written source, in 27:62–66.

Jews: Not the usual translation, "Judeans," since this is not a report about Jesus and his time but the author's late first-century aside, an anachronism in his narrative.

• **28:16** *The eleven disciples:* The twelve (26:47) without Judas.

Jesus had not mentioned a *mountain* in Galilee. Perhaps, as with the "Sermon on the Mount" (chaps. 5–7), the author cannot imagine such a revelation as this except on a mountain.

• **28:17** *when they saw him:* Jesus was there, waiting for them.

worshipped him: See comment on vs 9.

some were skeptical: Evidently about whether it was Jesus, raised from death.

• **28:18** *All authority has been given to me . . . :* As in the Gospel of John, Jesus speaks as the divine Son of God.

• **28:19–20** The "Great Commission." The author intends his readers, I believe, to understand this as if spoken directly to them.

• **28:19** *make followers . . . baptize them:* There is

stole his body while we were asleep. ¹⁴If the governor should hear about this, we will deal with him; you need have no worries." ¹⁵They took the money and did as they had been instructed. And this story has been passed around among Jews until this very day.

¹⁶The eleven disciples went to the mountain in Galilee where Jesus had told them to go. ¹⁷And when they saw him, they worshipped him; but some were skeptical.

On a mountain in Galilee

¹⁸And Jesus approached them and spoke these words: "All authority has been given to me in heaven and on earth. ¹⁹You are to go and make followers of all peoples. You are to baptize them in the name of the Father and the son and the holy spirit. ²⁰Teach them to observe everything I commanded you. I'll be with you day in and day out, as you'll see, so long as this world continues its course."

---

no other indication in the synoptic gospels that baptism should be the way people become Jesus' followers.

make followers: This is a single word in Greek. The verb is directly related to the word for "disciple" *(mathêtês)*.

all peoples: The first followers of Jesus were of course Jewish, and this gospel has a strongly Jewish character. But by the evangelist's time, the so-called Gentile mission had been underway for sometime. Ever since Jesus' resurrection—according to this story—it has been justifiable, in fact essential.

in the name of the Father and the son and the holy spirit: This combination of the three nouns is found nowhere else in NT. Over the following centuries it became the basis for the concept of Trinity.

in the name of: See Glossary.

the holy spirit: See on 12:32.

• **28:20** *Teach them to observe everything I commanded you:* Jesus speaks to the disciples the way God spoke to Moses in Torah.

Interpretive Note: The Resurrection

Probably the most difficult issue for the modern Christian is the question of Jesus' resurrection. What actually happened? What did it mean that Jesus appeared to certain people? Was the tomb really empty? What kind of event is a resurrection?

To begin with the last: Resurrection is not just the resuscitation of a corpse, or of a person thought to be dead. According to Christian faith, Jesus did not have simply a near-death experience. A radical event took place, in the eyes of his followers, and with it Christianity was born—the belief that Jesus was now more than the healer and prophet and teacher he had been in his lifetime; he was the "first-born from the dead," as Paul put it, the only person whom God had "raised." And so he was, they understood, the Anointed one/the Christ/the Messiah, in fact the divine Son of God. But no one witnessed it; only its after-effects can be documented. And strictly speaking, resurrection is a trans-historical "event," by definition. The history of the man Jesus ends with his death.

The experience of the risen Jesus' appearances—in this gospel, to the women at the tomb, then to the Eleven; elsewhere to Peter, to his own brother James, to many disciples all at once, finally to Paul—is as well attested historically as anything in the gospels. What those appearances involved is a question that people will answer in various ways. But few would hold that they could have been recorded by camera. Various verbs are used, the most common can be translated either "was seen" or "appeared." It was these experiences that had such a profound effect that Jesus' dispirited followers went back to Jerusalem, the place of catastrophe and of danger.

The empty tomb story is technically a legend. And it appears for the first in Mark's gospel, unknown evidently to Paul, our earliest Christian writer. (There are scholars who think that Jesus was not carefully buried but that, like all crucified bodies, his would have been thrown by the soldiers into an open pit.) If he was buried on that Friday afternoon, the story that the tomb was empty on Sunday morning—a story perhaps created to prove the resurrection of Jesus—backfired. For the rumor then arose among non-believers, documented in Matthew, that the disciples had stolen Jesus' body. And so our author, alone, gives the account of guards being placed at the tomb, to prove that it was not the disciples who took away the body, but God—a story evidently created to counter the rumor.

Does a resurrection involve the dead person's remains? That was the belief that arose two centuries earlier, during the Maccabean revolt. The bones of the martyrs were carefully preserved for resurrection, at the end of the age (with Ezekiel 37 in mind). But the modern practice of cremation by Christians obviously does not hold to this belief.

So the issue is a tangle of questions. To accept the resurrection is simply a leap of faith, no more and no less. Historically it is not verifiable, nor can it be understood rationally. It is the fundamental mystery.

Appendix

A Prison Dialogue on the Parable
of the Entrusted Money

From time to time I would take students in one of my undergraduate Bible courses for an evening of discussion with a select group of inmates at a maximum-security prison near to our college. This weekly meeting of prisoners was known as the Exodus group. Not, of course, because it was organized to plan escape . . . but because the members used the Biblical story of the exodus as a metaphor for finding their own way out of the slavery of their mentality, a mentality to a large extent adopted unconsciously from the Black ghetto society out of which most of them had come. Those evenings usually proved intellectually stimulating for all of us making the visit. These men, despite the misleading sound of their street-talk, were the cream of the prison population, selected for their self-discipline, by which most of them had completed a badly disrupted education, first finishing high school or even primary school, then college, and in some cases a post-graduate degree . . . entirely behind prison walls. At the same time, most of them represent the underclass in America and they view the world from that perspective.

One year I organized a visit for a college seminar that for a semester had been studying the parables of the historical Jesus. I was a bit uncomfortable that the inmates, invited to choose a parable from those we had not examined, opted for Matthew's so-called Parable of the Talents. Uncomfortable, because I had never been able to understand that parable; I was quite sure that it was not the banal allegory to the effect that we should make the most of those strengths of character that God has given us. But I was hopeful that some insight might break through. In fact most of that session was highly frustrating. Here is an abbreviated reconstruction of what was said.

247

The Characters:

Teacher—that's me, and as you'll see, I was often floundering, fearing a total flop.

Student(s)—anonymous and mostly silenced by the inmates' eagerness and ability to talk.

Inmates—combined into just three individuals and identified by fictitious names (Pedro, Smitty, and Red). Several of those who took part have consented to our using the dialogue that the students and I later reconstructed and had no objection to the attempt to reproduce some of the flavor of their speech . . . slightly cleaned up.

Teacher [after the parable had been read aloud]: The agenda, which our hosts have chosen, is the parable we've just heard, usually called "the Talents." I propose that we try to go behind the text in Matthew to discover if we can what Jesus' original story was, maybe sixty years earlier, and what it might mean.

Pedro [evidently reporting what the inmates' group had concluded in a preparatory session]: Well, we all know that. It about our talents God gave us, how we should use 'em.

Teacher: Are you sure?

A chorus of inmates: 'Course. What else could it mean? Hell yes. [etc.]

Teacher: But why would Jesus tell this long and complicated story just to say that?

Smitty: You tell us, Prof; that's your thing. [Laughter, but not unfriendly]

Teacher: Well, I'm not sure I know. [Murmuring] And anyway, I'd like us all to try and discover that together.

Red: Pedro told you what it mean. Ain't he right?

Teacher: I'm not so sure.

Inmates: Then why it talkin' 'bout talents?

A student [to the teacher's relief]: It can't be about what we call talents today, because back then that word just meant a whole lot of money and didn't have anything to do with our abilities.

Red: Well, look at the story. It says, To each accordin' to his ability. Don't that mean talent?

Student [taken aback]: Well, maybe . . . .

Smitty: Prof, what she mean, Maybe? What you teachin' these kids?

Teacher: We try to keep on looking at the text . . . and . . . and Red has gotten us started.

Pedro: Yeah, like I say, the story mean we should use our abilities what God gave us. Some does better at that than some others [looking around with a grin].

Smitty: Hey, Pedro; what use you got for talents? You in here for life, man.

[Laughter—easy and affectionate from the inmates, nervous from the visitors.]

Teacher [trying hard]: People usually assume that the rich man who went away stands for God. But is that so?

Various inmates: Sure, it's obvious. All these stories 'bout God. Yeah! the Kingdom of God.

A student: But that makes the story into an allegory. And Jesus didn't tell allegories about God. He talked about money and the rich and stuff like that.

Teacher [pleased, but wanting to avoid the broad-scale argument this was sure to meet with]: Look, let's study the story for a moment, just for the way it's told. What do you think of these three slaves?

Red: They just servants in my Bible.

Teacher: Yes, but it was translated by whites. The Greek clearly means slaves. [Mixed consternation and interest.] So what do you think of them?

Smitty: Two of them smart, but that third one, kinda slow. That's plain.

Teacher: So the man with the money was right to punish him?

Smitty: 'Course the rich dude oughta nail him; he was this slothful servant . . . uh, I mean slave.

Red: Yeah, my Bible say he worthless.

Teacher: But do you think he was worthless?

Inmates: Why not?

Teacher: Well, it's only the boss who calls him worthless.

Smitty: But he's God, ain't he?

Teacher [deciding to risk the argument after all]: No, in the story he's just a rich man.

Smitty [impatient]: In the story, of course, but . . .

Pedro: Prof, this gettin' us nowhere. We all understands this story; let's talk about somethin' useful.

Teacher [getting a little desperate]: Wait a minute, Pedro; you guys chose it, and you're making it into just a piece of white, middle-class advice. [Pauses, then grasps at a straw]: Which of those three slaves in the story do you like the best?

Smitty [after general silence, and with a little smile]: Why Prof, I kinda dig that third dude.

Teacher [suspecting a trick but having no alternative]: OK, go with that. Let's say you're that guy. You get the least, but you still get a lot of money. A single talent was worth about fifteen years' wages for a poor laborer.

Inmates [whistles, various forms of strong language].

Smitty: You mean, we're talkin' big money.

Teacher: Right. So, Smitty, how do you feel about the boss who left with you all this money to invest for him?

Smitty [a pause, then very slowly]: Why, that son-of-a-bitch!

Teacher: Why?

Smitty: He just part of the System. He tryin' to use me to make his money for him.

Teacher: And if you don't?

Smitty: I get it pinned on me. He exploitin' me, man!

Teacher: So is he God?

Smitty [grinning]: 'Course not. Who sayin' that? [Laughter]

Red: Time's up, Prof.

Teacher [frustrated but relieved]: Well, we got started . . . and just maybe Smitty has discovered the key to a way of understanding the story.

This remarkable discussion took place more or less as I've reported it. And Smitty's sudden perspective on the story was quite unexpected by any of us, including himself. The question I put ("Which of those three do you like most?") was just a lucky stab.

The people Jesus mostly addressed were the disenfranchised, the marginalized and oppressed—victims of the System who'd fallen thru the cracks in a society with no safety nets. And they are represented today more nearly by Smitty and his fellow inmates than by us visitors. If anything, most of us are like those Jesus spoke against, the pious and the comfortable. The inmates simply speak for the underclass. However guilty of particular crimes, they all to some degree or other were set up by their society to lead lives of crime. It can hardly be accidental that almost all of today's prison population in America are very poor Blacks or Hispanics. Those prisoners who are conscientized understand this; they have become especially sensitive to issues of exploitation. So perhaps Smitty's startling hunch provides a valid point of departure for looking at this difficult parable, helps us discover more nearly how Jesus may have meant it. If Smitty is right, it's the third slave that we must pay attention to. The first two are more or less faceless, and duplicates of each other: both make a 100% return on the money they have invested, both are eager to please the master, and both get warmly rewarded by him in the end.

The third slave's handling of the money he got is usually seen as laziness, or lack of concern. In fact, burying the money was a responsible way of keeping it safe. But in his owner's eyes he is a "no good" slave. And whether we entirely approve of the master or not, it is probably with him that we unconsciously identify. Smitty sees through that and pays attention to what the third slave says about the master's business practice. He honors that slave's refusal to be co-opted into that corrupt practice, identifies him as blowing a whistle on his boss.

(See further my essay, "Reading Jesus' Parable of the Talents through Underclass Eyes.")

Glossary and Abbreviations

1 Cor: Paul's First Letter to the Corinthians.

1 Kgs: The First Book o Kings.

1 Sam: The First Book of Samuel.

1 Thess: Paul's First Letter to the Thessalonians.

2 Chr: The Second book of Chronicles.

2 Cor: Paul's Second Letter to the Corinthians.

2 Kgs: The Second Book of Kings.

2 Sam: The Second book of Samuel.

aphorism: A brief saying of Jesus, usually a "one-liner," that is pithy and memorable. Together with the parables (see below), the aphorisms, or many of them, constitute the probably authentic database of Jesus' teaching.

allegory: A story told not for its own sake, but conveying some other meaning. Each important detail in the story stands for something else outside it. For example, in the allegorized version of the parable of the Leased Vineyard (21:33–43) the landlord is meant to stand for God, the slaves for the prophets, the son for Jesus, and the farmers for wicked Israel.

angel: See below on "Messenger of the Lord."

the Anointed [one]: See the Translation Note, p. 34.

apocalyptic: Vividly imaginative description of what will take place at the end of the age and the events leading up to it. Mark 13 is often called "the Apocalyptic Discourse," and Matthew's version of it is chapters 24–25. See the Interpretive Note, p. 216.

Aramaic: A Semitic language very close to Hebrew. Jesus' mother tongue. (He may have spoken some Greek as well.) It had been the lingua franca of the Persian empire.

the author: See "the evangelist," below.

Babylonian exile: The deportation of the leaders of Judah to Babylon in Mesopotamia when the Southern Kingdom, surviving the collapse of the Northern in 722 BCE, fell in 587 and the Jewish Dispersion began.

beatitude: A saying conveying God's blessing (Latin *beatus*) on certain people or certain traits. In SV the usual "blessed" is changed to "Congratulations . . . !" See the Translation Note, p. 63.

BCE: "Before the common [or Christian] era." It is equivalent to the older term, BC, but more ecumenical. See "CE" below.

blasphemy: Speaking irreverently of God or of anything associated with God, such as the Jerusalem temple; claiming to be God; perhaps also questioning the power of God ("blasphemy against the spirit"?).

canonical: Found in the Biblical "canon," that is, in the finally accepted list of books to be included. The "New Testament canon" is the second part of the Christian Bible, following the "Old Testament" (see OT, below).

catchword: A word or phrase in one saying that reminds of another, which is then appended to the first. This often begins a string of sayings.

CE: "In the common [or Christian] era," equivalent to "AD." See "BCE," above.

ch, chs: Chapter(s). The principal divisions in the text of a biblical book.

christological: Having to do with Jesus' messiahship (the belief that he is the Christ, the Anointed one expected in Judaism), or with his divinity, or his status in general. Often demonstrating that status.

Dan: The Book of Daniel.

demons: Evil spirits, understood to be in the devil's power and by inhabiting people causing human illness.

Deut: The Book Deuteronomy.

elders: This can refer either to Jewish ancestors, as perhaps at 15:2, or to senior leaders in Jerusalem at the time of Jesus.

esp: especially.

Esth: The Book of Esther.

eschatology, eschatological: Literally, having to do with "eschaton," the end or the final things. Thus, having ultimate theological significance, particularly in the salvation history of Israel and its Christian continuation. Sometimes but not always involves apocalyptic (see above), the expectation of a final disaster ("the impending doom" of 3:7) before "the End of the age," which is not the end of time but the beginning of the New Age.

the evangelist: The author of the Gospel according to Matthew, whatever that author's actual name—see Introduction, 3, pp. 12–14.

Exod: The Book Exodus.

exorcise: To expel an unclean spirit and make a person well.

Ezek: The Book of Ezekiel.

the Fourth Gospel: The Gospel according to John.

Gal: Paul's Letter to the Galatians.

Gehenna: The mythical name for a place of damnation. The idea seems to have derived from Jerusalem's town dump, in the Valley of Hinnom. "Gehenna" comes from this name. The valley was usually burning with a terrible stench. It became a metaphor for what we would call Hell.

Gen: The Book Genesis.

Hebrew Scriptures: The Jewish Bible, known to Christians as the Old Testament.

Hell: Sometimes translating the Greek "Hades" (11:23, 16:18), sometimes the Hebraic "Gehenna" (23:15, 33; see above).

Horeb: An alternative name for "the mountain of God" where Moses was believed to have received the Torah. See also Sinai.

Hos: The Book of Hosea.

irony: Saying or portraying one thing, when the hearer or reader should understand that something else, sometimes the opposite, is true. For example, the soldiers horseplay with the condemned Jesus (27: 27–31). They mock him as if he were a king, when in fact, as the reader understands, he was a king, the Anointed.

in the name of: A phrase, very common in OT, that is hard to unfold. It can mean, for example, "on behalf of," "for the sake of," "in the place of," or "with the authority of." And it usually assumes allegiance to the one named.

Isa: The Book of Isaiah.

Jer: The Book of Jeremiah.

Jesus Seminar: A long-term collaborative project by scholars seeking to recover what can be known of the historical Jesus—his sayings and his deeds. See the books edited by Funk in the Bookshelf.

John: This name refers mainly to John the Baptist. But a reference like "John 6:12" means a passage in the Gospel according to John, also known as the Fourth Gospel.

Jordan: The river that runs south from the Sea of Galilee to the Dead Sea.

Josh: The Book of Joshua.

Judea: The Roman name for ancient Judah, part of the province of Syria.

Judean: See the Translation Note, p. 41.

Judg: The Book of Judges.

kerygmatic: From the word *kerygma* (an announcement, a proclamation). Having to do with the Christian message and so, often, to be distinguished from what is [merely] historical or factual.

KJV: The King James Version, the classic translation of the Christian Bible into English. It was commissioned by King James I of England and published in

1611. In Britain it has since been known as the Authorized Version, since it alone was approved by the crown.

(the) Law: The first five books of the Hebrew Scriptures. In Hebrew, Torah; in Greek, the Pentateuch. These consisted of much narrative, but were valued chiefly for the commandments they also contained. Also known as the Law of Moses, believed to have been handed down to him by God on Mount Sinai/Horeb.

legend: See below on "myth."

Lev: The Book Leviticus.

Lukan: Having to do with the Gospel according to Luke, or its author.

LXX: See "Septuagint," below.

Mal: The Book of Malachi.

Markan: Having to do with the Gospel according to Mark, or its author.

Matthean: Having to do with the gospel, or the author, of Matthew.

messenger of the Lord [or **God's messenger**]: In most versions the Greek word *(angelos)* is simply transliterated, as "angel." But its meaning is more basic, one who carries a message for God.

the messianic secret: In Mark especially (to a lesser degree in Matthew and Luke) anyone who understands who Jesus is—that he is the Anointed or the Son of God—whether because healed by him or in some other way, is enjoined to silence, an enjoinder that fails. Before long Jesus is widely known, which undoubtedly reflects actual fact. The theme of the so-called messianic secret, is undoubtedly a Markan creation, emphasizing that Jesus is only to be understood as a crucified messiah.

ms(s): Manuscript(s). Old copies of the Greek text of Matthew, or sometimes of translations (into Latin or Syriac, for instance). None of the original documents have survived. All manuscripts were of course copied by hand. So changes from the manuscript copied would be made. Either by accident, or by the scribe's opinion that something needed to be corrected or improved. Thereafter copyists would normally pass on the change. See Introduction, p. 22.

Mic: The Book of Micah.

MT: The classical Hebrew text of the OT, called the "Masoretic Text."

myth: See the Introduction, p. 8. In the gospels there is a good deal of *legend*—stories that perhaps have no basis in fact, or are not in any way accurate historically. This would describe the different, and conflicting stories of Jesus' birth in the opening chapters of Matthew and Luke.

But there is also *myth*—not untruth, but stories or segments of stories told just as matter-of-factly but which cannot describe earthly events, for they involve supernatural and divine figures: for instance, the story of Jesus' testing by the devil (4:1–11), or his so-called transfiguration (17:1–13). The ordinary ancient reader or hearer would not make the above distinctions, but for the modern they are inevitable—or should be, I believe. Not that we discard the stories. On the contrary, myth in particular is a powerful way of conveying theological truth, and to take them as simply factual is to miss that affirmation, or an essential element in it.

NRSV: The New Revised Standard Bible, completed in 1989. One of the most important of the modern translations of the Old and New Testaments.

NT: The New Testament, the second part of the Christian Bible, perhaps better called the Second Testament.

Num: The Book of Numbers.

OT: The Old Testament, the Christian name for the Hebrew Scriptures.

pagan: Or "Gentile," that is, not Jewish.

parable: A fictional story, told not for its own sake but metaphorically, to suggest something else, usually about God's imperial rule, which however is at most hinted at in the story. The plot is not about God or Jesus or religion but some aspect of everyday life, recognizable to Jesus' peasant hearers—debt, farming, employer/employee relations, and so forth. There is usually something startling or shocking in the story and the hearer is left to make sense of it. Jesus' parables were not allegories that needed to be explained or decoded, although several of them have become allegorical by the time the gospels were written. Most of them, together with aphorisms (see above), make up the authentic teaching of Jesus.

Pharisees: Members of a sect, or movement, in the Judaism of Jesus' and the evangelist's time. They advocated stringent observance of the Law, in order to reform Israel. After the Jewish War (66–70 CE) they inherited the leadership of Judaism. In Matthew they are usually portrayed as opponents of Jesus. They had certainly become opponents of the church by our author's time. See Interpretive Note, p. 198.

Prov: The Book of Proverbs.

Ps(s): Psalm(s).

Q: A source used by the authors of Matthew and of Luke. The designation comes from *Quelle,* German for "source." It contained almost nothing but sayings of Jesus not found in Mark. It is sometimes called the Sayings Source, or even Sayings Gospel. See Introduction, p. 11.

Rabbinic tradition: Interpretation of the Hebrew Bible that was handed down in oral form for a number of generations. Much of it was amplification of Jewish law found in the first five books of the scriptures. The Pharisees and scholars were especially concerned with it.

ranking priests: Conventionally translated "high priests," but there was only one High Priest at a time.

redaction: The creative editing of a source by the author of a later document.

resurrection: An idea that developed in late Judaism prior to the rise of Christianity. It meant the—perhaps only eventual—restoration to new life from the dead. Most often it was imagined as an element of the new age, following the Last Judgment.

Rev: The Book of Revelation/The Apocalypse.

Rom: Paul's Letter to the Romans.

Sadducees: A party or class of men in first century Jerusalem who under Rome held considerable power. They were perhaps descendants of Zadok the priest of 2 Sam 8:17, or claimed or were thought to be; hence their name. They were theologically conservative. For example they evidently did not believe in resurrection of the dead, unlike Pharisees, insisting that the idea was not based on scripture. In the time of the Jewish War (66–70 CE) they seem to have disappeared.

Sanhedrin: The word is from the Hebrew, transliterated into Greek as *synedrion*. It was the ruling body of Judean Jewry. Usually translated "Council."

scholars: In earlier translations, usually called scribes, but they weren't merely copyists of the Bible. The Greek is *grammateis*—"those who have to do with the scriptures." They studied and interpreted them. Like modern Biblical exegetes. The evangelist may have been a former "scholar" who perhaps describes himself at 13:52. With the Pharisees, they became leaders of Judaism after the Jewish war (66–70 CE).

Scholars Version (SV): A fresh translation of the gospels into modern American English by fellows of the Jesus Seminar (see above). Not intended just *for* scholars; rather, it was made *by* scholars . . . that is, not under the auspices of any church or denomination, not for public use. See Introduction, section 7.

scribe: Not used here to indicate a Judean "scholar" (see above). Rather, a copyist of one of the Christian documents, after the original was written.

Septuagint (LXX): The standard ancient translation of the Hebrew scriptures into Greek. Usually designated by the Roman numeral "LXX" since "Septuagint" comes from the Latin for 70. Legend had it that there were seventy translators.

Sinai: The more common name for "the mountain of God" where Moses was believed to have received the Torah. Also known as Horeb.

Son of Adam: See the Translation Note, pp. 80–81.

soteriological: Having to do with salvation, God's activity in history.

spirit: Sometimes "the [or "a"] holy spirit, suggesting a power or effective force from God. Or "an unclean spirit," a force believed in the ancient world to "possess" people and cause them to be ill or deranged; see "demon," above.

synoptic gospels: The first three gospels in the NT canon. The term "synoptic" comes from Greek. They can be understood to be called this because they can "be viewed [*optic*] side-by-side [*syn*]."

SV: See "Scholars Version," above.

testament: A term given in the early English versions to the two parts of the Christian bible, the Old and New Testaments. Today the more accurate translation of the original Greek term is "Covenant": the so-called Old, or First, Covenant is the story of Israel and—as Christians hold—the New, or Second, the story of the New Israel, the Church.

text-critical: Having to do with the varying readings of ancient mss. See Introduction, p. 22.

Thom: The Gospel of Thomas. See the next notice.

Thomas: Except for the one mention of the apostle by name (10:3), this refers to the so-called Gospel of Thomas, cited by Logion (= saying) number. See Introduction, p. 12.

toll collector: More commonly translated "tax collector." Since passage on Roman roads was not free, the toll was itself a form of taxation. And its collectors were evidently Jews regarded by other Jews as disloyal to their people. Hence, they are often linked with "sinners."

Torah: The first five books of the Hebrew Scriptures—the Pentateuch—most often known as "the Law."

tradition (especially **oral tradition**) Literally, something handed down from listener to listener. In the case of the gospels, this material was passed along in small units—a single story about Jesus, or a parable that he was believed to have told. That is why the gospel narrative is made up of small units. It seldom has the form of continuous narrative, as a single writer, such as a novelist today, would create.

version: As a technical term this means a particular translation of the Bible—like the King James Version, the New Revised Standard Version, the Scholars Version (the one used here).

vs, vss: Verse(s). The small units into which a chapter has been divided. Sometimes a single sentence

YHWH: The ancient Israelite name for God, probably pronounced Yahweh, when it was believed that other gods existed, such as the Canaanite Baal. Sometimes this name has been (incorrectly) transliterated in English as "Jehovah." In English it is often represented by the Lord.

Zech: The book of Zechariah.

Bookshelf of Works Cited and
for Further Reading

Aland, Kurt, et al., eds. *The Greek New Testament.* 3rd ed. United Bible Societies, 1975. The best published text, better in the view of the SV translators than the 4th ed. of 1983 and later ones.

Balch, David L., ed. *Social History of the Matthean Community: Cross-Disciplinary Approaches.* Minneapolis: Fortress Press, 1991.

Bauer, David R. *The Structure of Matthew's Gospel: A Study in Literary Design.* Sheffield: Almond Press, 1988.

Carter, Warren. *Matthew and the Margins: A Sociopolitical and Religious Reading.* The Bible and Liberation Series. Maryknoll, NY: Orbis Books, 2000.

———. *Matthew and Empire: Initial Explorations.* Harrisburg; Trinity Press International, 2001

Catchpole, David. *Resurrection People: Studies in the Resurrection Narratives of the Gospels.* Sarum Theological Lectures. London: Darton, Longman and Todd Ltd., 2000.

Davies, W. D., and Allison, Dale C., Jr. *A Critical and Exegetical Commentary on the Gospel according to Matthew.* International Critical Commentary. 3 vols. Edinburgh: T. & T. Clark, 1988–97. An exhaustive consideration of every important word and phrase of the Greek text.

Fortna, Robert T. "Reading Jesus' Parable of the Talents Through Underclass Eyes—Matt 25:14–30," *Foundations and Facets Forum,* 8,3–4 (September–December 1992). 211–28.

———. "'You have made them equal to us' (Mt 20:1–16)," *Journal of Theology for Southern Africa,* 72 (September 1990), 66–72.

Funk, Robert W, Roy W. Hoover, and The Jesus Seminar. *The Five Gospels: The Search for the Authentic Words of Jesus.* New York: Macmillan Publishing Co., 1993. The first half of the Jesus Seminar's report.

Funk, Robert W, and the Jesus Seminar. *The Acts of Jesus: The Search for the Authentic Deeds of Jesus.* A Polebridge Press Book. New York: HarperSanFrancisco, 1998. The second half of the Jesus Seminar's report.

Harrington, Daniel J., SJ. *The Gospel of Matthew.* Sacra Pagina Vol. 2. Collegeville, MN: Liturgical Press, 1991.

Horsley, Richard A. *Hearing the Whole Story: The Politics of Plot in Mark's Gospel.* Louisville: Westminster John Knox, 2001.

Lachs, Samuel Tobia. *A Rabbinic Commentary on the New Testament: The Gospels of Matthew, Mark, and Luke.* Hoboken: Ktav Publishing House, 1987.

Luz, Ulrich. *Matthew 1-7: A Continental Commentary.* Tr. W. C. Linss. Minneapolis: Fortress Press, 1989.

———. *Matthew 8-20: A Commentary.* Tr. James E. Crouch. Ed. Helmut Koester. Hermeneia. Minneapolis: Fortress Press, 2001.

Malina, Bruce J., and Richard L. Rohrbach. *Social-Science Commentary on the Synoptic Gospels.* Minneapolis: Fortress Press, 1992.

May, Herbert G., et al., eds. *Oxford Bible Atlas.* New York: Oxford, 1984.

Miller, Robert J. *The Complete Gospels: Annotated Scholars Version.* Revised and expanded. Sonoma, CA: Polebridge, 1994.

———. *Born Divine: The Births of Jesus and Other Sons of God.* Santa Rosa: Polebridge Press, 2003.

Pritchard, James B. ed. *The Harper Atlas of the Bible.* New York: Harper & Row, 1987.

Schmidt, Daryl D. *The Gospel of Mark, with Introduction, Notes, and Original Text.* The Scholars Bible. Sonoma, CA: Polebridge Press, 1990.

Smith, Morton. *Jesus the Magician.* New York: Harper & Row, 1978.

Smith, Robert H. *Matthew.* Augsburg Commentary on the New Testament. Minneapolis: Augsburg Publishing House, 1989.

Stanton, Graham N. *A Gospel for a New People: Studies in Matthew.* Louisville: Westminster/John Knox Press, 1992.

Throckmorton, Burton H., Jr., ed. *Gospel Parallels: A Comparison of the Synoptic Gospels.* 5th ed. Nashville: Thomas Nelson, 1992.

Wink, Walter. *The Human Being: Jesus and the Enigma of the Son of the Man.* Minneapolis: Fortress Press, 2002.

Index of Ancient Texts

Hebrew Scriptures/ Old Testament

New Testament

NT Apocrypha

Index of Modern Authors